THE BIG BOOK
of
COUNTRY LIVING

THE BIG BOOK
of
COUNTRY LIVING

ERNEST THOMPSON SETON

LYONS
PRESS

Essex, Connecticut

An imprint of Globe Pequot, the trade division of
The Rowman & Littlefield Publishing Group, Inc.
4501 Forbes Blvd., Ste. 200
Lanham, MD 20706
www.rowman.com

Distributed by NATIONAL BOOK NETWORK

The special contents of this edition copyright © 2000 by The Lyons Press
Introduction copyright © 2000 by Noel Perrin
New Lyons Press edition published in 2024.

British Library Cataloguing in Publication Information available

Library of Congress Cataloging-in-Publication Data available

ISBN 978-1-4930-8152-3 (paper : alk. paper)
ISBN 978-1-4930-8610-8 (electronic)

∞™ The paper used in this publication meets the minimum requirements of
American National Standard for Information Sciences—Permanence of Paper
for Printed Library Materials, ANSI/NISO Z39.48-1992.

CONTENTS

v

Contents

Contents

Contents

Contents

Contents

Contents

Contents

Contents

Contents

Contents

xv

Contents

xvi

Contents

xvii

Contents

Contents

Contents

FOREWORD

A hundred years ago, nearly every street in the Latin Quarter of Paris resounded with spoken English. You'd almost think it was the Anglo-Saxon Quarter, so many Americans and Englishmen and Canadians were strolling about. Most of these young men and women were art students. The serious ones spent their weekdays enrolled in classes and their weekends in tiny ateliers, painting on their own. The less serious sat around in cafés.

One not-so-young Canadian, however, spent about half *his* time at the Paris zoo. A fanatic outdoorsman, he felt cramped in art school. Besides, he had discovered that one of the zoo's wolves—a particularly handsome one—spent almost every afternoon sleeping on the ground, with his nose on his left forepaw and his tail curled aesthetically around his flank. Cold though it was in January and February of 1891, Ernest Thompson Seton devoted some thirty afternoons to painting this wild animal. He entered *The Sleeping Wolf* for inclusion in the 1891 Grand Salon, and it was accepted. Not only accepted, but hung "on the line," at eye level, the most favored position.

The next year, when he was thirty-two, he entered another wolf painting, a much more alarming one. It shows five wolves in a snowy landscape. Sharing the scene is an almost-consumed human body. One wolf has the skull in his jaws and is trying to crack it like a nut. That painting—*The Triumph of the Wolves*—did not get accepted for the Salon, though a year later it was being prominently displayed in Chicago.

Seton differed from most of his fellow students not only in preferring to paint outdoors, even in winter, but also in preferring to be away from Paris a lot. About once a year he would feel a longing for the Canadian woods and go home for two or three months to hunt and explore and take canoe trips. In the past he had hunted wolves. While home he also did a good deal of nature writing—chiefly articles on birds for sober publications like *Canadian Science Monthly*.

In May of 1892, shortly after *The Triumph* had been rejected by the Grand Salon, Seton sailed for New York, en route to Toronto. A friend from art school traveled on the same ship. She was a beautiful girl from a rich New Jersey family, Miss Virginia Fitz-Randolph, coming home to get married. At her invitation he paid a visit to the Fitz-Randolphs before going on to Canada.

Naturally her family heard about the wolf paintings. Her father was particularly interested in the second one, because he felt himself a victim of real-life wolves. Metaphorically, at least, eaten by them.

Among other properties, Mr. Fitz-Randolph owned a big cattle ranch in New Mexico, and it was losing money. The chief cause was wolves. They kept killing the cattle. The cowboys could never get close enough to shoot them; trappers failed to trap them. Poison bait, so successful with coyotes, they contemptuously spurned.

Mr. Fitz-Randolph, impressed with the tall artist-woodsman and his great knowledge of animal behavior, made Seton an offer. If he would go to New Mexico and spend at least one month on the ranch—if he would "hunt and destroy wolves, and show cowboys how to do the same"—Fitz-Randolph would pay all expenses. Seton could collect all the bounties and sell all the hides.

Despite his strong and growing sympathy with wildlife (not every painter would have titled the second painting from the point of view of the wolves; indeed, French friends had specifically advised him to call it "Awaited in Vain," since in the far distance one can see the cottage where the dead man's family is waiting for him to come home to supper), Seton jumped at the offer. Short of being transported back to medieval myth, where kings send knights to slay dragons, it

Foreword

was about as thrilling an assignment as a man could ask for, at least a man of Seton's romantic and wilderness-loving temperament. The only important difference from the medieval tales was that instead of offering one of his five beautiful daughters as a reward (they were thoroughly independent young women, and he couldn't have), or half his estate, Mr. Fitz-Randolph contented himself with letting Seton have a crack at the cash bounties paid by the territory of New Mexico, and at the pelt fees paid by furriers. That may be one of the differences between a businessman and a king.

In October 1893, Seton arrived at Fitz-Randolph's L. Cross F Ranch in Clayton, New Mexico. He found that in the three days before his arrival, wolves had killed seven young horses and five sheep. He further found that local ranchers claimed that each grown wolf could and did kill about a thousand dollars' worth of cattle each year, a figure that translates to something like forty thousand dollars now. He heard about one especially large and clever wolf, so famous locally that he had acquired a name and an identity, as Moby Dick once did among whalemen.

Seton stayed in New Mexico much longer than planned. It took him four months to trap Lobo. By then he was using 130 traps. He had the somewhat unwilling assistance of numerous cowhands (setting a trap Seton-style is a lot of work), and in the end he got inadvertent help from one of the wolves in Lobo's small pack. He was almost sorry to catch and kill so fine a wolf. And the wolf's spirit he did not kill; he absorbed it. Later he would use Lobo's paw print as part of his signature.

From New Mexico, Seton came back to New York, where he sometimes worked as an illustrator. Occasionally, he made trips to Paris to paint or to the Canadian woods to study wildlife and have adventures. Apart from the little essays for *Canadian Science Monthly*, he had not yet begun to write, but he had acquired a reputation as a raconteur. He now added the story of Lobo to his repertoire. New Yorkers liked it so much that he decided to try writing it down, and then to see

Foreword

if he could sell it to a popular magazine and actually be paid. He could. It came out in 1894, with illustrations by the author.

Four years later he published his first book. It took so long partly because he had not yet come to see himself primarily as a writer. Twice more he went back to Paris to study painting. He continued to spend part of almost every year in the woods, practicing woodcraft. (Much later he was to write, with a bit of humorous exaggeration, that his theory of life was to "take two trips into the wilderness each year, and spend six months on each trip.") He got married—to another young artist, Grace Gallatin, who came from a family as formidably rich and prominent as Miss Fitz-Randolph's. Naturally the young couple needed a place to live. What they settled on was a thirty-room house with a two-hundred-acre backyard, in the outer suburbs of New York. Fixing the place up took time and energy as well as money.

But by the summer of 1898 he had a finished manuscript of the book that was to be called *Wild Animals I Have Known* (Lobo was one of them). All that remained was to find a publisher. Seton had his eye on Scribner's. And fortunately Charles Scribner had his eye on Seton. They just needed to come to terms.

Literary agents were a rarity in those days. Author and publisher normally sat down together and worked out a deal.

Scribner opened negotiations by telling Seton that publishing was a terribly hazardous business, and that most books were failures and cost the firm money, and that the best he could possibly do on royalties was a straight ten percent.

Seton was intensely proud of his Scottish ancestry, and among the qualities he saw as the patrimony of all Scots were canniness and the ability to drive a stiff bargain. He countered Mr. Scribner's tale of woe by asking how many copies a book had to sell to break even. Two thousand, he was told. Then he offered to forego any royalty whatsoever on the first two thousand copies of his book, thus partially ensuring the firm against loss.

Foreword

In return, Scribner's would have to pay him a double royalty—20 percent—on all subsequent copies. He assured Mr. Scribner that there would be lots and lots of subsequent copies. "Remember," he said, "my plan is not simply to throw this into the hopper with a hundred other new books. I am going forth to talk about it, give exhibitions of my illustrations, and sell copies in every town where I lecture." (That was a lot of towns. In the course of a long life, Seton gave around 4,000 lectures, and he spellbound nearly every audience.)

How can you refuse an author tour when the author is paying for it himself? How can you refuse an author's royalty proposal when he has just offered to assume much of your risk for you? Scribner reluctantly agreed to the deal, and it was the beginning of the fortune that Seton eventually acquired. The first edition (two thousand copies) sold out in three weeks. That was in October 1898. Two more printings sold out before Christmas. By early 1900 there had been nine printings, eight of them yielding a double royalty to the author.

Other books followed in a steady stream. *The Book of Woodcraft* came out in 1912, and was his fifteenth book. It was also one of his two longest—it kept growing over the years, rather like Whitman's *Leaves of Grass*. The book you are holding is the greatly enlarged edition of 1922.

Here Seton brings together practically all of his interests, with the exception of classical painting. He was much involved with the Boy Scout movement—he was the first Chief Scout—and there are numerous sections aimed both at the kids themselves and at scoutmasters. He loved trees as much as any modern tree-hugger, and for the edition of 1922 he folded in a book (he wrote it) called *The Foresters' Manual*. He admired American Indians above just about all other human beings, and six of the book's fifteen sections are at least partially concerned with Native American lore and ways of living.

In some ways the book is a slightly quirky encyclopedia of outdoor living. Naturally there's a full section devoted to natural history, with such subsections as "Forty Birds That

Foreword

Every Boy Should Know" and "The Secrets of the Trail."
(Why shouldn't girls know those birds and those secrets?
No reason except that ninety years ago most men thought
that most women were indoor creatures. That's why
American farmers a century ago, unless recent immigrants,
virtually never expected their wives or daughters to do farm-
work. They were to stay in the house and do housework:
pickling, bottling, sewing, mending, cleaning, nursing, washing, and a few more things like that. Anyhow, give Seton credit
for being a quick learner and, in this matter, ahead of his time.
In 1916, just four years later, he published *The Woodcraft
Manual for Girls*.)

In all, the book has around three hundred subsections.
They cover just about everything you might find useful in the
woods, from being able to identify safe mushrooms to knowing
how to start a fire using just a jackknife. Seton says he has
done the latter a thousand times—and adds casually that five
hundred of those times he was running experiments, testing
variations on the basic firedrill technique. Somewhat less
casually he tells you that he has made a fire in as little as thirty-
one seconds, which he is pretty sure is a world record. (No
Guinness Book of Records yet to confirm it.)

He really does cover an amazing variety of things. Forget
your flashlight? He tells you how to make one, if you have a
candle and an old tin can. He means the true focused beam of
a spotlight, not the dim glow of a candle just stuck in a can.
Or maybe it was your air mattress that you forgot. Seton is
delighted, because now he can show how to make a woodland
loom and weave a comfortable grass or sedge mattress.

You have questions about sex? Seton can answer them.
Don't bother to riffle through looking for *that*, though; what
he believes in is sublimation.

A person who truly learned all that Seton has to teach would
obviously be able to thrive in the woods. If male, he would
also stand a very good chance of making Eagle Scout. And
beyond that would know a good deal about Native American

Foreword

history and values. Ahead of his time in this matter, too, Seton had studied in detail the tragic history of the invasion of the continent by Europeans, and the long slow destruction of the Indian ways of life. Seton's ultimate aim is to enable whites to think and act more like pre-invasion Indians, and this volume offers many opportunities for doing this.

Today, some Native Americans will probably have reservations about Seton, thinking him a little too inclined to the Noble Red Man way of seeing Indian culture. So he was. But only a little. Seton had too many Indian friends, knew too much about tribal customs to do much stereotyping. But he *was* an artist. Few artists can resist touching things up just a little.

—Noel Perrin
Hanover, New Hampshire, 2000

PREFACE

For over thirty years I have been giving the talks and demonstrations that are gathered together in this book. Many of them have appeared in magazines or in the "Birch-Bark Roll" that has come out annually for eighteen years. But this is the first time in which a comprehensive collection has been made of the activities, customs, laws, and amusements that have been developed in my camps.

Some of the related subjects I have treated at too great length for enclosure in one book. Of this class are the "Life Histories of Northern Animals," "Animal Stories," and "Sign Language," which appear as separate works. All are merely parts of a scheme that I have always considered my life work, namely, the development or revival of Woodcraft as a school for Manhood.

By Woodcraft I mean outdoor life in its broadest sense and the plan has ever been with me since boyhood.

Woodcraft is the first of all the sciences. It was Woodcraft that made man out of brutish material, and Woodcraft in its highest form may save him from decay.

As the model for outdoor life in this country I took the Indian, and have thus been obliged to defend him against the calumnies of those who coveted his possessions. In giving these few historical extracts to show the Indian character, it must be remembered that I could give hundreds, and that practically all the travelers who saw with their own eyes are of one mind in the matter.

Commissioner Robert G. Valentine, of the Indian Bureau, the first Indian Commissioner we have ever had who knew and sympathized with the Indians, writes after reading my manuscript:

Preface

"On the question of the character of the Indians I am in absolute accord with you on everything that I believe any one would consider a basic point. In speech after speech I have fought the idea that Indians were cruel or lazy or vicious, and dwelt on their positive virtues — among these their sense of humor, and their deep reverence."*

The portions of the manuscript called "Spartans of the West," and "Campfire Stories of Indian Character," have been submitted to George Bird Grinnell, of New York, whose life has been largely spent among the Indians, and have received from him a complete endorsement.

In a similar vein I have heard from Dr. Charles A. Eastman, and from nearly all of the many who have seen the manuscript. Some of my friends at the Smithsonian Institution take exception to certain details, but no one denies the main contentions in regard to the character of the Indian, or the historical accuracy of the "Campfire Stories."

Gen. Nelson A. Miles, for example, writes me: "History can show no parallel to the heroism and fortitude of the American Indians in the two hundred years' fight during which they contested inch by inch the possession of their country against a foe infinitely better equipped with inexhaustible resources, and in overwhelming numbers. Had they even been equal in numbers, history might have had a very different story to tell."

I was taught to glorify the names of Xenophon, Leonidas, Spartacus, the Founders of the Dutch Republic or the Noble Six Hundred at Balaclava, as the ideals of human courage and self-sacrifice, and yet I know of nothing in all history that will compare with the story of Dull Knife as a narrative of magnificent heroism and human fortitude.

While I set out only to justify the Indian as a model for our

---

*The great racial defects of the Indians were revengefulness and disunion, and, latterly, proneness to strong drink. They taught the duty of revenge; so that it was easy to begin a feud, but hard to end one. Instead of a nation, they were a multitude of factions, each ready to join an outsider for revenge on its rival neighbor. This incapacity for team play prevented the development of their civilization and proved their ruin.

Preface

boys in camp, I am not without hope that this may lead to a measure of long-delayed justice being accorded him. He asks only the same rights as are allowed without question to all other men in America — the protection of the courts, the right to select his own religion, dress, amusements, and the equal right to the pursuit of happiness so long as his methods do not conflict with the greater law of the land.

This book is really the eleventh edition of the "Birch-Bark Roll," which I have published yearly and expanded yearly since 1902. On the first day of July that year I founded the first band of Woodcraft Indians. Since then the growth of the movement has called for constant revision and expansion. In the present volume, for the first time, I have fully set forth a justification of my Indian Ideal.

I am deeply indebted to my friend, Edgar Beecher Bronson, for permission to include the History of Chief Dull Knife's March, which appeared in his "Reminiscences of a Ranchman." It is a story that should be known to all the world.

I have also to express my obligations to Messrs. Charles Scribner's Sons for permission to quote from Capt. J. O. Bourke's writings, to J. W. Schultz for the use of his charming story of "No-Heart," to Messrs. The Fleming H. Revell Co., for permission to quote F. W. Calkins' story of the "Two Wilderness Voyagers," to Miss Alice C. Fletcher for the use of two Indian songs from her book "Indian Story and Song," as noted, to Edward S. Curtis for the use of Sitting Bull's "War Song," to Dr. Clinton L. Bagg for help in the "First Aid," to Dr. C. C. Curtis for the identification of toadstools, to Dr. Charles A. Eastman (Ohiyesa) for general criticism and for special assistance in the chapters on "The Indian's Creed," "Teepee Etiquette," and the "Teachings of Wabasha I."

Also to Robert G. Valentine (Indian Commissioner) and George Bird Grinnell of New York for critical reading of the historical parts of the book.

The section on Forest Trees appeared originally as a separate handbook called "The Foresters' Manual" in 1912. In it I aim

Preface

to give the things that appealed to me as a boy: First the identification of the tree, second where it is found, third its properties and uses, and last, various interesting facts about it.

I have included much information about native dyes, because it is all in the line of creating interest in the trees; and because it would greatly improve our color sense if we could return to vegetable dyes, and abandon the anilines that have in many cases displaced them. So also because of the interest evoked as well as for practical reasons I have given sundry medical items; some of these are from H. Howard's "Botanic Medicine," 1850. Several of the general notes are from George B. Emerson's "Trees and Shrubs of Massachusetts," 1846.

As starting point I have used Britton and Brown's "Illustrated Flora" (Scribner, 1896) and have got much help from Harriet L. Keeler's "Our Native Trees" (Scribner, 1900).

The illustrations were made by myself from fresh specimens in the woods, or in some cases from preserved specimens in the Museum of the New York Botanical Garden at Bronx Park.

The maps were made for this work by Norman Taylor, Curator of Plants in the Brooklyn Botanic Garden, N. Y., with corrections in Canada by Prof. John Macoun of the Geological Survey at Ottawa, Canada.

To Dr. N. L. Britton, Norman Taylor, and Prof. John Macoun, I extend my hearty thanks for their kind and able assistance.

The names of trees are those used in Britton's "North American Trees," 1908.

When I was a boy I hungered beyond expression for just such information as I have tried herein to impart. It would be a great joy to me if I could reach and help a considerable

Preface

number of such heart-hungry boys tormented with an insa-
tiate instinct for the woods, and if I fail of this, I shall at least
have the lasting pleasures of having lived through these things
myself and of having written about them.

ERNEST THOMPSON SETON'S
BIG BOOK OF COUNTRY LIVING

I. Principles of Woodcraft

Nine Important Principles of Woodcraft

THIS is a time when the whole nation is turning toward the Outdoor Life, seeking in it the physical regeneration so needful for continued national existence — is waking to the fact long known to thoughtful men, that those live longest who live nearest to the ground — that is, who live the simple life of primitive times, divested, however, of the evils that ignorance in those times begot.

Consumption, the white man's plague since he has become a house race, is vanquished by the sun and air, and many ills of the mind also are forgotten when the sufferer boldly takes to the life in tents.

Half our diseases are in our minds and half in our houses. We can safely leave the rest to the physicians for treatment.

Sport is the great incentive to Outdoor Life; Nature Study is the intellectual side of sport.

I should like to lead this whole nation into the way of living outdoors for at least a month each year, reviving and expanding a custom that as far back as Moses was deemed essential to the national well-being.

Not long ago a benevolent rich man, impressed with this idea, chartered a steamer and took some hundreds of slum boys up to the Catskills for a day in the woods. They were duly landed and told to "go in now and have a glorious time." It was like gathering up a netful of catfish and throwing them into the woods, saying, "Go and have a glorious time."

The boys sulked around and sullenly disappeared. An hour later, on being looked up, they were found in groups under the bushes, smoking cigarettes, shooting "craps," and playing cards — the only things they knew.

Thus the well-meaning rich man learned that it is not enough to take men out of doors. We much also teach them to enjoy it.

The purpose of this book is to show how Outdoor Life may be followed to advantage.

Nine leading principles are kept in view:

(1) This movement is essentially for *recreation*.

(2) *Camp-life.* Camping is the simple life reduced to actual practice, as well as the culmination of the outdoor life.

Camping has no great popularity to-day, because men have the idea that it is possible only after an expensive journey to the wilderness; and women that it is inconvenient, dirty, and dangerous.

These are errors. They have arisen because camping as an art is not understood. When intelligently followed, camp-life must take its place as a cheap and delightful way of living, as well as a mental and physical savior of those strained or broken by the grind of the over-busy world.

The wilderness affords the ideal camping, but many of the benefits can be got by living in a tent on a town lot, a piazza, or even a housetop.

(3) *Self-government with Adult Guidance.* Control from without is a poor thing when you can get control from within. As far as possible, then, we make these camps self-governing. Each full member has a vote in affairs.

(4) *The Magic of the Campfire.* What is a camp without a campfire? — no camp at all, but a chilly place in a

landscape, where some people happen to have some things.

When first the brutal anthropoid stood up and walked erect — was man, the great event was symbolized and marked by the lighting of the first campfire.

For millions of years our race has seen in this blessed fire, the means and emblem of light, warmth, protection, friendly gathering, council. All the hallow of the ancient thoughts, hearth, fireside, home is centred in its glow, and the home-tie itself is weakened with the waning of the home-fire. Not in the steam radiator can we find the spell; not in the water coil; not even in the gas log; they do not reach the heart. Only the ancient sacred fire of wood has power to touch and thrill the chords of primitive remembrance. When men sit together at the campfire they seem to shed all modern form and poise, and hark back to the primitive — to meet as man and man — to show the naked soul. Your campfire partner wins your love, or hate, mostly your love; and having camped in peace together, is a lasting bond of union — however wide your worlds may be apart.

The campfire, then, is the focal centre of all primitive brotherhood. We shall not fail to use its magic powers.

(5) *Woodcraft Pursuits*. Realizing that *manhood, not scholarship*, is the first aim of education, we have sought out those pursuits which develop the finest character, the finest physique, and which may be followed out of doors, which, in a word, *make for manhood*.

By nearly every process of logic we are led primarily to Woodcraft — that is, Woodcraft in a large sense — meaning every accomplishment of an all-round Woodman — Riding, Hunting, Camper-craft, Scouting, Mountaineering, Indian-craft, First aid, Star-craft, Signaling, and Boating. To this we add all good Outdoor Athletics and Sports, including Sailing and Motoring, and Nature Study, of which Wild Animal Photography is an important branch; but above all, Heroism.

Over three hundred deeds or exploits are recognized in these various departments, and the members are given decora-tions that show what they achieved. (See Woodcraft Manual.)

(6) *Honors by Standards.* The competitive principle is responsible for much that is evil. We see it rampant in our colleges to-day, where every effort is made to discover and develop a champion, while the great body of students is neglected. That is, the ones who are in need of physical development do not get it, and those who do not need it are over-developed. The result is much unsoundness of many kinds. A great deal of this would be avoided if we strove to bring all the individuals up to a certain standard. In our non-competitive tests the enemies are not "*the other fellows,*" but *time and space*, the forces of Nature. We try *not to down the others*, but *to raise ourselves*. A thorough appli-cation of this principle would end many of the evils now demoralizing college athletics. Therefore, all our honors are bestowed according to world-wide standards. (Prizes are not honors.) (See Woodcraft Manual.)

(7) *Personal Decoration for Personal Achievements.* The love of glory is the strongest motive in a savage. Civil-ized man is supposed to find in high principle his master impulse. But those who believe that the men of our race, not to mention boys, are civilized in this highest sense, would be greatly surprised if confronted with figures. Nevertheless, a human weakness may be good material to work with. I face the facts as they are. All have a chance for glory through the standards, and we blazon it forth in personal decorations that all can see, have, and desire.

(8) *A Heroic Ideal.* The boy from ten to fifteen, like the savage, is purely physical in his ideals. I do not know that I ever met a boy that would not rather be John L. Sullivan

than Darwin or Tolstoi. Therefore, I accept the fact, and seek to keep in view an ideal that is physical, but also clean, manly, heroic, already familiar, and leading with certainty to higher things.

(9) *Picturesqueness in Everything.* Very great importance should be attached to this. The effect of the picturesque is magical, and all the more subtle and irresistible because it is not on the face of it reasonable. The charm of titles and gay costumes, of the beautiful in ceremony, phrase, dance, and song, are utilized in all ways.

THE IDEAL

When two or three young people camp out, they can live as a sort of family, especially if a grown-up be with them; but when a dozen or more are of the party, it is necessary to organize.

What manner of organization will be practical, and also give full recognition to the nine principles of scouting? What form of government lends itself best to —

Recreation;
Outdoor Life;
Self-rule;
The Campfire;
Woodcraft traditions;
Honors by standards;
Personal decoration for personal achievement;
A heroic ideal;
Picturesqueness in all things?

In my opinion, the Tribal or Indian form of organization.

Fundamentally, this is a republic or limited monarchy, and many experiments have proved it best for our purpose. It makes its members self-governing; it offers appropriate things to do outdoors; it is so plastic that it can be adopted in whole or in part, at once or gradually; its picturesqueness takes immediate hold of all; and it lends itself so well to our object that, soon or late, other forms of organization are forced into its essentials.

No large band of boys ever yet camped out for a month without finding it necessary to recognize a *leader*, a *senior form* (or ruling set whose position rests on merit), some *wise grown person* to guide them in difficulties, and a place to display *the emblems* of the camp; that is, they have adopted the system of the Chief, Council, Medicine Man and Totem-pole.

Moreover, the Ideal Indian stands for the highest type of primitive life. He was a master of woodcraft, and unsordid, clean, manly, heroic, self-controlled, reverent, truthful, and picturesque always.

America owes much to the Redman. When the struggle for freedom came on, it was between men of the same blood and bone, equal in brains and in strength. The British had the better equipment perhaps. The great advantage of the American was that he was trained in Woodcraft, and this training which gave him the victory, he got from the Redman.

But the Redman can do a greater service now and in the future. He can teach us the ways of outdoor life, the nobility of courage, the joy of beauty, the blessedness of enough, the glory of service, the power of kindness, the super-excellence of peace of mind and the scorn of death. For these were the things that the Redman stood for; these were the sum of his faith.

II. The Spartans of the West

NO WORLD-MOVEMENT ever yet grew as a mere doctrine. It must have some noble example; a living, appealing personality; some man to whom we can point and say, "This is what we mean." All the great faiths of the world have had such a man, and for lack of one, many great and flawless truths have passed into the lumber-room.

To exemplify my outdoor movement, I must have a man who was of this country and climate; who was physically beautiful, clean, unsordid, high-minded, heroic, picturesque, and a master of Woodcraft, besides which, he must be already well-known. I would gladly have taken a man of our own race, but I could find none. Rollo the Sea-King, King Arthur, Leif Ericsson, Robin Hood, Leatherstocking, all suggested themselves, but none seemed to meet the requirements, and most were mere shadows, utterly unknown. Surely, all this pointed the same way. There was but one figure that seemed to answer all these needs: that was the *Ideal Indian* of Fenimore Cooper and Longfellow.

For this reason, I took the Native American, and called my organization "Woodcraft Indians." And yet, I am told that the prejudice against the word "Indian" has hurt the movement immensely. If so, it is because we do not know what the Indian was, and this I shall make it my sad and hopeful task, at this late day, to have our people realize.

We know more about the Redman to-day than ever we did. Indeed, we knew almost nothing of him twenty years ago. We had two pictures offered us; one, the ideal savage of Longfellow, the primitive man, so noble in nature that he was incapable of anything small or mean or wicked; the other was presented by those who coveted his possessions, and, to justify their robberies, they sketched the Indian as a dirty, filthy, squalid wretch, a demon of cruelty and cowardice, incapable of a human emotion, and never good till dead.

Which of these is the true picture? Let us calmly examine the pages of history, taking the words and records of Redmen and white, friends and foes of the Indian, and be prepared to render a verdict, in absolute accordance with that evidence, no matter where it leads us.

Let us begin by admitting that it is fair to take the best examples of the red race, to represent Indian philosophy and goodness; even as we ourselves would prefer being represented by Emerson, Tolstoi, Lincoln, Spencer, Peabody, General Booth, or Whitman, rather than by the border ruffians and cut-throat outlaws who were the principal exemplars of our ways among the Indians.

It is freely admitted that in all tribes, at all times, there were reprobates and scoundrels, a reproach to the people; just as amongst ourselves we have outcasts, tramps, drunkards, and criminals. But these were despised by their own people, and barely tolerated.

We must in fairness judge the Indian and his way of life and thought by the exemplifications of his best types: Hiawatha, Wabasha I, Tshut-che-nau, Ma-to-to-pa, Tecumseh, Kanakuk, Chief Joseph, Dull Knife, Washakie, and many that loved their own people and were in no wise touched by the doctrines of the whites.

If from these men we gather their beliefs, their teachings, and the common thoughts that guided their lives, we may fairly assume that we have outlined the creed of the best Indians.

THE INDIAN'S CREED

These are the main thoughts in the Redman's creed:

(1) While he believed in many gods, he accepted the idea of one Supreme Spirit, who was everywhere all the time; whose help was needed continually, and might be secured by prayer and sacrifice.

(2) He believed in the immortality of the soul, and that its future condition was to be determined by its behavior in this life.

(3) He reverenced his body as the sacred temple of his spirit; and believed it his duty in all ways to perfect his body, that his earthly record might be the better.

We cannot, short of ancient Greece, find his equal in physical perfection.

(4) He believed in the subjection of the body by fasting, whenever it seemed necessary for the absolute domination of the spirit; as when, in some great crisis, that spirit felt the need for better insight.

(5) He believed in reverence for his parents, and in old age supported them, even as he expected his children to support him.

(6) He believed in the sacredness of property. Theft among Indians was unknown.

(7) He believed that the murderer must expiate his crime with his life; that the nearest kin was the proper avenger, but that for accidental manslaughter compensation might be made in goods.

(8)   He believed in cleanliness of body.

(9)   He believed in purity of morals.

(10)   He believed in speaking the truth, and nothing but the truth.   His promise was absolutely binding.   He hated and despised a liar, and held all falsehood to be an abomination.

(11)   He believed in beautifying all things in his life.

He had a song for every occasion — a beautiful prayer for every stress.   His garments were made beautiful with painted patterns, feathers, and quill-work.   He had dances for every fireside.   He has led the world in the making of beautiful baskets, blankets, and canoes; while the decorations he put on lodges, weapons, clothes, dishes, and dwellings, beds, cradles, or grave-boards, were among the countless evidences of his pleasure in the beautiful, as he understood it.

(12)   He believed in the simple life.

He held, first, that land belonged to the tribe, not to the individual; next, that the accumulation of property was the beginning of greed that grew into monstrous crime.

(13)   He believed in peace and the sacred obligations of hospitality.

(14)   He believed that the noblest of virtues was courage, and that, above all other qualities, he worshipped and prayed for.   So also he believed that the most shameful of crimes was being afraid.

(15)   He believed that he should so live his life that the fear of death could never enter into his heart; that when the last call came he should put on the paint and honors of a hero going home, then sing his death song and meet the end in triumph.

If we measure this great pagan by our Ten Commandments, we shall find that he accepted and obeyed them, all

but the first and third: that is, he had many lesser gods
besides the one Great Spirit, and he knew not the Sabbath
Day of rest.   His religious faith, therefore, was much the
same as that of the mighty Greeks, before whom all the
world of learning bows; not unlike that of many Christians
and several stages higher than that of the Huxley and
other modern schools of materialism.

THE DARK SIDE

These are the chief charges against the Indian:
First: He was cruel to his enemies, even torturing them
at the stake in extreme cases.   He knew nothing about for-
giving and loving them.

In the main, this is true.   But how much less cruel he was
than the leaders of the Christian Church in the Middle
Ages!   What Indian massacre will compare in horror with
that of St. Bartholomew's Eve or the Massacre of Glencoe?
Read the records of the Inquisition, or the Queen Mary
persecutions in England, or the later James II. abominations for further light!

There was no torture used by the Indians that was not
also used by the Spainards.   Every frontiersman of the
Indian days knows that in every outbreak the whites were
the aggressors; and that in every evil count — robbery,
torture and massacre — they did exactly as the Indians did.   "The ferocity of the Redman," says Bourke,
"has been more than equaled by the ferocity of the
Christian Caucasian."   ("On the Border with Crook,"
p. 114.)

There are good grounds for stating that the Indians were
cruel to their enemies, but it is surprising to see how little of
this cruelty there was in primitive days.   In most cases the
enemy was killed in battle or adopted into the tribe; very,

very rarely was he tortured.   Captain Clark says of the Cheyennes:

"There is no good evidence that captives have been burned at the stake, flayed alive, or any other excruciating torture inflicted on persons captured by these fierce, war-loving and enterprising barbarians."   (" Sign Language," p. 106.)

But we know now that the whites did use diabolical tortures in their dealings with the Indian, and deliberately and persistently misrepresented him in order to justify their own atrocities.

The whites, however, had print to state their case, while the Indians had none to tell their story or defend them. Furthermore, it is notorious that all massacres of Indians by the whites were accomplished by treachery *in times of peace*, while all Indian massacres of whites were *in time of war*, to resist invasion.   At present, I know of no exception to this rule.*

In almost every case, it must be said that the army officers and men were personally guiltless.   They were impressed with the heroism of the Indians, admired them for their bravery, were horrified by the wickedness of the orders sent them, and did all they could to mitigate the atrocious policies of the shameless Indian Bureau.   But there were instances in which the army officers showed themselves the willing tools of the politicians.   Among the notorious cases was the cold-blooded massacre, in 1864, by Col. J. H. Chivington, of several hundred Cheyennes. Men, women, and children had surrendered and disarmed, and were, indeed, at the time, under military protection. The fiendish cruelty and cowardice of that one attack on these defenseless beings was enough to more than justify

---

*Many supposed massacres by Indians are now known to have been the work of whites disguised as Indians.

everything the Cheyennes have ever done to the race of the assassins. (See "Century of Dishonor," pp. 341-358.)

Still worse was the Baker massacre of Blackfeet, on January 23, 1870.

A border ruffian, a white man named Clark, had assaulted a young Indian, beating him severely, and the Indian, in retaliation, had killed Clark and gone off into Canada. Without troubling to find the guilty party, or even the band he belonged to, Brevet Col. E. M. Baker, major Second Cavalry, stationed at Fort Shaw, marched out, under orders from Gen. Philip H. Sheridan, to the nearest Indian village, on Marias River; as it happened, they were peaceable, friendly Indians, under Bear's Head. Without warning, the soldiers silently surrounded the sleeping village. But the story is better told by Schultz, who was on the spot later, and **heard** it all from those who saw:

"In a low tone Colonel Baker spoke a few words to his men, telling them to keep cool, aim to kill, to spare none of the enemy; and then he gave the command to fire. A terrible scene ensued. On the day previous, many of the men of the camp had gone out toward the Sweetgrass Hills on a grand buffalo hunt; so, save for Chief Bear's Head and a few old men, none were there to return the soldiers' fire. Their first volley was aimed low down into the lodges, and many of the sleeping people were killed or wounded in their beds. The rest rushed out, men, children, women, many of the latter with babes in their arms, only to be shot down at the doorways of their lodges. Bear's Head, frantically waving a paper which bore testimony to his good character and friendliness to the white men, ran toward the command on the bluff, shouting to them to cease firing, entreating them to save the women and children; down he also went with several bullet holes in his body. Of the more than four hundred souls in camp at the time, very few escaped. And when it was all over, when the last wounded woman and child had been put out of misery, the soldiers piled the corpses on overturned lodges, firewood and household property, and se, fire to it all.

"Several years afterward I was on the ground. Everywhere scattered about in the long grass and brush, just where the wolves and foxes had left them, gleamed the skulls and bones of those who had been so ruthlessly slaughtered. 'How could they have done it?' I asked myself, time and time again. 'What manner of men were these soldiers who deliberately shot down defenseless women and innocent children?' They had not even the excuse of being drunk; nor was their commanding officer intoxicated; nor were they excited or in any danger whatever. Deliberately, coolly, with steady and deadly aim they shot them down, killed the wounded, and then tried to burn the bodies of their victims. But I will say no more about it. Think it over, yourself, and try to find a fit name for men who did this." ("My Life as an Indian," pp. 41–2.)

According to G. B. Grinnell, one hundred and seventy-six innocent persons were butchered on this day of shame; ninety of them women, fifty-five babies, the rest chiefly very old or very young men, most of the able-bodied hunters being away on a hunt. No punishment of any kind was given the monster who did it.

There is no Indian massacre of whites to compare with this shocking barbarity, for at least the Indian *always had the excuse that war had been declared*, and he was acting on the defensive. Of a similar character were the massacres at Cos Cob, 1641; Conestoga, 1763; Gnadenwhütten, 1782; Coquille River, 1854; Wounded Knee, 1890; and a hundred more that could be mentioned. And no punishment was ever meted out to the murderers. Why? First, because apparently the Bureau at Washington approved; second, because "An Indian has no legal status; he is merely a live and particularly troublesome animal in the eye of the law." (New York *Times*, February 21, 1880.) (See "Century of Dishonor," p. 367.) Governor Horatio Seymour says:

"Every human being born upon our continent, or who comes here from any quarter of the world, whether savage or civilized, can go to our courts for protection — except those who belong to the tribes who once owned this country.   The cannibal from the islands of the Pacific, the worst criminals from Europe, Asia or Africa, can appeal to the law and courts for their rights of person and property — all save our native Indians, who, above all, should be protected from wrong." (Century of Dishonor," title-page.)

And this is the land whose Constitution grants equal rights to all alike.   This is the land that waxes virtuously indignant when Russia expels or massacres Nihilists, Poles or Jews.   Have we not enough courage left to face the simple truth that every crime of despotism in Russia has been more than doubled in atrocity by what has but recently been done in America?   Nihilists, Jews and Poles were certainly breaking the law, usually plotting against the Government, when attacked.   Russia never used burnings at the stake, as did the American unofficial Indian-killers. And never did Russia turn batteries of machine-guns on masses of men, women and children who were absolutely quiet, unarmed, helpless and submissive: who had indeed thrown themselves on the mercy of the Government, and were under its protection.

Americans were roused to a fury of indignation by doubtful newspaper accounts of Spanish misrule in Cuba.   But the atrocities so credited to Spain pale into insignificance beside the unspeakable abominations proved against the United States by records of its own officials in its dealings with the native American race during the last hundred years.

There are many exceptions to this charge that the Indian is cruel to his enemies, enough, almost, to justify a complete rebuttal, and among these was none more honorably distinguished than Tecumseh, the war chief of the Shawnees; perhaps the greatest of all historic Indians. Like a new incarnation of Hiawatha, he planned a defensive federation of the whole red race, and led them in war, that he might secure for them lasting peace. All great Indians had taught the doctrine "Love your friend." But Tecumseh was the first in authority to extend the heaven-taught precept, so they should be *kind*, at least, to their enemies; for he put an end in his nation to all torturing of prisoners.

Above all whose history is fully known, Tecumseh was the ideal noble Redman realized; nevertheless, he was not alone; Wabasha, Osceola, Kanakuk, and Wovoka must be numbered among those whose great hearts reached out in kindness even to those who hated them.

Tecumseh taught, "Love your enemy after he is conquered"; Kanakuk preached non-resistance to evil; Wovoka, "Be kind to all men."

Second: The Indian had no property instincts. He was a Socialist in all matters of large property, such as land, its fruits, rivers, fish, and game.

So were the early Christians. "And all that believed were together; had all things in common, and sold their possessions and goods, and parted them to all men, as every man had need." (Acts, ii., 44–45.)

They considered that every child had a right to a bringing up, and every old person to a free living from the tribe. We know that it worked well, for there was neither hunger nor poverty, except when the whole tribe was in want. And we know also that there were among them no men of shameful, monstrous wealth.

Third: He was improvident. He is *now*, just like our own drunkards. He was *not*, until after the Great Degradation that we effected in him. All the old travelers, testify that each Indian village had its fields of corn, beans, and pumpkins. The crops were harvested and safely carried them over long periods when there was no other supply. They did not believe in vast accumulations of wealth, because their wise men had said that greed would turn their hearts to stone and make them forget the poor. Furthermore, since all when strong contributed to the tribe, the tribe supported them in childhood, sickness and age. They had no poor; they had no famine until the traders came with whiskey and committed *the crimes for which we as a nation have yet to answer.*

Fourth: He was dirty. Many dirty habits are to be seen to-day among the Reservation Indians, but it was not so in the free days. A part of the old Indian's religion was to take a bath every day the year round for the helping of his body. Some tribes bathed twice a day. Every village had a Turkish bath in continual use. It is only the degraded Indian who has become dirty, and many of the whites who oftenest assail him as filthy never take a bath from birth to judgment day.

Fifth: He was lazy. No one who saw the Indian in his ancient form has preferred this charge. He was not fond of commercial manufacturing, but the regular work of tilling his little patch of corn and beans he did not shirk, nor the labor of making weapons and boats, nor the frightful toil of portaging, hunting and making war. He undertook these at all times without a murmur.

Many men will not allow their horses to bear such burdens as I saw the Chipewyans bear daily, without a thought of hardship, accepting all as a part of their daily lot.

Sixth: He degraded woman to be a mere beast of burden. Some have said so, but the vast bulk of evidence to-day goes to show that while the women did the household drudgery and lighter tasks, the men did all the work be-

yond their partners' strength. In making clothes, canoes,
and weapons, as well as in tilling of the fields, men and
women worked together. The woman had a voice in all
the great affairs, and a far better legal position than in most
of the civilized world to-day.

Seventh: He was treacherous. Oh! how ill it becomes *us*
to mention such a thing! Every authority tells us the
same — that primitive Redman never broke a treaty; his
word was as good as his bond; that the American Government broke every treaty as soon as there was something to
gain by doing so. Captain J. G. Bourke thus scores the
continual treachery of the whites: "The occasional treachery of the aborigines," says he, "has found its best excuse
in the unvarying Punic faith of the Caucasian invader."
("On the Border with Crook," p. 114.)

THE BRIGHT SIDE

But let us look for evidence of the Indian's character
among those who saw with their own eyes, and had no object to serve by blackening the fair fame of the bravely
dying race.

It would be easy to fill a large volume with startling and
trustworthy testimony as to the goodness of the old Indian
of the best type; I shall give a few pages bearing on the
Indian life and especially relating to the various character-
istics for which the Redman has been attacked, selecting the
testimony preferably from the records of men who knew the
Indian before his withering contact with the white race.

REVERENCE

In 1832 George Catlin, the painter, went West and spent
eight years with the unchanged Indians of the Plains. He
lived with them and became conversant with their lives.
He has left one of the fullest and best records we have of the

Redman. From his books I quote repeatedly. Concerning the Indian's religion, he says:

"The North American Indian is everywhere, in his native state, a highly moral and religious being, endowed by his Maker with an intuitive knowledge of some great Author of his being, and the Universe, in dread of whose displeasure he constantly lives, with the apprehension before him of a future state, where he expects to be rewarded or punished according to the merits he has gained or forfeited in this world.

* * * * * * *

"Morality and virtue I venture to say the civilized world need not undertake to teach them.

* * * * * * *

"I never saw any other people of any color *who spend so much of their lives* in humbling themselves before and worshipping the Great Spirit." (Catlin's "N. A. Indian," Vol. II., p. 243.)

"We have been told of late years that there is no evidence that any tribe of Indians ever believed in one overruling power; yet, in the early part of the seventeenth century, Jesuits and Puritans alike testified that tribes which they had met, believed in a god, and it is certain that, at the present time, many tribes worship a Supreme Being who is the Ruler of the Universe." (Grinnell's "Story of the Indian," 1902, p. 214.)

"Love and adore the Good Spirit who made us all; who supplies our hunting-grounds, and keeps us alive." (Teachings of Tshut-che-nau, Chief of the Kansas. J. D. Hunter's "Captivity Among the American Indians," 1798–1816, p. 21).

And, again, Hunter says (p. 216):

"A day seldom passes with an elderly Indian, or others who are esteemed wise and good, in which a blessing is not asked, or thanks returned to the Giver of Life, sometimes audibly, but more generally in the devotional language of the heart.

"Every Indian of standing has his sacred place, such as a tree, rock, fountain, etc., to which he resorts for devotional exercise, whenever his feelings prompt to the measure; sometimes many resort to the same place." (P. 221).

A typical prayer is recorded for us by Grinnell.

A Pawnee, in dire distress and despair, through a strong enemy, decided to sacrifice his horse to the unseen powers, that they might intercede for him with the Creator, and thus prayed beforehand:

"My Father [who dwells] in all places, it is through you that I am living. Perhaps it was through you that this man put me in this condition. You are the Ruler. Nothing is impossible with you. If you see fit, take this [trouble] away from me. Now you, all fish of the rivers, and you, all birds of the air, and all animals that move upon the earth, and you, O Sun! I present to you this animal. You, birds in the air, and you, animals upon the earth, we are related; we are alike in this respect, that one Ruler made us all. You see how unhappy I am. If you have any power, intercede for me." (Grinnell's "Story of the Indian," p. 213.)

Capt. W. P. Clark, one of our best authorities on the Plains Indians, says: "There are no people who pray more than Indians." ("Indian Sign Language," 1885, p. 309.)

And, again, he says:

"Indians make vocal petitions to the God or Force which they wish to assist them, and also make prayer by pointing the long stem of the pipe. The Poncas call the sun God or Grandfather, and the earth Grandmother, and pray to both when making supplications. Running Antelope, a chief of the Uncapapa Band of Sioux, said in regard to pointing the pipestem, that the mere motion meant, 'To the Great Spirit: give me plenty of ponies; plenty of meat; let me live in peace and comfort with my wife, and stay long with my children. To the Earth, my

Grandmother: let me live long; hold me good and strong. When I go to war, give me many ponies and let me count many "coups." In peace, let not anger enter my heart.'" (P. 309.)

But the best account of the Indian's belief and mode of worship is given to us by Dr. Charles A. Eastman, himself a Sioux Indian; he has written of the things that were his daily life in youth.   He says:

"When food is taken, the woman murmurs a 'grace' as she lowers the kettle, an act so softly and unobtrusively performed that one who does not know the custom usually fails to catch the whisper: 'Spirit partake!'   As her husband receives the bowl or plate, he likewise murmurs his invocation to the spirit. When he becomes an old man, he loves to make a notable effort to prove his gratitude.   He cuts off the choicest morsel of the meat and casts it into the fire — the purest and most ethereal element."   ("Soul of the Indian," 1911, pp. 47–48.)

"The first *hambeday*, or religious retreat, marked an epoch in the life of the youth, which may be compared to that of confirmation or conversion in Christian experience.   Having first prepared himself by means of the purifying vapor bath, and cast off, as far as possible, all human or fleshly influences, the young man sought out the noblest height, the most commanding summit in all the surrounding region.   Knowing that God sets no value upon material things, he took with him no offerings or sacrifices, other than symbolic objects, such as paints and tobacco.   Wishing to appear before Him in all humility, he wore no clothing save his moccasins and breech-clout.   At the solemn hour of sunrise or sunset, he took up his position, overlooking the glories of earth, and facing the 'Great Mystery,' and there he remained, naked, erect, silent, and motionless, exposed to the elements and forces of His arming, for a night and a day to two days and nights, but rarely longer.   Sometimes he would chant a hymn without words, or offer the ceremonial 'filled pipe.'   In this holy trance or ecstasy the Indian mystic found his highest happiness, and the motive power of his existence."   ("Soul of the Indian," Eastman, pp. 7–8.)

"In the life of the Indian there was only one inevitable duty, the duty of prayer — the daily recognition of the Unseen and Eternal. His daily devotions were more necessary to him than daily food. He wakes at daybreak, puts on his moccasins and steps down to the water's edge. Here he throws handfuls of clear cold water into his face, or plunges in bodily. After the bath, he stands erect before the advancing dawn, facing the sun as it dances upon the horizon, and offers his unspoken orison. His mate may precede or follow him in his devotions, but never accompanies him. Each soul must meet the morning sun, the new, sweet earth, and the Great Silence alone!

"Whenever, in the course of the daily hunt, the red hunter comes upon a scene that is strikingly beautiful or sublime — a black thunder-cloud, with the rainbow's glowing arch above the mountain; a white waterfall in the heart of a green gorge; a vast prairie tinged with the blood-red of sunset — he pauses for an instant in the attitude of worship. He sees no need for setting apart one day in seven as a holy day, since to him all days are God's." ("Soul of the Indian," Eastman; pp. 45–6.)

In the light of all this evidence, is it to be wondered that most of the early historians who lived with the primitive Indians of the Plains, were led to believe, from their worship of God, their strict moral code, their rigid laws as to foods clean and unclean, and their elaborate system of bathings and purifications, that in these red men of the New World, they had indeed found the long-lost tribes of Israel?

CLEANLINESS

Nothing will convince some persons but that "Yankees have tails," because, in their nursery days, these persons always heard it was so. That is exactly the attitude of the world on the subject of dirty Indians.

Alexander Henry II., a fur and whiskey trader, who did his share in degrading the early Indians, and did not love them, admits of the Mandans, in 1806:

"Both men and women make it a rule to go down to the river and wash every morning and evening." ("Journal," Vol. I., p. 325.)

"These people, like their neighbors, have the custom of washing, morning and evening." ("Journal," Vol. I., p. 348.)

Catlin, after eight years in their lodges (1832–40) says that notwithstanding many exceptions, among the wild Indians the "strictest regard to decency and cleanliness and elegance of dress is observed, and there are few people, perhaps, who take more pains to keep their persons neat and cleanly, than they do." (Vol. I., p. 96.)

"In their bathing and ablutions at all seasons of the year, as a part of their religious observances — having separate places for men and women to perform these immersions — they resemble again [the Jews]." (Vol. II., p. 233.)

J. W. Schultz, who spent his life among the Blackfeet, comments on their wonderful hardiness. During the intensest zero weather, he, himself, wore twice as much clothing as they did, and yet was suffering severely, while "They never froze, nor even shivered from the cold. They attributed their indifference to exposure, to the beneficial effect of their daily baths, which were always taken, even if a hole had to be cut in the ice for the purpose. And they forced their children to accompany them, little fellows from three years of age up, dragging the unwilling ones from ther beds, and carrying them under their arms to the icy plunge." ("My Life as an Indian," pub. 1907; p. 63.)

This same experienced observer says:

"I have seen hundreds of white homes — there are numbers of them in any city — so exceedingly dirty, their inmates so slovenly, that one turns from them in absolute disgust, but I have seen nothing like that among the Blackfeet." (P. 413.)

Friendly enthusiasts like Catlin may sometimes get only part of the facts, but the trained observers of the Smith-

sonian Institution usually have absolute and complete
evidence to offer. Here is J. O. Dorsey's paragraph on
Omaha cleanliness:

"The Omahas generally bathe (hica) every day in warm
weather, early in the morning and at night. Some who wish to
do so, bathe also at noon. Jackson, a member of the Elkgens,
bathes every day, even in winter. He breaks a hole in the ice
on the Missouri River, and bathes, or else he rubs snow over
his body. In winter the Omahas heat water in a kettle and wash
themselves (kigcija). . . .   The Ponkas used to bathe in
the Missouri every day." (Dorsey, 3th Ann. Dep. Eth.;
p. 269.)

Every Indian village in the old days had a Turkish bath,
as we call it; a "Sweat Lodge," as they say, used as a
cure for inflammatory rheumatism, etc. Catlin de-
scribes this in great detail, and says:

"I allude to their vapor baths, or *sudatories*, of which
each village has several, and which seem to be a kind of
public property — accessible to all, and resorted to by all, male
and female, old and young, sick and well." (Vol. I., p. 97.)

The "Sweat Lodge" is usually a low lodge covered with
blankets or skins. The patient goes in undressed and sits
by a bucket of water. In a fire outside, a number of stones
are heated by the attendants. These are rolled in, one or
more at a time. The patient pours water on them. This
raises a cloud of steam. The lodge becomes very hot.
The individual drinks copious draughts of water. After
a sufficient sweat, he raises the cover and rushes into the
water, beside which, the lodge is always built. After this,
he is rubbed down with buckskin, and wrapped in a robe
to cool off.

This was used as a bath, as well as a religious purification.

I have seen scores of them.   Clark says they were "common
to all tribes," (p. 365).   Every old-timer knows that they
were in daily use by the Indians and scoffed at by the white
settlers who, indeed, were little given to bathing of any kind.

CHASTITY

About one hundred years ago the notorious whiskey-
trader, Alexander Henry, already mentioned, went into
the Missouri region.   He was a man of strange character,
of heroic frame and mind, but unscrupulous and sordid.
His only interest and business among the Indians was
beating them out of their furs with potations of cheap
alcohol.   This fearless ruffian penetrated the far Northwest, was the first trader to meet certain Western tribes,
and strange to tell he wrote a full, straightforward and
shocking account of his wanderings and methods among the
red folk he despised for not being white.   In spite of arrogance and assumed superiority, his narrative contains
much like the following:

"The Flatheads on the Buffalo Plains, generally encounter the
Piegans and fight desperately when attacked.   They never
attempt war themselves, and have the character of a brave and
virtuous people, not in the least addicted to those vices so
common among savages who have had long intercourse with
Europeans.   Chastity is particularly esteemed, and no woman
will barter her favors, even with the whites, upon any mer-
cenary consideration.   She may be easily prevailed upon
to reside with a white man as his wife, according to the custom
of the country, but prostitution is out of the question —she will
listen to no proposals of that nature.   Their morals have not
yet been sufficiently debauched and corrupted by an intercourse
with people who call themselves Christians, but whose licentious
and lecherous manners are far worse than those of savages.   A
striking example is to be seen throughout the N. W. country, of
the depravity and wretchedness of the natives, but as one

advances into the interior parts, vice and debauchery become less frequent. Happy those who have the least connection with us, for most of the present depravity is easily traced to its origin in their intercourse with the whites. That baneful source of all evils, spirituous liquor, has not yet been introduced among the natives of the Columbia. To the introduction of· that subtle poison among the savage tribes may be mainly attributed their miserable and wretched condition." [So at once he set about introducing it. E. T. S.] (A. Henry's Journal, 1811; pp. 710-11.)

Jonathan Carver, who traveled among the Sioux from 1766-9, says:

"Adultery is esteemed by them a heinous crime, and punished with the greatest rigor." (Travels, 1796; p. 245.)

George Catlin, after his eight years among the wild Mandans of the Missouri (1832), says of them:

"Their women are beautiful and modest — and amongst the respectable families, virtue is as highly cherished and as inapproachable, as in any society whatever." (Vol. I., p. 121.)

Colonel R. I. Dodge, an Indian fighter and hater, says:

"The Cheyenne women are retiring and modest, and for chastity will compare favorably with women of any other nation or people . . . almost models of purity and chastity." ("Hunting-grounds of the Great West," p. 302.)

I am well aware that the Crows, the Arapaho and some West coast tribes were shockingly immoral in primitive times, but these were the exceptions, and in consequence they were despised by the dominant tribes of the Plains.

BRAVERY

Old-time travelers and modern Indian fighters agree that there was no braver man on earth, alive or in history, than the Redman. Courage was the virtue he chiefly honored. His whole life and training were with the pur-

pose of making him calm, fearless and efficient in every
possible stress or situation.

Father Lafitau said of the Eastern Indians, in 1724:

"They are high-minded and proud; possess a courage equal to
every trial; an intrepid valor; the most heroic constancy under
torments, and an equanimity which neither misfortune nor
reverses can shake." (Moeurs des Sauv. Amer.)

"An Indian meets death, when it approaches him in his hut,
with the same resolution he has often faced him in the field.
His indifference relative to this important article, which is the
source of so many apprehensions to almost every other nation,
is truly admirable. When his fate is pronounced by the physician, and it remains no longer uncertain, he harangues those
about him with the greatest composure." (Carver's "Travels
Among the Sioux," 1766–9; p. 261.)

"The greatest insult that can be offered to an Indian, is, to
doubt his courage." (J. D. Hunter, "Captivity"; 1798–1816;
p. 301.)

"These savages are possessed with many heroic qualities, and
bear every species of misfortune with a degree of fortitude which
has not been outdone by any of the ancient heroes either of
Greece or of Rome." (Carver's "Travels Among the Sioux,"
1766–9; pp. 221–2.)

None of us are likely to question the Redman's prowess when
we remember for example that Black Hawk with 40 warriors
utterly routed 270 American riflemen in 1832, Chief Joseph in 1877
with inferior weapons beat the American soldiers over and over
again with half their number, and in 1878 Dull Knife with 69 warriors fought and defied 2000 American troops for over four months.

Every Indian village in the old days had its granaries of
corn, its stores of dried beans, berries, and pumpkin-strips,
as well as its dried buffalo tongues, pemmican and deer's
meat. To this day all the Fisher Indians of the north and
west dry great quantities of fish, as well as berries, for the
famine months that are surely coming.

Many of the modern Indians, armed with rifles, have

learned to emulate the white man, and slaughter game for the love of slaughter, without reference to the future. Such waste was condemned by the old-time Indians, as an abuse of the gifts of God, and which would surely bring its punishment.

When, in 1684, De la Barre, Governor of Canada, complained that the Iroquois were encroaching on the country of those Indians who were allies of the French, he got a stinging reply from Garangula, the Onondaga Chief, and a general statement showing that *the aborigines had game-laws*, not written, indeed, but well known, and enforced at the spear-point, if need be: "We knock the Twightwies [Miamis] and Chictaghicks [Illinois] on the head, because they had cut down the trees of peace, which were the limits of our country. They have hunted beaver on our lands. They have acted contrary to the customs of all Indians, for they left none of the beavers alive, they killed both male and female." (Sam G. Drake's "Indian Biog." 1832, p. 111.)

Hunter says of the Kansas Indians:

"I have never known a solitary instance of their wantonly destroying any of those animals [buffalo, elk, and deer], except on the hunting-grounds of their enemies, or encouraged to it by the prospect of bartering their skins with the traders." (Hunter's "Captivity," 1798-1816, p. 279.)

"After all, the Wild Indians could not be justly termed improvident, when the manner of life is taken into consideration. They let nothing go to waste, and labored incessantly during the summer and fall, to lay up provisions for the inclement season. Berries of all kinds were industriously gathered and dried in the sun. Even the wild cherries were pounded up, stones and all, made into small cakes, and dried, for use in soups, and for mixing with the pounded jerked meat and fat to form a much-prized Indian delicacy." ("Indian Boyhood," Eastman; pp. 237-8.)

Their wise men were not blind to the dangers of greed, as we know, from many sources, and, in particular, their attitude toward money-getting is full of interest:

"The Indians, except those who live adjoining to the European colonies, can form to themselves no idea of the value of money; they consider it, when they are made acquainted with the uses to which it is applied by other nations, as the source of innumerable evils. To it they attribute all the mischiefs that are prevalent among Europeans, such as treachery, plundering, devastations and murder." (Carver's "Travels," p. 158.)

Could we have a more exact paraphrase of "The love of money is the root of all evil?"

Beware of greed which grows into crime and makes men forget the poor. A man's life should not be for himself, but for his people. For them he must be ready to die.

This is the sum of Indian economic teaching. (See Eastman "Soul of Indian," pp. 94 and 99–103.)

CHEERFULNESS OR THE MERRY INDIAN

Nothing seems to anger the educated Indian, to-day, more than the oft-repeated absurdity that his race was of a gloomy, silent nature. Any one that has ever been in an Indian village knows what a scene of joy and good cheer it normally was. In every such gathering there was always at least one recognized fun-maker, who led them all in joke and hilarious jest. Their songs, their speeches, their fairy-tales are full of fun and dry satire. The reports of the Ethnological Bureau sufficiently set forth these facts.

Eastman, the Sioux, says on this subject:

"There is scarcely anything so exasperating to me as the idea that the natives of this country have no sense of humor and no

faculty for mirth. This phase of their character is well understood by those whose fortune or misfortune it has been to live
among them, day in and day out, at their homes. I don't
believe I ever heard a real hearty laugh away from the Indians'
fireside. I have often spent an entire evening in laughter with
them, until I could laugh no more. There are evenings when
the recognized wit or story-teller of the village gives a free
entertainment which keeps the rest of the community in a
convulsive state until he leaves them. However, Indian humor
consists as much in the gestures and inflections of the voice, as
in words, and is really untranslatable." ("Indian Boyhood," p.
267.)

And, again, Grinnell:

"The common belief that the Indian is stoical, stolid, and
sullen, is altogether erroneous. They are really a merry people,
good-natured and jocular, usually ready to laugh at an amusing
incident or a joke, with a simple mirth that reminds one of
children." ("Ind. To-day," p. 9.)

There is, however, an explanation of our widespread misconception. Many a time in Indian camp or village, I have
approached some noisy group of children or hilarious ring of
those more grown. My purpose was wholly sympathetic, but
my presence acted as a wet-blanket. The children were hushed
or went away. I saw shy faces, furtive glances, or looks of dis-
trust. They hate us; they do not want us near. Our presence
is an evil influence in their joy. Can we wonder?

OBEDIENCE — REVERENCE FOR THEIR PARENTS AND FOR
THE AGED

We cannot, short of the Jews or the Chinese, perhaps, find
more complete respect for their parents than among the
Indians. Catlin says:

"To each other I have found these people kind and honorable,
and endowed with every feeling of parental, of filial, and con-

jugal affection, that is met in more enlightened communities. I have found them moral and religious; and I am bound to give them credit for their zeal, which is often exhibited in their modes of worship, however insufficient they may seem to us, or may be in the estimation of the Great Spirit." (Vol. II., p. 242.)

While Hunter, after living with the Kansas Indians for nineteen years, says:

"They are very assiduous and attentive to the wants and comforts, particularly, of the aged; and kind to all who require their assistance. And an Indian who failed in these respects, though he otherwise merited esteem, would be neglected and despised. To the credit of their morals, few such are to be found, except where debauched by the vices of the white people." (Hunter's "Captivity," 1798-1816; p. 251.)

Among the maxims laid down by the venerable Chief of the Kansas, was:

"Obey and venerate the old people, particularly your parents." ("Teachings of Tshut-che-nau, Chief of the Kansas;" Hunter; p. 21.)

Father J. F. Lafitau, the Jesuit missionary, was far from being predisposed in favor of savage ways or views, yet says of the Eastern Indians:

"Toward each other, they behave with a natural politeness and attention, entertaining a high respect for the aged." (Moeurs des Sauv. Am., 1724.)

"The Indians always took care of their aged and helpless. It was a rare exception when they did not." (Francis La Flesche, Conversation, April 27, 1912.)

There have been cases of Indians abandoning their very aged to die, but it was always done by request of the victims, under dire stress of hunger or travel, and was dis-approved and denounced by all their great teachers.

During my Northern journey in 1907 I selected for one of my guides a fine young Indian named Freesay. At the end of our first journey I said to him: "Would you like to go with me still farther, to the Far North country, and see the things your people have not yet seen? I will give you good wages and a big present."

He replied: "Yes; I would like to go very much, but my uncle [his adoptive father] told me not to go beyond Pike's Lobstick, and so I cannot go." And he did not, though his uncle was 350 miles away. This was one case out of several noted, and many heard of. The Fifth Commandment is a very big, strong law in the wigwam.

KINDNESS

At every first meeting of red men and whites, the whites were inferior in numbers, and yet were received with the utmost kindness, until they treacherously betrayed the men who had helped and harbored them. Even Christopher Columbus, blind and burnt up with avarice as he was, and soul-poisoned with superstition, and contempt for an alien race, yet had the fairness to write home to his royal accomplices in crime. the King and Queen of Spain:

"I swear to your Majesties that there is not a better people in the world than these; more affectionate, affable or mild. They love their neighbors as themselves, and they always speak smilingly. (Catlin, "N. A. Indian," II., p. 246.)

Jonathan Carver, who lived among the Sioux from 1766–9, after speaking of their severity in dealing with enemies, says:

"But if they are thus barbarous to those with whom they are
at war, they are friendly, hospitable, and humane in peace. It
may with truth be said of them, that they are the worst enemies
and the best friends of any people in the whole world." (" Travels," p. 157.)

"We shall likewise see them sociable and humane to those
whom they consider as their friends, and even to their adopted
enemies: and ready to partake with them of the last morsel, or
to risk their lives in their defence." (P. 269.)

And, again:

"No people are more hospitable, kind and free than the
Indians." (P. 171.)

"Nothing can exceed the tenderness shown by them to their
offspring." (P. 247.)

Catlin, writing of the Plain Indians generally, says:

"To their friends, there are no people on earth that are more
kind; and cruelties and punishments (except for capital offences)
are, amongst themselves, entirely dispensed with." (Vol. II.,
p. 241.)

Schultz evidently went among the Blackfeet with the
usual wrong ideas about the Indians, but he soon wrote:

"I have read, or heard, that an Indian's loss of to-day is forgotten on the morrow. That is certainly not true of the Blackfeet, nor the Mandans. Often and often I have heard many of
the Blackfeet mourn for one dead long years since." ("My
Life as an Indian," p. 154.)

And again:

"I have often heard the Blackfeet speak of various white men
as utterly heartless, because they had left their parents and their
youthful home to wander and seek adventure in a strange land.
They could not comprehend how one with right feeling might

absent himself from father and mother, as we do, for months and years. 'Hard hearts,' 'stone hearts,' they call us, and with some reason." (Schultz, p. 155.)

"There are few people so generous as the Indians.

*   *   *   *   *   *   *

In their religious and war ceremonies, at their feasts, festivals, and funerals, the widows and orphans, the poor and needy are always thought of; not only thought of,   . . .   but their poverty and necessity are relieved.

*   *   *   *   *   *   *

"I have seen white men reduced to the last 'hard tack,' with only tobacco enough for two smokes, and with no immediate prospect of anything better than horse-meat 'straight.' A portion of the hard bread was hidden away, and the smokes were taken in secret. An Indian, undemoralized by contact with the whites, under similar circumstances, would divide down to the last morsel." (Clark's "Sign Language," p. 185 and 186.)

HOSPITALITY

This is a point that needs little discussing, even the sworn enemy was safe, once he was admitted to an Indian lodge "as a guest."

Carver says of the Sioux, in 1766 ("Travels," p. 172):

"No people are more hospitable . . .   and free than the Indians."

And, again, I found them ready to share with their friends the last morsel of food they possessed. (P. 269.)

The Jesuits testify of the Iroquois, 1656:

"Hospitals for the poor would be useless among them, because there are no beggars; those who have are so liberal to those who are in want, that everything is enjoyed in common. The whole village must be in distress before any individual is left in necessity." ("Century of Dishonor," p. 379.)

Catlin, in 1832–40, enthusiastically writes of the Plains Indians and their hospitality:

"I have been welcomed generally in their country, and treated to the best that they could give me [for eight years], without any charges made for my board." (Vol. I., p. 9.)

"No matter how great the scarcity of food might be, so long as there was any remaining in the lodge, the visitor received his share without grudging." (Grinnell, "Ind. of To-day," p. 9.)

The same authority writes me:

"When Lone Chief had gone into the Lodge of the Chief of the enemy, and food and water had been given to him, the Chief stood up and spoke to his tribespeople saying, 'What can I do? They have eaten of my food, I cannot make war on people who have been eating with me and have also drunk of my water.'" ("Pawnee Hero Stories," pp. 59–60.)

TREATMENT OF THEIR WOMEN

"The social condition of the North Americans has been greatly misunderstood. The place of woman in the tribe was not that of a slave or of a beast of burden. The existence of the gentile organization, in most tribes, with descent in the female line, forbade any such subjugation of woman. In many tribes, women took part in the councils of the chiefs; in some, women were even the tribal rulers; while in all, they received a fair measure of respect and affection from those related to them." (Grinnell's "Story of the Indian," p. 244.)

This is Grinnell's summing up of what every student of Indians has known for long. Here in addition are the statements of other good authorities:

"I have often heard and read that Indian women received no consideration from their husbands, and led a life of exceedingly hard and thankless work. That is very wide of the truth, so

far as the natives of the northern plains were concerned. It is
true, that the women gathered fuel for the lodge — bundles of
dry willows, or limbs from a fallen cottonwood. They also did
the cooking, and, besides tanning robes, converted the skins of
deer, elk, antelope, and mountain sheep, into soft buckskin for
family use. But never a one of them suffered from overwork;
when they felt like it, they rested; they realized that there were
other days coming, and they took their time about anything
they had to do. Their husbands, never interfered with them,
any more than they did with him in his task of providing the
hides and skins and meat, the staff of life. The majority —
nearly all of them — were naturally industrious, and took pride
in their work; they joyed in putting away parfleche after parfleche of choice dried meats and pemmican; in tanning soft robes
and buckskins for home use or sale, in embroidering wonderful
patterns of beads or colored porcupine quills upon moccasin
tops, dresses, leggings and saddle trappings. When robes were
to be traded, they got their share of the proceeds." (Schultz,
p. 64.)

"It has often been asserted that the 'Indian' did no work,
even leaving the cultivation of the corn and squashes to the
women. That the women in some of the tribes tended the crops,
is true, but in others, like the Pueblos, they seldom or never
touched hoe or spade. The Eastern men were hunting or building boats, or were on the war-path, hence it was necessary for the
women to look after the fields." ("The N. A. of Yesterday,"
by F. S. Dellenbaugh, p. 333.)

Schultz tells us that the men had to make their own
clothing. ("My Life as an Indian," p. 180.)

Prof. J. O. Dorsey writes of Omaha manners:

"Politeness is shown by men to women. Men used to help
women and children to alight from horses. When they had to
ford streams, the men used to assist them, and sometimes they
carried them across on their backs." (Dorsey, 270-1; 3rd Ann.
Rep. Ethn.)

"One of the most erroneous beliefs relating to the status and
condition of the American Indian woman is, that she was, both
before and after marriage, the abject slave and drudge of the

men of her tribe, in general. This view, due largely to inaccurate observation and misconception, was correct, perhaps, at times, as to a small percentage of the tribes and peoples whose social organization was of the most elementary kind politically and ceremonially, and especially of such tribes as were non-agricultural." ("Handbook of American Indians," Bur. Am. Ethn., p. 968.)

"Among the Iroquoian tribes—the Susquehanna, the Hurons, and the Iroquois — the penalties for killing a woman of the tribe were double those exacted for the killing of a man, because in the death of a woman, the Iroquoian lawgivers recognized the probable loss of a long line of prospective offspring." ("Handbook American Indian," p. 971.)

"In most, if not in all, the highly organized tribes, the woman was the sole master of her own body." ("Handbook North American Indian," p. 972.)

"The men are the warriors and hunters, though an old woman of rank usually steers the war-canoe." ("Coast Indian"; Niblack; 1889; p. 253.)

"A mother possessed the important authority to forbid her sons going on the war-path, and frequently the chiefs took advantage of this power of the woman, to avoid a rupture with another tribe." ("Handbook North American Indian," p. 971.)

"Roger Williams, with reference to another subject, brings this same respect for woman to view; he wrote: 'So did never the Lord Jesus bring any unto his most pure worship, for he abhors, as all men, yea, the very Indians, an unwilling spouse to enter into forced relations." ("Handbook North America," p. 972.)

"At a later day, and in the face of circumstances adverse to the Indians, Gen. James Clinton, who commanded the New York Division in the Sullivan expedition in 1779, against the hostile Iroquois, paid his enemies the tribute of a soldier, by writing in April, 1779, to Colonel Van Schaick, then leading the troops against the Onondaga, the following terse compliment: 'Bad as the savages are, they never violate the chastity of any woman, their prisoners.'"

"Among the Sioux and the Yuchi, men who made a practice of seduction were in grave bodily danger, from the aggrieved women and girls, and the resort by the latter to extreme measures was sanctioned by public opinion, as properly avenging a gross violation of woman's inalienable right — the control of her own body. The dower or bride-price, when such was given, did not confer it, it seems, on the husband, absolute right over the life and liberty of the wife: it was rather compensation to her kindred and household for the loss of her services." ("Handbook American Indian," pp. 972,3.)

"It is the universal testimony, as voiced by Portlock (1787), that they [the Coast Indians] treat their wives and children with much affection and tenderness." ("Voyages," p. 290.) "In the approach to political and industrial equality of the sexes, and in the respect shown for the opinions of their females, these Indians furnish another refutation of the old misconception concerning the systematic mal-treatment of the women by savages. Such a thing is incompatible with the laws of nature. Good treatment of the female is essential to the preservation of the species, and it will be found that this ill-treatment is more apparent than real." (Niblack, "Coast Indian," 1889, p. 238–9.)

That is, the sum of evidence, according to all reliable authority, plainly shows that the condition of the women among the primitive Indians was much as with white folks. They had the steady, dreary work of the household, while the men did the intermittent, yet much harder work of portaging, hunting and fighting. But the Indian woman had several advantages over her white sister. She owned the house and the children. She had absolute control of her body. There could be no war without her consent; she could and often did become the Head Chief of the Nation.

Awashonks, the Woman Chief of Seconset, R. I. (1671), and Wetamoo, the beautiful woman Sachem of the Massachusetts Wampanoags (1662) were among the many famous women whose lives and positions give the lie to the tiresome calumny that the "Indian women were mere beasts of burden; they had no rights, nor any voice in their public affairs."

COURTESY AND POLITE BEHAVIOR

There has never been any question of the Redman's politeness. Every observer remarks it. I have seen countless cases of it, myself. The white who usurped his domain are immeasurably his inferiors in such matters.

For fuller testimony, let us note these records by early travelers:

"Toward each other, they behave with natural politeness and attention." (Pere Lafitau, 1724.)

Catlin says of the Mandans:

"They are handsome, straight, and elegant in their forms — not tall, but quick and graceful; easy and polite in their manners, neat in their persons, and beautifully clad." (Catlin; Vol. I., p. 96.)

"The next and second Chief of the [Mandan] tribe is Ma-to-to-pa (The Four Bears). This extraordinary man, though second in office, is undoubtedly the first and most popular man in the nation. Free, generous, elegant and gentlemanly in his deportment — handsome, brave and valiant; wearing a robe on his back with the history of his battles emblazoned on it, which would fill a book of themselves, if properly translated. This, readers, is the most extraordinary man, perhaps, who lives at this day, in the atmosphere of Nature's nobleman." (Catlin; Vol. I., p. 92.)

Omaha politeness: "When persons attend feasts, they extend their hand and return thanks to the giver. So, also, when they receive presents.

    *   *   *   *   *   *   *

"If a man receives a favor and does not manifest his gratitude, they exclaim, 'He does not appreciate the gift; he has no manners!'

    *   *   *   *   *   *   *

"Mothers teach their children not to pass in front of people, if they can avoid it." (Dorsey, 3d Ann. Rep. Bur. Eth. 1881-2, p. 270.)

TEEPEE ETIQUETTE — THE UNWRITTEN LAW OF THE LODGE

(Gathered chiefly from observations of actual practice, but in many cases from formal precept.)

Be hospitable.

Always assume that your guest is tired, cold, and hungry.

Always give your guest the place of honor in the lodge, and at the feast, and serve him in reasonable ways.

Never sit while your guest stands.

Go hungry rather than stint your guest.

If your guest refuses certain food, say nothing; he may be under vow.

Protect your guest as one of the family; feed his horse, and beat your dogs if they harm his dog.

Do not trouble your guest with many questions about himself; he will tell you what he wishes you to know.

In another man's lodge follow his customs, not your own.

Never worry your host with your troubles.

Always repay calls of courtesy; do not delay.

Give your host a little present on leaving; little presents are little courtesies and never give offence.

Say "Thank you" for every gift, however small.

Compliment your host, even if you strain the facts to do so.

Never walk between persons talking.

Never interrupt persons talking.

Let not the young speak among those much older, unless asked.

Always give place to your seniors in entering or leaving the lodge; or anywhere.

Never sit while your seniors stand.

Never force your conversation on any one.

Speak softly, especially before your elders, or in presence of strangers.

Never come between any one and the fire.

Do not touch live coals with a steel knife or any sharp steel.

Do not stare at strangers; drop your eyes if they stare hard at you; and this, above all, for women.

The women of the lodge are the keepers of the fire, but the men should help with the heavier sticks.

Always give a word or sign of salute when meeting or passing a friend, or even a stranger, if in a lonely place.

Do not talk to your mother-in-law at any time, or let her talk to you.

Be kind.

Show respect to all men, but grovel to none.

Let silence be your motto till duty bids you speak.

Thank the Great Spirit for each meal.

HONESTY

Catlin says:

"As evidence of . . . their honesty and honor, there will be found recorded many striking instances in the following pages.

*   *   *   *   *   *   *

"I have roamed about, from time to time, during seven or eight years, visiting and associating with some three or four hundred thousands of these people, under an almost infinite variety of circumstances;

*   *   *   *   *   *   *

and under all these circumstances of exposure, no Indian ever betrayed me, struck me a blow, or stole from me a shilling's worth of my property, that I am aware of." (Vol. I., p. 9–10.)

"Never steal, except it be from an enemy, whom it is just that we should injure in every possible way." ("Teachings of Tshut-che-nau, Chief of Kansas," Hunter; p. 21.)

"Among [between] the individuals of some tribes or nations,

theft is a crime scarcely known." (Hunter's "Captivity Among American Indians," 1798-1816; p. 300.)

"Theft was unknown in an Indian camp." (G. B. Grinnell; "Indians of To-day," p. 8.)

Every traveler among the highly developed tribes of the Plains Indians tells a similar story, though, of course, when at war, it was another matter.

Even that rollicking old cut-throat, Alexander Henry II, says after fifteen years among the Wild Indians: "I have been frequently fired at by them and have had several narrow escapes for my life. But I am happy to say they never pillaged me to the value of a needle." ("Journal" 1799-1814, p. 452.)

In my own travels in the Far North, 1907, I found the Indians tainted with many white vices, and in many respects degenerated, but I also found them absolutely honest, and I left valuable property hung in trees for months, without fear, knowing that no wild Indian would touch it.

There is a story told of Bishop Whipple:

He was leaving his cabin, with its valuable contents, to be gone some months, and sought some way of rendering all robber-proof. His Indian guide then said: "Why, Brother, leave it open. Have no fear. There is not a white man within a hundred miles!"

On the road to a certain large Indian Ojibway village in 1904 I lost a considerable roll of bills. My friend, the white man in charge, said: "If an Indian finds it, you will have it again within an hour; if a white man finds it, you will never see it again, for our people are very weak, when it comes to property matters."

Finally, to cover the far Southwest, I found that the experience of most travelers agrees with the following:

"I lived among the Wild Indians for eight years (1872–1880); I know the Apaches, the Navajos, the Utes, and the Pueblos, and I never knew a dishonest Indian." (Robert A. Widenmann, West Haverstraw, N. Y.)

TRUTHFULNESS AND HONOR

"Falsehood they esteem much more mean and contemptible than stealing. The greatest insult that can be offered to an Indian, is, to doubt his courage: the next is to doubt his honor or truth!

*   *   *   *   *   *   *

"Lying, as well as stealing, entails loss of character on habitual offenders; and, indeed, an Indian of independent feelings and elevated character will hold no kind of intercourse with any one who has been once clearly convicted." (Hunter's "Captivity Among Indians," 1797–1816, p. 301.)

"This venerable, worn-out warrior [the Kansas Chief, Tshut-che-nau, Defender of the People], would often admonish us for our faults and exhort us never to tell a lie." (Hunter, p. 21.)

"On all occasions, and at whatever price, the Iroquois spoke the truth, without fear and without hesitation." (Morgan's "League of the Iroquois," p. 330.)

"The honor of their tribe, and the welfare of their nation is the first and most predominant emotion of their hearts; and from hence proceed in a great measure all their virtues and their vices. Actuated by this, they brave every danger, endure the most exquisite torments, and expire triumphing in their fortitude, not as a personal qualification, but as a national characteristic." (Carver's "Travels," p. 271.)

The Indian's assent to a treaty was always binding. I cannot discover a case of breach, excepting when the whites first broke it; and this does not mean the irresponsible whites, but the American Government. The authorities at Washington never hesitated to break each and every treaty apparently, as soon as some material benefit seemed likely to accrue.

Col. R. I. Dodge says:

"The three principal causes of wars with the Indians are:
"First, Non-fulfilment of treaties by the United States Government.
"Second, Frauds by the Indian agents.
"Third, Encroachments by the whites." ("Hunting-grounds of the Great West," 1878, pp. XLIII–XLIV.)

Captain John G. Bourke, who served under General Crook in 1872, when the Apaches were crushed by overwhelming numbers and robbed of their unquestioned heritage, says:

"It was an outrageous proceeding, one for which I should still blush, had I not long since gotten over blushing for anything that the United States Government did in Indian matters." ("On the Border with Crook," p. 217.)
"The most shameful chapter of American history is that in which is recorded the account of our dealings with the Indians. The story of our Government's intercourse with this race is an unbroken narrative of injustice, fraud and robbery." (Grinnell's "Blackfoot Lodge Tales," 1892, p. IX.)

In brief, during our chief dealings with the Redman, our manners were represented by the border outlaws, the vilest criminals the world has known, absolute fiends; and our Government by educated scoundrels of shameless, heartless, continual greed and treachery.

The great exception on American soil was that of William Penn. He kept his word. He treated the Indians fairly; they never wronged him to the extent of a penny, or harmed him or his, or caused a day's anxiety; but continued his loyal and trusty defenders." (See Jackson's "Century of Dishonor.")

How is it that Canada has never had an Indian war or an Indian massacre? Because the Government honorably kept all its treaties, and the Indians themselves were honorable, by tradition; they never yet broke a treaty. In northwestern Canada, there were two slight outbreaks of half-breeds (1871 and 1885), but these were misunderstandings, easily settled. There was little fighting, no massacres, and no heritage of hate in their track.

What wonder that all who could, among the Indian tribes, moved over the "Medicine Line," and dwell in Canada to-day!

TEMPERANCE AND SOBRIETY

When the white traders struck into the West with their shameful cargoes of alcohol to tempt the simple savages, it was the beginning of the *Great Degradation* for which we must answer.

The leading Indians soon saw what the drink habit meant, and strove in vain to stem the rising current of madness that surely would sweep them to ruin.

About 1795, Tshut-che-nau, chief of the Kansas, did his best to save the youth of his people from the growing vice of the day.

"'Drink not the poisonous strong-water of the white people;' he said, 'it is sent by the Bad Spirit to destroy the Indians.' He preached, but preached in vain." (J. D. Hunter, p. 21.)

Pere Lafitau says, in 1724:

"They never permit themselves to indulge in passion, but always, from a sense of honor and greatness of soul, appear masters of themselves." (P. 378, "Century of Dishonor.")

In 1766, living among the Sioux, Carver writes:

"We shall find them temperate, both in their diet and potations (it must be remembered that I speak of those tribes who
have little communication with Europeans) that they withstand
with unexampled patience, the attacks of hunger, or the incle-
mency of the seasons, and esteem the gratification of their
appetites but as a secondary consideration.' ("Travels," p. 269.)

Concerning the temperance of the Wild Indian, Catlin
writes, in 1832:

"Every kind of excess is studiously avoided.

     *   *   *   *   *   *   *

"Amongst the wild Indians in this country, there are no beggars — no drunkards — and every man, from a beautiful
natural precept, studies to keep his body and mind in such a
healthy shape and condition as will, at all times, enable him to
use his weapons in self-defense, or struggle for the prize in their
manly games." (Catlin, Vol. I., p. 123.)

And, how was it he fell from these high ideals? Alas!
we know too well. G. B. Grinnell has sent me a record
which, in one form or another, might have been made about
every western tribe:

"The Reverend Moses Merrill, a missionary among the Oto
Indians from 1832 to the beginning of 1840, kept a diary from
which the following account is taken:
"'April 14, 1837. Two men from a trading expedition in the
Indian country called on me to-day. They state that one half
of the furs purchased in the Indian country are obtained in
exchange for whiskey. They also stated that the Shiennes, a
tribe of Indians on the Platte River, were wholly averse to drinking whiskey, but, five years ago — now (through the influence
of a trader, Captain Gant, who, by sweetening the whiskey,
induced them to drink the intoxicating draught), they are a
tribe of drunkards.'" ("Trans. and Repts. Nebraska State
Historical Society, IV.," p. 181.)

After describing the rigid dieting that formed part of the
Indian's training, Eastman adds:

"In the old days, no young man was allowed to use tobacco
in any form until he had become an acknowledged warrior and
had achieved a record." ("Ind. Boy.," p. 50.)

PHYSIQUE

We need but little evidence on this head. All historians,
hostile or friendly, admit the Indian to have been the finest
type of physical manhood the world has ever known.
None but the best, the picked, chosen and trained of the
whites, had any chance with them. Had they not been
crushed by overwhelming numbers, the Indians would
own the continent to-day.

Grinnell says ("Indians of To-day," p. 7.):

"The struggle for existence weeded out the weak and the
sickly, the slow and the stupid, and created a race physically
perfect, and mentally fitted to cope with the conditions which
they were forced to meet, so long as they were left to themselves."

Speaking of the Iroquois in *primitive condition*, Brinton
says that physically "they were unsurpassed by any other
on the continent, and I may even say by any other people
in the world." ("The American Race," p. 82.)

The most famous runner of ancient Greece was Phi-
dippides, whose record run was 152 miles in 2 days.
Among our Indians such a feat would have been considered very second rate. In 1882, at Fort Ellice, I saw a
young Cree who, on foot, had just brought in despatches
from Fort Qu' Appelle (125 miles away) in twenty-five hours.
It created almost no comment. I heard little from the traders but cool remarks like, "A good boy"; "pretty good run."
It was obviously a very usual exploit, among Indians.

"The Tarahumare mail carrier from Chihuahua to Batopilas, Mexico, runs regularly more than 500 miles a week; a Hopi messenger has been known to run 120 miles in 15 hours." ("Handbook American Indians," Part II., p. 802.)

The Arizona Indians are known to run down deer by sheer endurance, and every student of southwestern history will remember that Coronado's mounted men were unable to overtake the natives, when in the hill country, such was their speed and activity on foot.

We know that white men's ways, vices, and diseases have robbed them of much of their former physique, and yet, according to Dr. Daniel G. Brinton ("The American Race," 1891.)

"The five Companies (500 men) recruited from the Iroquois of New York and Canada, during the Civil War, stood first on the list among all the recruits of our army, for height, vigor, and corporeal symmetry." (Grinnell's "Indian of To-day," p. 56.)

The wonderful work of the Carlisle Indian School football team is a familiar example of what is meant by Indian physique, even at this late date, when the different life has done so much to bring them low.

(While this was in press the all round athletic championship of the world was won at the Olympic games (1912) by James Thorpe, a Carlisle Indian. He was at best the pick of 300,000, while against him were white men, the pick of 300,000,000.)

The whole case, with its spiritual motive, is thus summed up by Eastman in his inspiring account of the religion of his people, the Dakotas:

"The moment that man conceived of a perfect body, supple, symmetrical, graceful, and enduring — in that moment he had laid the foundation of a moral life.   No man can hope to maintain such a temple of the spirit beyond the period of adolescence, unless he is able to curb his indulgence in the pleasures of the senses. Upon this truth the Indian built a rigid system of physical training, a social and moral code that was the law of his life.

"There was aroused in him as a child a high ideal of manly strength and beauty, the attainment of which must depend upon strict temperance in eating and in the sexual relation, together with severe and persistent exercise. He desired to be a worthy link in the generations, and that he might not destroy by his weakness that vigor and purity of blood which had been achieved at the cost of so much self-denial by a long line of ancestors.

"He was required to fast from time to time for short periods and to work off his superfluous energy by means of hard running, swimming and the vapor bath. The bodily fatigue thus induced, especially when coupled with a reduced diet, is a reliable cure for undue sexual desires." (Eastman's "Soul of the Indian," pp. 90–92.)

In their wonderful physique, the result of their life-long, age-long training, in their courage, their fortitude, their skill with weapons, their devoted patriotism, they realize more than any other modern race has done the ideal of the Spartan Greek, with this advantage; that, in his moral code, the Indian was far superior.

IN GENERAL

"I admit," says Father Lallemant, of the Hurons, "that their habits and customs are barbarous in a thousand ways, but, after all, in matters which they consider as wrong, and which their public condemns, we observe among them less criminality than in France, although here the only punishment of a crime is the shame of having committed it." ("Century of Dishonor," p. 378.)

Even stronger is the summary of the Jesuit Father, J. F. Lafitau:

"They are high-minded and proud; possess a courage equal to every trial, an intrepid valor, the most heroic constancy under torments, and an equanimity which neither misfortunes not reverses can shake. Toward each other they behave with a natural politeness and attention, entertaining a high respect for the aged, and a consideration for their equals which appears scarcely reconciliable with that freedom and independence of which they are so jealous." (Moeurs des Sauv. Amer., 1724, quoted in "Century of Dishonor" p. 378.)

Long afterward the judicial Morgan in his League of the Iroquois, says, (p. 55):

"In legislation, in eloquence, in fortitude, and in military sagacity, they had no equals.
"Crimes and offences were so infrequent, under their social system, that the Iroquois can scarcely be said to have had a criminal code."

Captain John H. Bourke, who spent most of his active life as an Indian fighter, and who, by training, was an Indian hater, was at last, even in the horror of an Indian-crushing campaign, compelled to admit:

"The American Indian, born free as the eagle, would not tolerate restraint, would not brook injustice; therefore, the restraint imposed must be manifestly for his benefit, and the government to which he was subjected must be eminently one of kindness, mercy and absolute justice, without necessarily degenerating into weakness. The American Indian despises a liar. The American Indian is the most generous of mortals; at all his dances and feasts, the widow and the orphan are the first to be remembered." (Bourke's "On the Border with Crook," p. 226.)

"Bad as the Indians often are," says this same frontier veteran, "I have never yet seen one so demoralized that he was not an example in honor and nobility to the wretches who enrich themselves by plundering him of the little our Government apportions for him." (Bourke's "On the Border with Crook," p. 445.)

Catlin's summary of the race is thus:

"The North American Indian, in his native state, is an honest, hospitable, faithful, brave; warlike, cruel, revengeful, relentless — yet honorable — contemplative and religious being." (Vol. I., p. 8.)

Omitting here what he gives elsewhere, that the Redman is clean, virtuous, of splendid physique, a master of woodcraft, and that to many of his best representatives, the above evil adjectives do not apply.

Bishop Whipple thus sums up the wild Indian, after intimate knowledge, during a lifetime of associations, ("Century of Dishonor," Jackson; p. VII.):

"The North American Indian is the noblest type of a heathen man on the earth. He recognizes a Great Spirit; he believes in immortality; he has a quick intellect; he is a clear thinker; he is brave and fearless, and, until betrayed, he is true to his plighted faith; he has a passionate love for his children, and counts it a joy to die for his people. Our most terrible wars have been with the noblest types of the Indians and with men who had been the white man's friends. Nicolet said the Sioux were the finest type of wild men he had ever seen."

Why, then, has he so long been caluminated? "Because," explains the Bishop, "Ahab never speaks kindly of Naboth whom he has robbed of his vineyard. It soothes conscience to cast mud on the character of the one whom we have wronged."

When General Crook, after he had crushed, and enabled the nation to plunder the Apaches, was ordered to the northward on a similar expedition against the Sioux, a friend said to him, "It is hard to go on such a campaign," the General replied, "Yes, it is hard; but, sir, the hardest thing is to go and fight those whom you know are in the right." ("Century of Dishonor," p. VI.)

Finally, let me reproduce in full the account by Bonne ville, from which I have already selected portions:

In 1834, he visited the Nez Perces and Flatheads, and thus sums up these wholly primitive Indians, for they were as yet uncorrupted by the whiskey-trader or those who preached the love of money.

"They were friendly in their dispositions, honest to the most scrupulous degree in their intercourse with the white man." (P. 200.) "Simply to call these people religious would convey but a faint idea of the deep hue of piety and devotion which pervades their whole conduct. Their honesty is immaculate, and their purity of purpose and their observance of the rites of their religion are most uniform and remarkable. They are certainly more like a nation of saints than a horde of savages." ("Captain Bonneville's Narrative;" by Washington Irving, p. 171, 1837.)

It would, I know, be quite easy to collect incidents — true ones — that would seem to contradict each of these claims for the Redman, especially if we look among the degraded Indians of the Reservations. But I do not consider them disproofs any more than I consider our religion disproved by the countless horrors and wickedness recorded every day as our daily history, in every newspaper in every corner of the land. The fact remains that this was the ideal of the Indian, and many times that ideal was exemplified in their great men, and at all times the influence of their laws was strong.

One might select a hundred of these great Indians who led their people, as Plato led the Greeks or as Tolstoi led the Russians, and learn from each and all that dignity, strength, courtesy, courage, kindness, and reverence were indeed the ideals of the teepee folk, and that their ideal was realized more or less in all their history — that the noble Redman did indeed exist.

The earliest of the northern Indians to win immortal fame was the great Mohawk, Hiawatha. Although the Longfellow version of his life is not sound as history, we know that there was such a man; he was a great hero; he stood for peace, brotherhood, and agriculture; and not only united the Five Nations in a Peace League, but made provision for the complete extension of that League to the whole of America.

Pontiac, the Napoleon of his people; Tecumseh, the chevalier Bayard, who was great as warrior and statesman, as well as when he proclaimed the broad truths of humanity; Dull Knife, the Leonidas of the Cheyennes; Chief Joseph, the Xenophon of the Nez Perces; Wabasha, Little Wolf, Pita-Lesharu, Washakie, and a hundred others might be named to demonstrate the Redman's progress toward his ideals.

SUMMARY

Who that reads this record can help saying: "If these things be true, then, judging by its fruits, the Indian way must be better than ours. Wherein can we claim the better thought or results?"

To answer is not easy. My first purpose was to clear the memory of the Redman. To compare his way with ours, we must set our best men against his, for there is little difference in our doctrine.

One great difference in our ways is that, like the early Christians, the Indian was a Socialist. The tribe owned the ground, the rivers and the game; only personal property was owned by the individual, and even that, it was considered a shame to greatly increase. For they held that greed grew into crime, and much property made men forget the poor.

Our answer to this is that, without great property, that is

power in the hands of one man, most of the great business enterprises of the world could not have been; especially enterprises that required the prompt action impossible in a national commission. All great steps in national progress have been through some one man, to whom the light came, and to whom our system gave the power to realize his idea.

The Indian's answer is, that all good things would have been established by the nation as it needed them; anything coming sooner comes too soon. The price of a very rich man is many poor ones, and peace of mind is worth more than railways and skyscrapers.

In the Indian life there was no great wealth, so also poverty and starvation were unknown, excepting under the blight of national disaster, against which no system can insure. Without a thought of shame or mendicancy, the young, helpless and aged all were cared for by the nation that, in the days of their strength, they were taught and eager to serve.

And how did it work out? Thus: Avarice, said to be the root of all evil, and the dominant characteristic of our race, was unknown among Indians, indeed it was made impossible by the system they had developed.

These facts long known to the few are slowly reaching all our people at large, in spite of shameless writers of history, that have done their best to discredit the Indian, and to that end have falsified every page and picture that promised to gain for him a measure of sympathy.

Here are the simple facts of the long struggle between the two races:

There never yet was a massacre of Indians by whites — and they were many — except in time of peace and made possible by treachery.

There never yet was an Indian massacre of whites except in times of declared war to resist invasion.

There never yet was an Indian war but was begun by the whites violating their solemn treaties, encroaching on the Indians' lands, stealing the Indians' property or murdering their people.

There never yet was a successful campaign of whites against Indians except when the whites had other Indians to scout, lead and guide them; otherwise the Redmen were too clever for the whites.

There never yet was a successful war of whites against Indians except when the whites were in overwhelming numbers, with superior equipments and unlimited resources.

There cannot be the slightest doubt that the Indian was crushed only by force of superior numbers. And had the tribes been united even, they might possibly have owned America to-day.

Finally, a famous Indian fighter of the most desperate period thus summarizes the situation and the character of the dispossessed:

"History can show no parallel to the heroism and fortitude of the American Indians in the two hundred years' fight during which they contested inch by inch the possession of their country against a foe infinitely better equipped, with inexhaustible resources, and in overwhelming numbers. Had they even been equal in numbers, history might have had a very different story to tell." (Gen. Nelson A. Miles, U. S. A., Letter, February 16, 1912.)

I never yet knew a man who studied the Indians or lived among them, without becoming their warm friend and ardent admirer. Professor C. A. Nichols, of the South-western University, a deep student of Indian life, said to me, sadly, one day last autumn: "I am afraid we have stamped out a system that was producing men who, taken all around, were better than ourselves."

Our soldiers, above all others, have been trained to hate the Redmen, and yet the evidence of those that have lived years with this primitive people is, to the same effect as that of missionaries and travelers, namely, that the high-class Indian was brave; he was obedient to authority. He was kind, clean and reverent. He was provident, unsordid, hospitable, dignified, courteous, truthful, and honest. He was the soul of honor. He lived a life of temperance and physical culture that he might perfect his body, and so he achieved a splendid physique. He was a wonderful hunter, a master of woodcraft, and a model for outdoor life in this country. He was heroic and picturesque all the time. He knew nothing of the forgiveness of sin, but he remembered his Creator all the days of his life, and was in truth one of the finest types of men the world has ever known.

We set out to discover the noble Redman. Have we entirely failed?

Surely, it is our duty, at least, to do justice to his memory, and that justice shall not fail of reward. For this lost and dying type can help us in many ways that we need, even as he did help us in the past. Have we forgotten that in everything the white pioneer learned of woodcraft, the Indian was the teacher? And when at length came on the white man's fight for freedom, it was the training he got from the Redman that gave him the victory. So again, to fight a different enemy to-day, he can help us. And in our search for the ideal outdoor life, we cannot do better than take this Indian, with his reverence and his carefully cultured physique, as a model for the making of men, and as a pattern for our youth who would achieve high manhood, in the Spartan sense, with the added graces of courtesy, honor and truth.

The world knows no higher ideal than the Man of Galilee; nevertheless, oftentimes, it is helpful to the Plainsmen climbing Mount Shasta, if we lead them, first, to Sheep-Rock Shoulder, before attempting the Dome that looks down upon the clouds.

* * * * * * *

STANDARD INDIAN BOOKS

"Drake's Indian Chiefs, the lives of more than 200 Indian Chiefs, by Samuel G. Drake. Boston. 1832.

"Adventures of Captain Bonneville," by Washington Irving, in 3 vols. London. 1837. An amazing record of the truly noble Redmen.

"North American Indians," by George Catlin, in 2 vols. London. 1866. A famous book; with many illustrations.

"Life Amongst the Modocs," by Joaquin Miller, Bentley & Son. London. 1873. A classic. The story of a white boy's life among the uncontaminated Redmen.

"Indian Sign Language," by W. P. Clark. Philadelphia, Pa. 1884. A valuable cyclopedia of Indian life, as well as the best existing treatise on Sign Language.

"A Century of Dishonor," by Helen Jackson (H. H.). Boston. 1885. Treats of the shameful methods of the U. S. in dealing with Indians, an unbroken record of one hundred years of treachery, murder and infamy.

"On the Border With Crook," by John G. Bourke, U. S. A. Scribner's Sons. New York. 1891. A soldier account of the Apache War. Setting out an Indian hater, he learned the truth and returned to make a terrible arraignment of the U. S. Government.

"Indian Boyhood," by Charles A. Eastman, M. D. Mc-

Clure, Phillips & Co. New York. 1902. A Sioux
Indian's story of his own boyhood.

"The Story of the Indian," by G. B. Grinnell. Appleton
& Co. New York. 1902.

"Two Wilderness Voyagers," by F. W. Calkins. Fleming
H. Revell Co. New York. 1902. The Indian Babes
in the Woods.

"Lives of Famous Indian Chiefs," by W. B. Wood. American Indian Hist. Pub. Co. Aurora, Ill. 1906.

"My Life as an Indian," by J. W. Schultz. Doubleday,
Page & Co. New York. 1907. A white man's life
among the Blackfeet in the old days.

"Handbook of American Indians," by F. W. Hodge and
associates. Pub. in 2 large vols. by Smithsonian Institution, Washington, D. C. 1907. This is a concise
and valuable encyclopedia of Indian names and matters.

"Famous Indian Chiefs I have Known," by Gen. O. O.
Howard. U. S. A. The Century Co. New York.
1908. Treats of Osceola, Washakie, etc. from the
white man's standpoint.

"The Soul of the Indian," by Charles A. Eastman.
Houghton, Mifflin Co. Boston & New York. 1911. A
Sioux Indian's account of his people's religion.

"Legends of Vancouver," by Pauline Johnson. McClel-
land, Goodchild & Stewart, Ltd., Toronto, Ont. 1912.
A valuable collection of charming legends gathered on the
West coast.

"Sign Talk," by Ernest Thompson Seton. Doubleday,
Page & Co., Garden City, New York. 1918. A universal signal code without apparatus, for use in army,
navy, camping, hunting, and daily life.

Besides these the Annual Reports of the Bureau of Ethnology (1878 to date, Smithsonian Institution, Washington,
D. C.), are full of valuable information about Indians.

III. Woodland Songs, Dances, and Ceremonies

THE OMAHA TRIBAL PRAYER.

Harmonized by Prof. J. C. Fillmore.)

(By permission from Alice C. Fletcher's " Indian Story and Song.")

Translation:

    Father a needy one stands before thee;
    I that sing am he.

SITTING BULL'S WAR SONG—Indian Words

(By permission from E. S. Curtis' North American Indians, Vol. III, p. 149)

Moderato.

Ma-ka Si-to-mi-ni....... i Chaz he - may-a.......

to-pe - lo   Bè-li hĕ-i-chey awaon-jel - o.

Ma - ka... Si-to.. mi-ni, Ma-ka.. Si-to-mi-

ni.......... Be-li-chey a • • wa-on ye - lo

Bèl - cheï.. chey.. a-po, Bèl.. ch-e-I

chey a • po.   Ma - ka,... Ma - ka....

Si - - to • mi - • • ni.

SITTING BULL'S WAR SONG—English Words

Moderato.

Earth wide is my fame,...... They are shouting my name;..

Sing ho! the ea - gle   soul....   Who follows Sitting Bull.

THE GHOST DANCE SONG

(From Prof. Jas. Mooney's "The Ghost Dance Religion," 14th. Ann. Rep. Bur. Ethn. p. 977.)

ANI'QU NE'CHAWU'NANI'

Ani'qu ne'chawu'nani',
Ani'qu ne'chawn'nani';
Awa'wa biqǎna'kaye'na,
Awa'wa biqǎna'kaye'na;
Iyahu'h ni'bithi'ti,
Iyahu'h ni'bithi'ti.

Translation

Father, have pity on me,
Father, have pity on me;
I am crying for thirst,
I am crying for thirst;
All is gone—I have nothing to eat,
All is gone—I have nothing to eat.

This is the most pathetic of the Ghost-dance songs. It is sung to a plaintive tune, sometimes with tears rolling down the cheeks of the dancers as the words would bring up thoughts of their present miserable and dependent condition. It may be considered the Indian paraphrase of the Lord's prayer.

Also translated:

Father have pity on me,
My soul is ever hungry for thee;
I am weeping,
There is nothing here to satisfy me.

THE PEACE PIPE CEREMONY

The Medicine Man, standing in front of the ready-laid fire, opens Council thus: "*Meetah Kola nayhoon-po omnicheeyay nee-chopi* — Hear me, my friends, we are about to hold a council.

"Now light we the Council Fire after the manner of the Forest children, not in the way of the white man, but — even as Wakonda himself doth light his fire — by the rubbing together of two trees in the storm-wind, so cometh forth the sacred fire from the wood of the forest."

(He uses the drill; the smoke comes, the flame bursts forth.) "Now know we that Wakonda, whose dwelling is above the Thunder-bird, whose messenger is the Thunder-bird, hath been pleased to smile on his children, hath sent down the sacred fire. By this we know he will be present at our Council, that his wisdom will be with us.

"This is a Council of Peace, so light we first the Pipe of Peace."

(Kneeling at the fire he lights the pipe. As soon as it is going, he lifts the pipe grasped in both hands, with the stem toward the sky, saying):

To *Wakonda;* that his wisdom be with us. *Hay-oon-kee-ya. Noon-way.*

(All answer): *Noon-way.* (Amen, or this is our prayer.)

To *Maka Ina*, Mother Earth, that she send us food, *Hay-oon-kee-ya. Noon-way.*

(All answer): *Noon-way.*

To *Weeyo-peata*, the Sunset Wind, that he come not in his strength upon us. *Hay-oon-kee-oon-ee-ya-snee. Noon-way.* (Then blows smoke and holds the stem to the west.)

(All answer): *Noon-way.*

To *Wazi-yata*, the Winter Wind, that he harm us not with his cold, *Hay-oon-kee-oon-ee-ya-snee*. *Noon-way*. (Pipe as before.)

(All answer): *Noon-way*.

To *Weeyo-hinyan-pata*, the Sunrise Wind, that he trouble us not with his rain. *Hay-oon-kee oon-ee-ya-snee*. *Noon-way*. (Pipe as before.)

(All answer): *Noon-way*.

To *Okaga*, the Hot Wind, that he strike us not with his fierce heat, *Hay-oon-kee-oon-ee-ya-snee*. *Noon-way*. (Pipe as before.)

(All answer): *Noon-way*.

Then the Medicine Man stands holding the pipe in one hand and proclaims aloud: "Now with the Blessing of Wakonda and respite from the *Tah-tee-yay To-pa*, we may deal with business of gravest import, doubting nothing, for wisdom from above is with us."

THE SCALP DANCE

If the assemblage is mixed, each brave selects a squaw for this, ten to thirty couples taking part; otherwise, twenty braves can do it. They come out of the woods in procession, form a circle about the fire; standing with both hands raised they look upward and sing the Omaha Tribal Prayer (see page 61). They sit in a large circle, alternately brave and squaw. Each squaw has a club by her side.

Squaws begin to sing the *Coona* song (*Cahuilla Bird Dance Song*) (next page) or *Omaha Love Song* (p. 50, Fletcher), guided by Medicine Man and drum.

BIRD DANCE SONG.

CAHUILLA TRIBE.

At length the song stops.   Squaws begin nudging the braves and pointing forward.   New music by the Medicine Man begins.   The Zonzimondi, The Mujje Mukesin* or

other dance song.   The braves jump up, dance around once, with heads high in air, almost held backward and not crouching at all.   (*They carry no clubs yet.*)

---

*This Moccasin Song is from Fred R. Burton's American "Primitive Music," 1909.

There are many fine airs and dances in Alice C. Fletcher's "Indian Story and Song," Small, Maynard & Co., 1900. ($1.00.)

After going once around, each is back again near his squaw, and she holds out to him the war club and utters the little squaw yelp.   Each brave takes his club, and now begins the crouch dance.   Going three times around, and each time crouching lower while the squaws stand or sit in a circle, arms down tight to side, but bodies swaying in time to music.   In the fourth round all are crouching very low and moving sideways, facing inward.

The music suddenly changes, and all do the slow sneak toward the centre with much pantomime.   The squaws watch eagerly and silently, leaning forward, shading their eyes with one hand.   All the braves strike the fire together, utter the loud war whoop, and stand for a moment with hands and weapons raised high, then, in time to the fast drum, dance quickly erect with high steps and high heads to the squaws who utter the squaw yelp for welcome, and all sit down as before.

The squaws begin the singing again, repeat the whole scene, but this time the chief falls when the block is struck, and is left lying there when the other braves retire.

His squaw stands up, and says: "*Mee-heheenna tuk-tay-ay-hay natang ee-tang-chang-keeng.*"   ("Where is my chief, he who led you to battle?")

All look and whisper; his wife gets up to seek.   Soon she finds him, and flinging herself on his breast with clasped hands, breaks forth in the lament for the dead, which is a high-pitched, quavering wail.   The warriors lift him up and slowly carry him off the scene, out of sight, followed by the squaws, who, with heads bent, sing:

THE LAMENT

Our chief our war-rior true is
lost to all to me and you to me and you to
me and you Dire fall our ven-geance due on
those who slew our war-rior true Our war-rior true Our
war-rior true Dire fall our ven-geance due On
those who slew our war-rior true Our war-rior true Our war-rior true

Music from F. R. Burton's American Primitive Music, by permission.

Repeat it many times; as they disappear, the music dies away, fainter and fainter.

If no girls take part, let the braves enter in procession, singing, and carry their clubs throughout, and at the end one of them made up like an Indian woman goes out and finds the dead chief.

THE CARIBOU DANCE

The easiest of our campfire dances to learn, and the best for quick presentation, is the Caribou Dance. I have put it on for public performance, after twenty minutes' rehearsing, with fellows who never saw it before; and it does equally well for indoor gymnasium or for campfire in the woods.

In the way of fixings for this, you need four pairs of horns and four tails. I have seen real deer horns used, but they are scarce and heavy. It is better to go out where you can get a few crooked limbs of oak, cedar, hickory, or apple tree; and cut eight pair, as near like *a*, *b*, *c*, in the cut as possible, each about two feet long and one inch thick at the butt. Peel these; point the square ends of the branches,

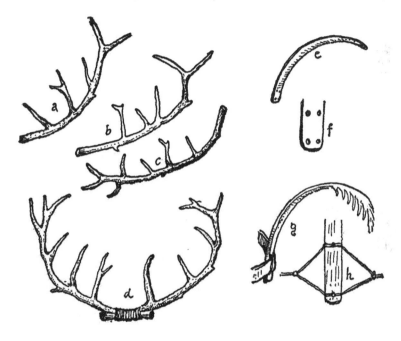

then lash them in pairs, thus (*d*). A pair, of course, is needed for each caribou. These are held in the hand and above the head, or in the hand resting on the head.

The tails are made each out of one third of a flat barrel hoop of wood. At one end of the hoop make four holes in pairs, an inch apart; thus (see *f* in cut). These are for cords that pass over the wearer's belt and through the hoop.

The hoop is then wrapped with white muslin and finished with a tuft of white muslin strips on the end. The tail finished, looks (*g*), and is stuck inside the wearer's belt, which goes through the two cord loops. (*h*), shows a way of fastening on the tail with cord only.

The four caribou are best in white. Three or four hunters are needed. They should have bows but no arrows. The Medicine Man should have a drum and be able to sing the Mujje Mukesin, as given, or other Indian dance tune. One or two fellows who can howl like wolves should be sent off to one side, and another that can yell like a lynx or a panther on the other side, well away from the ring. Now we are ready for

THE DANCE OF THE WHITE CARIBOU

The Medicine Man begins by giving three thumps on his drum to call attention; then says in a loud, singing voice: "The Caribou have not come on our hunting grounds for three snows. We need meat. Thus only can we bring them back, by the big medicine of the Caribou Dance, by the power of the White Caribou."

He rolls his drum, then in turn faces each of the Winds, beckoning, remonstrating and calling them by name. Kitchi-nodin (West); Keeway-din, (North); Wabani-nodin (East); Shawani-nodin (South). Calling last to the quarter whence the caribou are to come, finishing the call with a long *Ko — Kee — Na*. Then as he thumps a slow single beat the white caribou come in at a stately pace timed to the drum. Their heads are high, and they hold the horns on their heads, with one hand, as they proudly march around. After going round once in a sun circle (same way as the sun), they go each to a corner. The drum stops; all four approach to salute the great mystery in the middle, the fire. They bow to it together, heads low, tails high, uttering a long bellow.

Then they circle once, close to the fire; stop on opposite sides of it, facing outward; march each to a corner or compass point; and then bow or honor that *wind*, bellowing long.

Now the Medicine Man begins any good dance song and beats double time. The caribou dance around once in a circle. The music stops. The first and second, and third and fourth, close in combat. They lower their heads, lock horns held safely away from the head, lash tails, snort, kick up the dust, and dance around each other two or three times.

The music begins again, and they circle once.

The music stops. Now the first and fourth and second and third lock horns and fight.

After a round or so, the music begins again and they circle, dancing as before.

Now the howling of wolves is heard in the distance, from the fellows already posted.

The caribou rush toward that side and face it in a row, threatening, with horns low, as they snort, stamp, and kick up the dust.

The wolf-howling ceases. The caribou are victorious. They turn away and circle once to the music, holding their heads high.

The wolf-howling, panther-yelling (or other menacing sound) is now heard in the other direction.

Again the caribou line up and defy it. When it ceases, they dance proudly around, heads up, chests out as they step, for they have conquered every foe.

But a band of hunters appears, crawling flat on their breasts and carrying bows. They crawl half around the ring, each telling those behind by signs, "Here they are; we have found them." "Four big fellows." "Come on," etc. When they come opposite the caribou, the first hunter lets off a short "yelp." The caribou spring to the opposite side of the ring, and then line up to defy this new noise; but do not understand it, so gaze in fear. The hunters draw their bows together, and make as though each let fly an arrow, then slap their hands to make a loud "crack." The first caribou drops, the others turn in fear and run around about half of the ring, heads low, and not dancing; then they dash for the timber. The hunters run forward with yells. The leader holds up the horns. All dance and yell around the fallen caribou and then drag it off the scene.

The Medicine Man says: "Behold, it never fails; the Caribou dance brings the Caribou. It is great medicine. Now there is meat in the lodge."

For a large ring, the number of caribou might be doubled, and variations introduced whenever we find some one who can make good imitation of any animal or bird.

THE DOG DANCE

This is a Shoshoni celebration.* A procession is formed. The leader carries a bucket, a stool, or a basket upside down, for a low stand. The next one carries a dog's skull, or something like one. We have used a loaf of bread, provided with eyes and teeth, or a big puff ball. The next has a dish or a flat Indian basket or tray. The next two or three have feathers, and the rest have crackers or candies. The last is fixed up with a dog's mask and tail and runs on all-fours.

The procession comes in dancing and barking to a little dance tune. Goes once around.

---

* For this I am chiefly indebted to Hamlin Garland.

Then the leader puts down the stand. The skull is set on it, and the tray on the ground before. The rest sit in a half circle in front.

The leader then kneels down and addresses the skull thus: "Dog! In the days of our fathers you were the one who dragged the lodge poles from camp to camp. Without you, we could have had no comfortable place in which to sleep. So I will dance and sing in your honor to-night."

He puts a feather in the dog's head, then dances his best dance, while the rest sing, "Yap-yap, Yap-yap, Yap-yap, Yow-w-w-o" in imitation of a dog barking on a rising scale, finishing with a long howl.

The leader has now danced to the other end of the half-circle and sits down.

The next comes and addresses the skull: "Dog! In times of war you were the one who guarded the camp at night. No one could surprise us when you were on watch. Nothing could make you betray us. So I will dance and sing in your honor to-night!"

He adds a feather and dances his best, while the rest "Yap" the dog chorus. Then he sits at the opposite end of the circle.

The next comes and says, perhaps "Dog! In the days of our fathers, you were the one who could follow the wounded deer. You made the hunting a success. So I will dance and sing in your honor to-night." He adds a feather or a candy, and dances. (Yap, yap, as before.)

The next says: "Dog! When I was a little pappoose, I wandered from the village and fell in the river. No one saw me. I should have been drowned, but you jumped in and pulled me out. So I will dance and sing in your honor to-night." He adds his contribution and dances.

The next says, "Dog! You were the one who cleaned up the camp, so we were not troubled with flies."

Others thank the dog for finding the lost children, for giving alarm when an enemy approached, for killing a rattler, for finding the lost medicine bag, etc.

Then the last one, the boy dog, comes up and barks at the head.

Finally, the leader resumes, saying: "Yes, Dog! You were the one that dragged the lodge poles. You were the one that found the wounded deer, etc. And best of all, first, last, and all the time, you were our faithful friend, and all you asked in return was a bite to eat and a place to lie down. And so long as the blue sky is above the green grass you will be the friend of the prairie children. Then, when at last we cross over the great river, and see behind the Divide, we hope we shall find awaiting us our old friend, the Dog that we may take up our friendship again, and continue on and on in the good country where no white man or smallpox ever comes."

Then they pass around the dish and eat the crackers and candies; offering things to the dog, and honoring him as much as possible with a variety of stage "business." Finally, all go off, carrying the various things and barking as they came.

OJIBWA SNAKE DANCE

Select a good dancer for leader. All form line, holding hands, carefully graded so the least is last. Then dancing in step to the music, they set out in a line, follow-my-leader style, doubling the line on itself, and evoluting around the fire. Sometimes the dancers face alternately — that is, all the even numbers in the line look one way and the odd another.

A good finish is to curl in a tight spiral around the head, when the tail boy mounts on the back of the one before him and shakes a rattle, like a rattler rattling on its coil.

THE HUNTING OF MISHI-MOKWA THE BIG BEAR

Any number of hunters up to twenty can take part in this game. Each one is armed with a war club. This is made of straw tied around two or three willow switches, and tightly sewn up in burlap. It should be about three feet long, one inch thick at the handle, and three or four inches through at the top.

Each hunter must make a wooden claw two inches long (see Cut*) and a wooden bead three quarters of an inch long. The bead is usually a piece of elder with the pith pushed out. The claw is painted black toward the base. The tip is left the natural color of the wood. The bead is painted red. These beads and claws are strung alternately to form a necklace. There should be twenty in each. Finally, a toy balloon is blown up tight and put in a small bag; this is the bear's heart.

Now select a bear. Take the biggest, if several offer. He may be made realistic with wool or fur. Put the necklace on him; strap the bag on his back; then give him a club, also three dens or mountains about one hundred yards apart.

First, the Big Bear comes in and addresses the audience:

"I am fearless Mishi-Mokwa,
I, the mighty Mountain Grizzly,
King of all the Western prairies.
When the roving bands of Indians
Come into my own dominion
I will slay as I have slain them.
They shall not invade my country.
I despise those puny creatures."

Then he stalks off to his den.

*For cuts and details, see p. 203 among the games

Now the hunters come in, and, facing the audience, the leader says:

> "I am Chief of the Ojibwa,
> These are all my chosen warriors.
> We go hunting Mishi-Mokwa,
> He the Big Bear of the mountains;
> He that ravages our borders.
> We will surely seek and slay him;
> Or, if we should fall before him,
> We will die like men of valor,
> Dying, winning deathless glory."

Or, as an alternative prose reading, he says:

"I am Chief of the Black Hawk Band. These are my chosen warriors; the pick of my tribe. We go to hunt the Mishi-Mokwa, the Big Bear of the mountains. He is big and terrible. He kills our people every day. Many of us may die in the fight, but living or dead, we shall win glory. Now we dance the war dance."

All give the war whoop and dance, imitating a bear on his hind legs. At intervals, when the music changes, every other one strikes his neighbor on the back with his club, at which he turns and growls horribly.

Chief: "Now we go to seek the foe."

They set out, looking for the trail. They find it and follow, studying the ground, smelling it, peeking and pointing here and there till they get pretty close to the Big Bear, whereupon he rouses up with a growl. The warriors spring back, but, encouraged by the Chief, they form a circle and approach the bear. The Chief shouts:

"Ho, Mishi-Mokwa, we have found you. Come forth now, for I mean to club your head, and take that necklace for my own neck. Come forth now. You are very brave when you find an old squaw picking berries, but you do not like the looks of this band. If you do not come before I count a hundred, I shall brand you a coward wherever I go."

(As alternative reading, a verse):

"Mishi-Mokwa, we have found you,
Come you forth and try our mettle.
For I mean to club and brain you;
Mean to take that magic necklace;
Wear it for my own adorning.
What! you dare not, valiant creature!
You are absolutely fearless
When you find a lot of children
With their baskets, picking berries,
But you do not like our war clubs;
Noble creature, dauntless Grizzly!"

The bear springs forth, growling. He uses his club freely, trying to knock the hunters' hats off. Once a hat is off, the owner is dead and must drop beside it.

The bear makes for his second mountain or den, and he is safe as long as he is in, or touching, a den. But again the hunters force him to come out, by taunts and by counting. He must continue to go the rounds of his three dens till either the bear or all the hunters are killed.

One good blow on the bear's heart breaks it with a loud "bang." Then the bear must fall; he is dead. The warrior who dealt the fatal blow, no matter who, now becomes the leader, the others join in with war whoops. He takes the necklace from the bear's neck. Then, standing with one foot on the bear, he brandishes his club, shouting, "Ha, ha, how, now, Mishi-Mokwa! Yesterday you did not know me. Now you know me; know my war club. I am none but Hiawatha."

The surviving hunters drag the bear before the grandstand. The Medicine Man or Woman shouts, "Welcome, mighty Hiawatha, you have killed the Mishi-Mokwa."

Hiawatha replies:

> "Yes, we've killed the Mishi-Mokwa,
> But my band is now a remnant.
> On the hillsides, in the valleys,
> Many fighting men are lying.
> Many of my chosen warriors,
> Killed by fearful Mishi-Mokwa."

(Medicine Man): "What! is it true?"

(All answer): "Yes; Gray Wolf is dead; Whooping Crane," and so on.

(Medicine Man):

> "Here bring me earth and fire and water,
> Bring me wood and plume of eagle,
> Bring me hair of Mishi-Mokwa."

(All run to get these things.)

The Medicine Man makes a fire, throws in the things, and as the smoke goes up, he blows it with his robe to the four quarters of the heavens, saying:

> "Hear me, Oh, ye four wind spirits,
> Though these warriors' souls have left us,
> Ye who have them in your keeping,
> Bring them back into their bodies.
> I command you by the magic
> Of the med'cine I have made me
> Of the scalp of Mishi-Mokwa,
> Hear me, Oh, ye stricken warriors."

(They all stir a little.)

> "Hear! Though dead, you all must hear me."

(They stir again.)

"Hear me! Ho!"

(They all jump up and join the circle amid cheers and greetings from the others.)

(The Medicine Man now says):

> "Honor be to Hiawatha,
> He hath saved his loving people.
> On his neck we place the necklace
> Of the bear claws and the wampum.
> So the tribes shall still remember
> He it was killed Mishi-Mokwa."

All join in a war-dance to drum, around the body of the bear.

If, on the other hand, all the hunters are killed by the bear, he comes forward and hands the necklace to the Medicine Man, saying:

> "I'm the mighty Mountain Grizzly;
> Dead are those who sought to slay me.
> Mortal man cannot subdue me,
> But I bow me to your magic."

The Medicine Man takes the necklace, holds it up, and replies:

> "Mishi-Mokwa of the mountains,
> You are chief of all the mighty,
> Keep the sacred wampum necklace,
> You have won it, wear it, keep it."

(He puts it on the bear's neck.)

> "You have won a name of glory,
> Henceforth all the tribes shall tremble
> At the name of Mishi-Mokwa.

But a truce I now command you:
Manitou, whose children all are,
Made the land for all his children;
There is room for Bear and Hunters.
Rise up, Brethren, greet your Brother,
Valor always honors valor."

(All jump up now, cheering. They dance around the bear, shaking his paw, and grunting, "How, how, how.")

The winner, whether bear or chief, keeps the necklace as his own, and may have the title if he desires it; in one case, of Mishi-Mokwa, in the other of Hiawatha, Bear-killer, or Grizzly-chief.

INDIAN SONG BOOKS

Alice Fletcher's "Indian Song and Story." (Small & Maynard) $1.00.

F. R. Burton's "American Primitive Music." (Moffat, Yard, & Co.) $5.00.

Natalie Curtis. "The Indians' Book" (Harper & Bros.) $7.50.

Frances Densmore. "Chippewa Music" (Smithsonian Institution).

THE WEASEL IN THE WOOD

This is a French song game. Somewhat like our "Button, Button," or the Indian Moccasin Game. The players sit in a circle with hands on a cord which goes all around. On the cord is a ring, which is passed secretly from one to another as they sing the song on next page. Each time the singing ends, the one in the middle has to guess who holds the ring. If he fails he pays a forfeit. If he wins the loser takes his place.

LE FURET

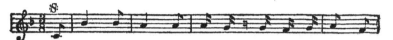

Il court, il court le fu - ret du bois mes-da - mes,

Il court, il court le fu - ret du bois jo - li;

Il a pas - sé par i - ci le fu - ret du bois mes-da-mes,

Il a pas - sé par i - ci le fu - ret du bois jo - li.

(English Substitute)

He runs, he runs, the wea-sel in the wood, my boys,

He runs, he runs, the wea - sel in.... the wood;

He has pass'd by here, he's pass'd, you'd catch him if you could, my boys,

He has pass'd by here, he's pass'd, you'd catch him if you could.

ROUSER OR REVEILLÉ

Ho, sleepers, a - rise! the sun's in the skies, The summer mist

flies from the lake and the lea. The Red Gods do call: Ho,

high, Hi-kers all, Come drink of the Life-cup you nev-er will see.

Then blow ye winds high, or blow ye winds low, Or blow, ye wet

east wind o - ver the sea. We'll face ye and fight, and

laugh when you smite, For storm was the trainer that toughened the tree.

Yo ho!   a - rise, a - rise! A - rise, a - rise, ye be -

IV. Suggested Programs

A Monthly Series

January, the Snow Moon
OUTDOORS:
Tracks in the snow.
Gather mosses in the woods for home study.
Take a bird census.
Look for cocoons and dormant insects.
Dig out borers in dead timber for home study.
INDOORS:
Make a target.
Make a warbonnet.
Study Sign Language, picture-writing, wig-wag; knots, splices.
Learn compass signs.
Qualify in first aid.

February, the Hunger Moon
OUTDOORS:
Snowshoeing and skiing.
Look for rock tripe; roast and boil it as emergency food.
Go to every aspen and study the cause of the scars on its trunk; each one is full of history.
Cut lodge poles.
Play the game "Watching by the Trail."

INDOORS:

>Make a war shirt of sheepskins and beads.
>Make Indian furniture.
>Study signaling by semaphore, Myer, Morse, etc.
>Also by blazes, stone signs, grass signs, smoke fires.
>Hand wrestling.

March, the Wakening Moon
OUTDOORS:

>Cut the rods for a willow bed.
>Cut wood for bow and arrows.
>Study geology.
>Take a new bird census.
>Get up an animal scouting for points.
>Make a quiver of canvas or leather.

INDOORS:

>Make willow bed and other woodland equipment.
>Make bird boxes to sell.
>Make rustic furniture.
>Make a wooden buffalo skull.

April, the Green Grass Moon
OUTDOORS:

>Note spring birds' arrivals.
>Collect spring flowers.
>Note early butterflies.
>Do your half-mile track work with irons.
>Mal your four-mile walk for the degree of Mini-
> sino.

INDOORS:

>One-legged chicken fights.
>Make tracking irons.
>Make tilting spears for tub work, on land or
> for water.
>Carve souvenir spoons.

May, the Planting Moon

OUTDOORS:

Make collection of wild flowers.

Take first over-night hikes.

Nature compass signs.

Begin sleeping out your hundred nights.

INDOORS:

Make a dummy deer for the deer hunt.

Make straw clubs for bear hunt.

Work on willow or Indian bed.

June, the Rose Moon

OUTDOORS:

Fishing, swimming, Indian signs.

Practise judging distances.

Learn ten trees.

INDOORS:

Initiate new Woodcraft boys.

Study camp hygiene.

Make a Navaho loom and use it;

July, the Thunder Moon

OUTDOORS:

Camping, canoeing, or hiking.

Play scout messenger.

Make a sweat lodge.

UNDERCOVER:

Make camp mattress of grass.

Learn the history of Tecumseh and Dull Knife.

Practise camp cooking.

Boil water against time, given only one match, a log, a pail, and a quart of water.

August, the Red Moon

OUTDOORS:

Camping, canoeing, or hiking.

Water sports.

Medley scouting in camp, each in turn being called on to dance, sing, tell a story, produce the leaf of a given tree, imitate some animal, or do the four-medley race namely, row a hundred yards, swim a hundred, walk a hundred and run a hundred, for honors.

INDOORS:

Make a war club, each, for use in dancing.

Make a hunter's lamp.

Make a camp broom.

September, the Hunting Moon

OUTDOORS:

Camping, over-night hikes, etc.

Now the water is low, make dams and docks at swimming place for next year.

INDOORS:

Make a collection of spore prints, and portraits of fungus.

When raining: Practise tribal calls, story telling, and games like Rattler and Feather-blow.

Make a Peace Pipe of wood.

October, the Leaf-falling Moon

OUTDOORS:

Make a collection of leaves and study trees.

Make a collection of nuts.

Gather wood for bows and arrows.

INDOORS:

Arrange, mount, and name specimens.

Learn knots. First aid.

November, the Mad Moon
> OUTDOORS:
>> This is the Moon of Short Hikes.
>> Now build a cabin for winter use.
>> Study evergreens.
>> This is the Moon of Gloom and Sadness, so study fire lighting; rubbing-stick fire.
> INDOORS:
>> Study Sign Language and picture writing.
>> Carve horns, spoons, and cups, decorating with record pictography.
>> Take up taxidermy.
>> Decorate the Tally Book.

December, the Long Night Moon.
> OUTDOORS:
>> This is the time to learn the stars. Also study evergreens, making a collection of their twigs and cones.
> INDOORS:
>> Make bead work for costumes.
>> Get up entertainments to raise money.
>> Make an Indian Council, or a Wild-West Show.
>> Learn the War dances.

SUGGESTIONS FOR EVENINGS

1st Hour:
> Roll call.
> Train new fellows, if need be, in knots, and laws; or prepare others for 1st and 2d degrees.

2d Hour:
> Lesson in one or other of the following subjects:
>> Semaphore, Myer code, tracks, animals, birds. Sign Language, trees, basketry, carving, stars, fire-lighting, box-making, bed-making,

3d Hour:
>   Lessons in Indian dances.
>   Learn some song.
>   Tell a story.
>   Close, singing National Anthem or the Omaha Tribal
>   Prayer.

ANIMAL STORY BOOKS FOR EVENINGS

Written by Ernest Thompson Seton.
Published by Charles Scribner's Sons
153 5th Ave., New York City.

WILD ANIMALS I HAVE KNOWN, 1898.
>   The stories of Lobo, Silverspot, Molly Cottontail,
>   Bingo, Vixen, The Pacing Mustang, Wully, and
>   Redruff.   Price, $2.

LOBO, RAG AND VIXEN, 1900.
>   This is a school edition of the above, with some of
>   the stories and many of the pictures left out.
>   Price, 50c. net.

THE TRAIL OF THE SANDHILL STAG, 1899.
>   The story of a long hunt that ended without a tragedy.
>   Price, $1.50.

THE LIVES OF THE HUNTED, 1901.
>   The stories of Krag, Randy, Johnny Bear, The Mother
>   Teal, Chink, The Kangaroo Rat, and Tito, The
>   Coyote.   Price, $1.75, net.

KRAG AND JOHNNY BEAR, 1902.
>   This is a school edition of the above, with some of
>   the stories and many of the pictures left out.
>   Price, 50c. net.

MONARCH, THE BIG BEAR OF TALLAC, 1904.
>   The story of a big California Grizzly that is living
>   yet.   Price, $1.25 net.

ANIMAL HEROES, 1905.
The stories of a Slum Cat, a Homing Pigeon, The Wolf That Won, A Lynx, A Jack-rabbit, A Bull-terrier, The Winnipeg Wolf and A White Reindeer. Price $1.75 net.

Published by The Century Company,
Union Square, New York City.

BIOGRAPHY OF A GRIZZLY, 1900.
The story of old Wahb from Cubhood to the scene in Death Gulch. Price, $1.50.
WOODMYTH AND FABLE, 1905.
A collection of fables, woodland verses, and camp stories. Price, $1.25 net.
BIOGRAPHY OF A SILVER FOX, 1909.
The story of a New England silver fox. Price, $1.50. (A companion to the Grizzly.)

Published by Doubleday, Page & Company,
Garden City, N. Y.

TWO LITTLE SAVAGES, 1903.
A book of adventure and woodcraft and camping out for boys, telling how to make bows, arrows, moccasins, costumes, teepee, warbonnet, etc., and how to make a fire with rubbing sticks, read Indian signs, etc. Price, $2.00 net.
ROLF IN THE WOODS, 1911.
The Adventures of a Boy Scout with Indian Quonab and little dog Skookum. More than 200 drawings by the author. Price, $2.00 net.
WILD ANIMALS AT HOME, 1913.
With more than 150 sketches and photographs by the

author. 226 pages. Price, $2.00 net. In this Mr. Seton gives for the first time his personal adventures in studying wild animals.

WILD ANIMAL WAYS, 1916.

Seven wild animal stories. The history of a Razor-back Hog, a Coon, a Wild Horse, etc. More than 200 drawings by the author. 247 pages. Price, $2.00 net.

THE PREACHER OF CEDAR MOUNTAIN, 1917.

A tale of the open country. Founded on real life in the West. Mr. Seton's first novel. Price, $1.90 net.

SIGN TALK of the Indians, 1918. Price, $3.00 net.

INDOOR OR WINTER ACTIVITIES

Handicraft:

Make a willow bed (see later); teepee; war club for cere-monial use in dance; boat; skiff; bird boxes; wall pocket for camp; bow and arrows; paddle and paint it; fire sticks for rubbing-stick fire; drum; baskets of spruce, raffia or rattan, etc.; and decorate the Tally Book. Map-making.

Games (see Index):

Learn the Games: Tree the coon. Quicksight. Farsight. Let each imitate some animal, or all the same animal. Practise cockfight. Practise spearfight on tubs. Feather-blow. Bear hunt. Rat on-his-lodge (with little sawdust bags.)

Learn: The flags of some other nations. The flags of the weather bureau. The stars. The evergreen trees. The Indian blazes and signs.

Learn: First aid. Sign Languge. Signaling.

Songs: Some songs for camp. War song of Sitting Bull. Omaha Tribal Prayer.

Dances: The War dance. The Dog dance. Snake dance. Caribou dance.

ROBE OR WAR SHIRT CONTEST

It will be found stimulating to offer a grand prize for the individual that scores the highest in the whole campout, according to a given scale of points. We usually call this a Robe Contest, because the favorite prize is a Sagamore's robe—that is, a blanket decorated with figures in colored wools or in appliqué work. A war shirt also makes a good prize. The standard for points used at our last camp was as follows: All events for which the fixed standards allow more than 5 minutes, 20 and 5 points as winner and loser. All less than 5 minutes, 10 and 2.

Sturgeon: The crews get, each, 10 for every sturgeon they land.

Deer hunt: The winners score 10 for each deer hunted; the losers score 2 for each deer hunted.

Each fellow who wished to be in it was allowed for his contribution to the Council entertainment: For songs: up to 25 points each; for long stories, up to 25 points each; for jokes, up to 25 points each; for stunts, up to 25 points each; for hand wrestling and other competitions, 5 on for winner, 5 off for loser. All challenges not given in Council must be handed to the committee for approval, three hours before running off.

Prizes: 1st man, 15; 2d, 10; 3d, 5 points.

All competitions must be on the present camp ground. Extra points up to 25 per day for neatness and extra service. Campfire up to 25 for each of the two keepers. Dock up to any number for breach of laws. For each hour of camp service, 10 points per hour. Articles made since camp began up to 50 points. All points must be handed in as soon as made. The Council may refuse those held back. Those who have won robes are not to enter for present contest. Those under 14, or over 35, get 10 per cent. handicap; those over 14 and under 18, get 5 per cent.

SUGGESTED CAMP ROUTINE

6.30 A.M.	Turn out, bathe, etc.
7.00 "	Breakfast.
8.00 "	Air bedding, in sun, if possible.
8.15 "	Business Council of Leaders.
9.00 "	Games and practice.
11.00 "	Swimming.
12.00 "	Dinner.
1.00 P.M.	Talk by Leader.
2.00 "	Games, etc.
4.00 "	Swimming.
6.00 "	Supper.
7.00 "	Evening Council.
10.00 "	Lights out.

GOOD PROGRAM OF ENTERTAINMENT AT A COUNCIL

Indian Formal Opening.
Peace Pipe.
Braves to be sworn in.
Honors.
Names.
First aid.
Initiations.
Fire-making.
Challenges.
Water-boiling.
Caribou dance.
Close by singing the Omaha Prayer.

INDOOR COMPETITION FOR A PRIZE

Each must get up and tell a short story. No excuses allowed. It is better to try and fail, than not to try. The one who *fails to try is a quitter.*

Mark off on a stick your idea of a yard, a foot, and an inch.

Show a war club made by yourself.

Dance a step.

Sing a song "Mary's Little Lamb" — if you can do no better.

Lay a pole to point to true north.

Draw a map of North America from memory in ten minutes.

Show a piece of wood-carving by yourself, it may be a picture frame, a spool, an image, a doll, a box, or a peach basket — but do it.

Give an imitation of some animal — dog, cat, monkey, mouse, bird, or any wild creature you have seen.

Let each, in turn, read some one poem, and try who can do it best.

Play the part of an Indian woman finding her warrior dead.

ONE-DAY HIKES

I think it is a good rule in hiking, never to set out with the determination that you are going to show how *hardy* you are. It is as bad as setting out to show how *smart* you are. "Smart Aleck" always lands in the gutter. Do not set out to make a record. Record breakers generally come to grief in the end. Set out on your hike determined *to be moderate*. That is, take a *few* fellows; not more than a dozen. Plan a *moderate* trip, of which not more than half the time must be consumed in going and coming.

For example, if it is Saturday afternoon, and you must be home by six o'clock, having thus four hours, I should divide it in two hours' travel, going and coming, and two hours' exploration. Three miles is a moderate walk for one hour, so that should be the limit of distance that ordinarily you tramp from your starting point. At five o'clock all hands should gird up their loins and face homeward.

These are some rules I have found good in hiking:

Do not go in new shoes.

Be sure your toe nails and corns are well pared before going.

Do not take any very little or weak fellows.

Be prepared for rain.

Take a pair of dry socks.

Travel Indian file in woods, and double Indian file in roads.

Take a Book of Woodcraft along.

Always have with you a rule and tape line, knife, some string, and some matches.

Take a compass, and sometimes a pocket level.

Take a map, preferably the topographical survey.

Take a notebook and a pencil.

Do not waste time over things you can do as well, or better, at home.

And last, and most important, it is wise to *set out with an object.*

Here are samples of the ideas I have found useful as objects for a short hike in winter:

To determine that hard maple (or other timber) does or does not grow in such a woods.

To prove that a certain road runs north and south.

To decide whether the valley is or is not higher than the one across the divide.

To prove that this or that hill is higher than such a one.

To get any winter fungi.

To look for evergreen fern.

To get, each, 100 straight rods, 30 inches long, to make Indian bed, of willow, hazel, kinnikinik, arrowwood, etc.

To get wood for rubbing-sticks, or for a fire-bow.

To get horns for a Caribou dance.

If there is snow, to take, by the tracks, a census of a given woods, making full-size drawings of each track — that is, four tracks, one for each foot; and also give the distance to the next set.

If there is snow, to determine whether there are any skunk dens in the woods, by following every skunk trail until it brings you to its owner's home.

Now, be it remembered that, though I always set out with an object, I find it wise to *change* whenever, after I get there, some much more alluring pursuit or opportunity turns up. Any one who sticks to a plan, merely because he started that way, when it turns out to be far from the best, is not only unwise, he is stupid and obstinate.

V General Scouting Indoors

Handicraft Stunts

LET each Scout carve a *fork* and *spoon* out of wood, with his band totem on handle.

Make a *needle case* out of a fowl's leg or wing bone, thus: Clean and smooth about three inches of the bone plug up one end with a soft wood plug and make a, wooden stopper for the other end. Then with the point of a knife decorate the bone. The lines should be scratched in deeply and then have black paint rubbed into them. If no black paint is handy make a mixture of soot and pine gum, with a little grease, butter or oil.

Make a *tackle box* or *ditty box* 2 x 2 x 6 inches carved out of solid wood.

Make *peach-stone baskets*, of a peach-stone shaped with a file.

Turkey call. An interesting curio is the turkey call. Take a small cigar box and cut off the end as in the figure. Get a piece of slate about 2 x 3 inches long, or, failing slate, take a flat piece of wood and rub it well with rosin. Draw the two curved edges of the box lightly up this one way, and it will make a wonderfully good imitation of a turkey call.

A Chicken squawk. This is another call easily made. Take any small round tin box — a condensed milk tin is good — and make a hole through the bottom and into this put a cord. A knot on the inside prevents the cord from

slipping through. Rosin the cord and draw the fingers down it with short and long jerks. This give a good imitation of a cackling hen.

Picture frames as in the above illustrations.

Also make *beds* of willow rods, grass rugs, baskets of spruce roots, etc. as described elsewhere.

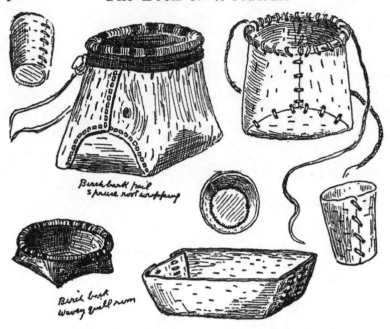

Birch-bark pail
spruce root wrapping

Birch bark
Wavey quill rim

Birch-bark boxes and *baskets*. These are easily made if the bark be softened in hot water before you shape it. The lacing is spruce roots, also softened with hot water.

(See "How to Make Baskets," by Mary White, Double-day, Page & Co., $1 plus 10 cents postage.)

SOUVENIR SPOONS

A good indoor activity of Scouts is the making of souve-nir spoons. Some craftsmen are clever enough to make these out of wood or of silver. I have found that the best, easy-working material is bone, deer antler or horn. Go to any big drug shop and get one of the 25-cent horn spoons. It is already of a good spoon-shape, of course. The handle is hard, smooth, and ready to be ornamented with any device, cutting it with knife or file, into the owner's totem, or the clan or the tribal totems which naturally suggest themselves

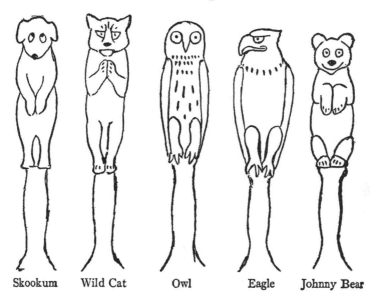

| Skookum | Wild Cat | Owl | Eagle | Johnny Bear |

The design should be sketched on with pencil or ink, then realized by shaping the outline with file or knife. The inner lines are merely scratched on the surface.

In general, one should avoid changing the main outline of the spoon handle or cutting it .enough to weaken it. Always, rather, adapt the animal to fill the desired space.

There are several purposes the spoon can answer: First as a spoon in camp, especially when prizes are offered to the camp that makes most of its own equipment; next, as a salable article; third, as exhibition article when it is desired to get up a fine exhibit of handicraft products illustrating camp life.

KNOTS

The following are standard knots that an accomplished camper should know. Remember a perfect knot is one that's neither jambs nor slips.

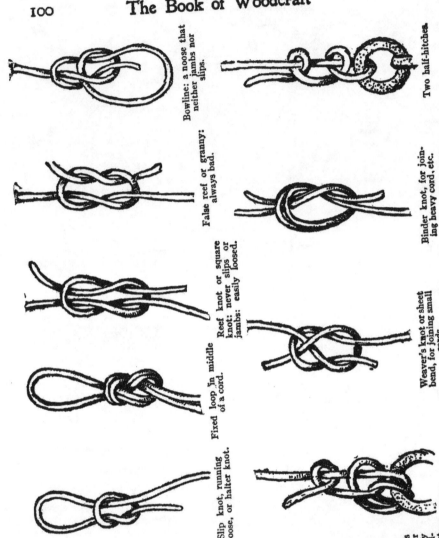

Bowline: a noose that neither jambs nor slips.

Two half-hitches.

False reef or granny: always bad.

Binder knot, for joining heavy cord, etc.

Reef knot or square knot: never slips or jambs: easily loosed.

Weaver's knot or sheet bend, for joining small cords.

Fixed loop in middle of a cord.

Slip knot, running noose, or halter knot.

The fisherman's knot. It never slips; is easily opened by pulling the two short

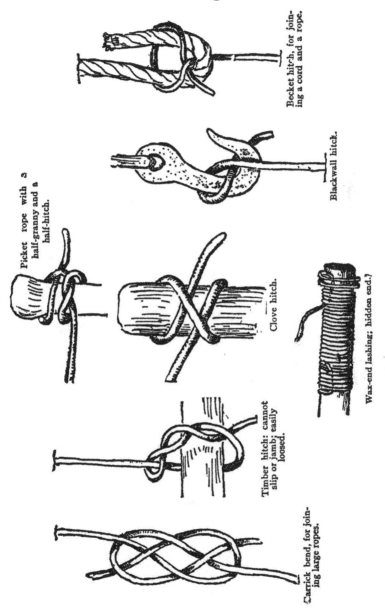

Becket hitch, for joining a cord and a rope.

Blackwall hitch.

Picket rope with a half-granny and a half-hitch.

Clove hitch.

Wax-end lashing; hidden end.?

Timber hitch: cannot slip or jamb; easily loosed.

Carrick bend, for joining large ropes.

FIRESIDE TRICK

An Indian showed me this, though I have since seen it among whites!

Put your hands together as in the drawing, palms also touching.

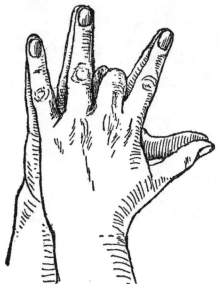

The thumbs are you and your brother. You can separate easily — like that.

The first fingers are you and your father, you can separate not quite so easily — like that:

The little fingers are you and your sister, you can separate, but that comes a little harder still — like that.

The middle fingers are you and your mother, you can separate, but it is hard — see that.

The ring fingers are you and your sweetheart, you cannot separate without everything else going first to pieces.

THE LONE STAR TRICK

A Texan showed me an interesting trick on the table. He took six wooden toothpicks, bent them sharply in the middle, and laid them down in the form shown in "A."

"Now," he says, "when our people got possession of Texas, it was nothing but a wilderness of cactus spines.

See them there! Then they began irrigating. (Here he put a spoonful of water in the centre of the spines.) And then a change set in and kept on until they turned into the Lone Star State."

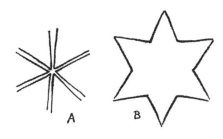

As we watched, the water caused the toothpicks to straighten out until they made the pattern of a star as in "B."

BIRD BOXES OR HOUSES

A good line of winter work is making bird boxes to have them ready for the spring birds.

Two styles of bird houses are in vogue; one a miniature house on a pole, the other is an artificial hollow limb in a tree.

First — the miniature cabin or house on a pole. This is very good for martins, swallows, etc., and popular with most birds, because it is safest from cats and squirrels. But most of us consider it far from ornamental.

To make one, take any wooden box about six inches square put a wooden roof on it (a in Cut), then bore a hole in the middle of one end, making it one and one half inches wide; and on the bottom nail a piece of two-inch wood with an inch auger hole in it (b). Drive in a nail for a perch below the door and all is ready for a coat of soft, olive-green paint. After this is dry, the box is finished. When you set it in place, the end of the pole is shaved to fit tight into the auger hole in the bottom, and the pole then set up, or fastened to the end of the building. In the latter case a six or eight foot pole is long enough. In some neighborhoods it is necessary to put tin as a cat and rat guard, on the pole, as shown (c and d). Some elaborate these bird houses, making a half dozen compartments. When this is done the pole goes right through the lowest floor and fits into a small hole in the floor above.

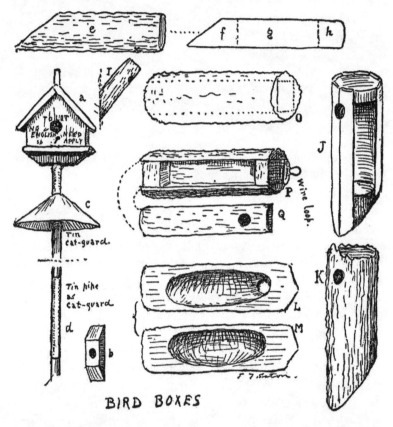

BIRD BOXES

These large apartment houses are very popular with the purple martin, as well as with the English sparrow if they are set up in town.

Alexander Wilson tells us that the Choctaw and Chicasaw Indians used to make bird houses for the purple martins thus: "Cut off all the top branches from a sapling, near their cabins, leaving the prongs a foot or two in length, on each of which they hang a gourd, or calabash properly hollowed out for their convenience."

But the wild-wood box or hollow limb is more sightly and for some birds more attractive. There are several ways of using the natural limb. One is, take a seven or eight inch stick of chestnut about twenty inches long, split four slabs off it: (O) then saw off three inches of each end of the "core" and nail the whole thing together again (P and Q), omitting the middle part of the core.

Another way is to split the log in half and scoop out the interior of each half (L and M). When nailed together again it makes a commodious chamber, about five inches wide and a foot or more deep.

Another plan is: Take a five-inch limb of green chestnut, elm, or any other tough-barked tree. Cut a piece eighteen inches long, make a long bevel on one end (e). Now carefully split the bark on one side and peel it. Then saw the peeled wood into three pieces (f g h), leave out g and put the bark on again. Cut a hole in the bark on the longest side, at the place farthest from the beveled end (x in e), and your bird nest is finished. The beveled end is there to make it easily nailed up; when in place, it is as at I. The front — that is, the side where the door is — should always be the under one; and the door in each case should be near the top.

But these methods presuppose a fine big stick of wood. I have more often found it convenient to work with scraps.

Here is one easy way that I have long used: From a four or five inch round log saw off two sections each two inches thick, or failing a log, cut out two circles from a two-inch plank, for top and bottom parts (like f and h);

then using six or seven laths instead of bark, make a hol‹ low cylinder (J). Cover the hollow cylinder with a large piece of bark and cut the hole (K). Cut your entry at the top, half on each of a pair of laths. Cover the whole thing with bark nailed neatly on; or failing the bark, cover it with canvas and paint a dull green mottled with black and gray.

This last has the advantage of giving most room in a small log. Of course, if one can find a hollow limb, all this work is saved. By way of variety this one can be put up hanging from a nail, for which the wire loop is made.

To a great extent the size of hole regulates the kind of bird, as most birds like a tight fit.

For wrens make it about one inch; for bluebirds, and tree-swallows one and one half inches; for martins two and one half inches.

For latest ideas send to The Jacobs Bird House Company, 404 So. Washington Street, Waynesburg, Pa.

See also the "Making of a Hollow Tree," By E. T. Seton, *Country Life in America*, November, 1908, and seq.

"Putting up Bird Boxes," By B. S. Bowdish (special leaflet), Audubon Society, 141 Broadway, New York. 15 cents per dozen.

"Useful Birds and Their Protection," By E. H. Forbush, Massachusetts State Board Agriculture, p. 388.

HOW TO RAISE SOME MONEY

A good Woodcrafter always "travels on his own steam." When you want to go camping, don't go round begging for the cash, but earn it. And a good time to do this is in the winter when you are forced to stay indoors.

How? One way, much in the line of our work, is making

some bird houses. I know a number of persons who would gladly put up bird houses, if they could get them easily. See article on Bird Houses.

You can either sell them in a lot to a man who has already a shop for garden stuff or hardware, or put them on a hand cart and sell them at much better prices yourself. It is useless to take them to a farmer, or to folks in town, but a ready sale will be found among the well-to-do in the suburbs, in a country town, or among the summer residents of the country. The simple boxes might fetch 50 cents each, the more elaborate $1.00 or $2.00 according to the labor they have cost you.

Another way is the manufacture of Indian stuff such as furniture, birch-bark boxes, baskets, rustic seats, etc., as described elsewhere in the book. See index.

VI. General Scouting Outdoors

Rubbing-Stick Fire

I HAVE certainly made a thousand fires with rubbing-sticks, and have made at least five hundred different experiments. So far as I can learn, my own record of thirty-one seconds from taking the sticks to having the fire ablaze is the world's record, and I can safely promise this: That every boy who will follow the instructions I now give will *certainly succeed* in making his rubbing-stick fire.

Take a piece of dry, sound, balsam-fir wood (or else cedar, cypress, tamarac, basswood or cottonwood, in order of choice) and make of it a drill and a block, thus:

Drill. Five eighths of an inch thick, twelve to fifteen inches long; roughly rounded, sharpened at each end as in the cut (Cut 1 a).

Block, or *board,* two inches wide, six or eight inches long, five eighths of an inch thick. In this block, near one end, cut a side notch one half an inch deep, wider on the under side; and near its end half an inch from the edge make a little hollow or pit in the top of the block, as in the illustration (Cut 1 b).

Tinder. For tinder use a wad of fine, soft, very dry, dead grass mixed with shredded cedar bark, birch bark or even cedar wood scraped into a soft mass.

Bow. Make a bow of any bent stick two feet long, with a strong buckskin or belt-lacing thong on it (Cut 1 c).

Socket. Finally, you need a socket. This simple little thing is made in many different ways. Sometimes I use a pine or hemlock knot with a pit one quarter inch deep, made by boring with the knife point. But it is a great help to have a good one made of a piece of smooth, hard stone or marble, set in wood; the stone or marble having in it a smooth, round pit three eighths inch wide and three eighths inch deep. The one I use most was made by the Eskimo. A view of the under side is shown in Cut 1 (fig. d).

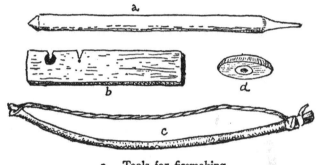

1. Tools for firemaking

Now, we are ready to make the fire:

Under the notch in the fire-block set a thin chip.

Turn the leather thong of the bow once around the drill: the thong should now be quite tight. Put one point of the drill into the pit of the block, and on the upper end put the socket, which is held in the left hand, with the top of the drill in the hole of the stone (as in Cut 2). Hold the left wrist against the left shin, and the left foot on the fire-block. Now, draw the right hand back and forth steadily on level and the *full length* of the bow. This causes the drill to twirl in the pit. Soon it bores in, grinding out powder, which presently begins to smoke. When there is a great volume of smoke from a growing pile of black powder, you know that you have the spark. Cautiously lift the block, leaving the smoking powder on the chip. Fan this with your hand till the live coal appears. Now, put a wad

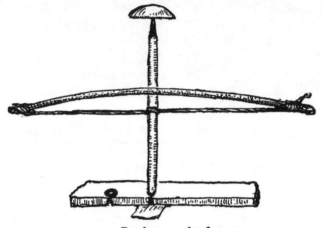

2. Ready to make fire

of the tinder gently on the spark; raise the chip to a convenient height, and blow till it bursts into flame.

N. B. (1) *The notch must reach the middle of the fire-pit.*

(2) You must hold the *drill steadily* upright, and cannot do so without bracing the left wrist against the left shin, and having the block on a firm foundation.

(3) You must begin lightly and slowly, pressing heavily *and sawing fast after there is smoke.*

(4) *If the fire does not come, it is because you have not followed these instructions.*

HIKING IN THE SNOW

In the suggested programs I have given a number of outlines for one-day hikes. For those who wish to find out what animals live near there is no time better than when the snow is on the ground.

I remember a hike of the snow-track kind that afforded myself and two boy friends a number of thrills, more than twenty-five years ago.

There were three of us out on a prowl through the woods, looking for game. We saw no live thing, but there had been a fall of soft snow, a few days before; tracks were abundant, and I proposed that each of us take a track and follow it through thick and thin, until he found the beast, which, if living and free, was bound to be at the other end of the line; or, until he found its den. Then, each should halloa to let the others know that his quarry was holed. Close by were the tracks of a mink and of two skunks. The

Mink track

mink-track was my guide. It led southward. I followed it through swamps and brushwood, under logs, and into promising nooks. Soon I crossed the trail of the youngest boy, closely pursuing his skunk. Later, I met my friend of skunk No. 2, but our trails diverged. Now I came to a long hill down which my mink had tobogganed six or eight feet, after the manner of the otter. At last the trail came to an end in a perfect labyrinth of logs and brush. I went all around this. The snow was clear and smooth. My mink was certainly in this pile. So I let off a long halloa and got an answer from one of the boys, who left his trail and came to me within a few minutes. It happened that this one, Charlie, was carrying a bag with a ferret in it, that we had brought in the hope that we might run to earth a rabbit; and this particular ferret was, like everything his owner had, "absolutely the best in Canada." He claimed that it could kill rats, six at a time; that it could drive a fox out of its hole; that it was not afraid of a coon; while a skunk or a mink was simply beneath its notice. I now suggested that this greatest of ferrets be turned in after the mink, while we watched around the pile of logs.

I never did like a ferret. He is such an imp of murder incarnate. It always gives me the creeps to see the blood-thirsty brute, like a four-legged snake, dive into some hole,

Skunk track

with death and slaughter as his job. I hate him; but, after all, there is something thrilling and admirable about his perfectly diabolical courage. How would one of us like to be sent alone into a dark cave, to find out and fight some unknown monster, much larger than ourselves, and able, for aught we know, to tear us into pieces in a moment!

But the ferret never faltered; he dived into the log laby-rinth. It was a small ferret and a big mink; I awaited anxiously. After a long silence, we saw our four-footed partner at the farther end, unruffled, calm and sinuous.

Nothing had happened. We saw no mink, but I knew he was there. The ferretteer said, "It just proved what he had claimed — 'a mink was beneath his ferret's notice'!" Maybe?

Now, we heard the shout of hunter No. 2. We answered. He came to us to say that, after faithfully following his skunk-trail leader for two hours, through forest, field and fen, he had lost it in a host of tracks in a ravine some half-a-mile away.

So we gave our undivided attention to skunk No. 1, and in a few minutes had traced him to a hole, into which there led a multitude of trails, and from which there issued an odor whose evidence was beyond question. Again we submitted the case to our subterranean representative, and nothing loth the ferret glided down. But presently reappeared, much as he went, undisturbed and unodorized. Again and again he was sent down, but with the same result. So at length we thrust him ignominiously into the bag. The ferret's owner said there was no skunk; the rest of us said there was, but that the ferret was "scared," "no good," etc. Then, a plan suggested itself for clearing or convicting that best of all ferrets. We plugged up the skunk hole, and went back to the house. It seemed that the youngest brother of one of my companions had a tiny pet dog, a toy, the darling of his heart — just such a dog as you read about; a most miserable, pampered, cross, ill-bred, useless and snarling little beast, about the size of a large rat. Prince was his name, for Abraham, his little master, never lost an opportunity of asserting that this was the prince of all dogs, and that his price was above rubies. But Prince had made trouble for Bob more than once, and Bob was ready to sacrifice Prince on the altar of science, if need be. Indeed, Satan had entered into Bob's heart and sketched there a plausible but wicked plan. So this boy set to work and coaxed Prince to leave the house, and beguiled him with soft words, so that he came with us to the skunk's den in the woods. It required but little encouragement, then, to get that aggressive little beast of a doglet to run into the hole and set about making himself disagreeable to its occupant. Presently, we were entertained with a succession of growlets and barklets, then a volley of howlets, followed by that awful smell — you know.

Soon afterward, Prince reappeared, howling. For some minutes he did nothing but roll himself in the snow, rub his eyes and yell. So that after all, in spite of our ferret's evidence, there *was* a skunk in the hole, and the ferret had really demonstrated a vast discretion; in fact, was probably the discreetest ferret in Canada.

We had got good proof of that skunk's existence but we did not get him, and had to go home wondering how we should square ourselves for our sacrilege in the matter of the pet dog. It was Bob's job to explain, and no one tried to rob him of the glory. He began by sowing a few casual remarks, such as, "Pears to me there must be a skunk under the barn." Then, later, when Prince bounded in, "Phew! 'pears to me that there fool purp has been after that skunk!"

Poor little Prince! It made him lose his nightly couch in Abraham's bosom and condemned him to be tubbed and scrubbed every day, and to sleep outdoors for a week. But he had his revenge on all of us; for he barked all night, and every night, under our windows. He couldn't sleep; why should we? And we didn't.

Of course, this instance is given rather as a dreadful example of error than as a model for others.

We got back from our hike that time with a lot of interesting wild animal experience, and yet you will note we did not see any wild animal all the time.

OLD WEATHER WISDOM

When the dew is on the grass,
Rain will never come to pass.

When the grass is dry at night,
Look for rain before the light.

When grass is dry at morning light,
Look for rain before the night.

Three days' rain will empty any sky.

A deep, clear sky of fleckless blue
Breeds storms within a day or two.

When the wind is in the east,
It's good for neither man nor beast.
When the wind is in the north,
The old folk should not venture forth,
When the wind is in the south,
It blows the bait in the fishes' mouth.
When the wind is in the west,
It is of all the winds the best.

An opening and a shetting
Is a sure sign of a wetting.

(Another version)

Open and shet,
Sure sign of wet.

(Still another)

It's lighting up to see to rain.

Evening red and morning gray
Sends the traveler on his way.
Evening gray and morning red
Sends the traveler home to bed.

Red sky at morning, the shepherd takes warning;
Red sky at night is the shepherd's delight.

If the sun goes down cloudy Friday, sure of a clear Sunday.

If a rooster crows standing on a fence or high place, it will clear. If on the ground, it doesn't count.

Between eleven and two
You can tell what the weather is going to do.

Rain before seven, clear before eleven.

Fog in the morning, bright sunny day.

If it rains, and the sun is shining at the same time, the devil is whipping his wife and it will surely rain to-morrow.

If it clears off during the night, it will rain shortly again.

Sun drawing water, sure sign of rain.

A circle round the moon means "storm." As many stars as are in circle, so many days before it will rain.

Sudden heat brings thunder.

A storm that comes against the wind is always a thunderstorm.

The oak and the ash draw lightning. Under the birch the cedar, and balsam you are safe.

East wind brings rain.

West wind brings clear, bright, cool weather.

North wind brings cold.

South wind brings heat. (On Atlantic coast.)

The rain-crow or cuckoo (both species) is supposed by all hunters to foretell rain, when its "Kow, kow, kow" is long and hard.

So, also, the tree-frog cries before rain.

Swallows flying low is a sign of rain; high, of clearing weather.

The rain follows the wind, and the heavy blast is just before the shower.

OUTDOOR PROVERBS

What weighs an ounce in the morning, weighs a pound at night.

A pint is a pound the whole world round.

Allah reckons not against a man's allotted time the days he spends in the chase.

If there's only one, it isn't a track, it's an accident.

Better safe than sorry!

No smoke without fire.

The bluejay doesn't scream without reason.

The worm don't see nuffin pretty 'bout de robin's song.— (Darkey.)

Ducks flying over head in the woods are generally pointed for water.

If the turtles on a log are dry, they have been there half an hour or more, which means no one has been near to alarm them.

Cobwebs across a hole mean "nothing inside."

Whenever you are trying to be smart, you are going wrong. Smart Aleck always comes to grief.

You are safe and winning, when you are trying to be kind.

The Stars

A settlement worker once said to me: "It's all very well talking of the pleasures of nature study, but what use is it to my little Italians and Polish Jews in the slums of New York? They get no chance to see the face of nature."

"If they do not," I replied, "it is their own fault. They watch the pavements too much for coppers; they are forever looking down. To-night you ask them to *look up*. If the sky is clear, they will have a noble chance."

Yes! the stars are the principle study for outdoors at night and above all in winter time; for not only are many of the woodcraft pursuits impossible now, but the nights are long, the sky is clear, and some of the most famous star-groups are visible to us only in winter.

So far as there is a central point in our heavens, that point is the Pole Star — Polaris. Around this all the stars

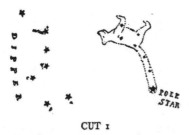

CUT 1

in the sky seem to turn once in twenty-four hours. It is easily discovered by the help of the Pointers, or Dipper, known to every country boy in America.

Most of the star-groups are known by the names of human figures or animals. The modern astronomers laugh at and leave out these figures in the sky; but we shall find it a great help to memory and interest if we revive and use them; but it is well to say now that it is not because the form of the group has such resemblance, but because there is some traditional association of the two. For example:

The classical legend has it that the nymph Callisto, having violated her vow, was changed by Diana into a bear, which, after death was immortalized in the sky by Zeus. Another suggestion is that the earliest astronomers, the Chaldeans, called these stars "the shining ones," and their word happened to be very like the Greek *Arktos* (a bear). Another explanation (I do not know who is authority for either) is that vessels in olden days were named for animals, etc. They bore at the prow the carved effigy of their namesake, and if the "Great Bear," for example, made several very happy voyages by setting out when a certain constellation was in the ascendant, that constellation might become known as the Great Bear's Constellation.

It is no doubt, because it is so conspicuous, that the Great Bear is the oldest of all the constellations, in a human historical sense. Although it has no resemblance to a Bear, the tail part has obvious resemblance to a *Dipper*, by which name it is known to most Americans. Therefore, because so well known, so easily pointed out, and so helpful in pointing out the other stars, this Dipper will be our starting point and shall prove our Key to the whole sky.

If you do not know the Dipper, get some one who does to point it out; or look in the northern sky for the shape shown in Cut, remembering that it goes around the Pole Star every twenty-four hours, so that at different times it is seen at different places.

Having found the Dipper, note carefully the two stars marked b and a; these, the outer rim of the Dipper bowl are called the Pointers, because they point to, or nearly to, the Pole Star; the latter being about three dipper rims (a d) away from the Dipper.

Now, we have found the great Pole Star, which is called by Indians the "Star that never moves" and the "Home

Star." Note that it is in the end of the handle of a Little Dipper, or, as it is called, the Little Bear, *Ursa minor;* this Bear, evidently, of an extinct race, as bears, nowadays, are not allowed such tails.

Now, let us take another view of the Dipper. Its handle is really the tail of the Great Bear, also of the extinct long-tailed race. (Cut 2.) Note that it is composed of seven stars, hence its name, "The Seven Stars." Four of these are in the bowl and three in the handle; the handle is bent at the middle star, and this one is called Mizar. Just above Mizar is a tiny star called Alcor. Can you see Alcor? In all ages it has been considered a test of good eyesight to see this little star, even among the Indians. They call the big one the Old Squaw, and the little one the "pappoose on her back." Keep this in mind as a test. *Can you see the pappoose?*

If I give you the Latin names of the stars and the scientific theories as to their densities and relations, you certainly will not carry much of it away. But let us see if the old animal stories of the sky are not a help.

In Cut No. 2 of the Great Bear Hunt, for instance, you see the Dipper in the tail of the long-tailed Bear; and not only is this creature hunted, but in many other troubles. Thus, there is a swarm of flies buzzing about his ear, and another on his flank below b of the Dipper. These swarms are really *nebulæ* or clusters of very small stars.

Close below the Bear are two Hounds of Boötes in leash and in full pursuit of Ursa. They also have annoyances, for there is a swarm of flies at the ear of each. On Ursa's haunch are two areas that, according to the star maps, belong to the Hounds, so we must consider them the bites the hounds are going to take out.

Last, and leading, is the great hunter "Boötes." If you follow the Dipper, that is, the Bear's tail, in a curve for the length of two tails, it will bring you to Arcturus, the wonderful star that the Bear hunter wears like a blazing jewel in his knee.

Just above the head of Boötes is another well-known constellation, the Northern Crown. (*Corona borealis.*) This very small and very beautiful star-group has been called the "Diamond Necklace in the sky." because it looks like

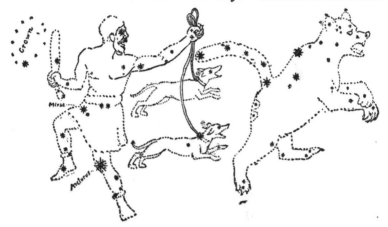

CUT 2. Boötes Hunting the Great Bear

a circle of jewels with one very large one in the middle of the string. The Indians call it the Camp Circle of the Gods.

If you draw a line from the back rim of the Dipper through Mizar, that is, the star at the bend of the handle and continue about the total length of the Dipper, it will touch the Crown.

The step from the Crown to the Cross is natural, and is easy in the sky. If you draw a line upward from the middle of the Dipper bowl, straight across the sky, about three total Dipper lengths, until it meets the Milky Way, you reach the Northern Cross, which is also called *Cygnus,* the

NORTHERN CROSS

Swan. You note it is on the opposite side of the Pole Star from the Dipper, and about one and a half Dipper lengths from the Pole.

One more easily known group is now in sight, that is, Cassiopeia in her chair. It is exactly opposite the Big Dipper on the other side of the Pole Star, and about as far from the latter as the Big Dipper is, that is, the Big Dipper and Cassiopeia balance each other; as the one goes up, the other goes down.

There is yet another famous constellation that every one should know; and that is "Orion, the great hunter, the Bull-fighter in the sky." During the summer, it goes on in day-time, but in winter it rises in the evening and passes over at the best of times to be seen. February is a particularly happy time for this wonder and splendor of the blue.

CASSIOPEIA

If you draw a line from the inner rim of the Dipper, through the outer edge of the bottom, and continue it about two and a half total lengths of the Dipper, it will lead to the Star "Procyon" the "Little Dogstar," the principal light of the constellation *Canis minor*. Below it, that is, rising later, is Sirius the "Great Dogstar," chief of the Constellation *Canis major*, and the most wonderful star in the sky. It is really seventy times as brilliant as the Sun, but so far away from us, that if the Sun's distance (92,000,000 miles) be represented by one inch, the distance of Sirius would be represented by *eight miles;* and yet it is one of the nearest of the stars in the sky. If you see a star that seems bigger or brighter than Sirius, you may know it is not a star, but a planet, either Venus, Jupiter or Mars.

Having located the Dogstar, it is easy to go farther to the southward, and recognize the Great Hunter Orion. The

three Kings on his belt are among the most striking of all
the famous stars in our blue dome.   And, having found
them, it is easy to trace the form of the Giant by the bright
stars, Betelgeuse (orange), in his right shoulder, and Bella-
trix in his left, Saiph in his right knee, and Rigel in his left
foot.   In his left hand he shakes the lion skin to baffle the
bull while his right swings the mighty club that seems already to have landed on the bull's head, for the huge crea-

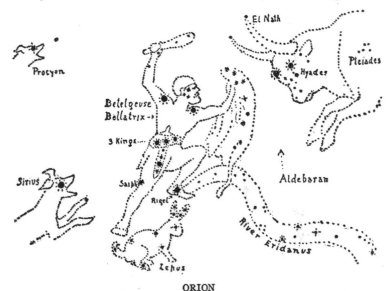

ORION

ture's face is spotted all over with star-groups called the
"Hyades." The wonderful red star, Aldebaran, is the Bull's
right eye and the Pleiades are the arrow wounds in the
Bull's shoulder.

Serviss tells us that the Pleiades have a supposed
connection with the Great Pyramid, because "about
2170 B. C., when the beginning of spring coincided
with the culmination of the Pleiades at midnight, that
wonderful group of stars was visible just at midnight,

through the mysterious southward-pointing passage of the Pyramid."

Out of Orion's left foot runs the River Eridanus, to wander over the sky; and, crouching for protection at the right foot of the Great Hunter, is *Lepus* the Hare.

Now, how many constellations have you learned? In Woodcraft you need fifteen. This sounds hard but here you have already got seventeen, and I think will have little trouble in remembering them.

And why should you do so? There are many reasons, and here is one that alone would, I think, make it worth while:

An artist friend said to me once: "I am glad I learned the principal star groups when I was young. For my life has been one of wandering in far countries, yet, wherever I went, I could always look up and see something familiar and friendly, something that I knew in the dear bygone days of my boyhood's home, and something to guide me still."

PLEIADES AS A TEST OF EYESIGHT

This star group has always been considered a good test of eyesight.

I once asked a group of boys in camp how many of the Pleiades they could count with the naked eye. A noisy, forward boy, who was nicknamed "Bluejay," because he was so fond of chattering and showing off, said, "Oh, I see hundreds."

"Well, you can sit down," I said, "for you can do nothing of the kind."

Another steadier boy said, "I believe I see six," and he proved that he did see them, for he mapped them out properly on a board with six pebbles.

That boy had good eyes, because poor eyes see merely a haze, but another boy present had better eyes, for he saw, and proved that he saw, seven. This is considered first-class. The Indians as a rule see seven, because they call them the Seven Stars. But, according to Flammarion, it is possible to exceed this, for several persons have given proof that they distinguished ten Pleiades. This is almost the extreme of human eyesight. There is, however,

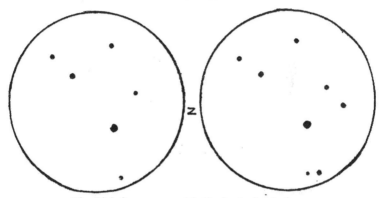

The Pleiades as seen with the best of naked eyes

according to the same authority, a record of thirteen Pleiades having been actually seen by the unaided human eye.

The telescope reveals some 2,000 in the cluster.

The Indians call them the "Seven Dancers," and tell a legend that seems to explain their dancing about the smallest one, as well as the origin of the constellation.

Once there were seven little Indian boys, who used to take their bowl of succotash each night and eat their suppers together on a mound outside the village. Six were about the same size, one was smaller than the rest, but he had a sweet voice, and knew many songs, so after supper the others would dance around the mound to his singing, and he marked time on his drum.

When the frosty days of autumn were ending, and winter

threatened to stop the nightly party, they said, "Let us ask our parents for some venison, so we can have a grand feast and dance for the last time on the mound."

They asked, but all were refused. Each father said, "When I was a little boy, I thought myself lucky to get even a pot of succotash, and never thought of asking for venison as well."

So the boys assembled at the mound. All were gloomy but the little singer, who said:

"Never mind, brothers! We shall feast without venison, and we shall be merry just the same, for I shall sing you a new song that will lighten your hearts."

First, he made each of them fasten on his head a little torch of birch bark, then he sat down in the middle and thumped away at his little drum and sang:

> Ki yi yi yah
> Ki yi yi yah

And faster

> Ki yi yi yah
> Ki yi yi yah

And faster still, till now they were spinning round. Then:

> Ki yi yi yah
> Ki yi yi yah
> Whoooooop

They were fairly whirling now, and, as the singer gave this last whoop of the last dance on the mound, they and he went dancing over the treetops into the sky; light of heart and heels and head, they went, and their parents rushed out in time to see them go, but too late to stop them. And now you may see them every clear autumn night as winter draws near; you may see the little torches sparkling as they

dance, the six around the little one in the middle. Of
course, you can't hear his song, or even his drum, but you
must remember he is a long way off now.

There is another story of a little Indian girl called
Two-Bright-Eyes. She was the only child of her parents.
She wandered away one evening seeking the whippoorwill
and got lost — you see, even Indians get lost sometimes.
She never returned. The mourning parents never learned
what became of her, but they thought they saw a new pair
of twin stars rising through the trees not long after, and
when their grief was so softened by time that they could
sing about it, this is the song they made about their loss:

THE TWIN STARS

Two-Bright-Eyes went wandering out
   To chase the whippoorwill.
Two-Bright-Eyes got lost, and left
   Our teepee, oh, so still!

Two-Bright-Eyes was lifted up
   To sparkle in the skies,
And look like stars, but we know well
   That that's our lost Bright-Eyes.

She is looking for the camp,
   She would come back if she could;
She is peeping thro' the trees to find
   The teepee in the wood.

The Planets

The stars we see are suns like our Sun, giving out light
to worlds that go around them as our world goes around our
Sun; as these worlds do not give out light, and are a long

way off, we cannot see them. But around our own Sun are several worlds besides ours. They are very near to us, and we can see them by the reflected light of the Sun. These are called "planets" or "wanderers," because, before their courses were understood, they seemed to wander about, all over the sky, unlike the fixed stars.

They are so close to us that their distance and sizes are easily measured. They do not twinkle.

There are eight, in all, not counting the small Planetoids; but only those as large as stars of the first magnitude concern us. They are here in order of nearness to the Sun:

1. MERCURY is always close to the Sun, so that it is usually lost in the glow of the twilight or of the vapors of the horizon, where it shows like a globule of quicksilver. It has phases and quarters like the Moon. It is so hot there "that a Mercurian would be frozen to death in Africa or Senegal" (*Flammarion*).

2. VENUS. The brightest of all the stars is Venus; far brighter than Sirius. It is the *Morning Star*, the *Evening Star*, the Shepherd's Star, and yet not a star at all, but a planet. It has phases and quarters like the Moon. You can place it only with the help of an almanac.

3. THE EARTH.

4. MARS. The nearest of the other worlds to us. It is a fiery-red planet. It has phases like the Moon.

5. JUPITER, like a very large star of the first magnitude, famous for its five moons, and really the largest of the planets.

6. SATURN, noted for its rings, also like a very large star of the first magnitude.

7. URANUS and (8) NEPTUNE, are too small for observation without a telescope.

THE MOON

The Moon is one fifth the diameter of the Earth, about one fiftieth of the bulk, and is about a quarter million miles away. Its course, while very irregular, is nearly the same as the apparent course of the Sun. But "in winter the full Moon is at an altitude in the sky near the limit attained by the Sun in summer, . . . and even, at certain times, five degrees higher. It is the contrary in summer, a season when the Moon remains very low" (*F.*).

The Moon goes around the Earth in twenty-seven and a quarter days. It loses nearly three quarters of an hour each night; that is, it rises that much later.

"Astronomy with an Opera Glass." Garrett P. Serviss, D. Appleton & Co., New York City. Price, $1.50.

MAKING A DAM

When I was a boy we had no natural swimming pool, but there was a small stream across our farm; and I with my two friends succeeded in making a pool, partly by dam-

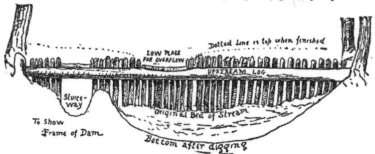

ming up the little stream, and partly by digging out the place above the dam.

The first things needed were two logs long enough to

reach from bank to bank. These we placed across with the help of the team, and fixed them firmly three feet apart. Inside of each and tight against it we drove a row of strong stakes leaving a gap or sluiceway for the water to run until

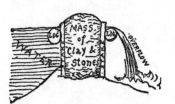

the rest of the dam was finished.

This cribbing we now filled with clay dug out of the bed of the brook above the dam. Hammering it down hard, and covering the top with flat stones.

Finally we closed up the sluice-way with stakes and clay like the rest of it, and in one night the swimming hole filled up. Next morning there was a little cataract over the low place I had purposely left for an overflow. The water was four feet deep and many of us there learned to swim.

WHEN LOST IN THE WOODS

If you should miss your way, the first thing to remember is, like the Indian, "You are not lost; it is the teepee that is lost." It isn't serious. It cannot be so, unless you do something foolish.

The first and most natural thing to do is to get on a hill, up a tree, or other high lookout, and seek for some landmark near the camp. You may be so sure of these things:

You are not nearly as far from camp as you think you are.

Your friends will soon find you.

You can help them best by signaling.

The worst thing you can do is to get frightened. The truly dangerous enemy is not the cold or the hunger, so much as the fear. It is fear that robs the wanderer of his judgment and of his limb power; it is fear that turns the passing experience into a final tragedy. Only keep cool and all will be well.

If there is snow on the ground, you can follow your back track.

If you see no landmark, look for the smoke of the fire. Shout from time to time, and wait; for though you have been away for hours it is quite possible you are within earshot of your friends. If you happen to have a gun, fire it off twice in quick succession on your high lookout then wait and listen. Do this several times and wait plenty long enough, perhaps an hour. If this brings no help, send up a distress signal — that is, make two smoke fires by smothering two bright fires with green leaves and rotten wood, and keep them at least fifty feet apart, or the wind will confuse them. Two shots or two smokes are usually understood to mean "I am in trouble." Those in camp on seeing this should send up one smoke, which means "Camp is here."

In a word, "keep cool, make yourself comfortable, leave a record of your travels, and help your friends to find you."

INDIAN TWEEZERS

Oftentimes, a camper may need a pair of tweezers or forceps to pull out a thorn or catch some fine end. If he happens to be without the real thing, he can supply the place with those of Indian style — these are simply a small pair of clam-shells, with edges clean and hinge unbroken.

The old-time Indians had occasionally a straggly beard. They had no razor, but they managed to do without one. As a part of their toilet for special occasion they pulled out each hair by means of the clam-shell nippers.

A HOME-MADE COMPASS

If you happen to have a magnet, it is easy to make a compass. Rub a fine needle on the magnet; then on the side of your nose. Then lay it gently on the surface of a cup full of water. The needle will float and point north. The cup must not be of metal.

AN INDIAN CLOCK, SHADOW CLOCK OR SUNDIAL

To make an Indian shadow clock or sundial, prepare a smooth board about fifteen inches across, with a circle

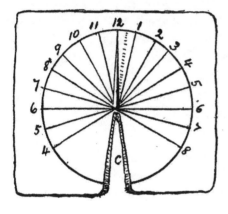

divided by twenty-four rays into equal parts. Place it on a level, solid post or stump in the open. At night set the dial so that the twelve o'clock line points exactly north, as determined by the Pole Star and nail it down. Then, fix a stick or pointer with its upper edge on the centre and set it exactly pointing to the Pole Star (a b); that is, the same angle as the latitude of the place, and fix it there immov-

ably; it may be necessary to cut a notch (c) in the board to permit of a sight line. The hours eight at night to four next morning may as well be painted black. As a time-piece, this shadow clock will be found roughly correct.

The Indians of course used merely the shadow of a tree, or the sun streak that fell on the lodge floor through the smoke opening.

LIGHTS

For camp use, there is nothing better than the Stone-bridge folding lantern, with a good supply of candles. A temporary torch can readily be made of a roll of birch bark, a pine knot, or some pine-root slivers, in a split stick of green wood.

HUNTER'S LAMP

A fairly steady light can be made of a piece of cotton cloth or twisted rag, stuck in a clam-shell full of oil or melted grease. An improvement is easily made by putting the cotton wick through a hole in a thin, flat stone, which sets in the grease and holds the wick upright.

Another improvement is made by using a tin in place of the shell. It makes a steadier lamp, as well as a much larger light. This kind of a lamp enjoys wide use and has some queer names, such as slot-lamp, grease-jet, hunter's lamp, etc. (See Cut on next page.)

WOODMAN'S LANTERN

When nothing better is at hand, a woodman's lantern can be made of a tomato can. Make a big hole in the bottom for the candle, and punch the sides full of small holes, preferably from the inside. If you have a wire to make a hanger, well and good; if not, you can carry it by the bottom. This lets out enough light and will not go out in the wind. If you want to set it down, you must make a hole in the ground for the candle, or if on a table, set it on two blocks. (Cut on next page.)

Another style is described in a recent letter from Hamlin Garland:

"Apropos of improved camp lights, I had a new one 'sprung on me,' this summer: A forest ranger and I were visiting a miner, about a mile from our camp. It came on dark, pitch dark, and when we started home, we could not follow the trail.

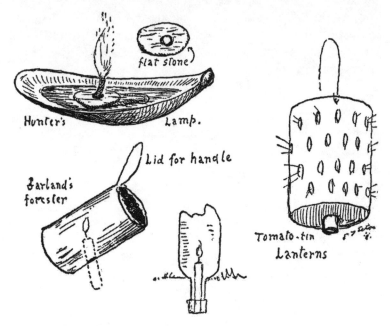

flat stone

Hunter's Lamp.

Lid for handle

Garland's forester

Tomato-tin Lanterns

It was windy as well as dark, and matches did very little good. So back we went to the cabin. The ranger then picked up an old tomato can, punched a hole in the side, thrust a candle up through the hole, lighted it, and took the can by the disk which had been cut from the top. The whole thing was now a boxed light, shining ahead like a searchlight, and the wind did not affect it at all! I've been camping, as you know, for thirty years, but this little trick was new to me. Perhaps it is new to you." H. G.

Still another style, giving a better light, is made by

heating an ordinary clear glass quart bottle pretty hot in the fire, then dipping the bottom part in cold water; this causes the bottom to crack off. The candle is placed in the neck, flame inside, and the bottle neck sunk in the ground.

CAMP LOOM AND GRASS MATS

The chief use of the camp loom is to weave mats for the beds of grass, straw, hay, or, best of all, sedge. I have made it thus:

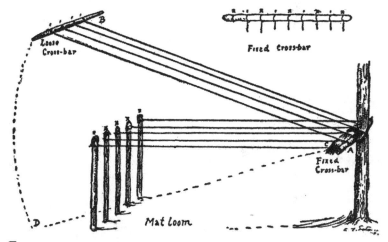

Mat loom

A 3-foot cross-bar *A* is fast to a small tree, and seven feet away, even stakes are driven into the ground 8 inches apart, each 3 feet out of the ground.

Five stout cords are tied to each stick, and to the cross-bar, keeping them parallel. Then, between each on the cross-bar is attached another cord (four in all) the far end of which is made fast to a loose cross-bar, *B*.

One fellow raises the loose cross-bar *B*, while another lays a long bundle of grass tight in the corner *C*. Then *B* is lowered to *D*, and another roll of grass or sedge is tucked in on the under side of the stake cords. Thus the bundles are laid one above and one below, until the mat is of the the required length. The cords are then fastened, the cross-bars removed, and the mat, when dried, makes a fine bed. When added to the willow bed, it is pure luxury; but lawful, because made of wildwood material.

NAVAHO LOOM

A profitable amusement in camp, is weaving rugs or mats of inner bark, rags, etc., on a rough Navaho loom.

The crudest kind, one which can be made in an hour is illustrated on next page. I have found it quite satisfactory for weaving rough mats or rugs. (A and B) are two trees or posts. (C) is the cross piece. (D) is the upper yarnbeam, wrapped its whole length with a spiral cord. (E) is the lower yarn-beam, similarly wrapped. (F F) are stout cords to carry the frame while the warp is being stretched between the yarn-beams. (G G) is a log hung on for weight. (H H) is a round stick fastened between the yarns, odds on one side, evens on the other, to hold the yarns open until the rug is all done, but about one inch when it is drawn out.

Now with a needle, the yarns or strings for the warp are stretched from one yarn-beam to another, as a continuous string. The exact method is shown on a larger scale in the upper figure (I I) The batten or spreader (J) is a piece of light wood two inches wide and one half inch thick, with square edges, but thin sharp· point, and about as long as the yarn beam.

Now we are ready to begin. Run the batten between the yarns under the sticks (H H.) Then drop it to the bottom and turn it flatwise, thus spreading the yarns apart

in two rows. Lay a line of soft bark, rags, or other woof
in this opening on top of the batten, making sure that it
projects a couple of inches at each end. Double these
long ends around the strong cords (*F F*) then back along
themselves. Now draw out the spreading batten and press
the woof down tight.

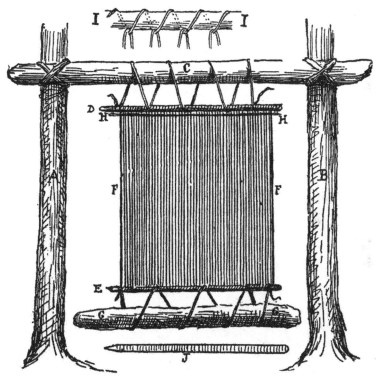

Run the batten through alternate threads again, but
the reverse way of last, and this time it goes more slowly
for the lack of a guide rod.* Lay a new line of woof as

---

*This is done much more quickly by help of a heald-rod, that is, a horizontal stick as
wide as the blanket, with every other strand of the warp loosely looped to it by a running
cord near the top. When this rod is pulled forward it reverses the set of the threads and
allows the batten to drop in at once.

above. When the rug is all finished except the top inch or more, draw out the rod (*H H*) and fill the warp to the top.

Finally cut and draw out the spiral cords on each yarn-beam. This frees the rug, which is finished, excepting for trim and binding, when such are desired.

Those who want full details of the best Navaho looms and methods will find them in Dr. Washington Matthew's article on Navaho Weavers, 3d Annual Report, Bur. of Ethnology, 1881–2. Washington 1884.

CAMP RAKE

A camp rake is made of forked branches of oak, beech, hickory, or other hard wood, thus: Cut a handle an inch

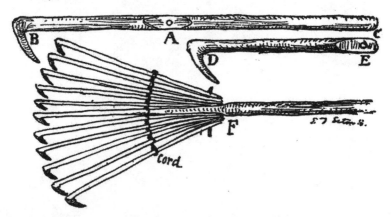

thick (*B C*) and 4 feet long, of the shape shown. Flatten it on each side of *A*, and make a gimlet-hole through. Now cut ten branches of the shape *D E*, each about 20 inches long. Flatten them at the *E* end, and make a gimlet-hole through each. Fasten all together, 5 on each side of the handle, as in *F*, with a long nail or strong wire through all the holes; then, with a cord, lash them together, spacing them by putting the cord between. Sharpen the points of the teeth, and your rake is ready.

CAMP BROOM

There are two ways of making a camp broom. First, the twig broom. This is easily made as follows: Cut a handle

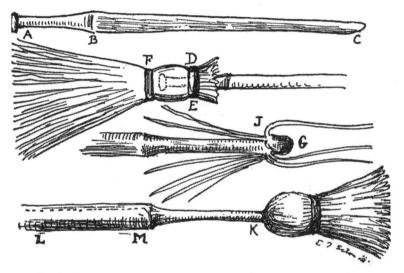

an inch thick, and shape it to a shoulder, as in *A B C*. Lash on birch or other fine twigs, one layer at a time, until sufficiently thick, as *D E*. Now at *F*, put a final lashing of cord. This draws the broom together, and binds it firmly to the handle. Trim the ends even with the axe, and it is ready for use.

The other style is the backwoods broom. This was usually made of blue-beech or hickory. A 4-foot piece of a 4-inch green trunk is best. Slivers 18 inches long are cut down, left attached at *J*, and bent back over the end until there is a bunch of them thick enough; when they are bound together with a cord and appear as in *K*. Now thin down the rest of the handle *L M*, and the broom needs only a little drying out to be finished.

BUILDING A BOAT

Most camp sites are selected with a view to boating; certainly no camp is complete without it.

Winter is a good time to build a boat, if you have a workshop big enough to hold it.

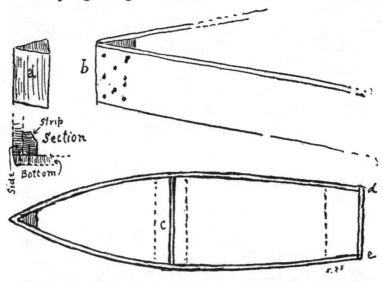

The simplest kind of a craft is the best to start with. Get two boards, smooth and with as few knots as possible, 15 in. wide, and 15 ft. long; about 50 sq. ft. of tongue and groove flooring; a piece of 2 x 6 in. scantling, 15 in. long; and plenty of 3-in. nails.

Begin by beveling the stern post to an edge (a). Set

this on the ground and nail two of the boards to it, one on each side (b).

At a point about 7 feet from the bow, put in a temporary cross piece 3½ ft. long (c), which can have the ends either plumb, or spreading wider toward the top.

Around this, bend the two side boards till their stem ends are but 3 ft. apart. Nail on an end piece (d e) to hold them there.

Now cut a strip of 1 x 2 in. stuff, and nail it inside along the lower edge of the side board, so as to give a double thickness on which to nail the bottom.

Turn the boat upside down and nail on the tongue and groove stuff to form the bottom.

Now, turn her over, remove the shaping board, put in the necessary stern and mid seats (see dotted lines), nail on a piece of board to double the thickness where the rowlocks are needed — each about 12 inches abaft the mid seat, add rowlocks, and the carpenter work is done.

Tar all the seams, caulking any that are gaping, and when the tar has set, paint her inside and out. As soon as this is dry, she is ready for the water.

She may leak a little at first, but the swelling of the wood has a tendency to close the seams.

This is the simplest form of boat. Great improvement can be made by making the sides deeper, and cutting the lower edge so that the bottom rises at bow and stern, also by setting the stem or bow-post at an angle, and finally by adding a keel.

If you cannot get a 15-in. board, use two or more narrow ones. Their joints can be made tight by caulking.

A DUGOUT CANOE

Basswood, tulip wood, and white pine were the favorite woods for a dugout canoe, though no one made one when they could get birch bark. The method of making was simple but laborious. Cut your log to the exact shape desired on the outside, then drive into it, all along the side, thin wire nails, an inch long, so that there should be one every two feet along the side, and more on the bottom. Now, hollow out the inside with adze or axe, till the nail points are reached. Sometimes longer nails were used for the bottom. The wood at bow and stern was, of course, much thicker.

CAMP HORN

I wish every Camp would get a good camp horn or Michigan lumberman's horn. It is about four feet long, has a six-inch bell-mouth, and is of brass. Its sounds are made by mouth, but a good player can give a tune as on a post horn. Its quality is wonderfully rich, mellow and far-reaching, and it can be heard for three or four miles. It is a sound to stir the echoes and fill the camp with romantic memories.

SLEEP OUTDOORS

As you drive through New England in the evening, summer or winter, you must notice a great many beds out of doors, on piazza or on sun-deck. Many of these are beds of persons who are suffering from lung trouble. They have found out that this is the way to cure it. Some of them are the beds of persons who fear lung trouble, and this they know is the way to evade it.

Take, then, this lesson: If possible, every brave should *sleep out of doors* as much as possible; *not on the ground*, and not in the wind, but in a bed, warm, dry, and rainproof, and he will be the better for it.

THE GEE-STRING CAMP

Whenever complete isolation from summer resorts or mixed company make it permissible, we have found it well to let the fellows run all day during warm weather, clad only in their shoes and their small bathing trunks, breech-clout or gee-string. This is the Gee-String or Indian Camp. Its value as a daily sun bath, a continual tonic and a mentally refreshing hark back to the primitive, cannot be overestimated.

VII. Signaling and Indian Signs

Sign Language

DO YOU know the Sign Language?

If not, do you realize that the Sign Language is an established mode of communication in all parts of the world without regard to native speech?

Do you know that it is so refined and complete that sermons and lectures are given in it every day, to those who cannot hear?

Do you know that it is as old as the hills and is largely used in all public schools? And yet when I ask boys this question, "Do you use the Sign Language?" they nearly always say "No."

The first question of most persons is "What is it?" It is a simple method of asking questions and giving answers, that is talking, by means of the hands. It is used by all the Plains Indians, and by thousands of white people to-day, in cities, as well as in the western country, and to an extent that surprises all when first they come to think of it.

Not long ago I asked a boy whether the policemen on the crowded streets used Sign Language. He said, "No!" at least he did not know if they did.

I replied: "When the officer on Fifth Avenue wishes to *stop* all vehicles, what does he do?"

"He raises his hand, flat with palm forward," was the reply.

"Yes, and when he means 'come on,' what does he do?"

"He beckons this way."

"And how does he say 'go left, go right, go back, come, hurry up, you get out?'" Each of these signs I found was well known to the boy.

The girls are equally adept and equally unconscious of it. One very shy little miss — so shy that she dared not speak — furnished a good illustration of this:

"Do you use the Sign Language in your school?" I asked. She shook her head.

"Do you learn any language but English?" She nodded.

"What is the use of learning any other than English?" She raised her right shoulder in the faintest possible shrug.

"Now," was my reply, "don't you see you have already given me three signs of the Sign Language, which you said you did not use?"

After collecting popular signs for several years I found that I had about one hundred and fifty that are in established use in the schools of New York City.

Here are some of the better known. Each boy will probably find that he has known and used them all his schooldays:

You (pointing at the person);

Me (pointing at one's self);

Yes (nod);

No (head shake);

Go (move hand forward, palm first);

Come (draw hand toward one's self, palm in);

Hurry (same, but the hand quickly and energetically moved several times);

Come for a moment (hand held out back down, fingers closed except first, which is hooked and straightened quickly several times);

Stop (one hand raised, flat; palm forward);

Gently or *Go easy* (like "stop," but hand gently waved from side to side);

Good-bye (hand high, flat, palm down, fingers wagged all together);

Up (forefinger pointed and moved upward);

Down (ditto downward);

Silence or *hush* (forefinger across lips);

Listen (flat hand behind ear);

Whisper (silently move lips, holding flat hand at one side of mouth);

Friendship (hands clasped);

Threatening (fist shaken at person);

Warning (forefinger gently shaken at a slight angle toward person);

He is cross (forefinger crossed level);

Shame on you (right forefinger drawn across left toward person several times);

Scorn (turning away and throwing an imaginary handful of sand toward person);

Insolent defiance (thumb to nose tip, fingers fully spread);

Surrender (both hands raised high and flat to show no weapons);

Crazy (with forefinger make a little circle on forehead then point to person);

Look there (pointing);

Applause (silently make as though clapping hands);

Victory (one hand high above head as though waving hat);

Indifference (a shoulder shrug);

Ignorance (a shrug and headshake combined);

Pay (hand held out half open, forefinger and thumb, rubbed together);

Poverty (both hands turned flat forward near trouser pockets);

Bribe (hand held hollow up behind the back);

Knife (first and second fingers of right hand used as to whittle first finger of left);

I am thinking it over (forefinger on right brow and eyes raised);

I forgot (touch forehead with all right finger tips, then draw flat hand past eyes once and shake head);

I send you a kiss (kiss finger tips and move hand in graceful sweep toward person);

The meal was good (pat stomach);

I beg of you (flat hands tight together and upright);

Upon my honor (with forefinger make a cross over heart);

Bar up, fins, or *I claim exemption* (cross second finger of right hand on first finger and hold hand up);

.*Give me* (hold out open flat hand pulling it back a little to finish);

I give you (the same, but push forward to finish);

Give me my bill (same, then make motion of writing);

Get up (raise flat hand sharply, palm upward);

Sit down (drop flat hand sharply, palm down);

Rub it out (quickly shake flat hand from side to side, palm forward);

Thank you (a slight bow, smile and hand-salute, made by drawing flat hand a few inches forward and downward palm up);

Do you think me simple? (forefinger laid on side of nose);

Will you? or, *is it so?* (eyebrows raised and slight bow made);

Will you come swimming? (first and second fingers raised and spread, others closed);

Also of course, the *points of the compass*, and the *numerals* up to twenty or thirty.

My attention was first directed to the Sign Language in 1882, when I went to live in western Manitoba. There I found it used among the Crees and Sioux, the latter especially being expert sign-talkers. Later, I found it a daily necessity for travel among the natives of New Mexico and Montana.

One of the best sign talkers I ever met was the Crow Indian, White Swan, who had been one of Custer's Scouts. He was badly wounded by the Sioux, clubbed on the head, and left for dead. He recovered and escaped; but ever after was deaf and dumb. However sign talk was familiar to all his people and he was at little disadvantage in daytime. From him I received many lessons in Sign Language and thus in 1897 began to study it seriously.

Now I wish to teach it to the Scouts. If each of them would learn to use with precision the one hundred and fifty schoolboy signs and then add twice as many more, they would become fairly good sign-talkers. These additional signs they can find in the "Dictionary of the Sign Language."*

Why should you talk the Sign Language? There are many reasons:

In this code you can talk to any other Scout, without a outsider knowing or understanding.

It makes conversation easy in places when you must not speak aloud, as in school, during music, or by the bedside of the sick.

It is a means of far-signaling much quicker than semaphore or other *spelling* codes, for this gives one or more words in one sign.

It will enable you to talk when there is too much noise to be heard, as across the noisy streets.

*Issued by Doubleday, Page & Co.

It makes it possible to talk to a deaf person.

It is a wonderful developer of observation.

It is a simple means of talking to an Indian or a Scout of another nationality whose language you do not understand. This indeed is its great merit. It is *universal*. It deals not with words but with ideas that are common to all mankind. It is therefore a kind of Esperanto already established.

So much for its advantages; what are its weaknesses? Let us frankly face them:

It is useless in the dark;

It will not serve on the telephone;

It can scarcely be written;

In its pure form it will not give new proper names.

To meet the last two we have expedients, as will be seen, but the first two are insurmountable difficulties.

Remember then you are to learn the Sign Language because it is *silent, far-reaching*, and the one *universal language*.

Since it deals fundamentally with ideas, we avoid words and letters, but for proper names it is very necessary to know the one-hand manual alphabet,

For *numbers* we use the fingers, as probably did the earliest men who counted.

Yes. The sign for "yes" is so natural that one can see it instinctively made if we offer food to a hungry baby. That is simply a nod. That is if you are near, but far off, make your right hand with all fingers closed except index and thumb which are straight and touching at top, advance, bend toward the left side as though bowing, then returned and straight again.

No. This also is a natural sign, we can see it if we offer bitter medicine to a baby. The sign for "No," when near, is shake the head; but, when too far for that to be seen, hold the closed right hand in front of the body, then sweep it

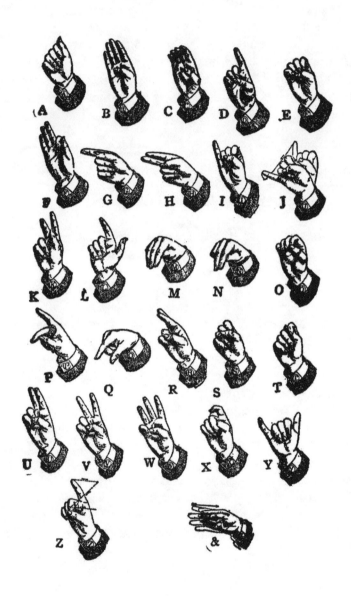

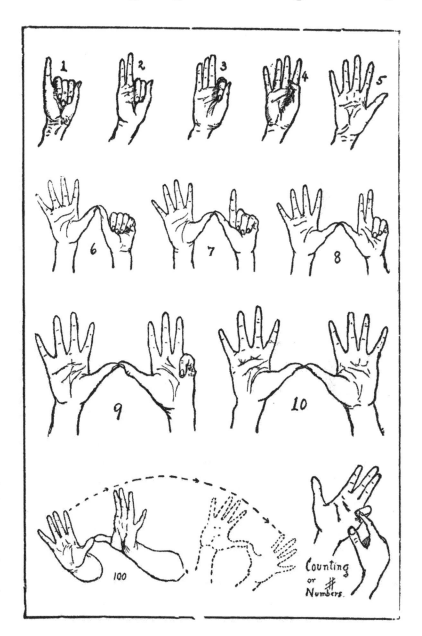

outward and downward, at the same time turn the palm up as though throwing something away.

Query. The sign for *Question* — that is, "I am asking you a question," "I want to know" — is much used and important. Hold up the right hand toward the person, palm forward, fingers open, slightly curved and spread. Wave the hand gently by wrist action from side to side. It is used before, and sometimes after all questions. If you are very near, merely raise the eyebrows.

The following are needed in asking questions:

How Many? First the *Question* sign, then hold the left hand open, curved, palm up, fingers spread, then with right digit quickly tap each finger of left in succession, closing it back toward the left palm, beginning with the little finger.

How Much? Same as *How many?*

What? What are you doing? What do you want? What is it? First give *Question*, then hold right hand palm down, fin-

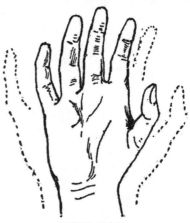

QUERY SIGN

gers slightly bent and separated, and, pointing forward, throw it about a foot from right to left several times, describing an arc upward.

When? If seeking a definite answer as to length of time, make signs for *Question, How much*, and then specify time by sign for hours, days, etc. When asking in general "*When*" for a date, hold the left index extended and vertical, other and thumb closed, make a circle round left index tip with tip of extended right index, others and thumb closed; and when the index reaches the starting point, stop it and point at tip of left index (what point of shadow?).

Where? (What direction) *Question*, then with forefinger sweep the horizon in a succession of bounds, a slight pause at the bottom of each.

Which? *Question*, then hold left hand in front of you with palm toward you, fingers to right and held apart; place the end of the right forefinger on that of left forefinger, and then draw it down across the other fingers.

Why? Make the sign for *Question*, then repeat it very slowly.

Who? *Question*, and then describe with the right forefinger a small circle six inches in front of the mouth.

Eat. Throw the flat hand several times past the mouth in a curve.

Drink. Hold the right hand as though holding a cup near the mouth and tip it up.

Sleep. Lay the right cheek on the right flat hand.

My, *mine*, *yours*, *possession*, etc. Hold out the closed fist, thumb up, and swing it down a little so thumb points forward.

House. Hold the flat hands together like a roof.

Finished or *done*. Hold out the flat left hand palm to the right, then with flat right hand chop down past the ends of the left fingers.

Thus "*Will you eat?*" would be a *Question, you eat,* but *Have you eaten* would be, *Question, you eat, finished.*

Way or *road.* Hold both flat hands nearly side by side, palms up, but right one nearer the breast, then alternately lift them forward and draw them back to indicate track or feet traveling.

The Indian had much use for certain signs in describing the white trader. The first was:

Liar. Close the right hand except the first and second

fingers; these are straight and spread; bring the knuckles of the first finger to the mouth, then pass it down forward to the left, meaning double or forked tongue.

The second sign, meaning "*very*" or "*very much*," is made by striking the right fist down past the knuckles of the left without quite touching them, the left being held still.

Another useful sign is *time*. This is made by drawing a circle with the right forefinger on the back of the left wrist. It looks like a reference to the wrist watch, but it is certainly much older than that style of timepiece and probably refers to the shadow of a tree. Some prefer to draw the circle on the left palm as it is held up facing forward.

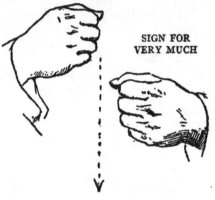

SIGN FOR VERY MUCH

If you wish to ask, "*What time is it?*" You make the signs *Question*, then *Time*. If the answer is "Three o'clock," you would signal:

Time and hold up *three* fingers of the right hand.

Hours are shown by laying the right forefinger as a pointer on the flat palm of the left and carrying it once around; *minutes* by moving the pointer a very little to the left.

If you wish to signal in answer 3:15. You give the signs for hours 3 and minutes 15. Holding all ten fingers up for 10, then those of one hand for 5.

It takes a good-sized dictionary to give all the signs in use, and a dictionary you must have, if you would become an expert.

I shall conclude with one pretty little Indian sign: First,

give the *Question* sign, then make an incomplete ring of your right forefinger and thumb, raise them in a sweep until above your head, then bring the ring straight down to your heart. This is the Indian way of asking, "Is the sun shining in your heart?" — that is, "Are you happy?" — your answer will, I hope, be made by the right hand and arm standing up straight, then bowing toward the left, followed by a sharp stroke of the right fist knuckles past those of the left fist without their touching, which means "Yes, the sun shines in my heart *heap strong.*"

PICTURE-WRITING

The written form of Sign Language is the picture-writing also called Pictography, and Ideography, because it represents *ideas* and not words or letters. It is widely believed that Sign Language is the oldest of all languages; that indeed it existed among animals before man appeared on earth. It is universally accepted that the ideography is the oldest of all writing. The Chinese writing for instance is merely picture-writing done with as few lines as possible.

Thus, their curious character for "*Hearing*" was once a complete picture of a person listening behind a screen, but in time it was reduced by hasty hands to a few scratches; and "*War,*" now a few spider marks, was originally a sketch of "two women in one house."

To come a little nearer home, our alphabet is said to be descended from hieroglyphic ideographs.

"A" or "Ah," for example, was the sound of an ox represented first by an outline of an ox, then of the head, which in various modifications, through rapid writing, became our "A."

"O" was a face saying "Oh," now simplified into the round shape of the mouth.

"S" was a serpent hissing. It is but little changed to-day.

We may also record our Sign Language in picture-writing, as was the custom of many Indian tribes, and we shall find it worth while for several reasons: It is the Indian special writing; it is picturesque and useful for decoration; and it can be read by any Indian no matter what language he

Some Indian Scout Pictographs

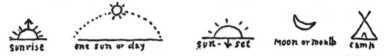

sunrise — one sun or day — sun-↓set — moon or month — camp

speaks. Indeed, I think it probable that a pictograph inscription dug up 10,000 years from now would be read, whether our language was understood or not. When the French Government set up the Obelisk of Luxor in Paris and wished to inscribe it for all time, they made the record, not in French or Latin, but in pictographs.

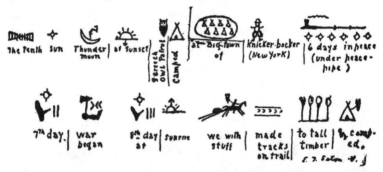

It is, moreover, part of my method to take the boy through the stages of our race development, just as the young bird must run for a send-off, before it flies, so pictography being its earliest form is the natural first step to writing.

In general, picture writing aims to give on paper the idea of the Sign Language without first turning it into sounds. In the dictionary of Sign Language I give the written form after each of the signs that has a well established or possible symbol. Many of these are drawn from the Indians who were among the best scouts and above all noted for their use of the picture-writing. A few of them will serve to illustrate.

Numbers were originally fingers held up, and five was the whole hand, while ten was a double hand. We can see traces of this origin in the Roman style of numeration.

A one-night camp, a more permanent camp, a village and a town are shown in legible symbols.

An enemy, sometimes expressed as a " snake," recalls our own "snake in the grass." A "friend," was a man with a

The picture on the teepee lining, to record Guy's Exploit

branch of a tree; because this was commonly used as a flag of truce and had indeed the same meaning as our olive branch. The "treaty" is easily read; it was a pair of figures like this done in Wampum that recorded Penn's Treaty.

"*Good*" is sometimes given as a circle full of lines all

straight and level, and for "*bad*" they are crooked and contrary. The wavy lines stood for *water*, so *good water* is clearly indicated. The three arrows added mean that at three arrow flights in that direction, that is a quarter mile, there is good water. If there was but one arrow and it pointed straight down that meant "good water here," if it pointed down and outward it meant "good water at a little distance." If the arrow was raised to carry far, it

——	Level		Snow Moon or January
——▶	Direction forward		Hunger Moon or February
◀——	Direction backward		March the Wakening or Crow Moon
	Sun or day		Grass Moon or April
	Sunrise		Planting Moon or May
	Sunset		Rose Moon or June
	Noon		Thunder Moon or July
	Night		Red Moon or Green Corn, August
	Day back one, or yesterday		Hunting Moon, September
	Day forward one, or to-morrow		Leaf - Falling Moon. October
	Moon, or month		Mad Moon, November
	Rain		Long Night Moon, December.
	Snow		
	Year (or snow round to snow)		

大	Man	⊜	Good
大	Woman	⊛	Bad
⊕	Baby	≋	Water
大	Scout	⊜	Good water
℧	Scouting	⊜→	Good water in 3 arrow flights
?	Question	柰	One-night camp
×	Yes	𝝙	More permanent camp
○	No	𝗫𝗫𝗫	Village
⊗	Doubtful	⬭	Town
⟨⟨⟨ or 𝓵 Peace		⌒	Heap or many
𝗫 or 𝓩 War		大	I have found
大	Surrender	🐻	Bear
大	Prisoner	🐻	Grizzly bear
大	Enemy	🐿	Chipmunk
大	Friend	🐻	Dead bear
		大大	Treaty of peace

meant good "water a long way off there." This sign was of the greatest value in the dry country of the southwest. Most Indian lodges were decorated with pictographs depicting in some cases the owner's adventures, at other times his prayers for good luck or happy dreams.

The old Indian sign for peace, three angles all pointing one way that is "agreed," contrasts naturally with the "war" or "trouble" sign, in which they are going different ways or against each other.

An animal was represented by a crude sketch in which its chief character was shown, thus chipmunk was a small animal with long tail and stripes. Bear was an outline bear, but grizzly bear, had the claws greatly exaggerated.

When the animal was killed, it was represented on its back with legs up.

Each chief, warrior and scout had a totem, a drawing of which stood for his name or for himself.

A man's name is expressed by his totem; thus, the above means, To-day, 20th Sun Thunder Moon. After three days "Deerfoot," Chief of the Flying Eagles, comes to our Standing Rock Camp.

When a man was dead officially or actually, his totem was turned bottom up.

Here is a copy of the inscription found by Schoolcraft on the grave post of Wabojeeg, or White Fisher, a famous Ojibwa chief. He was of the Caribou clan. On the top is his clan totem reversed, and on the bottom the White Fisher; the seven marks on the left were war parties he led.

The three marks in the middle are for wounds.

The moose head is to record a desperate fight he had with a bull moose, while his success in war and in peace are also stated.

This inscription could be read only by those knowing the story, and is rather as a memory help than an exact record.

BLAZES AND INDIAN SIGNS — BLAZES

First among the trail signs that are used by Scouts, Indians, and white hunters, and most likely to be of use to the traveler, are axe blazes on tree trunks. Among these some may vary greatly with locality, but there is one that I have found everywhere in use with scarcely any variation. That is the simple white spot meaning, *"Here is the trail."*

The Indian in making it may nick off an infinitesimal speck of bark with his knife, the trapper with his hatchet may make it as big as a dollar, or the settler with his heavy axe may slab off half the tree-side; but the sign is the same in principle and in meaning, on trunk, log or branch from Atlantic to Pacific and from Hudson Strait to Rio Grande. "This is your trail," it clearly says in the universal language of the woods.

There are two ways of employing it: one when it appears on back and front of the trunk, so that the trail can be run both ways; the other when it appears on but one side of each tree, making a *blind trail*, which can be run one way only, the blind trail is often used by trappers and prospectors, who do not wish any one to follow their back track.

But there are treeless regions where the trail must be marked; regions of sage brush and sand, regions of rock, stretches of stone, and level wastes of grass or sedge. Here other methods must be employed.

A well-known Indian device, in the brush, is to break a twig and leave it hanging. (*Second line.*)

Among stones and rocks the recognized sign is one stone set on top of another (*top line*) and in places where there is nothing but grass the custom is to twist a tussock into a knot (*third line*).

These signs also are used in the whole country from Maine to California.

INDIAN SIGNS

Signs in Stones

This is the Trail   Turn to the Right   Turn to the Left   Important Warning

Signs in Twigs

This is the Trail   Turn to the Right   Turn to the Left   Important Warning

Signs in Grass

This is the Trail   Turn to the Right   Turn to the Left   Important Warning

Signs in Blazes

This is the Trail   Turn to the Right   Turn to the Left   Important Warning

Code for Smoke Signals

Camp is Here   I am lost. Help!   Good News   All come to Council

Some Special Blazes used by Hunters & Surveyors

A Trap to Right   A Trap to Left   Camp is to Right   Camp is to Left   Special   Adirondack Special   Surveyor's Line Here

In running a trail one naturally looks straight ahead for the next sign; if the trail turned abruptly without notice one might easily be set wrong, but custom has provided against this. The tree blaze for turn "to the right" is shown in Number 2, fourth row; "to the left" in Number 3. The greater length of the turning blaze seems to be due to a desire for emphasis as the same mark set square on, is understood to mean "Look out, there is something of special importance here." Combined with a long side chip it means "very important; here turn aside." This is often used to mean "camp is close by," and a third sign that is variously combined but always with the general meaning of "warning" or "something of great importance" is a threefold blaze. (No. 4 on fourth line.) The combination (No. 1 on bottom row) would read "Look out now for something of great importance to the right." This blaze I have often seen used by trappers to mark the whereabouts of their trap or cache.

Surveyors often use a similar mark — that is, three simple spots and a stripe to mean, "There is a stake close at hand," while a similar blaze on another tree near by means that the stake is on a line between.

STONE SIGNS

These signs done into stone-talk would be as in the top line of the cut.

These are much used in the Rockies where the trail goes over stony places or along stretches of slide-rock.

GRASS AND TWIG SIGNS

In grass or sedge the top of the tuft is made to show the direction to be followed; if it is a point of great importance three tufts are tied, their tops straight if the trail goes straight on; otherwise the tops are turned in the direction toward which the course turns.

The Ojibways and other woodland tribes use twigs for a great many of these signs. (See second row.) The hanging broken twig like the simple blaze means "This is the trail." The twig clean broken off and laid on the ground across the line of march means, "Here break from your straight course and go in the line of the butt end," and when an especial *warning* is meant, the butt is pointed toward the one following the trail and raised somewhat, in a forked twig. If the butt of the twig were raised and pointing to the left, it would mean "Look out, camp, or ourselves, or the enemy, or the game we have killed is out that way." With some, the elevation of the butt is made to show the distance of the object; if low the object is near, if raised very high the object is a long way off.

These are the principal signs of the trail used by Scouts, Indians, and hunters in most parts of America. These are the standards — the ones sure to be seen by those who camp in the wilderness.

SMOKE SIGNALS

There is in addition a useful kind of sign that has been mentioned already in these papers — that is, the Smoke Signal. These were used chiefly by the Plains Indians, but the Ojibways seem to have employed them at times.

A clear hot fire was made, then covered with green stuff or rotten wood so that it sent up a solid column of black smoke. By spreading and lifting a blanket over this smudge the column could be cut up into pieces long or short, and by a preconcerted code these could be made to convey tidings.

But the simplest of all smoke codes and the one of chief use to the Western traveler is this:

One steady smoke — "Here is camp."

Two steady smokes — "I am lost, come and help me."

I find two other smoke signals, namely:

Three smokes in a row — "Good news."

Four smokes in a row — "All are summoned to council."

These latter I find not of general use, nor are they so likely to be of service as the first two given.

SIGNAL BY SHOTS

The old buffalo hunters had an established signal that is yet used by the mountain guides. It is as follows:

Two shots in rapid succession, an interval of five seconds by the watch, then one shot; this means, "where are you?" The answer given at once and exactly the same means "Here I am; what do you want?" The reply to this may be one shot, which means, "All right; I only wanted to know where you were." But if the reply repeats the first it means, "I am in serious trouble; come as fast as you can."

SPECIAL SIGNS

A sign much used among the Utes was three flocks of geese flying one way meaning, "All at Peace." But two one way and one the other meant, "Look out! there is a war afoot."

Another Indian sign was a little heap of stones, meaning "We camped here because one of us was sick." This originated in the hot stones used for making steam in the vapor bath that is so much favored by Indian doctors.

The Indians sometimes marked a spot of unusual importance by sinking the skull of a deer or a mountain sheep deep into a living tree, so that the horns hung out on each side. In time the wood and bark grew over the base of the horns and "medicine tree" was created. Several of these trees have become of historic importance. A notable example of this was the big Ramtree that by common consent demarked the hunting grounds of the Blackfeet from those of the Nez Perces. It was held by these Indians in religious veneration until some white vandal deliberately destroyed it by way of a practical joke.

It would be easy to record many other Indian signs; the sign for the "first crow" of spring; the sign for "buffalo in sight"; the sign for a "war party coming"; the sign that a certain man "wants the arrows," that another man owes him, and the sign that the owner of the teepee is "praying and must not be disturbed." But these are things that are quickly passing away and the Indians themselves are forgetting them.

The most important of the signs used by men of the wilderness are herein described. They are interesting as a crude beginning of literature. The knowledge of such things appeals to most boys. They find pleasure in learning this crudest of writing. Furthermore, many a one in the past has owed his life to an inkling of this woodcraft knowledge, and there is no reason to doubt that many a wilderness traveler in the future will find it of equally vital service.

WEATHER SIGNALS

(Adopted for general use by the United States Signal Service on and after March 1, 1887.)

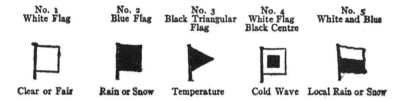

No. 1 White Flag	No. 2 Blue Flag	No. 3 Black Triangular Flag	No. 4 White Flag Black Centre	No. 5 White and Blue
Clear or Fair	Rain or Snow	Temperature	Cold Wave	Local Rain or Snow

No. 1, white flag, clear or fair weather, no rain.

No. 2, blue flag, rain or snow.

No. 3, black triangular flag, refers to temperature, and above Nos. 1 or 2, indicates warmer weather; below No. 1 or 2, colder weather, and when not displayed, stationary weather.

No. 4, white flag with black centre (cold wave flag), sudden fall in temperature; this signal is usually ordered at least twenty-four hours in advance of the cold wave. It is not displayed unless a temperature of forty-five degrees, or less is expected, nor is flag No. 3 ever displayed with it.

No. 5, means local rain or snow; with 3 above it means with higher temperature; with 3 below it means lower temperature.

A red flag with a black centre indicates that a storm of marked violence is expected.

DISPLAY EXAMPLES

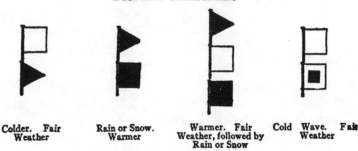

| Colder. Fair Weather | Rain or Snow. Warmer | Warmer. Fair Weather, followed by Rain or Snow | Cold Wave. Fair Weather |

STORM AND HURRICANE WARNINGS

| N. E. Winds. | S. E. Winds | N W Winds. | S. W. Winds. | Hurricane. |

STORM WARNINGS.—A red flag with a black centre indicates a storm of marked violence. The pennants displayed with flags indicate direction of wind—red, easterly; white, westerly; pennant above flag indicates wind from northerly quadrants; below, from southerly quadrants.

By night a red light indicates easterly winds, white light below red, westerly winds. Two red flags with black centres indicate approach of tropical hurricane. No night hurricane signals are displayed.

SIGNALS ON THE RAILWAY

Most of us are familiar with some of the signals given by brakemen, conductors, or engineers, but not so many of us have sat right down to inspect the code, as officially fixed. A conductor on the Canadian Pacific Railway allowed me to copy it out from his "Trainman's Book," 1909, and since then I have been told that this is the code in universal use, so I give it in full.

It consists of color signals, hand and lantern signals, toots, and cord-pulls. It will add a new interest to the journey, at least when you can read the "Signs of the Iron Trail," and the "Talk of the Iron Horse."

THE CODE

(From C. P. R. "Trainman's Book," 1909, No. 7563; but in general use.)

Colors:

Red = *Stop.*

Green = *Go ahead.*

Yellow = *Go cautiously.*

Green and White = *Flag station; stop at night.*

Blue = *Workmen busy under car.*

Hand, Flag and Lamp Signals:

Swung across track	*Stop.*
Raised and lowered vertically	*Go ahead.*
Swung at half-arms' length, in small circle across track, train standing	*Back up.*
Swung vertically in a big circle, at arms' length across the track, when train is running	*Train broken in two.*
Swung horizontally above head, when train is standing	*Put on air-brakes.*
Held at arms' length above the head, when train is standing	*Release air-brakes.*

Other Hand Signals, modifications of the above:

Hand (or hands) held out horizontally and waved up and down	*Go ahead.*
Hand (or hands) suddenly thrown flat and horizontal	*Stop.*
Sometimes hands raised and held palms forward	*All right.*
Arm thrust forward and swept back toward opposite shoulder, as in beckoning	*Come back.*

Signals by Engine Whistle:

(o a short toot. — a long one)

o = Stop; put on brakes.

— — = Take off brakes; get ready to start.

— ooo = Flagman go out to protect rear of train.
— — — — = Flagman return from west or south.
— — — — — = Flagman return from east or north.
— — — = (when running) Train broken in two.
To be repeated till answered by the same from the trainman, i. e., No. 4 in hand, flag and lamp signals. Similarly, this is the answer to No. 4 of hand, flag and lamp signals.

oo = (all right) the answer to any signal not otherwise provided for.

ooo = (when the train is standing) back up; also is the reply to signals to "back up."

oooo = Call for signals.

—oo = Calls attention of other trains to signals.

oo = The acknowledgment by other trains.

——oo = Approaching grade-crossings, and at whistle posts.

— = Approaching stations.

o— = (when double-heading) Air-brakes have failed on leading engine, and second engine is to take control of them. Second engine repeats same as soon as it has control.

●ooooooooo, etc. = Cattle (or persons) on the track.

Air-whistle or Cord-pull:

When the train is standing:
Two blasts = Start.
Three " = Back.
Four " = Put on or take off brakes.
Five " = Call in flagman.

When the train is running:
(All but the 2nd are answered by 2 blasts)

Two blasts = Stop at once.
Three " = Stop at next station.
Four " = Reduce speed.

Five	"	= Increase speed.
Six	"	= Increase steam-heat.
Seven	"	= Release air-brakes, or sticking brake.

The engineer responds to these with two short toots, meaning "All right," except in the second, when the engineer answers in three short toots.

VIII. Campercraft or The Summer Camp

Camping Out

EVERY boy looks forward to camping out. Then it is that he gets the best chance to practise the things that are peculiar to scouting; and camping out is the only complete outdoor life.

When a boy, I was of course eager for a chance to camp out, but I had a very wrong idea about it. I believed that one must undergo all sorts of hardships, in order to be really "doing it"; such as, sleep on the ground with one blanket, go without proper food, etc. I know some boys that were injured for life by such practices.

It is well, then, to keep in mind that camping out offers a number of priceless benefits, and is also beset by one or two dangers. Let us aim to *get all the good* and *avoid all the ill.*

The good things are: The pure air, especially at night; the bracing and lung-healing power of the woods; the sun bath; the tonic exercise; and the nerve rest.

The bad things are: The danger of rheumatism from sleeping on the ground, or in damp clothes; the exhaustion from bad nights, through insufficient bed-clothes or an uncomfortable bed; and the dangers arising from irregular meals and badly cooked food.

I have seen boys go back from an ill-run camp, tired out and but little benefitted; whereas, if properly guided, every camp-out should mean a new spell of life — a fresh start in vigor for every one concerned.

Many mothers ask with fear, "Won't my boy catch cold, if he camps out?" This is the last and least of dangers. Almost never does one catch cold in camp. I have found it much more likely that boys suffer through irregular hours of eating and sleeping; but these are troubles that the camp discipline is designed to meet.

The great evil that campers should beware of, is of course rheumatism. But none need suffer if they will take the simple precaution of changing their wet clothes when not in action, and never sleeping directly on the ground. A warm, dry place for the bed should be prepared in every tent and teepee.

As a rule, it is better to go on a trip with a definite object. If you go with a general vague determination to get healthy, you are likely to think too much about it. It is better to live correctly, and safely assume that you will be healthier for the trip. To illustrate: One of my trips was made to determine the existence of Wood Buffalo on the Great Slave River; another to prove that the Canadian Fauna reached the Lake of the Woods. Some of my friends have made trips to win the badge of expert canoe-man; others for the camper badge, and so forth, and I think it best to go a long way from home. Get as complete a change as possible.

OUTFIT FOR A PARTY OF SIX (CAMPING ONE WEEK IN FIXED CAMP)

1 12-foot teepee (if for cold weather), accommodating five or six men not forgetting a storm-cap,

Or, in summer, a 10 x 12 wall tent.

18 x 10 awning for kitchen and dining-room, in hot or wet weather.

5 yards mosquito-bar and some dope for stinging-insects.

3 or 4 one-gallon bags of cotton for supplies.

A few medicines and pill-kit or "first aid," including cold cream for sunburn.

1 strong clothes line; ball of cord; ball twine; of ball of strong linen pack-thread.

Axe.

A sharp hatchet.

Claw-hammer.

Whetstone.

Small crosscut saw.

Spade.

File.

Packing needles and sewing-kit for repairing clothes.

Nails: One lb. of 1½, two lbs. of 2½, two lbs. of 3½, and one lb. of 5-inch.

Pocket tool outfit (A, K, and B is good)

Soap.

Mirror.

Toilet-paper.

Waterproof match-box.

Book of Woodcraft

A locker.

Cooking outfit: Either a ready-made, self-nesting "Buzza-cot," or

3 cover-kettles, 10-qt., 4-qt., and 2-qt. (riveted, not soldered).

2 frying-pans, with handles and covers.

2 big spoons.

Coffee strainer.

1 Dutch oven.

1 wire grill.

2 bake-pans

1 butcher knife.

Salt and pepper casters.

Tin boxes to hold stock of same.

2 folding buckets.

2 folding wash-basins.

Dishpan.

Tea-pot (riveted).

Coffee-pot (riveted).

Dishcloths and towels.

Soap.

Folding lantern and supply of candles.

4 flat steel rods to cook on.

And for each man, plate, cup, saucer, and porringer (preferably enameled); also knife, fork, and spoon.

And such other things as are dictated by previous experience, or for use in the games to be played.

Besides which each member has his ordinary clothes, with a change, and toilet-bag, also:

A rubber blanket.

2 wool blankets.

1 cotton or burlap bed-tick, $2\frac{1}{2}$ x $6\frac{1}{4}$ ft.

Swimming-trunks.

A pair of brown sneaks.

A war-sack of waterproof.

Khaki suit.

Fishing tackle and guns, according to choice.

Pocket knife.

Food to last six fellows one week:

Oatmeal	6	lbs.
Rice	2	lbs.
Crackers	10	lbs.
Cocoa	3	lb.

Tea	½	lb.
Coffee	3	lbs.
Lard	5	lbs.
Sugar	6	lbs.
Condensed milk	12	tins
Butter	7	lbs.
Eggs	3	dozen
Bacon	15	lbs.
Preserves	5	lbs.
Prunes	3	lbs.
Maple syrup	3	quarts
Cheese	1	lb.
Raisins	3	lbs.
Potatoes	½	bushel
White beans	3	quarts
Canned corn	3	tins
Flour	25	lbs.
Baking-powder	1	lb.
Concentrated soups	½	lb.
Salt	2	lbs.
Pepper	1	ounce

Fresh fish and game are pleasant variations, but seem to make little difference in the grocery bill.

OUTFIT FOR EACH WOODCRAFTER

1 good 5-foot lancewood bow, complete with string.
6 standard arrows, 25 in. long, 3 feathers, steel points.
1 quiver of waterproof canvas or leather.
1 arm-guard.
1 head-band.
1 pair moccasins or "sneaks."
1 waterproof blanket.
2 Indian blankets of gray wool.

TENTS

There are many styles of small tents on the market; almost any of them answer very well. For those who wish to equip themselves with the latest and best, a 10 x 12-foot wall tent of 10-ounce double-filled army duck, stained or dyed yellow, brown, or dull green, is best. It will accommodate a party of five or six.

For tramping trips, light tents of waterproof silk are made. One large enough for a man weighs only two or three pounds.

Any of the established makers can supply what is needed if they know the size of the party and nature of the outing.

TEEPEES

The Indian teepee has the great advantage of ventilation and an open fire inside. It has the disadvantage of needing a lot of poles and of admitting some rain by the smoke-hole. (It is fully described on page 468.)

A new style of teepee, invented by myself some years ago, has been quite successful, since it combines the advan-

tage of teepee and tent and needs only four poles besides the smoke-poles. It is, however, less picturesque than the old style.

This gives the great advantage of an open fire inside, and good ventilation, while it is quite rainproof.

It can be put up with four long poles *outside* the canvas, the holes crossing at the top as in the Indian teepee. Of course the point of the cover is attached before the poles are raised.

THE CAMP GROUND

In selecting a good camp ground, the first thing is a dry, level place near good *wood* and good *water*. If you have horses or oxen, you must also have grass.

Almost all Indian camps face the east, and, when ideal, have some storm-break or shelter on the west and north. Then they get the morning sun and the afternoon shade in summer, and in winter avoid the coldest winds and drifting snows, which in most of the country east of the Rockies come from the north and west.

Sometimes local conditions make a different exposure desirable, but not often. For obvious reasons, it is well to be near one's boat-landing.

After pitching the tent or teepee, dig a trench around, with a drain on the low side to prevent flooding.

LATRINE

Each small camp or group of tents in a large camp, must have a latrine, that is a sanitary ditch or hole. For a small camp or short use, this is a narrow trench a foot wide, surrounded by a screen of bushes or canvas. It is made narrow enough to straddle. Each time after use, a shovelful of dry earth is thrown in.

But a large camp needs the regulation army latrine. This is a row of seats with lids over a long trench which has a layer of quicklime in the bottom. The wooden structure is banked up so no flies can get in. The lids are down tight when the seat is not in use. A shovelful of quicklime is then thrown in after each occasion. A running trough is arranged along side so it is tributary to the main trench; this also is kept coated with quicklime. The place should be thoroughly screened, but is as well without a roof except over the seats.

All camps should be left as clear of filth, scraps, papers, tins, bottles. etc., as though a human being had never been there.

ARRIVING ON THE CAMP GROUND

As soon as all are on the ground, with their baggage, let the Leader allot the places of each band or clan. Try to have each and every dwelling-tent about 25 feet from the next, in a place dry and easy to drain in case of rain and so placed as to have sun in the morning and shade in the afternoon.

Each group is responsible for order up to the halfway line between them and the next group.

Loose straw, tins, papers, bottles, glass, filth, etc., out of place are criminal disorder.

Pitch at a reasonable distance from the latrine, as well as from the water supply.

As much as possible, have each band or clan by itself.

As soon as convenient, appoint fellows to dig and prepare a latrine or toilet, with screen.

All will be busied settling down, so that usually there is no methodic work the first day.

But the second day it should begin.

CAMP OFFICERS AND GOVERNMENT

After the routine of rising, bathing, breakfast, etc., there should be called at eight o'clock a High Council. That is, a

Council of all the Leaders, Guides, Head Guides, and
Head Chief; that is, the Chief of the whole camp, appointed for that day. He is the Chief in charge, or Head
Man of the village. It is his duty to appoint all other officers
for the day, and to inspect the camp. In some camps this
High Council meets at night when the younger members are
asleep.

The other officers are:

Assistant Chief in Charge, who goes about with the Chief
and succeeds him next day.

Keeper of the Milk and the Ice-box, when there is ice for
the milk.

Keeper of the Letters. He takes all letters to the post and
brings back all mail.

Keeper of the Canoes. No boats may be taken without
his sanction, and he is responsible for the same.

Keeper of the Garbage. He must gather up and destroy all
garbage each day at a given hour; preferably late afternoon.

Keeper of the Latrine. He must inspect hourly, and see
that all keep the rules.

Keeper of the Campfire. He must have the wood cut and
laid for the Council-fire at night, with an extra supply for
all the evening, and must keep the Council-fire bright, not
big; but never dull.

Also, the High Council should appoint a Tally Keeper for
the whole camp; he is to serve throughout the whole period
of the encampments, keeping the records for every day.
Sometimes the work is divided, but one fellow can do it
better, if he is willing.

A band or clan prize for the whole term is always offered.
The competition for this is judged by points, and for each
of the above services to the camp, the band, to which the
scout belongs, gets up to 25 points per day, according to his
efficiency.

No fellow should leave camp without permission. If he does so, he may cause his Band to lose points.

THE DOG SOLDIERS

In every large camp it is found well to follow the Indian custom in forming a Lodge of Dog Soldiers. These are a band of eight or ten of the strongest and sturdiest fellows. They act as police when needed, but wear no badge. They must at once run to any place where the signal (a loud baying) is heard, and act promptly and vigorously.

When the Chief has selected the huskies he wishes to have in the Dog Lodge, he invites all to meet secretly in some quiet teepee at night, explains the purpose and adds "I have called on you who are here. If any do not wish to serve, now is the time to retire."

The sacred fire is lighted in the middle, all stand in a ring about it, each with his right hand on a war club above the fire, his left holding a handful of ashes. Then all repeat this vow:

"As a Dog Soldier I pledge the might of my manhood to the cause of law and justice in this Camp for the term of the Camp or until released by the Chief, and if at any time I fail in my duty through fear entering into my heart, may I be dropped, scorned and forgotten like these ashes."

Then he scatters the ashes.

It is customary for each Tribe to adopt further a secret sign and password, which is taught to the Dog Soldiers as a finish.

INSPECTION

Every day there is an inspection. It is best in the middle of the morning. The Chief and his second go from tent to tent. Each Clan is allowed 50 points for normal, then docked 1 to 10 points for each scrap of paper, tin, or rubbish left lying about; also for each disorderly feature or neglect of the rules of common sense, decency or hygiene, on their territory; that is, up to halfway between them and the next group. They may get additional points for extra work or inventions, or unusual services for the public good; but it is always as a Clan that they receive the points, though it was the individual that worked for them.

After the inspection, the Chief announces the winning Band or Clan saying: "The Horns of the High Hikers were won to-day by . . . . . Band." And the horns are accordingly hung on their standard, pole or other place, for the day. At the end of the camp, provided ten were present for at least a fortnight, Clan or Band that won them oftenest carries them home for their own; and ever afterward are allowed to put in one corner of their banner a small pair of black horns.

THE HORNS OF THE HIGH HIKERS

What are they? Usually a pair of polished buffalo horns with a fringed buckskin hanger, on which is an inscription saying that they were won by . . . . . Band at such a camp.

When buffalo horns cannot be got, common cow horns or even horns of wood are used.

COUNCIL-FIRE CIRCLE

In every large permanent camp I establish a proper Council-fire Circle or Council Camp. The uses and benefits of these will be seen more and more, as camp goes on.

For the Council-fire Circle, select a sheltered, level place that admits of a perfectly level circle 24 feet across; 18 feet has been used, but more room gives better results. On the outer rim of this, have a permanently fixed circle of very low seats; 8 inches is high enough, but they should have a back, and for this, the easiest style to make is that marked K. L. on page 481. Each Band or Clan should make its own seat, and always go there in Grand Council. On the back of the seat should be two loops of wire or string in which to put their standard. Back of the first row should be a slightly higher row. If the ground slopes up, all the better, but in any case there should be *fixed seats enough for all the camp*. The place should be carefully leveled and prepared, and kept always in order, for it will be used several times each day, either for councils or for games, dances and performances.

At one side of the ring in a conspicuous place should be the throne of the Chief (p. 481); close by this a desk and seat for the Tally Keeper and on the desk should be a lantern holder; in the exact middle of the ring is the Council-fire, never a bonfire.

TOTEM-POLE

Directly opposite the Chief's throne, on the outer edge of the camp, should be the Totem-pole. This I always set up as soon as possible in all permanent camps. Its purpose is, 1st, to typify the movement; 2nd, to display the Totems of all the Tribes, or Bands that camp here; 3rd, to serve as a place of notice. Any document posted on the Totem-pole is considered published.

a Totem-pole of the Sinawa Tribe (15 feet high)
b of Flying Eagles
c and *d* from Niblack's West Coast Indians. Eagles and Bears

COUNCILS

Three kinds of Councils are held in the Council Place:

1. The *High Council* of the Chiefs and the Guides every morning at 8 o'clock, and at other times when called.

2. The *General or Common Council* of all the fellows every night from seven to nine o'clock. At this we have some business (in the awarding of honors), some campfire stunts or challenges, and a little entertainment.

3. *Grand Council*. This is usually held once a week. Every one comes in full Scout or Indian dress. Visitors are invited. Business except when very interesting is dispensed with, and a program of sports and amusements, chiefly for the visitors, is carefully prepared. This is "Strangers' Night" and they should be entertained, not bored.

BEDS

Of all things, the camper's bed is the thing most often made wrong, and most easily made right, when one knows how; and of all things comfort at night is most essential.

Every dealer in camp outfits can produce an array of different camp beds, cots, and sleeping bags, that shows how important it is to be dry and warm when you sleep.

The simplest plan is the oldest one — two pair of blankets and waterproof undersheet on a neatly laid bed of evergreen boughs, dry leaves, or dry grass. The ideal way of laying the boughs is shown in the figure below.

> *When I can't get grub of the Broadway sort,*
> *I'll fatten on camper's fare,*
> *I'll tramp all day and at night resort*
> *To a bed boughed down with care.*

Log frame of Bed

Overlapping Boughs.

But there are few places now in eastern America where you are allowed to cut boughs freely. In any case you cannot take the bough bed with you when you move, and it takes too much time to make at each camp.

Sleeping bags I gave up long ago. They are too difficult to air, or to adjust to different temperatures.

Rubber beds are luxurious, but heavy for a pack outfit, and in cold weather they need thick blankets over them, otherwise they are too cool.

So the one ideal bed for the

camper, light, comfortable, and of wildwood stuff, is the Indian or willow bed, described on p 495.

WATER, OR THE INDIAN WELL

If there is swamp or pond, but no pure water at hand, you can dig an Indian well in half an hour. This is simply a hole about 18 inches across and down about 6 inches below water-level, a few paces from the pond. Bail it out quickly; let it fill again, bail it a second time, and the third time it fills, it will be full of filtered water, clear of everything except matter actually dissolved.

It is now well known that ordinary vegetable matter does not cause disease. All contamination is from animal refuse or excreta, therefore a well of this kind in a truly wild region is as safe as a spring.

MOSQUITOES, BLACK FLIES, ETC.

If you are camping in mosquito or fly season, the trip may be ruined, if you are not fully prepared.

For extreme cases, use the ready-made head-nets. They are hot, but effectual. You can easily get used to the net; no man can stand the flies. In my Arctic trip of 1907, we could not have endured life without the nets. Indians and all wore them.

Of the various dopes that are used, one of the simplest and best is Colonel N. Fletcher's, given in Kephart's "Book of Camping and Woodcraft":

"Pure pine tar . . . . 1 oz.
Oil pennyroyal . . . . . . 1 oz.
Vaseline . . . . 3 ozs.

Mix cold in a mortar. If you wish, you can add 3 per cent. carbolic acid to above. Some make it 1½ ozs. tar."

Most drug shops keep ready-made dopes under such names as Citronella, Repellene, Lollakapop, etc.

LICE AND VERMIN

In certain crowded camps there is danger of head lice and body vermin. I have heard washing in potato water recommended as a sure cure. Potato water is the water potatoes have been boiled in. Most drug shops have tobacco ointment and blue ointment; a very little of these applied to the body where there is hair is a sure cure.

SUGGESTED CAMP ROUTINE

6:30	A. M.	Turn out, bathe, etc.
7:00		Breakfast.
8:00		Air bedding in sun, if possible
8:15		High Council of Leaders.
9:00		Scouting games and practice.
11:00		Swimming.
12:00	M.	Dinner.
1:00	P. M.	Talk by leader.
2:00		Games, etc.
6:00		Supper.
7:00		Evening Council.
10:00		Lights out.
		Sometimes High Council for a few minutes instead of in the morning.

CAMPFIRES

The day Columbus landed (probably) the natives remarked; "White man fool, make big fire, can't go near; Indian make little fire and sit happy."

We all know that a camp without a campfire would be no camp at all; its chiefest charm would be absent.

Your first care, then, is to provide for a small fire and prevent its spreading. In the autumn this may mean very elaborate clearing, or burning, or wetting of a space around the fire. In the winter it means nothing.

Cracked Jimmy, in "Two Little Savages," gives very practical directions for lighting a fire anywhere in the timbered northern part of America, thus:

> *"First a curl of birch bark as dry as it can be,*
> *Then some twigs of soft wood, dead, but on the tree,*
> *Last of all some pine-knots to make the kittle foam,*
> *And there's a fire to make you think you're settin' right at*
>   *home."*

If you have no birch bark, it is a good plan to shave a dry soft-wood stick, leaving all the shavings sticking on the end in a fuzz, like a Hopi prayer stick. Several of these make a sure fire kindler. Fine splinters may be made quickly by hammering a small stick with the back of the axe.

In the case of a small party and hasty camp, you need nothing but a pot hanger of green wood for a complete

kitchen, and many hundreds of times, on prairie and in forest, I found this sufficient.

A more complete camp grate is made of four green logs (aspen preferred), placed as in the illustration. Set the top logs 3 inches apart at one end, 10 inches at the other. The top logs should be flattened in the middle of their top sides — to hold the pot which sits on the opening between the top logs. The fire of course is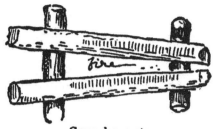

Green log grate

built on the ground, under the logs. Sometimes stones of right size and shape are used instead of the logs, but the stones do not contribute anything to the heat and are less manageable.

Camp kitchen

In addition to this log grate, more elaborate camps have a kitchen equipped with a hanger as below, on which are pot hooks of green wood.

In wet weather, an axeman can always get dry wood by

cutting into a standing dead tree, or on the under side of down timber that is not entirely on the ground.

On the prairies and plains, since buffalo chips are no more, we use horse and cow chips, kindled with dry grass and roots of sage-brush, etc.

To keep a fire alive all night, bank the coals: i. e., bury them in ashes.

Always put out the fire on leaving camp.
It is a crime to leave a burning fire.
Use buckets of water if need be.

COUNCIL-FIRE

The Council-fire is a very different thing from the cooking fire or the so-called bonfire. And there are just as many ways of making it wrong.

These are the essentials:

It must be easily started.

It must give a steady, bright light.

It must have as little heat as possible, for it is mostly used in the summer. Therefore, it must be small.

It is best built as in (c), about two and one half feet high; the bottom stick about three feet long; the rest shorter and smaller.

The small wood and chips to light it can be put either under or on top of the second layer.

It should be drawn in toward the top, so as to burn without falling apart.

It must contain a large proportion of dry, winter-seasoned wood, if it is to blaze brightly. The readiest seasoned wood is usually old lumber.

For an all-evening Council-fire, at least three times as much should be in stock as on the fire when started.

Here are some wrong methods.

The high pyramid or bonfire, (a) goes off like a flash, roasts every one, then goes dead.

The shapeless pile (b), is hard to light and never bright.

Bad   Bad   Good

The bonfire is always bad. It wastes good wood; is dangerous to the forest and the camp; is absolutely unsociable. A bonfire will spoil the best camp-circle ever got together. It should be forbidden everywhere.

FIREARMS

Experience shows that it is unwise to have firearms in camp. And no one under fourteen years of age should be allowed the use of a gun or pistol under any circumstances.

The didn't-know-it-was-loaded fool is the cause of more sorrow than the deliberate murderer.

For any one to point a firearm at another is a crime. If he didn't know it was loaded, he should be still more severely punished.

Never let the muzzle of the gun sweep the horizon.

Never carry a gun full-cock or hammer down. The half-cock is made for safety. Use it.

Never pull a gun by the muzzle.

Never shoot at anything about which you are in doubt.

CAMP COOKERY

(See Horace Kephart's "Book of Camping and Wood-craft.")

In most camps the staples are: Coffee (or tea), bacon, game, fish and hardtack, bannocks or biscuit, usually and most appropriately called "sinkers" and "damper."

To make these necessary evils, take

1 pint flour.

1 teaspoonful of baking-powder,

Half as much salt,

Twice as much grease or lard,

With water enough to make into paste, say one half a pint.

When worked into smooth dough, shape it into wafers, half an inch thick, and three inches across. Set in a greased tin, which is tilted up near a steady fire. Watch and turn the tin till all are browned evenly.

For other and better but more elaborate methods of making bread, see Kephart's book as above.

For cooking fish and game the old, simple standbys are the frying-pan and the stew-pan.

As a general rule, mix all batters, mush, etc., with cold water, and always cook with a slow fire.

There is an old adage:

> Hasty cooking is tasty cooking.
> Fried meat is dried meat.
> Boiled meat is spoiled meat.
> Roast meat is best meat.

This reflects perhaps the castle kitchen rather than the camp, but it has its measure of truth, and the reason why roast meat is not more popular is because it takes so much time and trouble to make it a success.

During my Barren Ground trip I hit on a remarkably successful roaster that, so far as I know, was never tried before.

The usual pot-stick is set in the ground (if no tree be near), and the roast hung by a wire and a cord; where they

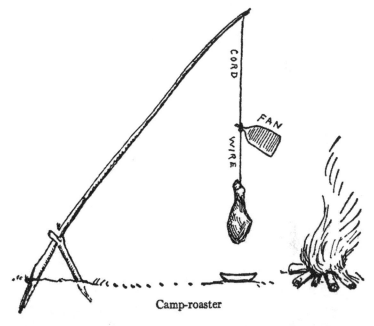

Camp-roaster

meet is a straight or flat piece of wood, or bark, set in a loop of the wire.

The wind strikes on this, causing the roast to turn; it goes till the cord is wound up then unwinds itself and goes on unceasingly. We used it every day. It was positively uncanny to see the way in which this thing kept on winding and unwinding itself, all day long, if need be.

WAR-SACK

Every brave in camp should have a war-sack. This is a
sack of waterproofed canvas to hold clothing and anything
that is unbreakable. It has several advantages over a
trunk. It is cheap ($1.50), waterproof, light, a comfortable
pack to carry or to stow in a canoe, collapsible when empty,
safe to float in an upset, and at night it serves as a pillow.

Its disadvantages are that it will not protect breakables,
and you have to take out most of the things to find an article
not on the top. Nevertheless, all old campers use the war-
sack. They can be had of any camp outfitter.

WOODCRAFT BUTTONS

On the Plains, when a button is lost or needed, it is easy
to make one of leather. Usually a piece of an old strap is
is used. Cut it the right size, make two holes in it, and sew
it on as an ordinary button. This never breaks or fails.
As the old plainsman who first showed me, said, "There's
a button that'll be right there when the coat's all wore away
from behind it."

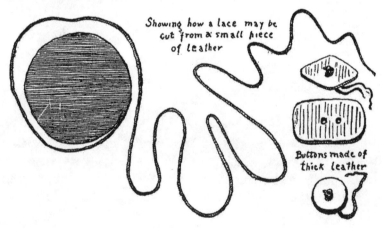

Showing how a lace may be cut from a small piece of leather

Buttons made of thick leather

LACE OR THONG

If you need a lace or thong and have no leather long enough, take a square piece, round the corners, then cut it round and round, till it is all used up. Pull and roll the thong produced, until it is small and even, without kinks.

IX. Games for the Camp

Interesting Pursuits

I HAVE always taken the ground that interest is as essential to exercise as relish is to digestion. And for this reason have no use for the Indian clubs or dumb-bells. An ideal exercise is in the open air, employing not only every member vigorously — not violently — but also the faculties including the great coördinating power that is the crowning gift of the athlete — the power to make all parts play the game in the measure needed to secure the best total result.

How needful is it then to have interesting pursuits that inspire the Scout to do and be his very best.

The appeal to the imagination that is assumed by such games as Spear-throwing and Dispatch-runner is the great-est and most elevating of all. Without some such magical power, no fellow really does the best that is in him. It makes a live wire of every fibre in his make-up.

TILTING SPEARS

A simple and useful part of the Tribe's outfit that should be made ready before going into camp is a supply of tilting-spears. I have seen a good many campers try tilting in the water or on the land, and make an utter failure of it, by reason of the absurdly clumsy, heavy spears used. A green sapling was cut for handle, and the end tied up in a bundle of rags that was 18 inches through. This was hard enough to lift, when dry, and as it usually soon fell into the water, and got sopping wet, its weight became trebled, and one could not use it as a spear at all.

The correct spears always used in our camps are made thus: Take 8 feet of the butt-end of an ordinary bamboo fishing-rod — or, if anything, a little heavier than ordinary. Get a 2-inch plank of any light wood, and from this cut a disk 3 inches across, bevel off and round the edges. Bore a hole (about $\frac{3}{4}$ inch) in the middle, and put this on the top of the bamboo, so that it sets against a shoulder or knot. Drive a circular plug in the hollow of the bamboo for a wedge, and make all secure with one or two very thin nails driven in (No. 7).

Wooden disk
No 7

Finished Head
No 8

Now pad the head an inch thick with the ordinary horsehair stuffing that is used in furniture, and bind all with strong burlap, sewing it at the seams, and lashing it around the bamboo with string (No. 8). This completes the dry land spear. If for use in the water, make a final cover out of rubber cloth. This keeps the spear dry. A completed spear weighs about $1\frac{1}{2}$ lbs.

Each band should have a half-dozen of these spears. They serve a number of purposes, some of them quite different from that originally intended.

TILTING IN THE WATER

When used in the water, the ordinary rules of canoe-tilting are followed. Each spearman stands in the bow of his boat, on the bow-seat. His crew bring him within 8 feet of his rival, and now he endeavors to put him overboard. Points are reckoned thus:

Forcing your enemy to put one foot down off
the seat 5
Forcing your enemy to put two feet down off
the seat 10
Forcing your enemy on one knee . . . 5
Forcing your enemy down on two knees 10
Forcing your enemy to lose his spear . 10
Forcing your enemy overboard . . . 25

It is a foul to strike below the knee, or to use the spear as a club.

The umpire may dock up to 25 points for fouls.

When canoes are used, the spearman stands on the bottom, so all points are by loss of spear, or by going overboard.

TUB-TILTING ON LAND

But by far the most of the tilting is done on land, around the campfire. For this we use two stools, about 14 inches across. These are set level, exactly a spear length apart, centre to centre.

Each fighter takes his place on a stool, and his game is to put the other off the other stool. To prevent accidents, we have usually a catcher behind each man. The umpire stands alongside, near the middle.

It is a foul to use the spear as a club, or to push below the knees, or to push the stool, or to seize the other man's spear in your hand, or to touch the ground with your spear.

A foul gives the round to the other man.

The round is over when one man is off.

It is a draw when botl go off together.

They change stools after each round.

If one drops his spear, and recovers it without going off, it is all right.

The battle is usually for 3, 5, or 7 rounds.

I do not know of any good thrusts having been invented, but several good parries are well known. One is to use your spear-handle as a single stick. The best players parry much by wriggling the body. Often, when over-balanced, one can regain by *spinning* completely around.

So much for the game. It is immensely popular at night by the blazing campfire, and is especially used in initiations.

STILL-HUNTING THE BUCK, OR THE DEER-HUNT

The deer is a dummy, best made with a wire frame, on which soft hay is wrapped till it is of proper size and shape, then all is covered with open burlap. A few touches of white and black make it very realistic.

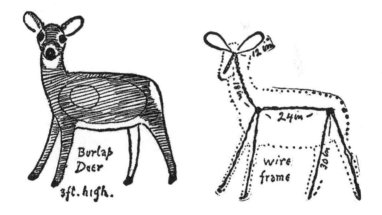

Burlap
Deer

3ft. high.

wire
frame

If time does not admit of a well-finished deer, one can be made of a sack stuffed with hay, decorated at one end with a smaller sack for head and neck, and set on four thin sticks.

The side of the deer is marked with a large oval, and over the heart is a smaller one.

Bows and arrows only are used to shoot this deer.

A pocketful of corn, peas, or other large grain is now needed for scent. The boy who is the deer for the first hunt takes the dummy under his arm and runs off, getting ten minutes' start, or until he comes back and shouts "ready!" He leaves a trail of corn, dropping two or three grains for every yard and making the trail as crooked as he likes, playing such tricks as a deer would do to baffle his pursuers. Then he hides the deer in any place he fancies, but not among rocks or on the top of a ridge, because in one case many arrows would be broken, and in the other, lost.

Wooden legged Deer

The hunters now hunt for this deer just as for a real deer, either following the trail or watching the woods ahead; the best hunters combine the two. If at any time the trail is quite lost the one in charge shouts "*Lost Trail!*" After that the one who finds the trail scores *two*. Any one giving a false alarm by shouting "*Deer*" is fined *five*.

Thus they go till some one finds the deer. He shouts "*Deer!*" and scores *ten* for finding it. The others shout "*Second,*" "*Third,*" etc., in order of seeing it, but they do not score.

The finder must shoot at the deer with his bow and arrow from the very spot whence he saw it. If he misses, the second hunter may step up five paces, and have his shot. If *he* misses, the third one goes five, and so on till some one hits the deer, or until the ten-yard limit is reached. If the finder is within ten yards on sighting the deer, and misses his shot, the other hunters go back to the ten-yard limit. Once the deer is hit, all the shooting must be from the exact spot whence the successful shot was fired.

A shot in the big oval is a *body wound;* that scores *five.* A shot outside that is a *scratch;* that scores *two.* A shot in the small oval or heart is a *heart wound;* it scores *ten,* and ends the hunt. Arrows which do not stick do not

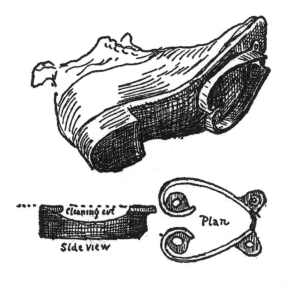

count, unless it can be proved that they passed right through, in which case they take the highest score that they pierced.

If all the arrows are used, and none in the heart, the deer escapes, and the boy who was deer scores *twenty-five.*

The one who found the dummy is deer for the next hunt. A clever deer can add greatly to the excitement of the game.

Originally we used paper for scent, but found it bad. It littered the woods, yesterday's trail was confused with that of to-day, etc. Corn proved better, because the birds and the squirrels kept it cleaned up from day to day, and thus the ground was always ready for a fresh start. But the best of all is the hoof mark for the shoe. These iron hoof marks are fast to a pair of shoes, and leave a trail much like a real deer. This has several advantages. It gives the hunter a chance to tell where the trail doubled, and which way the deer was going. It is more realistic, and a boy who can follow this skilfully can follow a living deer. In actual practice it is found well to use a little corn with this on the hard places, a plan quite consistent with realism, as every hunter will recall.

It is strictly forbidden to any hunter to stand in front of the firing line; all must be back of the line on which the shooter stands.

There is no limit to the situations and curious combinations in this hunt. The deer may be left standing or lying. There is no law why it should not be hidden behind a solid tree trunk. The game develops as one follows it. After it has been played for some time with the iron hoof mark as above, the boys grow so skilful on the trail that we can dispense with even the corn. The iron mark like a deer hoof leaves a very realistic "slot" or track, which the more skilful boys readily follow through the woods. A hunt is usually for three, five, or more deer, according to agreement, and the result is reckoned by points on the whole chase.

THE BEAR HUNT

This is played by half a dozen or more boys. Each has a club about the size and shape of a baseball club, but made of

Straw Club

straw tied around two or three switches and tightly sewn up in burlap.

One big fellow is selected for the bear. He has a school-bag tightly strapped on his back, and in that a toy balloon fully blown up. This is his heart. On his neck is a bear-claw necklace of wooden beads and claws. (See Cut.)

He has three dens about one hundred yards apart in a triangle. While in his den the bear is safe. If the den is a tree or rock, he is safe while touching it. He is obliged to come out when the chief hunter counts 100, and must go the rounds of the three till the hunt is settled.

The object of the hunters is to break the balloon or heart; that is, kill the bear. He must drop dead when the heart bursts. The hunter who kills him claims the necklace.

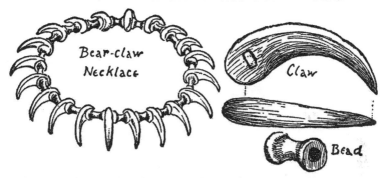

But the bear also has a club for defence. Each hunter must wear a hat, and once the bear knocks a hunter's hat off, *that one is dead* and out of this hunt. He must drop where his hat falls.

Tackling of any kind is forbidden.

The bear wins by killing or putting to flight all the hunters. In this case he keeps the necklace.

The savageness of these big bears is indescribable. Many lives are lost in each hunt, and it has several times happened that the whole party of hunters has been exterminated by some monster of unusual ferocity.

This game has also been developed into a play.

SPEARING THE GREAT STURGEON

This water game is exceedingly popular and is especially good for public exhibition, being spectacular and full of amusement and excitement.

The outfit needed is:

(1) A sturgeon roughly formed of soft wood; it should be about three feet long and nearly a foot thick at the head. It may be made realistic, or a small log pointed at both ends will serve.

The Wooden Sturgeon

Weight for ballast.

(2) Two spears with six-inch steel heads and wooden handles (about three feet long). The points should be sharp, but not the barbs. Sometimes the barbs are omitted altogether. Each head should have an eye to which is

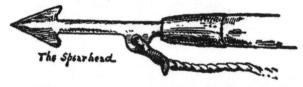

The Spearhead

attached twenty feet of one-quarter-inch rope. On each rope, six feet from the spearhead, is a fathom mark made by tying on a rag or cord.

(3) Two boats with crews. Each crew consists of a spearman, who is captain, and one or two oarsmen or paddlers, of which the after one is the pilot. All should be expert swimmers or else wear life belts during the game.

The game. Each boat has a base or harbor; this is

usually part of the shore opposite that of the enemy; or it obviates all danger of collision if the boats start from the same side. The sturgeon is left by the referee's canoe at a point midway between the bases. At the word "Go!" each boat leaves its base and, making for the sturgeon, tries to spear it, then drag it by the line to the base. When both get their spears into it the contest becomes a tug of war until one of the spears pulls out.

The sturgeon is landed when the prow of the boat that has it in tow touches its proper base, even though the spear of the enemy is then in the fish: or it is landed when the fish itself touches base if it is also in tow at the time. The boats change bases after each heat.

Matches are usually for one, three, or five sturgeon. Points are counted only for the landing of the fish, but the referee may give the decision on a foul or a succession of fouls, or the delinquent may be set back one or more boat-lengths.

Sometimes the game is played in canoes or boats, with one man as spearman and crew.

Rules: It *is not allowed* to push the sturgeon into a new position with the spear or paddle before striking.

It *is allowed* to pull the sturgeon under the boat or pass it around by using the line after spearing.

It *is allowed* to lay hands on the other boat to prevent a collision, but otherwise it is forbidden to touch the other boat or crew or paddle or spear or line, or to lay hands on the fish or to touch it with the paddle or oar, or touch your own spear while it is in the fish, or to tie the line around the fish except so far as this may be accidentally done in spearing.

It *is allowed* to dislodge the enemy's spear by throwing your own over it. The purpose of the barbs is to assist in this.

It *is allowed to run on to* the sturgeon with the boat.

It *is absolutely forbidden to throw the spear over the other boat or over the heads of your crew.*

In towing the sturgeon the fathom-mark must be over the gunwale — at least six feet of line should be out when the fish is in tow. It is not a foul to have less, but the spearman must at once let it out if the umpire or the other crew cries "Fathom!"

The spearman is allowed to drop the spear and use the paddle or oar at will, but not to resign his spear to another of the crew. The spearman must be in his boat when the spear is thrown.

If the boat is upset the judge's canoe helps them to right. Each crew must accept the backset of its accidents.

CANOE TAG

Any number of canoes or boats may engage in this. A rubber cushion, a hot-water bag full of air, any rubber football, or a cotton bag with a lot of corks in it is needed. The game is to tag the other canoe by throwing this *into* it.

The rules are as in ordinary cross-tag.

SCOUTING

Scouts are sent out in pairs or singly. A number of points are marked on the map at equal distances from camp, and the scouts draw straws to see where each goes. If one place is obviously hard, the scout is allowed a fair number of points as handicap. All set out at same time, go direct, and return as soon as possible.

Points are thus allowed:

Last back, *zero* for traveling.

The others count one for each minute they are ahead of the last.

Points up to 100 are allowed for their story on return.

Sometimes we allow 10 points for each Turtle they have seen; 10 for each Owl seen and properly named; 5 for each Hawk, and 1 each for other wild birds; also 2 for a Cat; 1 for a Dog.

No information is given the Scout; he is told to go to such a point and do so and so, but is fined points if he hesitates or asks how or why, etc.

THE GAME OF QUICKSIGHT

Take two boards about a foot square, divide each into twenty-five squares; get ten nuts and ten pebbles. Give to one player one board, five nuts, and five pebbles. He places these on the squares in any pattern he fancies, and when ready, the other player is allowed to see it for five

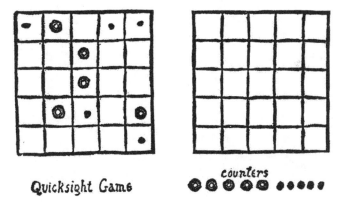

Quicksight Game   counters

seconds. Then it is covered up, and from the memory of what he saw the second player must reproduce the pattern on his own board. He counts one for each that was right, and takes off one for each that was wrong. They take turn and turn about.

This game is a wonderful developer of the power to see and memorize quickly.

FAR-SIGHT, OR SPOT-THE-RABBIT

Take two six-inch squares of stiff white pasteboard or whitened wood. On each of these draw an outline Rabbit, one an exact duplicate of the other. Make twenty round black wafers or spots, each half an inch across. Let one player stick a few of these on one Rabbit-board and set it

6 inches sq

up in full light. The other, beginning at 100 yards, draws near till he can see the spots well enough to reproduce the pattern on the other which he carries. If he can do it at 75 yards he has wonderful eyes. Down even to 70 (done 3 times out of 5) he counts high honor; from 70 to 60 counts honor. Below that does not count at all.

HOME STAR OR POLE STAR

Each competitor is given a long, straight stick, in daytime, and told to lay it due north and south. In doing this he may guide himself by sun, moss, or anything he can find in nature — anything, indeed, except a compass.

The direction is checked by a good compass corrected for the locality. The one who comes nearest wins.

It is optional with the judges whether the use of a time-piece is to be allowed.

RABBIT HUNT

The game of Rabbit-hunting is suited for two hunters in limited grounds.

Three little sacks of brown burlap, each about eight inches by twelve, are stuffed with hay.

At any given place in the woods the two hunters stand in a 10-foot circle with their bows and arrows. One boy is blindfolded; the other, without leaving the circle, throws the Rabbits into good hiding places on the ground. Then the second hunter has to find the Rabbits and shoot them without leaving the circle. The lowest number of points wins, as in golf. If the hunter has to leave the circle he gets one point for every step he takes outside. After he sees the Rabbit he must keep to that spot and shoot till it is hit once. One shot kills it, no matter where struck. For every shot he misses he gets five points.

After his first shot at each Rabbit the hider takes alternate shots with him.

If it is the hider who kills the Rabbit, the hunter adds ten points to his score. If the hunter hits it, he takes ten off his score.

If the hunter fails to find all the Rabbits, he scores twenty-five for each one he gives up.

The hider cannot score at all. He can only help his friend into trouble. Next time the two change places.

A match is usually for two brace of Rabbits.

ARROW FIGHT

This is a good one for challenges between two bands of equal numbers, say six on a side.

Each brave is armed with a bow and arrows (blunt preferred). ˙ Let the two bands stand in a row opposite a given bank, 10 to 20 yards away. Against this bank should be a row of 12-inch wooden or card disks (wooden dishes do well) set on edge lightly in stakes. Each brave is represented by a disk, which is opposite his enemy or corresponding number. Thus six disks, number one to six, represent the Wolf Band; they are opposite the Eagles, and vice-versa.

At the word *go* each shoots at the disks that represent his enemies. As soon as the disk that represents himself is shot, he must fall; he is out of the fight. The battle continues until all of one side are down. A truce may be arranged to recover the arrows.

HOSTILE SPY

Hanging from the Totem-pole is a red or yellow horsetail. This is the Grand Medicine Scalp of the band. The Hostile Spy has to capture it. The leader goes around on the morning of the day and whispers to the various braves, "Look out — there's a spy in camp." At length he goes secretly near the one he has selected for spy and whispers, "Look out, there's a spy in camp, and *you are it.*" He gives him at the same time some bright-colored badge, that he must wear as soon as he has secured the Medicine Scalp. He must not hide the scalp on his person, but keep it in view. He has all day till sunset to get away with it. If he gets across the river or other limit, with warriors in close pursuit, they give him ten arrowheads (two and one half cents each), or other ransom agreed on. If he gets away safely and hides it, he can come back and claim fifteen arrowheads from the Council as ransom for the scalp. If he is caught, he pays his captor ten arrowheads, ransom for his life.

THE SCOUT MESSENGER

This is played with a scout and ten or more Hostiles, or Hounds, according to the country; more when it is rough or wooded.

The scout is given a letter addressed to the "Military Commandant"* of any given place a mile or two away. He is told to take the letter to any one of three given houses, and get it endorsed, with the hour when he arrived, then return to the starting-point within a certain time.

The Hostiles are sent to a point halfway, and let go by a starter at the *same time* as the scout leaves the camp. They are to intercept him.

If they catch him before he delivers the letter he must ransom his life by paying each two arrowheads (or other forfeit) and his captor keeps the letter as a trophy. If he gets through, but is caught on the road back, he pays half as much for his life. If he gets through, but is over time, it is a draw. If he gets through successfully on time he claims three arrowheads from each Hostile and keeps the letter as a trophy.

They may not follow him into the house (that is, the Fort), but may surround it at one hundred yards distance. They do not know which three houses he is free to enter, but they do know that these are within certain narrow limits.

The scout should wear a conspicuous badge (hat, shirt, coat, or feather), and may ride a wheel or go in a wagon, etc., as long as his badge is clearly visible. He must not go in female dress.

A CHALLENGE FOR SCOUT MESSENGER

On ...... day, 1913, the Sinawa Tribe of Cos Cob, Conn., will send a letter by one man into the town of

---

*The "Military Commandment" is usually the lady of the house that he gets to.

Jellypot (two miles off) and will have him bring again an answer within the space of three hours; and hereby challenge any twenty picked warriors of the Flying Eagles of New Jersey to capture or hinder the delivery of said letter. On this the messenger will stake his scalp or any other agreed forfeit according to the rules of the game of Scout Messenger.

TREE THE COON

This is an indoor game, founded on the familiar "Hunt the Thimble."

We use a little dummy coon; either make it or turn a ready-made toy rabbit into one, by adding tail and black mask, and cropping the ears. Sometimes even a little rag ball with a face painted on it.

All the players but one go out of the room. That one places the coon anywhere in sight, high or low, but in plain view; all come in and seek. The first to find it sits down silently, and scores 1. Each sits down, on seeing it, giving no clue to the others.

The first to score 3 coons is winner, usually. Sometimes we play till every one but one has a coon; that one is the booby. The others are first, second, etc.

Sometimes each is given his number in order of finding it. Then, after 7 or 8 coons, these numbers are added up, and the *lowest* is winner.

NAVAJO FEATHER DANCE

An eagle feather hung on a horsehair, so as to stand upright, is worked by a hidden operator, so as to dance and caper. The dancer has to imitate all its motions. A marionette may be used. It is a great fun maker.

FEATHER FOOTBALL OR FEATHER-BLOW

This is an indoor, wet-weather game.

The players hold a blanket on the knees or on the table. A soft feather is put in the middle. As many may play as can get near. They may be in sides, 2 or 4, or each for himself. At the signal "Go!" each tries to blow the feather off the blanket at the enemy's side, and so count one for himself.

A game is usually best out of 7, 11, or 13.

COCK-FIGHTING

Make 2 stout sticks, each 2 feet long (broomsticks will do). Pad each of these on the end with a ball of rag. These are the spurs. Make an 8-foot ring. The two rivals are on their hunkers, each with a stick through behind his knees, his hands clasped in front of the knees, and the arms under the ends of the spurs.

Now they close; each aiming to upset the other, to make him lose his spurs or to put him out of the ring, any of which ends that round, and scores 1 for the victor. If both fall, or lose a spur, or go out together, it is a draw. Battle is for 3, 5, 7, 11, or 13 rounds.

ONE-LEGGED CHICKEN FIGHT

In this the two contestants stand upon one leg, holding up the ankle grasped in one hand behind. Points are scored as above, but it is a defeat also to drop the up leg.

STRONG HAND

The two contestants stand right toe by right toe, right hands clasped together; left feet braced; left hands free.

At the word "Go!" each tries to unbalance the other; that is, make him lift or move one of his feet. A lift or a shift ends the round.

Battles are for best out of 3, 5, 7, or 11 rounds.

BADGER-PULLING

The two contestants, on hands and knees, face each other. A strong belt or strap is buckled into one great loop that passes round the head of each; that is, crosses his nape. Halfway between them is a dead line. The one who pulls the other over this line is winner.

The contestant can at any time end the bout by lowering his head so the strap slips off; but this counts 1 against him.

Game is best out of 5, 7, 11, or 13 points.

STUNG, OR STEP ON THE RATTLER — SOMETIMES CALLED POISON

This is an ancient game. A circle about three feet across is drawn on the ground. The players, holding hands, make a ring around this, and try to make one of the number step into the poison circle. He can evade it by side-stepping, by jumping over, or by dragging another fellow into it.

First to make the misstep is "it" for the time or for next game.

Sometimes we use a newspaper with a switch lying across it. Each when stung sits down. When one only is left he is the Rattler, and may sting each of the others with the switch across their hand.

BUFFALO CHIPS

When I was among the Chipewyan Indians of Great Slave Lake, in 1907, I made myself popular with the young men, as well as boys, by teaching them the old game of hat-ball or Buffalo Chips.

The players (about a dozen) put their hats in a row near a house, fence, or log (hollows up) A dead-line is drawn 10 feet from the hats; all must stand outside of that. The one who is "it" begins by throwing a soft ball into one of the hats. If he misses the hat, a chip is put into his own, and he tries over. As soon as he drops the ball into a hat, the owner runs to get the ball; all the rest run away. The owner must not follow beyond the dead-line, but must throw the ball at some one. If he hits him, a chip goes into that person's hat; if not, a chip goes into his own.

As soon as some one has 5 chips he is the Buffalo; he wins the booby prize: that is, he must hold his hand out steady against the wall, and each player has 5 shots at it with the ball, as he stands on the dead-line.

RAT-ON-HIS-LODGE

Each player has a large, smooth, roundish stone, about 4 or 5 inches through. This is his rat. He keeps it permanently.

The lodge is any low boulder, block, stump, bump, or hillock on level ground. A dead-line is drawn through the lodge and another parallel, 15 feet away, for a firing line.

The fellow who is "it," or "keeper," perches his rat on the lodge. The others stand at the firing-line and throw their rats at his. They must not pick them up or touch them with their hands when they are beyond the dead-line. If one does, then the keeper can tag him (unless he reaches the firing-line), and send him to do duty as keeper at the rock.

But they can coax their rats with their feet, up to the dead-line, not beyond, then watch for a chance to dodge back to the firing-line, where they are safe at all times.

If the rat is knocked off by any one in fair firing, the keeper is powerless till he has replaced it. Meantime, most of the players have secured their rats and got back safe to the firing-line.

By using bean bags or sandbags instead of stones this may be made an indoor game.

WATCHING BY THE TRAIL

This is a game we often play in the train, to pass the time pleasantly.

Sometimes one party takes the right side of the road with the windows there, and the other the left. Sometimes all players sit on the same side.

The game is, whoever is first to see certain things agreed on scores so many points. Thus:

A crow or a cow counts	1
A horse	2
A sheep	3
A goat	4
A cat	5
A hawk	6
An owl	7

The winner is the one who first gets 25 or 50 points, as agreed.

When afoot, one naturally takes other things for points, as certain trees, flowers, etc.

TRAILING

A good trailing stunt to develop alertness and observation is managed thus: One fellow wearing the tracking irons is deer. He is given 100 beans, 30 slices of potato and 10 minutes start. He has to lay a track, as crooked as he pleases, dropping a bean every 3 or 4 yards and a slice

of potato every 20. After ten minutes' run the deer has
to hide.

The trailers follow him, picking up the beans and
potato slices. Each bean counts 1 point, each slice of
potato 2. The one who finds the deer scores 10 for it.

APACHE RELAY RACE

One band is pitted against another, to see who can carry
a message and bring a reply in shortest time, by means of
relays of runners. One mile is far enough for an ordinary
race. This divides up even 220 yards to each of eight
runners. The band is taken out by the Chief, who drops
scouts at convenient distances, where they await the arrival
of the other runner, and at once take the letter on to the
next, and there await the return letter.

A good band of 8 can carry a letter a mile and bring the
answer in about 9 minutes.

THE WEASEL IN THE WOOD

The old French Song game much like our game of "Button, Button," or the Indian Moccasin game, is given in the
Section on Songs, etc.

THROWING THE SPEAR

This was popular among Indians until the rifle made the
spear of little use.

The spear is of a straight, slender staff of ash or hickory,
about 7 feet long. It should have a steel point, the
weight should be chiefly in the head end; that is, the
balancing point should be 2 feet from the head. A tuft
of colored feathers or hair near the light end helps the spear
to fly straight, and is a distinctive ornament.

The target should be a burlap sack stuffed tight with straw and ranged as for archery. Make it big, 6 feet square, if possible, and always begin so close to it that you at least hit the sack nearly every time. Afterward you can work off to the correct range of 30 feet.

WATER-BOILING CONTEST

Given a hatchet and knife, 1 match, a 2-quart pail, 7 inches or less in diameter, one quart of water and a block of soft wood about 2 feet long and 5 or 6 inches through.

Any one should have the water boiling in 10 minutes. The record is said to be 7.59

First cut plenty of wood. Spend three minutes on it. Support your pail on four pegs driven in the ground. If water is handy dip the pegs in it before placing.

The water must be jumping and bubbling *all over the surface* or it is not boiling.

If the first match goes out, contestants are usually allowed a second, but are penalized by having 2 minutes added to their time.

MEDLEY SCOUTING

The following competition in Medley Scouting took place at one of my camps. A prize was offered for the highest points in the following:

At the word, "Go."

Bring a leaf of sugar-maple; and tell how it differs from other maples.

Tell a short story.

Bring a leaf of poison ivy (wrapped in a thick paper, to avoid touching it), and describe the poison, and mode of counteracting it.

Mark off on a stick your idea of a yard.

Bring a leaf of witch hazel, and tell what it is good for.

Show a bed made by yourself in camp of woods material.

Bring a leaf of beech, and tell how it differs from those most like it.

Show a dancer's war club made by yourself in camp, and tell what they are used for.

Dance a step; any — English, Irish, Scotch, or Indian.

Strike a match and light a lamp; both of them imaginary.

Show a birch-bark utensil or article made by yourself.

Make a map of North America from memory in 10 minutes.

Boil a quart of water in a 2-quart pail, given 1 match, a hatchet, and a stick of wood. You should do it inside of 12 minutes.

Give an imitation of some animal, actions or sounds.

Play the part of an Indian woman finding her warrior dead.

For each of the first 20 competitors, points were given; the prize adjudged by the total.

Some of these stunts may seem trivial, but there was a purpose in each, and that purpose was served. In the Indian widow, for example, we wished to select the best actor for play. Most of the fellows failed. Two were good, but one, nearly the smallest in camp, was so fine that he brought tears into the eyes of many.

The selection of the various leaves impressed these kinds on all, especially those who failed to bring the right ones.

The song and dance was introduced to cultivate the spirit of going fearlessly in and doing one's best, however poor it might be; and the elements of handicraft were recognized in birch-bark vessel and war club.

By the bed competition, all were taught how easy it is to make one's self comfortable in the woods.

The water-boiling was particularly instructive and was tried twice. The first time the winner took 14 minutes, and the second best 20. The last time, the winner's time was 8 minutes, and the second one's 10.

Even the imitations of monkey, lynx, cat, panther, moose, etc., developed a keen observation, and a lot of good natural history that was intensely interesting as well as amusing.

X. Health and Woodland Medicine

FIRST AID. (Rudimentary)

(Second Aid, and best, is bring the doctor)

TO REVIVE FROM DROWNING

AS SOON as the patient is in a safe place, loosen the clothing if any.

(2) Empty the lungs of water, by laying the body breast down, and lifting it by the middle, with the head hanging down. Hold thus for a few seconds, till the water is evidently out.

(3) Turn the patient on his breast, face downward.

(4) Give artificial respiration thus: by pressing the lower ribs down and forward toward the head, then release. Repeat about twelve times to the minute.

(5) Apply warmth and friction to extremities, rubbing toward the heart.

(6) DON'T GIVE UP! Persons have been saved after hours of steady effort, and after being under water over twenty minutes.

(7) When natural breathing is reëstablished, put the patient into warm bed, with hot-water bottles, warm drinks, or stimulants, in teaspoonfuls, fresh air, and quiet. Let him sleep, and all will be well.

SUNSTROKE

(1) Reduce the temperature of the patient and the place — that is, move the patient at once to a cooler spot, if possible, in the shade.

(2) Loosen or remove the clothing about the neck and body.

(3) Apply cold water or ice to the head and body, or even wrap the patient in sheets wet from time to time with cold water.

(4) Use no stimulant, but allow free use of cold water to drink.

BURNS AND SCALDS

Exclude the air by covering the burn with a thin paste of baking-soda, starch, flour, vaseline, olive oil, linseed oil, castor-oil, lard, cream, or cold cream. Cover the burn first with the smear; next with a soft rag soaked in the smear.

Shock always accompanies severe burns, and must be treated.

HEMORRHAGE, OR INTERNAL BLEEDING

This is usually from the lungs or stomach. If from the lungs, the blood is bright-red and frothy, and is coughed up; if from the stomach, it is dark, and is vomited. Cause the patient to lie down, with head lower than body. Small pieces of ice should be swallowed, and ice-bags, or snow, cold water, etc., applied to the place whence it comes. Hot applicati ns may be applied to the extremities, but avoid stimulants, unless the patient is very weak.

CUTS AND WOUNDS

After making sure that no dirt or foreign substance is in the wound, the first thing is tight bandaging — to close it and stop the bleeding. The more the part is raised above the heart — the force-pump — the easier it is to do this.

If the blood comes out in spurts, it means an artery has been cut; for this, apply a twister or tourniquet — that is, make a big knot in a handkerchief, tie it round the limb, with the knot just above the wound, and twist it round with a stick till the flow is stopped.

LIGHTNING

To revive one stunned by a thunderbolt, dash cold water over him.

SHOCK OR NERVOUS COLLAPSE

A person suffering from shock has pale, dull face, cold skin, feeble breathing, rapid, feeble pulse, listless, half-dead manner. Place him on his back with head low. Give stimulants, such as hot tea or coffee, or perhaps one drink of spirits. Never remove the clothing, but cover the person up. Rub the limbs and place hot-water bottles around the body. Most persons recover in time, without aid, but those with weak hearts need help.

FAINTING

Fainting is caused by the arrest of the blood supply to the brain, and is cured by getting the heart to correct the lack. To aid in this have the person lie down with the head lower than the body. Loosen the clothing. Give fresh air.

Rub the limbs. Use smelling-salts. Do not let him get up until fully recovered.

MAD DOG OR SNAKE BITE

Put a tight cord or bandage around the limb between the wound and the heart. Suck the wound many times and wash it with hot water to make it bleed. Burn it with strong ammonia or caustic or a white-hot iron; or cut out the wounded parts with a sharp knife or razor, if you cannot get to a doctor.

INSECT STINGS

Wash with oil or weak ammonia, or very salt water, or paint with iodine.

TESTS OF DEATH

Hold a cold mirror to the nostrils or mouth. This shows at once if there is any breath. Push a pin into the flesh. If living, the hole will close again; if dead, it will remain open.

CINDERS OR SAND IN THE EYE

Can be removed with the tip of a lead-pencil, or the wet end of a tiny roll of soft paper. I have seen a woman lick the cinder out of her child's eye when other means were lacking.

BOOKS RECOMMENDED

"First Aid" By Major Charles Lynch. P. Blakiston Sons & Co., 1017 Walnut St., Philadelphia, 1911. 30 cents.

Some Wildwood Remedies or Simples

(In case no standard remedies be at hand.)

For trees mentioned, but not illustrated here, see Forestry section.

Antiseptic or *wound-wash:* Strong, salt brine, as hot as can be borne: a handful of salt in a quart of water.

Balm for wounds: Balsam Fir. The gum was considered a sovereign remedy for wounds, inside or out; it is still used as healing salve, usually spread on a piece of linen and laid over the wound for a dressing.

Bleeding, to stop, nose or otherwise: Gather a lot of leaves of witch hazel, dry them, and powder them to snuff. A pinch drawn up the nose or on a wound will stop bleeding. The Indians used a pinch of powder from a puff ball.

Bowel complaint: Get about a pound of small roots of sassafras, or else two pounds of the bark, smashed up. Boil in a gallon of water till only one pint of the fluid is left. A tablespoonful of this three times a day is a good remedy for bowel trouble.

Chills and fever: Two pounds of white poplar or white willow bark, smashed up and soaked for twenty-four hours in a gallon of water and boiled down to a pint, make a sure remedy for chills and fever. A dessertspoonful four times a day is the proper dose.

A tea made of spice bush twigs is a good old remedy for chills and fever. Make it strong, and sip it hot all day.

Cold or fever cure: A decoction of the poplar bark or roots of flowering dogwood is a good substitute for quinine, as tonic and cold cure, bowel cure, and fever driver.

Cough remedy: (That is, to soften and soothe a cough:) Slippery elm inner bark boiled, a pound to the gallon, boiled down to a pint, and given a teaspoonful every hour.

Linseed is used the same way, and is all the better if licorice or sugar of any kind be added.

Spice bush.

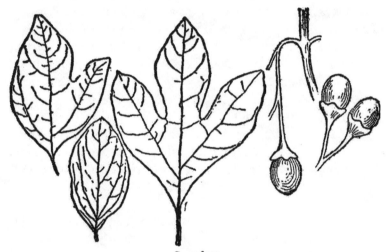

Sassafras.

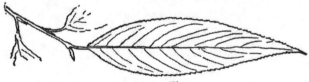

Golden willow.

Flowering dogwood.

Black cherry.

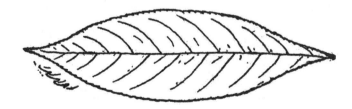

Cherry leaf — teeth enlarged.

Another woodland remedy is the syrup made by boiling down the sap of the sweet birch tree.

Cough and irritated throat: Mix a spoonful of sugar with two of butter, and eat it slowly. This usually stops a hacking cough that would keep the patient from sleep.

Cough and lung remedy: A pound of inner bark of black cherry, soaked twenty-four hours in a gallon of water and boiled down to one pint, makes a famous cough remedy and lung balm. A tablespoonful three or four times a day.

Diuretic: A decoction of the inner bark of elder is a powerful diuretic.

Face-ache: Heat some sand in the frying-pan, pour it into a light bag and hold it against the place. The sand should be as hot as can be borne. This treatment is good for most aches and pains.

Inflammation of the eyes or skin: Relieved by washing with strong tea of the bark of witch hazel.

Ink: The berries and leaves of red or staghorn sumac boiled together in water make a permanent black ink.

Lung balm: Infusion of black cherry bark, root preferred, is a powerful tonic for lungs and bowels. Good also as a skin wash for sores. When half wilted, the leaves are poisonous to cattle.

Nose-bleed: A snuff made of the dried leaves of witch hazel stops nose-bleed at once, or any bleeding.

Nose stopped up at night: Wet the nose outside, as well as in, with cold water, and prop the head up higher with pillows.

Pimples and skin rash: A valuable tonic or skin wash for such troubles is strong tea made of the twigs of alder.

Poison ivy sting, to cure: Wash every hour or two with soapy water as hot as can be borne, then with hot salt water. This relieves the sting, and is the best simple remedy. The sure cure is washing the parts two or three

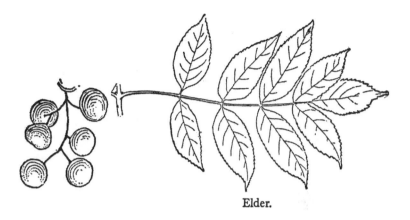

Elder.

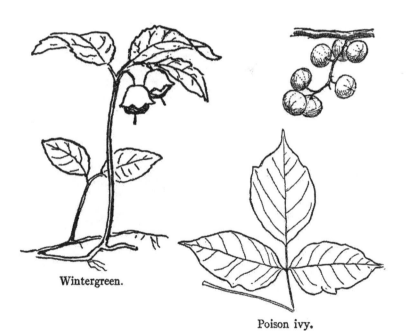

Wintergreen.

Poison ivy.

times in alcohol in which is dissolved sugar-of-lead, 20 to 1. This will cure the sores in three days unless the trouble is complicated with rheumatism, in which case you need a doctor. The same remarks apply to poison oak and poison sumac.

Witch hazel.

Purge, mild: A decoction of the inner bark of butternut, preferably of root, is a safe, mild purge. Boil a pound in a gallon of water till a quart only is left. A teaspoonful of it is a dose.

Purge, strong: The young leaflets of elder are a drastic purgative. They may be ground up and taken as decoction, boiling a pound in a gallon of water till it makes a quart. Use in very small doses — one teaspoonful.

Poison sumac.

Purge, fierce: The root, fresh or not long dry, of *blueflag*, should be powdered and given in twenty-grain doses. A grain is about the weight of a grain of wheat, or one twenty-fourth of an ounce; so twenty grains is what will cover a quarter-dollar to the depth of one sixteenth inch.

Rheumatism: Put the patient in bed. Make him drink

plenty of hot water, or better a thin extract of sassafras, or tea made of wintergreen leaves. Keep very warm, so as to get a good sweat. Rub him all over, especially the place afflicted, with grease or vaseline. The only use of these last things is to protect the skin. It is the rubbing that does the good.

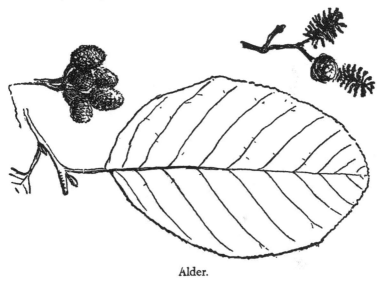

Alder.

The Indian treatment was a Turkish bath, as described later.

Sores and wounds: Can be cleansed by washing with hot brine, that is a handful of salt in a quart of water.

Sunburn: If you take your sunburn gradually, a little each day, it doesn't hurt. But if you are foolhardy at first, and expose your white skin, arms, or neck and back to the blaze of the summer sun for a few hours you will pay a heavy price. At night you will be in a torment of fever-fire. The punishment may last for days. Huge blisters will arise, and you may be obliged for a time to give up all active sports. As soon as you find you are overburnt, put cold cream, vaseline, sweet-oil, or grease of any kind on the place, and keep it covered up. In a day or two you will be well.

But it is best to go slow. Do not get overdone at all, and so have no damage to repair.

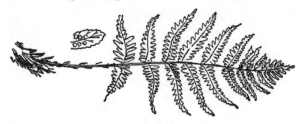

Male-fern.

Sweater: A famous woodman's sweater is tea made from the leaves and twigs of hemlock. Make a gallon of about two pounds of twigs, etc., and sip it all day.

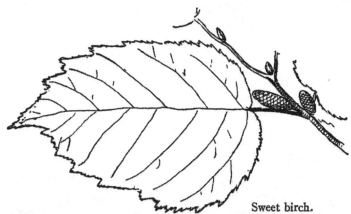

Sweet birch.

Tapeworm: Boil a pound of smashed-up male-fern or evergreen fern root in a gallon of water till but a pint of fluid is left. A teaspoonful three or four times a day — followed by a purge — is a famous remedy.

Tonic: An infusion or tea of black alder bark is a wonderful tonic, and a healer of the skin, inside and out. Boil a pound of bark in a gallon of water till a quart is left. Take half a cupful four times a day. This is a bracer for the feeble constitution.

Tonic: A fine tonic is made from the twigs of sweet birch, by boiling two pounds of twigs in a gallon of water, till it makes about a pint of strong brown tea, which should be sipped, about half a pint a day.

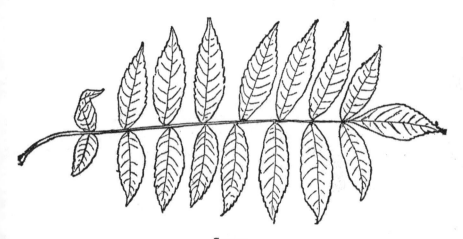

Sumac.

Tonic: A decoction, or boiled in water extract, of almost any part of the red sumac tree, is a powerful tonic. Make it of two pounds of sumac in a gallon of water boiled to a pint. Take a big spoonful twice a day.

Wash for sore throat: Inner bark of hemlock is a powerful astringent and good as a throat wash. A pound of bark in a gallon of water is boiled to a quart.

Worms: The berries of black alder used as tincture

(bruised in alcohol) are a powerful remedy for worms. A dessertspoonful three times a day is a dose.

Worms and tonic: The inner bark and root bark of tulip tree, either as dry powder or infusion, are powerful tonics and especially good for worms.

Wound-wash. See *Antiseptic.*

For other remedies, see Dr. Elisha Smith's "Botanic Physician," Cincinnati, 1844.

AN INDIAN BATH OR SWEAT LODGE

A Turkish bath in the woods is an interesting idea. The Indians have always used this style of treatment and, with their old-time regard for absolute cleanliness, took the bath once a week, when circumstances permitted.

Their plan was to make a low, round-topped lodge, about five feet high and as much across, by bending over a number of long willow poles with both ends stuck in the ground. A few slender cross-bars lashed on here and there completed the skeleton dome. This was covered over with a number of blankets, or waterproof covers of canvas, etc. A shallow pit was dug near one side. The patient stripped and went in. A fire was made previously close at hand, and in this a number of stones heated. When nearly red-hot, these were rolled in, under the cover of the Sweat Lodge into the pit. The patient had a bucket of water and a cup. He poured water on the hot stones, a dense steam arose, which filled the Lodge, causing the intense heat, which could be modified at will. The more water on the stones the greater, of course, the steam. Meantime, the patient drinks plenty of water, and is soon in a profuse sweat. Half an hour of this is enough for most persons. They should then come out, have a partial rub-down, and plunge into cold water, or have it thrown over them. After this a thorough rub-down finishes, and the patient should roll up in a blanket and lie down for an hour. Aromatic herbs or leaves are sometimes thrown on the stones to help the treatment.

This is fine to break up a cold or help a case of rheumatism. I have found it an admirable substitute for the Turkish bath.

LATRINE

Nothing in camp is more important than the latrine or toilet. It is fully described on page 178.

THE KEEN EYES OF THE INDIAN. DO YOU WISH TO HAVE THEM?

Near-sightedness. An eminent eye doctor, Dr. W. H. Bates of New York, has found out how you can have sight as keen and eyes as good as those of the Indians who live out of doors. After eight years' study of the subject he has established the following:

a. The defect known as near-sight or short-sight seldom exists at birth, but is acquired.

b. Besides being acquirable, it is preventable and in some cases curable.

c. It comes through continual use of the eye for near objects only, during the years of growth.

The Remedy. The remedy is, give the eye regular muscular exercise every day for *far-sight* by focussing it for a few minutes on distant objects. It is not enough to merely look at the far-off landscapes. The eye must be definitely focussed on something, like print, before the necessary muscular adjustment is perfect and the effect obtained.

The simplest way to do this is — get an ordinary eye testing card, such as is sold for a nickel at any optician's.

Hang it up as far off as possible in the schoolroom and use it each day. Train your eyes to read the smallest letters from your seat.

By such exercises during the years of growth almost all short-sight or near-sight, and much blurred sight or astigmatism, may be permanently prevented.

An interesting proof is found by Dr. Casey Wood in the fact that while wild animals have good sight, caged animals that have lost all opportunities for watching distant objects are generally myopic or short-sighted. In other words, nature adapts the tool to its job.

DRY SOCKS

A certain minister knowing I had much platform experience said to me once, "How is it that your voice never grows husky in speaking? No matter how well I may be my voice often turns husky in the pulpit."

He was a thin, nervous man, very serious about his work and anxious to impress. I replied: "You are nervous before preaching, which makes your feet sweat. Your socks are wet when you are in the pulpit, and the sympathy between soles and voice is well known. Put on dry socks just before entering the pulpit and you need not fear any huskiness."

He looked amazed and said: "You certainly have sized me up all right. I'll try next Sunday."

I have not seen him since and don't know the result, but I know that the principle is sound — wet feet, husky throat.

SHUT YOUR MOUTH AND SAVE YOUR LIFE

This was the title of an essay by George Catlin, a famous outdoor man, who lived among the Indians, and wrote about them 1825 to '40.   In this he pointed out that it is exceedingly injurious to breathe through your mouth; that, indeed, many persons injured their lungs by taking in air that was not strained and warmed first through the nose, and in many cases laid the foundation of diseases which killed them.

DON'T TURN OUT YOUR TOES MUCH

When you see a man whose toes are excessively turned out, you may know he was born and brought up on sidewalks.   He is a poor walker and will not hold out on an all day-tramp.

The mountaineer and the Indian scout always keep their feet nearly straight.   It is easier on the feet and it lengthens the stride; makes, in short, a better traveler.   A glance at his tracks will tell you how a person walks.

TOBACCO

No Indian was allowed to use tobacco until a proven warrior.   It was injurious to the young they said, but in the grown man if used only as a burnt sacrifice it helped in prayer and meditation.

Some of the finest Indians, Spotted-tail for example, never smoked as a habit.

In the New York *Literary Digest* for December 30, 1911, there appeared the following important article:

INJURIOUSNESS OF TOBACCO

The opinion that tobacco is injurious to the young and apparently harmless to adults, quoted in these pages recently from *American Medicine*, is adjudged by the editor of *Good Health* (Battle Creek, Mich., December) to be one of those half-truths which Tennyson tells us are "ever the blackest lies."

He agrees heartily with the first part of it, but asserts that no respectable medical authority will be found to endorse the other half of it. Has the editor of *American Medicine*, he asks, never heard of tobacco blindness? And how about cancer of the lip and of the throat, diseases almost confined to smokers? Bouchard, of Paris, an authority on diseases of the heart and blood-vessels, names tobacco, the writer goes on to say, as one of the leading causes of this deadly class of maladies. And this is by no means a new idea. Medical examiners tell us that nine tenths of the rejected applicants for the Army are refused on account of tobacco-heart. We read further:

"King Edward died of tobacco-heart. Mark Twain was another victim of this disease. A king of Hungary fell off his horse some time ago and lost his life because of defective vision due to smoking. The death-rate from disease of the heart and blood-vessels has increased, within the last ten years, from 6 per 100,000 to 24 per 100,000 or 400 per cent. Is there no evidence from these facts that it is not 'harmless to adults'?

"No experienced coach will allow men in training for athletic events to make use of tobacco, so well known are its effects upon the heart. A well-known physician said to the writer just before the Yale-Harvard boat-race: 'I am sure Yale will be beaten, for the coach permits the men to use tobacco.'

"The ill effects of tobacco upon the kidneys are familiar to all physicians. Statistics gathered some years ago showed that 10 per cent. of all smokers have albumen in the urine. The physician forbids the use of tobacco or very greatly restricts its use in cases of Bright's disease.

"But even on *a priori* grounds it may be safely said that tobacco is anything but harmless. The deadly effects of tobacco are well enough known. In very minute doses nicotin produces deadly effects. One tenth of a grain killed a goat, and a much smaller dose killed a frog. The farmer uses tobacco leaves and stems to kill ticks on sheep. An eminent German botanist has recently shown that tobacco, even in minute quantities, produces pernicious effects on plants.

"Numerous investigators have shown that pigeons are proof against anthrax, a disease very deadly to sheep. Charrin showed that after giving to a pigeon a very small dose of nicotin the creature quickly dies when infected with the anthrax germ

"Doctor Wright, of London, showed that nicotin lowers the tuberculo-opsonic index of the blood; that is, it lowers the power of resistance of the body against tuberculosis. He cited the case of a young man who was a great smoker and whose tuberculo-opsonic index was zero instead of 100. The young man was suffering from tuberculosis and died within a few weeks.

"Post-mortem examination made at the Phipps Institute showed that smokers are twice as subject to tuberculosis as non-smokers."

These are only a few of the thousand facts, the writer goes on, that might be cited on his side of the question. Nothing in them shows that there is any distinction between the child and the adult, and the fact that the effects are often less apparent in the latter is due, we are told, solely to the fact that they possess greater vital resistance than children. Finally, he remarks:

"We would remind the editor to review the study of physiologic chemistry and pathology, and consult a few up-to-date standard works on the practice of medicine in relation to the cause of Bright's disease, arteriosclerosis, angina pectoris and other maladies involving the heart and blood-vessels, the death-rate from which has kept even pace along with the increase of tobacco during the last thirty or forty years."

SEX MATTERS

Some of our best authorities tell us that more than half of our diseases, mental and physical, come from ignorance and consequent abuse of our sexual powers.

We have long known and realized vaguely that virtue and strength are synonymous; that the Puritan fathers, for example, notwithstanding their narrowness and their unlovely lives, were upon the whole a people of pure life, who reaped their reward in their wonderful mental, moral, and physical strength, not entirely gone to-day.

All men realize the desirability of virtue; and hitherto we have attempted to keep our young people virtuous by keeping them ignorant. Most thinking men to-day admit and maintain that as a protection *ignorance is a sad failure.*

It is far better for the parent to teach the child the truth — the sacred truth — by degrees, as he or she is ready for it. Most children are ready at seven or eight to know something about the process of procreation, especially if they live on a farm where they see it all about them.

No boy is any the worse for learning of these things. All are better for knowing them.

Rest assured of this, more nations have been wiped out by sex abuse than by bloody war. The nation that does not bring up its youth with pure ideals is certainly going to destruction.

Every leader of boys should talk frankly to his charges and read to them or have them read:

"From Youth Into Manhood," by Dr. Winfield S. Hall. Y. M. C. A. Press, 124 East Twenty-eighth Street, New York.

STARVATION FOODS IN THE NORTHERN WOODS

For a man who is lost, the three great dangers in order of importance, are *Fear, Cold,* and *Hunger.* He may endure extreme hunger for a week and extreme cold for a day, but *extreme fear may undo him in an hour.* There is no way of guarding against this greatest danger excepting by assuring him that he is fortified against the other two.

Starvation is rare in warm regions and I suppose that no one ever starved during the late summer and early autumn. The woods then are full of roots, nuts, and berries that, as a rule, are wholesome and palatable, and usually there is a large amount of small game at this season.

The greatest danger of starvation is in the far north *during winter.* By the far north I do not mean the Polar regions, where few go and where life usually depends on keeping touch with the ship, but the wooded regions of Canada and Alaska where there are hundreds, yes, *thousands* of travelers each year, and where each year one hears of some one dying of starvation, through ignorance of the few emergency foods that abound in that country.

Fish are not included among these foods, for the wanderer in the snow is not likely to be equipped with fish hook, spear or net. The fish, moreover, are in winter protected by ice of great thickness. Animal food is exceedingly scarce at such times, the forms most likely to be found are rabbits, mice, insect-borers, ants, and rawhide gear. Of course the mounted Indian never starved, because he would bleed his horse each day and live on the blood; taking care that his steed had fodder enough to keep up his strength. But we must assume that this source of food is not available — that our traveler is on foot.

A well-known explorer states in his book that northern expeditions should be undertaken chiefly or only in rabbit years — that is, when rabbits are at the maximum of their remarkable periodic increase. While there is some truth in this, we must remember, first, a rabbit year in one region is not necessarily a rabbit year in another, so we could not foretell with certainty what would be a season of abundant food in the region proposed for the expedition; second, men will at any risk go into the vast northern wilderness every year, for it is destined to be the great field for exploration, and every traveler there ought to know the foods he can count on finding at all times.

Rabbits. If when in straits for food he have the luck to be in a rabbit country, he should select a thicket in which their tracks and runs are very numerous. By quietly walking around it, he is likely to see one of these silent, ghostlike hares, and can easily secure it with his gun. Without a gun his next best reliance is on snares. String, a shoelace, a buckskin thong, or even a strip of clothing, may be used as a snare. There are many ways of making a rabbit snare, but the simplest is the best. The essentials are, first, the snare — an ordinary running noose; second, a twitch-up; that is either a branch bent down, or a pole laid in the crotch of a sapling. If the nearest sapling does not have a crotch the twitch-up can be fastened to it with a willow withe.

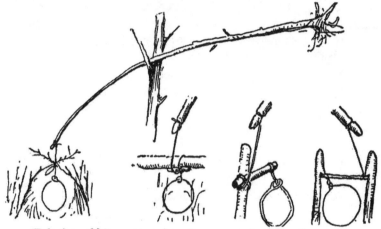

Pole for rabbit snare and various ways of setting the noose.

The snare is fast to the end of the pole, and spread open in a well-worn runway. The loop is about four inches across and placed four inches from the ground. The pole twitch-up is held down by placing the cross-piece of the snare under some projecting snag, as shown. The rabbit, bounding along, puts his head in the noose, a slight jerk frees the cross piece from its holder, and in a moment the rabbit is dangling in the air. The cross piece can be dispensed with if the snare be wrapped three or four times around a snag. The squaws often build a little hedge across a rabbit thicket, so as to close all but three or four runs, each of which is guarded by a snare. They then drive the rabbits back and forth, capturing several at each drive.

Mice swarm in all the northern country wherever there is heavy sedge, or where the ground is deeply buried in moss, and that means most of the Far North. If I were seeking for mice I should pick out a sedgy hollow, one evidently not actually a pond in summer, and dig through snow and tangle down to the runways, at the level of the ground. If one has traps they may be set here with the certainty of taking some game within a few hours. But usually the mice are so common that they may be caught by hand. I have frequently done this, taking a hint from the method of a fox hunting mice. He advances very slowly, watching for a movement in the cover. As soon as this is seen he seizes the whole tussock, and, after the death squeeze, separates his victim from the grass.

Deep snow, unfortunately, puts the mice beyond reach, and excludes them from the bill of fare when most needed.

Ants, the next on our list, are usually to be found dormant in dead and hollow trees, sometimes in great numbers. Bears and flickers eat them in quantities, and I have met with men who claim to have done so, but I never tried them myself and suspect that they are unpleasantly acid.

Insect-borers. These are the fat white grubs that winter under the bark of trees and in dead timber. They are accounted acceptable food by bears and by most birds, which is almost if not quite conclusive evidence that they are good for human food. Their claws, nippers, and spines should be removed. To get them one must have an axe.

Rawhide, or even *leather*, if boiled for hours, will make a nutritious soup. Many a man has bridged the awful gap by boiling his boots, whence the phrase to express the final extreme, "I'll eat my boots first." Mark Twain was once put to this final resort and recorded afterward that "the holes tasted the best."

But the hardest case of all is the best for present discussion. That is the case of the man who has not happened on a rabbit region and who has neither gun nor axe, string nor rawhide. He must look entirely to the vegetable world for sustenance, as do all the northern natives in times of direst famine.

Bark and buds. In the forest region are several foods that are available in the depth of winter. First of these is the thin green outer skin or bark, the white innermost bark, and the buds (not the middle brown bark) of quaking asp or white poplar. The brown bark is highly charged with a bitter principle, partly tannin, that makes it unpalatable as well as unwholesome. Aspen bark is a favorite food with elk, deer, beavers, squirrels, rabbits, and mice in winter. I found that by boiling it for some hours it is reduced to a gelatinous and apparently nutritious mass. I have also found the buds of basswood a palatable food supply. In my early days, in the backwood of Canada, we children frequently allayed our hunger with basswood buds and spruce and tamarac shoots.

Dr. C. C. Curtis informs me that in British Columbia the natives eat the *inner* bark of willows, hemlock, and other trees, and I have often heard of the Indians eating the innermost bark of birch.

All these are common foods with herbivorous animals. Man, having a less capable stomach, will do well to pre-digest such by roasting or long boiling.

Toadstools. There is yet another supply that is commonly shunned, namely—toadstools. No toadstool growing on trees is known to be poisonous, and most contain nutriment — especially the birch polyporus, which grows on birch trees and has pores instead of gills. A toadstool gnawed by mice or squirrels is usually good. References to the article on toadstools will show that none but the Amanitas are deadly, and these are well known by their white or yellow gills, their parasol shape, the ring on their upper stem, and the cup out of which they spring. They grow on the ground in the woods.

Lichens. But the surest food supply of all is that from the lowly *lichens*, which exist in enormous quantities throughout the great land of big hunger and little sticks. Doctor C. C. Curtis says:

"All lichens are rich in carbohydrates; lichen starch or lichenin, constituting 40 to 60 per cent. of the bulk of the higher forms."

They supply winter food to all the northern quadrupeds. The reindeer, the white hare, the musk-ox, and the lemming find in them their chief support; and those which do not live directly on the lichen do so indirectly by preying on those who do.

They are not choice dainties for human food. But Richardson, the famous northern naturalist, and the party with him, as well as unnumbered Eskimos and travelers, have lived for weeks on the lichens when other food has failed.

The kinds most useful are the Iceland moss (*Cetraria icelandica*), the reindeer moss (*Cladonia rangiferina*), and the rock-tripe or famine-food (*Umbilicaria arctica*), and other species. To these we might add the *Lucanora esculenta* or manna lichen, the manna of the Bible; but as this is an old-world species it is not within the intended scope of this article.

The Iceland moss is a rigid, erect, branching moss, almost like a seaweed, and of brown color. It abounds in most northern latitudes. Richardson speaks of the Barren Grounds being covered with *Cetraria* of two species. When boiled for an hour, it is highly nutritious. Those who wish to familiarize themselves with its appearance as a preliminary of northern travel can see it in most drug shops.

The reindeer moss is by far the most abundant of the food lichens. There are thousands of square miles in the barren northern country, deeply covered with reindeer moss. It is indeed the most abundant form of vegetable life, the

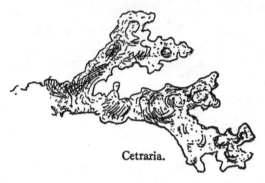

Cetraria.

main support of the reindeer, and the ever-present and obvious guarantee to the traveler that he need not starve. It is readily known by its soft gray-green color and its branching like a little tree without leaves. It grows on rocks or on the ground, and masses sometimes like sponges. It is said to be a nutritious food. It is gritty unless collected carefully and washed. This latter, fortunately, is easily done, for grit sinks in the water and the moss floats when fresh.

Boiling is the usual way of cooking it. Reindeer moss from Connecticut, however, I boiled for several hours without producing any evident change. It continued to be tough and unpalatable, and tasteless except for a slight suggestion of fish oil.

Roasting was more successful than boiling. When carefully browned, I found it tasted not unlike burnt bread

crumbs, and, of course, was easily chewed.   While roasting
it gave off a smell, like seaweed.

Rock-tripe.   But the last, the *rock-tripe* or *famine-food*
of the Indians, has proved the most satisfactory of all the
starvation foods that I have experimented with.   Every
one knows it as the flat leathery crinkle-edged lichen that

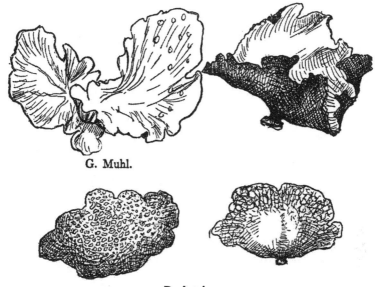

G. Muhl.

Rock-tripes.

grows on rocks.   It is blackish and brittle in dry weather,
but dull dark greenish on the upper side in wet.   It is
largely composed of nutritious matter that can be assimi-
lated by the human stomach.   Unfortunately it is also a
powerful purge, unless dried before being boiled, as food.
Specimens gathered from the rocks in Connecticut — it is
very widely distributed even in New England — after drying and two or three hours boiling, produced a thick mucilaginous liquid and a granular mass of solid jelly, that were

mild and pleasant to the taste, entirely without the bitter-
ness of *Cetraria*, etc.   Indeed, it was sweetish, with a slight
flavor of licorice and of sago, far from unpalatable at any
time, and to a starving man, no doubt, a boon from heaven.
It is less abundant in the north country than the reindeer
moss, but yet of general distribution and to be found in
great quantities and at all seasons of the year.

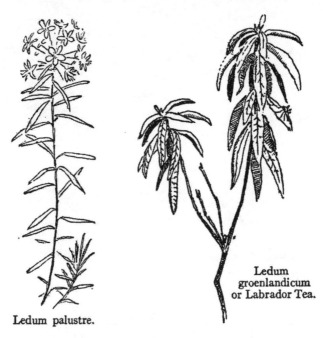

Ledum
groenlandicum
or Labrador Tea.

Ledum palustre.

Rock-tripe is the food that saved the life of Sir John
Franklin and Dr. J. Richardson on their long and desperate journey for three months, in the summer and autumn
of 1821, on foot from Fort Enterprise to the Polar Sea and
back.   The record of that expedition shows that when they
were out of game, as soon happened, their diet was varied
with burnt bones when they could find them and toasted

leather and hide; but the staple and mainstay was rock-tripe. It is not delicious food, nor is it highly nutritious, but it will sustain life, and every traveler should know what it is like and how to use it.

Drinks.   It will be a fitting conclusion to this question of foods if we note one or two possible drinks.   Franklin and Richardson used *Labrador tea* as a hot drink.   This is an infusion of the plants figured here.   But good and slightly nourishing drinks are made also of the buds, sprouts, or inner bark of spruce, basswood, tamarac, birch, and especially of slippery elm.

XI. Natural History

Our Common Birds or Forty Birds that Every Boy Should Know

THE Bald Eagle or White-headed Eagle (*Haliæetos leucocephalus*) is the emblem of America. It is three to four feet from beak to tail, and six or seven feet across the wings. When fully adult it is known by its white head, neck and tail, and the brown body; but when young it is brownish black, splashed and marked with dull white.

The only other eagle found in the United States is the *Golden or War Eagle (Aquila chrysaëtos)*. This is a little larger. When full grown it is dark brown, with the basal half of tail more or less white. The plumage of the young birds is somewhat like that of the young Bald Eagle; but the two species may always be distinguished by the legs. The War Eagle wears leggings — his legs are feathered to the toes. He is ready for the warpath. The Bald Eagle has the legs bald, or bare on the lower half.

Redtailed Hawk or Henhawk (Buteo borealis). The common hawks of America are very numerous and not easy to distinguish. The best known of the large kinds is the Redtail. This is about two feet long and four feet across the wings. In general it is dark brown above and white beneath, with dark brown marks; the tail is clear reddish with one black bar across near the tip. In young birds the tail is gray with many small bars. It has four primaries notched on the inner web. The legs are bare of feathers for a space above the toes. It is common in North

Bald Eagle　　　　Redtailed Hawk or Henhawk.

America east of the Rockies up to mid-Canada. It does much good, killing mice and insects. It is noted for its circling flight and far-reaching whistle or scream.

The Barred or Hoot Owl (Strix varia). This Owl is known at once by the absence of horns, the black eyes and the plumage barred *across* the chest and *striped* below that. It is about twenty inches long, in general gray-brown marked with white. It is noted for its loud hooting; it is the noisiest owl in our woods. Found in the wooded parts of America up to about latitude 50 degrees, east of the Plains.

Great Horned Owl or Cat Owl (Bubo virginianus). This is the largest of our Owls. About twenty-four inches long and four feet across the wings. It is known at once by its great ear tufts, its yellow eyes, its generally barred plumage of white, black and buff, and its white shirt front. This is the winged tiger of the woods. Noted for its destruction of game and poultry, it is found throughout the timbered parts of North America.

Screech Owl (Otus asio). This is not unlike the Horned Owl in shape and color but is much smaller — only ten inches long. Sometimes its plumage is red instead of gray. It feeds on mice and insects and has a sweet mournful song in the autumn — its lament for the falling leaves. It is found in the timbered parts of North America.

Turkey Vulture or Buzzard (Cathartes aura). The Turkey Vulture is about two and a half feet long and about six feet across its wings. It is black everywhere except on the under side of the wing which is gray, and the head which is naked and red. It is known at once by the naked head and neck, and is famous for its splendid flight. It is found from Atlantic to Pacific and north to the Saskatchewan. It preys on carrion.

In the Southern States is another species — the Black Vulture or Carrion Crow — which is somewhat smaller and wears its coat collar up to its ears instead of low on the neck; also its complexion is dusky not red.

Loon (Gavia immer). The common Loon is known by its size — thirty-two inches long and about four feet across the wings — and its brilliant black and white plumage. It is noted for its skill as a fisher and diver. Its weird rolling call is heard on every big lake in the country.

Common Seagull (Larus argentatus). The common Seagull is twenty-four inches long and four feet across. The plumage is white with blue-gray back, when adult; but

Barred or Hoot Owl.

Great Horned Owl.

Turkey Vulture or Buzzard.

Screech Owl.

splashed brown when young, and with black tips to the wings. Its beak is yellow with red spot on the lower mandible. It is found throughout North America.

Loon.

Common Seagull.

Pelican (*Pelecanus erythrorhynchos*).   The white Pelican is known at once by its great size — about five feet long and eight feet across the wings — by its long beak, its pouch, and its feet fully webbed.   Its plumage is white, but the wing tips are black.   It is found in the interior of America up to Great Slave Lake.

Wild Duck or Mallard (*Anas platyrhynchos*).   Of all our numerous wild ducks this is the best known.   It is about twenty-three inches long.   Its bottle-green head, white

collar, chestnut breast, penciled sides and curled up tail
feathers identify it. The female is streaky brown and
gray. It is found in all parts of the continent, up to the
edge of the forest. This is the wild duck from which tame
ducks are descended.

Pelican.

Wood Duck or Summer Duck (Aix sponsa). This beautiful duck is about eighteen inches long. Its head is
beautifully variegated, bottle-green and white. Its eye is
red, its breast purplish chestnut, checkered with white
spots, while its sides are buff with black pencilings. This

Wild Duck or Mallard

Wood Duck or Summer Duck

Wild Goose, Canada Goose or Honker

is one of the wildest and most beautiful of ducks. It nests in hollow trees and is found in North America up to about latitude 50 degrees.

Wild Goose, Canada Goose or Honker (*Branta canadensis*). This fine bird is about three feet long. Its head and neck are black; its cheek patch white; its body gray; its tail black with white coverts above and below. It is found up to the Arctic regions, and breeds north of about latitude 45 degrees. It is easily tamed and reared in captivity.

Swan. There are two kinds of Swan found in America: The Trumpeter (*Olor buccinator*), which is almost extinct, is very large and has a black bill, and the Whistling Swan (*Olor columbianus*), which is smaller —about five feet long and seven feet across. Its plumage is pure white; its bill black, with a *yellow spot* near the eye. It is found generally throughout North America but is rare now.

Bittern (*Botaurus lengtiginosus*). This bird of marshes is about twenty-eight inches long and can stand nearly three feet high. Its general color is warm yellowish brown splashed with dark brown. The black mark on the side

Bittern   Great Blue Heron

of the neck is a strong feature, and its bright green legs and beak are very distinctive. It is famous for its guttural call notes in the marshes, and is found throughout North America up to about latitude 60 in the interior.

Great Blue Heron (*Ardea herodias*). This bird is commonly called Blue Crane. Its great size will distinguish it. In general it is blue-gray above, white below; head, white, with black hind head, crest and marks on neck, and shoulders. Its thighs are chestnut. It is found throughout North America to the limit of heavy timber.

Quail or Bobwhite (Colinus virginianus). This famous and delicate game bird is about ten inches long. Its plumage is beautifully varied with reddish brown, lilac, and black markings, on a white ground. Its whistle sounds like "Bob White." It is found in eastern North America up to Massachusetts and South Ontario.

Quail or Bobwhite   Ruffed Grouse or Partridge

Ruffed Grouse or Partridge (Bonasa umbellus). It is known by its mottled and brown plumage, its broad and beautiful fan tail, and the black ruffs on each side of the neck. It is noted for **its** drumming, which is usually a love song — a call to **its** mate. Found in the heavy woods of North America, north of the Gulf States.

Dove (Zenaidura macroura). This is an abundant inhabitant of the farming country as far north as wheat is now grown. It is about twelve inches long, and known by its pigeon-like look, and its long wedge-shaped tail, with black and white marks on the feathers. Its breast is soft purplish gray. Its extinct relation, the once plentiful Passenger Pigeon, was eighteen inches long and had a reddish breast.

Downy Woodpecker (Dryobates pubescens). About six and and a half inches long, black and white. In the male the nape is red, the outer tail feathers white, with black spots. Carefully distinguish this from its large relation the Hairy Woodpecker which is nine and a half inches long and has no black spots on the white outer tail feathers. A familiar inhabitant of orchards the year round, it is found in woods throughout eastern North America.

Flicker or Highhole (Colaptes auratus). This large and beautiful woodpecker is twelve inches long. Its head is ashy gray behind, with a red nape in the neck, and brown-gray in front. On its breast is a black crescent. The spots below and the little bars above are black, and the under side of wings and tail are bright yellow. The rump is white. Its beautiful plumage and loud splendid "clucker" cry make it a joy in every woodland. It is found throughout North America, east of the Rockies up to the limit of trees.

Ruby-throated Hummingbird (Trochilus colubris). Every one knows the Hummingbird. The male only has the throat of ruby color. It is about four inches long from tip of beak to tip of tail. This is the only Hummingbird found in the Northern States or Canada east of the Prairies.

Kingbird (Tyrannus tyrannus). This bird is nearly black in its upper parts, white underneath, and has a black tail with white tip. Its concealed crest is orange and red. It is eight and a half inches long. Famous for its intrepid attacks on all birds, large and small, that approach its nest, it is found in North America east of the Rockies, into Southern Canada.

Bluejay (*Cyanocitta cristata*). This bird is soft purplish blue above, and white underneath. The wings and tail are bright blue with black marks. It is found in the

Dove.   Flicker.

Downy
Woodpecker.   Kingbird.

woods of America east of the plains to about latitude 55. The Bluejay is a wonderful songster and mimic, but it is mischievous — nearly as bad as the crow indeed.

Common Crow (Corvus brachyrhynchos). The Crow is black from head to foot, body and soul. It is about

Bluejay.

Bobolink
or Reedbird.

eighteen inches long and thirty wide. It makes itself a nuisance in all the heavily wooded parts of E. North America.

Bobolink or Reedbird (Dolichonyx oryzivorus). This bird is about seven and a half inches long. The plumage is black and white, with brown or creamy patch on nape; and the tail feathers all sharply pointed. The female, and the male in autumn, are all yellow buff with dark streaks. Though famous for its wonderful song as it flies over the meadows in June, it is killed by the thousands to supply the restaurants in autumn and served up under

the name Reedbird.   It is found in North America, chiefly
between north latitude 40 and 52 degrees.

Baltimore Oriole (Icterus galbula).   The Oriole is about
eight inches long, flaming orange in color, with black head
and back and partly black tail and wings.   The female
is duller in plumage.   Famous for its beautiful nest, as

Baltimore Oriole.   Purple Grackle or Crow Blackbird.

well as its gorgeous plumage and ringing song, it is abundant
in Eastern North America in open woods up to Northern
Ontario and Lake Winnipeg.

Purple Grackle or Crow Blackbird (Quiscalus quiscala).
This northern bird of paradise looks black at a distance
but its head is shiny blue and its body iridescent.   It is
twelve inches long.   When flying it holds its long tail with
the edge raised like a boat, hence "boat tail."   In various
forms it is found throughout the eastern States, and in
Canada up to Hudson Bay.

Snowbird (Plectrophenax nivalis).   About six and a half
inches long, this bird is pure white, overlaid with brown

on the crown, back and sides. The wings, back and tail are partly black. The Snowbird nests in the Arctic regions and is common in most of temperate agricultural America, during winter, wherever there is snow.

Snowbird.

Song-sparrow.   Scarlet Tanager.

Song-Sparrow (*Melospiza melodia*). The Song-sparrow is about six and a half inches long — brown above — white underneath. It is thickly streaked with blackish marks on flanks, breast and all upper parts. All the tail feathers are plain brown. There is a black blotch on the jaw and another on the middle of the breast. Always near a brook.

It is noted for its sweet and constant song, and is found in all well wooded and watered parts of North America.

Scarlet Tanager (Piranga erythromelas). This gorgeous bird is about seven inches long. The plumage of the male is of a flaming scarlet, with black wings and tail; but the female is dull green in color. The Scarlet Tanager is found in the woods of eastern America, up to Ottawa and Lake Winnipeg.

Purple Martin (Progne subis). About eight inches in length, with long wings and forked tail, the Purple Martin

Purple Martin.   Barn Swallow.

is everywhere of a shiny bluish or purplish black. Like the Kingbird it attacks any intruder on its lower range. This swallow is found in the wooded regions of east temperate America, north to Newfoundland and the Saskatchewan.

Barn Swallow (Hirundro erythrogaster). About seven inches long, this bird is steel-blue above, chestnut on

throat and breast, buffy white on belly. It is known by
the long forked tail which is dark with white spots.
Famous for its mud nest, it is found in open country
'bout barns in America generally.

Mockingbird (*Mimus polyglottos*). About ten inches
long, soft gray above, dull white beneath, wings and tail

Catbird.

Mockingbird.

black and white, with *no* black on head — the Mockingbird is famous for its song, and is found in United States
north to New Jersey.

Catbird (*Dumetella carolinensis*). This northern Mockingbird is about nine inches long, dark slate in color, with
a black-brown cap, black tail and a red patch "on the
seat of its pants." It abounds in the Eastern States
and Canada, north to Ottawa, Saskatchewan and British
Columbia.

Common House Wren (*Troglodytes aëdon*). This little
fairy is about five inches long; soft brown above and brown-

ish gray below, it is barred with dusky brown on wings
and tail. It nests in a hole, and is found in wooded
America east of the plains, north to Saskatchewan. Ottawa
and Maine.

Chickadee (Penthestes atricapillus). This cheerful little
bird is five and a half inches long. Its cap and throat are

Common House Wren.

Robin.   Chickadee.

black. Its upper parts are gray, its under parts brownish
its cheeks white, no streaks anywhere. It does not migrate,
so it is well known in the winter woods of eastern America
up to the Canadian region where the Brown-Capped or
Hudson Chickadee takes its place. Its familiar song
chickadee dee dee has given it its name.

Wood Thrush (Hylocichla mustelinus). About eight

inches long, cinnamon-brown above, brightest on head, white below, with black spots on breast and sides, this thrush is distinguished from the many thrushes in America much like it, by the reddish head and round black spots on its under sides. It is found in the woods of eastern North America up to Vermont and Minnesota.

Robin (*Planesticus migratorius*). The Robin is about ten inches long, mostly dark gray in color, but with black on head and tail, its breast is brownish red. The spots

Wood Thrush.

Bluebird.

about the eye, also the throat, the belly and the marks in outer tail feathers are white. Its mud nest is known in nearly every orchard. Found throughout the timbered parts of America north to the limit of trees.

Bluebird (*Sialia sialis*). About seven inches long, brilliant blue above, dull red-brown on breast, white below. Found in eastern North America, north to about latitude 50 degrees in the interior, not so far on the coast.

BOOKS RECOMMENDED

"Handbook of the Birds of Eastern North America," By F. M. Chapman, Appleton, N. Y. Price $3.00. (Technical.)

"Handbook of Birds of the Western United States," By Florence Merriam Bailey. Houghton, Mifflin & Co. Price, $3.50. (Technical.)

"Bird Homes," By A. R. Dugmore. Doubleday, Page & Co. (Popular.)

"Bird Neighbors," By Neltje Blanchan. Doubleday, Page & Co. (Popular.)

"Birds That Hunt and Are Hunted," By Neltje Blanchan. Doubleday, Page & Co. (Popular.)

How to Stuff a Bird

(By E. T. S. from *Country Life*, July, 1904)

A boy found a bird that was lying dead in the woods. Its beautiful plumage, its form and its markings delighted his eye. He carried it home to show to his mother and to ask its name. She admired it with him but she could not tell him what it was, and at length said, "Now go and bury it before it begins to smell."

The boy had not given a thought to the history of the bird, nor had its death caused him a touch of sorrow. He was interested in it as a strange and beautiful thing, and the idea of burying all that beauty, or — worse — seeing it corrupt, now gave him a deep regret.

"How I wish I knew how to stuff it," he said, feeling that then he might always renew his present enjoyment. He was expressing the feeling of most young people when they see a dead bird. All would like to save its beautiful plumage at least. They know it can be done, but have an idea that it is a very difficult thing. In a sense this is true. It is so difficult to stuff a bird *well*, that not many men in the world to-day can do it. As with all arts, there can be but few masters. But the main process itself is easy to learn; and if the boy who tries to do it fails in making a life-like bird of his specimen, he at least does three things: he saves its beautiful plumage; he adds to his bird acquaintance; and he gains a keener appreciation of the work of others.

While each taxidermist has his own methods, all agree in the main. The directions here given are those, recommended by good authorities, and that I have found most practical in my own work.

There are two ways of preserving a bird:

(a) By making a skin.

(b) By mounting the bird.

MAKING A SKIN

The first is removing and preserving the skin in such a way that it may always serve to show what the bird's plumage is like. Most naturalists prefer to keep their specimens as skins, not only because it is easier and cheaper to do so, but because then they take up less room, and the skin may be properly mounted at any later time.

These are the tools and materials used in making a skin:

A sharp knife, a pair of stout, short scissors, and a pair of small forceps. (It is, however, quite possible to dispense with all but the knife and scissors in making a bird skin. I rarely use any tool but the scissors.)

For materials you will need cotton wool, needle and thread, arsenical soap (some naturalists prefer dry white arsenic) and cornmeal (or fine hardwood sawdust). Some plaster of paris and benzine will also be required if the specimen is soiled with grease.

The hardest birds to begin on are the very large ones, and the next hardest, perhaps, are the very small ones. The easiest birds are those about the size of a robin or bluejay (leaving out the woodpeckers).

Supposing the specimen to be skinned is a robin:

First put a little plug of cotton wool in its throat and mouth, also into any wounds the bird may have, to stanch the flow of blood, etc. This should be done the moment the bird comes into your possession.

Now lay the bird on its back, tail toward your right hand, part the feathers, and make a slit from near the end of the breast-bone into the vent (S.V. Fig. 1 p. 356), taking care to cut only the skin, not the walls of the abdomen. Separate the skin from the flesh by pushing it with the finger-nail or knife-blade. As soon as the flesh is exposed, put a pinch of meal on it to keep the feathers from sticking, and also to soak up oil, blood, etc. Some use plaster for this; but plaster is disagreeable under the finger nails, it takes the gloss off the feathers, and if the specimen happens to be a game-bird it injures the meat for the table. The plaster is better however for white, fluffy birds, as meal or sawdust lodges in the down.

Push the skin from the body till the leg is reached. Work the leg out of the skin till the knee-joint is clear on the inside of the skin; (H L, Fig. 2) cut the leg off at the knee, taking great care not to cut or tear the skin. The severed leg now hangs to the skin. When both legs are thus cut, work around the base of the tail, freeing the skin. Then cut straight through the bone and all, with the scissors, at the part marked with arrow and black line in Fig. 3 — leaving the tail bone with the tail hanging to the skin.

This is one of the most difficult parts of the skinning. It is so hard to get at, and so easy to tear the skin, that one is to be congratulated if in the first lesson he safely "rounds Cape Horn."

At all stages keep the meal applied to the body as fast as it is exposed, and in quantity enough to soak up all moisture; and avoid stretching the skin.

With the tail and legs free, there is no difficulty in pushing the skin off until stopped by the wings.

Cut them off at the shoulder joint deep in the muscles of the breast (W. W, Fig. 4), leaving them attached to the skin, just as the legs and tail are.

The skin is now inside out. It can readily be worked along the neck and onto the head. Here it is stopped by the ears. In the robin these are like pockets of skin tucked into the small skull and may be easily pulled out without cutting. In large birds the knife must be used. The next and last difficulty is the eyes. The skin must be cut free from them, carefully avoiding injury to the eyelids or the eyeballs.

Now the skin is attached only to the forepart of the skull (Fig. 4). Cut off the neck at the back of the skull and the skin is freed from the body, but needs careful cleaning.

Dig the eyes out of the sockets, taking great care not to break the eyeballs, as their liquid is very difficult to remove from the feathers. Cut out a section of the skull so as to enlarge the hole behind by extending it downward and sideways, as shown in Fig. 5, and remove the brains through this. Cut off any lumps of flesh left about the jaws, but do not break the jaw bone or its joints.

Next turn attention to the wings. Push the skin back to the first joint (the elbow) in each. Cut and scrape the meat from the bone. But there is a joint beyond

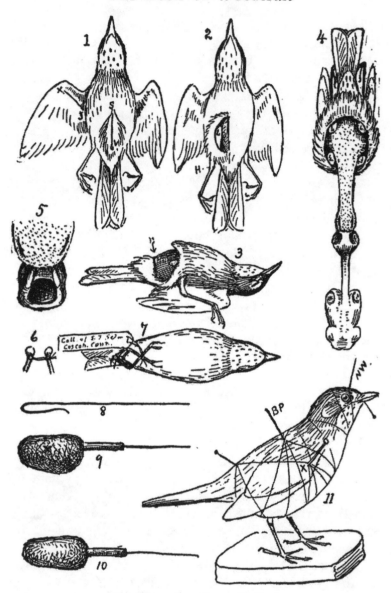

Skinning and stuffing a Robin

this — the one that corresponds with our forearm.
This must be reached in a different way. There are
two bones in this, and the space between them is full
of meat. The quill feathers on its under side hold the
skin tight. In birds up to the size of a robin, this can
be cut out after the skin is forced a little farther back
than the elbow joint on the upper side, but in large birds
it is well to slit the skin under the wing from X to J (Fig.
1), along the line between the two bones.

Clean off the leg bones in the same way as the first wing
joint, turning the skin back as far as the heel joint (H in
Fig. 2). Carefully scrape off any lumps of fat left on the
skin, and especially remove the grease and flesh about
the tail bones.

Now this is the time I have usually found most convenient to remove stains from the plumage.

If of blood, hold the stained feathers on the inside
rim of a cup of lukewarm water and wash till clear. Then
dry the feathers with cornmeal. The shaking and turning
they get in the next operation will make them fluff out
as before.

If the stain is grease, use a cream made of benzine
and plaster of Paris. Let this dry on the feathers. It
dries as powder and falls off, taking the grease with it.

The next thing I now do is to tie the wing bones with
a stout linen thread, so that their ends are shackled
together as far apart as in life, (Fig. 6.) Some do not do
this, but it strengthens the skin, and I find it a great
help in several ways.

Now comes the poisoning. After trying dry arsenic
for long, I have come back to the old-fashioned arsenical
soap. It is much less liable to poison any one, since it
is not blown about by the wind. It does not look like
anything but soap and hence is unlikely to be mistaken

for something good to eat. And last of all the soap in it takes care of the grease in the skin.

Every part of the under side of the skin and of the bones exposed is to be painted with this cream of the soap. It is well now to lay a thin film of cotton over the skin or sprinkle it lightly with sawdust to keep the feathers from sticking in the soap.

Make two tight round plugs of cotton each as big as the eyeball, put one into each eye-socket.

Now push the head back into its place. This is easy when the neck is slippery with the soap. Work the wing and legs back into their places after wrapping each of the bones with enough cotton to take the place of the flesh cut off. This wrapping is not necessary with very small birds, but the larger the bird, the more it is needed.

Make a neck of the cotton, push it with the forceps up the neck skin, and well into the skull. Let it hang into the body part, under the string that joins the wing bones. Push another soft wad up the neck and into the throat.

Shape a large piece of cotton for the body; set it in place, and draw the skin gently over it till the opening is closed. In large birds it is well to stitch this up, but it is not needed in small ones. All that is needed now is the prinking. Use a needle through the openings of the eyes to fluff out the cotton balls in each, till they fill out the sides of the head properly.

Set the innermost wing bones parallel with each other. Aim to arrange the feathers by arranging the skin and bones to which they are attached, rather than by prinking the feathers themselves.

If the wing was slit open as at X J, (Fig. 1), fill the space with cotton and close with a few stitches.

If at any time it is necessary to leave the specimen half

finished, wrap it in a damp cloth and put it in a close tin box. This will keep it from getting dry.

In skinning large birds, a strong hook, attached to a string from the wall in front and above, is a great help. As soon as the tail is cut off stick this hook into the bony pelvis. It holds the bird away from you and answers as a third hand.

Finally, make a little shroud out of a sheet of cotton and wrap the bird in this before setting it to dry.

Cross the legs as in Fig. 7, and attach a label to these, giving date, sex and place where the bird was taken.

The work is now done. But it is wise to lift the skin the next morning and see if all goes well. In a few days it will be dry and safe from ordinary corruption, but must be protected from moth and insects.

This is a museum skin. It can be kept indefinitely in this shape, or at any time it can be softened up and mounted.

MOUNTING THE BIRD

For mounting the bird some additional tools and materials are needed, namely:

A pair of wire cutters.

A pair of pliers.

A file,

Some glass eyes,

Some annealed or soft iron wire of several sizes,

Some tow, and a ball of stout packthread with needle to match.

A few ordinary carpenter tools are needed to make the stand, but that is another department.

The first part of the mounting is the skinning carried out exactly as in making the skin, up to the point where the cotton is put in. Now there is a difference. You cannot put a wire through cotton, therefore use no cotton in a bird to be mounted; use tow instead. Plug the eyes, wrap the legs and wings as before, but with tow.

If it is a dry skin that is to be mounted remove the cotton body and replace it with a lump of cotton soaked with water. Wrap damp cloth or cotton around the outside of each leg, and on the bend of each wing. Shut this up in a tin box for twenty-four hours and it will be soft and can be treated like a fresh skin.

Cut a wire (of stovepipe size) about a foot long. File a sharp point at one end and bend the other end into a hook (Fig. 8). Take tow in long strips and lash it tight over, around and through the hook — stitching it tight and binding it on with plenty of packthread — until you have a body the size and shape of the one you took out of the robin, with a neck on it also, like the bird's own neck (Figs. 9 and 10). Of course the real body should be at hand to give the measurements. Keep the neck lower than it appears, because the real neck is supple and drops low between the shoulders in a way not possible for the substitute. This body should be hard enough to hold a pin or needle driven into it; indeed some taxidermists use bodies carved out of cork.

Put the point of the wire up the neck, and out through the top of the skull between the eyes (N. W. Fig. 11). Gently work the neck up to the back of the skull and the body into its place.

Now make two other sharpened wires. Work one up through each foot under the skin of the leg, under the wrapping, and on straight through the hard body — which it enters about the middle of the side (X in Fig. 9). When this is far enough through clinch it and drive it back firmly into the body; taking care to avoid tearing the skin, by easing up the leg on the wire, as it is drawn back.

Do the same for the other leg. Get the tail into its right place; drive a sharpened 3-inch wire through the pope's nose or tail bone into the body to hold it there; work the skin together till the opening can be closed with a few stitches; and now we are ready for the stand. The simplest is the best for the present purpose. A piece of a board slightly hollowed on the under side is got ready in a few minutes. With an awl bore two holes through this about one inch apart and run a foot-wire through each. Clinch them on the under side, fastening them firmly with tacks or small staples. Now we are ready to give the robin its natural pose. This is done by bending the wires in the neck and legs. A wire or a large pin will have to be driven into each wing to hold it to the side, at least while drying (X, Fig. 11); and another in the middle of the back (B P, Fig. 11).

The prinking of the specimen is now done chiefly with needles reaching through the feathers to the skin. Pins may be driven into the body anywhere to hold the skin or feathers in place; and cotton thread may be lashed around the body or the wings and around the projecting wire till everything is held in the position that is wished. Then the bird is set away to dry.

In a week the specimen should be ready for the finishing touch — the putting in of the eyes. A plug of damp cotton is fastened on each eye-place the night before. In the morning the eyelids are once more soft. The eyes are put through the opening in the sockets, the lids neatly set around them. Some prefer to set them in a bed of putty or plaster of paris. Cut off the projecting wires flush, so that the feathers hide what is left, remove the thread lashings and the mounting of the robin is finished.

The process is much the same for all birds, but the larger

the bird the more difficult. Seabirds, ducks, and divers are usually opened at the back or under the side. Woodpeckers and owls and some others have the head so large that it will not come through the neck skin. This calls for a slit down the nape of the neck, which, of course, is carefully sewn up in finishing.

If the bird is to have its wings spread, each wing must be wired to the body in the way already set forth for the legs.

If the bill keeps open when you want it shut, put a pin through the lower jaw into the palate toward the part in front of the eyes, or even wind a thread around the bill behind the pin (see Fig. 11).

The mistakes of most beginners are: making the neck too long, stuffing it too full, or putting the body so far into it as to stretch the skin and show bare places.

To make good accessories for a group of mounted birds is another very special business. It involves a knowledge of wax flowers, imitation woods, water, stones, etc., and is scarcely in the line of the present book. Therefore the beginner is advised to use the simplest wooden stands.

Not every one has the taste for natural history, but those who have will find great pleasure in preserving their birds. They are not urged to set about making a collection, but simply to preserve such specimens as fall in their way. In time these will prove to be many, and when mounted they will be a lasting joy to the youthful owner. If the museum should grow too large for the house, there are many public institutions that will be glad to offer their hospitality and protection.

There is, moreover, a curious fatality attending a beginner's collection. It hardly ever fails. He speedily has the good luck to secure some rare and wonderful specimen that has eluded the lifelong quest of the trained and professional expert.

(From *Country Life*, June 1904)

OWL-STUFFING PLATE (P. 280)

Fig. 1. The dead owl, showing the cuts made in skinning it: A to B, for the body; El to H, on each wing, to remove the meat of the second joint.

Fig. 2. After the skinning is done, the skull remains attached to the skin, which is now inside out. The neck and body are cut off at Ct. Sn to Sn shows the slit in the nape needed for owls and several other birds.

Fig. 3. Top view of the tow body, neck end up, and neck wire projecting.

Fig. 4. Side view of the tow body, with the neck wire put through it. The tail end is downward.

Fig. 5. The heavy iron wire for neck.

Fig. 6. The owl after the body is put in. It is now ready to close up, by stitching up the slit on the nape, the body slit B to C, and the two wing slits El to H on each wing.

Fig. 7. A dummy as it *would look* if all the feathers were off. This shows the proper position for legs and wings on the body. At W is a glimpse of the leg wire entering the body at the middle of the side.

Fig. 8. Another view of the body without feathers. The dotted lines show the wires of the legs through the hard body, and the neck wire.

Fig. 9. Two views of one of the eyes. These are on a much larger scale than the rest of the figures in this plate.

Fig. 10. The finished owl, with the thread wrappings on and the wires still projecting. Nw is end of the neck wire. Bp is back-pin, that is, the wire in the centre of the back, Ww and Ww are the wing wires. Tl are the cards pinned on the tail to hold it flat while it dries. In the last operation remove the thread and cut all these wires off close, so that the feathers hide what remains.

STUFFING AN ANIMAL

Mounting a mammal, popularly called *animal*, is a much more difficult thing than mounting — that is, *stuffing* — a bird.

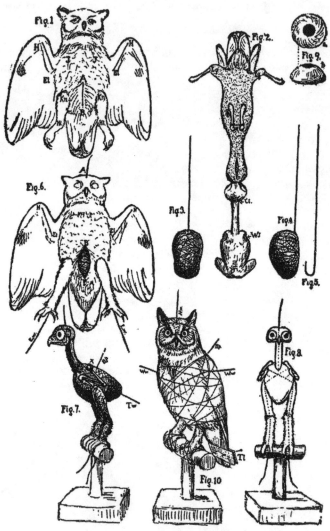

To illustrate the mounting of a Horned Owl.

It is so difficult that I do not advise any boy to try it unless he has the time and patience to go into it seriously. To do this he should get some standard treatise on Taxidermy, such as:

"Taxidermy and Zoölogical Collecting," by W. T. Hornaday. (Scribners. $2.50) or

"The Art of Taxidermy," by John T. Rowley. (Macmillan's. $1.75.)

Nevertheless all may learn to preserve the skins of small animals for cabinet collections, or for mounting at some later time.

The best instructions for this are those issued by the Biological Survey of the United States Department of Agriculture. I reproduce them.

PRESERVING SMALL MAMMAL SKINS

By Dr. C. Hart Merriam

Directions for Measurement

The tools necessary for measuring mammals are a pair of compasses or dividers, a steel rule graduated in millimeters, and two large pins. Dividers with round points are better than those with triangular points.

All measurements should give the distance *in a straight line* between the points indicated. They should be taken by means of dividers, or by driving pins into a board to mark the points between which the measurement is desired. They should never be made with a tape-line over the convexities or inequalities of the surface.

The three most important measurements, and those which should always be taken in the flesh are: (1) *total length;* (2) *length of tail;* (3) *length of hind foot.*

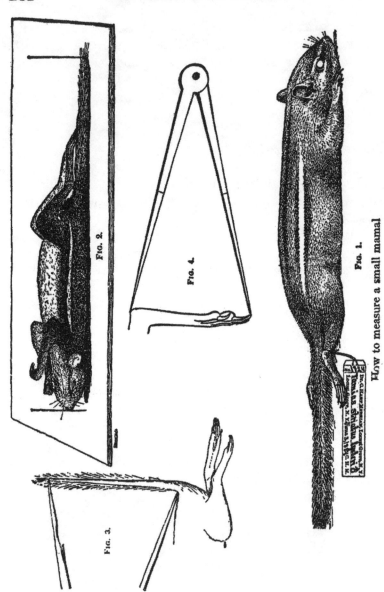

Fig. 2.

Fig. 4.

Fig. 3.

Fig. 1.

How to measure a small mamal

(1) The TOTAL LENGTH is the distance between the tip of the nose and the end of the tail vertebræ. It is taken by laying the animal on a board, with its nose against a pin or upright post, and by straightening the back and tail by extending the hind legs with one hand while holding the head with the other; a pin is then driven into the board at the end of the vertebræ. (See Fig. 2.)

(2) The LENGTH OF TAIL is the length of the caudal vertebræ. It is taken by erecting the tail at right angle to the back, and placing one point of the dividers on the backbone at the very root of the tail, the other at the tip end of the vertebræ. (See Fig. 3.)

(3) The HIND FOOT is measured by placing one point of the dividers against the end of the heel (*calcaneum*), the other at the tip of the longest claw, the foot being flattened for this purpose. (See Fig. 4.)

DIRECTIONS FOR THE PREPARATION OF SKINS

Skin all mammals as soon as possible after death.

Lay the animal on its back, and make an incision along the middle of the belly from just behind the fore legs nearly to the vent. Be careful not to stretch the skin while removing it, and exercise great caution in skinning around the eyes and lips, which are easily cut. Skin as far down on the feet as possible, but leave in the bones of the legs. Remove the bone from the tail by pulling it between the fingers (in the larger species a split stick answers well). Take out the skull, being careful not to cut or injure it in any way, and wash out the brains by means of a syringe or jet of water. Remove the tongue, and cut off the thick flesh from the sides and base of the skull. Tie a tag to the skull, bearing the same number that is attached to the skin, and dry in the shade. In damp weather it is sometimes necessary to use powdered borax to prevent the remaining flesh from decomposing. Never put arsenic or salt on a skull.

Remove all fat and tags of flesh that adhere to the skin. In cleaning off blood or dirt that may have soiled the hair an old toothbrush and a liberal supply of corn-meal will be found serviceable.

Poison all parts of the skin with dry arsenic (or better still, with a mixture of powdered arsenic and alum in the proportion of four parts arsenic to one part alum), being particular to put an extra supply in the feet and tail. Put a wire in the body, letting it extend to the extreme tip of the tail, but be careful not to stretch the tail. Use annealed iron wire of as large size as will fit easily into the tip end of the tail. In rabbits, foxes, and wildcats put wires in the legs also.

Stuff the skin to nearly its natural size with cotton or tow (never use wool, feathers, or other animal substances); sew it up along the belly, and place it flat on a board to dry (belly down), with the fore legs extended in front and parallel to the body (*i. e.*, not projecting sideways), and the hind legs and tail directed backward. The accompanying cut (Fig. 1) shows the appearance of a well-made skin.

Attach to each skin a label bearing the same number that is given the skull. On this label should be stated the sex, locality, date of capture (name of *month* should always be written in full), and name of collector.

All skins should be thoroughly dry before they are packed for shipment. They should be carefully wrapped in cotton and packed in small wooden boxes. Cigar-boxes do very well for the smaller species.

WASHINGTON, D. C., March, 1889.

TRAPPING ANIMALS

Trapping wild animals with steel traps is a wretchedly cruel business and will doubtless be forbidden by law before long. The old-fashioned deadfall which kills the animal at once is quite sufficient for all the legitimate work of a trapper. But many boys wish to capture animals alive without doing them any injury, and this is easily managed for most species if a ketchalive is used. The

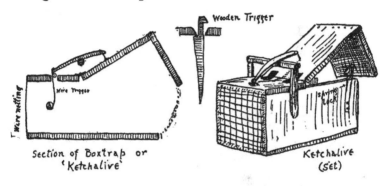

Section of Boxtrap or 'Ketchalive'

Wooden Trigger

Ketchalive (Set)

ketchalive or old-fashioned box trap is made in a hundred different ways; but the main principles are shown in the illustration. The lock on the side is necessary for some species, such as skunks, that would easily lift the lid and escape.

For skunks, cats, weasels, mink, rats, etc., use a piece of chicken as bait.

For rabbits use bread, turnip, apple, or other vegetable.

The trap should be visited every morning or not used at all.

THE SECRETS OF THE TRAIL

It was Fenimore Cooper who first put the good Indian on paper — who called the attention of the world to the wonderful woodcraft of these most wonderful savages.

It was he who made white men realize how far they had got away from the primitive. It was he who glorified the woodman and his craft. Yet nowhere do we find in Cooper's novels any attempt to take us out and show us this woodcraft. He is content to stand with us afar off and point it out as something to be worshiped — to point it out and let it die.

Fenimore Cooper has had many imitators, just as Uncas has had many successors. The fine art of trailing is still maintained in the Far West, and it has always seemed strange to me that none has endeavored to give it permanent record, other than superlative adjectives of outside praise.

TRAILING

What is trailing? The fox-hunter has some idea when he sees a superb pack follow a faint scent through a hundred perplexing places, discerning just which way the fox went, and about how long ago. The detective does another kind of trailing when he follows some trifling clue through the world of thought, tracing the secret of an unknown man along an invisible path, running it to earth at last in the very brain that conceived it. In his trailing the Indian uses the senses of the "animal" to aid the brain of the man. To a great extent his eyes do the work of the hound's nose, but the nose is not idle. When the trail disappears, he must do the human detective work; but under all circumstances his brains must be backed by the finest senses, superb physique, and ripe experience, or he cannot hope to overmatch his prey.

HARD TO PHOTOGRAPH TRACKS

When, in 1882, I began my dictionary of tracks (see "Life Histories of Northern Animals"), I found that there was

no literature on the subject.   All facts had to be gathered
directly from Nature.   My first attempts at recording
tracks were made with pencil and paper.   Next, realizing
how completely the pencil sketch is limited by one's own
knowledge, I tried photography; but it invariably happens
that not one track in ten thousand is fit for photographing,
and it cannot be taken except when the sun is about thirty
degrees above the horizon — that is, high enough to make
a picture, and low enough to cast a shadow of every detail.
Thus photography was possible only for about an hour in
the early morning and an hour in the late afternoon.   But
the opportunity in the meanwhile usually was gone.   I then
tried making a plaster cast of the tracks in the mud.   Only
one such in a million was castable.   As a matter of fact,
none of the finest were in the mud; and the much more
interesting dust-tracks were never within reach of this
method.   For most practical purposes I have been forced
to make my records by drawing the tracks.

NO TWO TRACKS ALIKE

The trailer's first task is to learn the trails he means
to follow.   The Red Indian and the Bushman, of course,
simply memorize them from their earliest days, but we
find it helpful and much easier to record them in some way.
Apart from other considerations, a form is always better
comprehended if we reproduce it on paper.   As a general
principle, no two kinds of animals leave the same track.
As a matter of fact, no two individuals leave the same
trail.   Just as surely as there are differences in size and
disposition, so there will be corresponding differences in
its trail; but this is refining beyond the purposes of prac-
ticability in most cases, and for the present we may be
satisfied to consider it a general rule that each species

leaves its own clearly recognizable track. One of my daily pastimes when the snow is on the ground — which is the easiest and ideal time for the trailer, and especially for the beginner — is to take up some trail early in the morning and follow it over hill and dale, carefully noting any change and every action as written in the snow, and it is a wonderfully rewarding way of learning the methods and life of an animal. The trail records with perfect truthfulness everything that he did or tried to do at a time when he was unembarrassed by the nearness of his worst enemy. The trail is an autobiographic chapter of the creature's life, written unwittingly, indeed, and in perfect sincerity.

Whenever in America during the winter I have found myself with time to pass between trains, I endeavor to get out into the country, and rarely fail to find and read one of these more or less rewarding chapters, and thus get an insight into the life of the animal, as well as into the kinds that are about; for most quadrupeds are nocturnal, and their presence is generally unsuspected by those who do not know how to read the secrets of the trail.

DOG AND CAT

The first trails to catch the eye and the best for first study are those nearest home. Two well-marked types are the tracks of cat and dog. Most anatomists select the cat as the ideal of muscular and bony structure. It is the perfect animal, and its track also is a good one to use for standard. (Illustration 1, p. 290.)

In these separate prints the roundness of the toe-pads tells the softness; their spread from each other shows the suppleness of the toes; the absence of claw-marks tells of the retractability of these weapons. The front and hind feet are equal in length, but the front feet are broader. This is the rule among true quadrupeds. The series of tracks — that is, its trail — shows the manner of the cat in walking. In this the animal used apparently but two legs, because the hind foot falls exactly on the trail made by the front foot, each track being really doubled. This is perfect tracking. There are several advantages in it. Every teamster knows that a wagon whose hind wheels do not exactly follow the front wheels is a very bad wagon to haul in sand, snow, or mud. The trail for it has to be broken twice, and the labor increased, some say, 50 per cent. This same principle holds good in the case of the cat track: by correct following the animal moves more easily. But there is still a more important reason. A hunting cat sneaking through the woods after prey must keep its eyes on the woods ahead or on the prey itself. At the very most it may pick out a smooth, safe, silent place for its front feet to tread on. Especially at the climax of the hunt all its senses are focussed on the intended victim; it cannot select a safe spot for each hind foot in turn, even though the faintest crunch of a dry leaf will surely spoil the stalk. But there is no danger of that; the cat can see the spots selected for the front feet, and the hind feet are so perfectly trained that they seek unerringly the very same spots — the safe places that the front feet have just left. Thus perfect stepping is silent stepping, and is essential to all creatures that stalk their prey. The opposite kind of stepping is seen in very heavy animals which frequent marshy ground; to them it would be a positive disadvantage to set the hind foot in the tread of the front foot, where so much of the support has just been destroyed. The ox illustrates this. These principles are applicable in geology, where the trails are the only biographical records of certain species._ From the manner

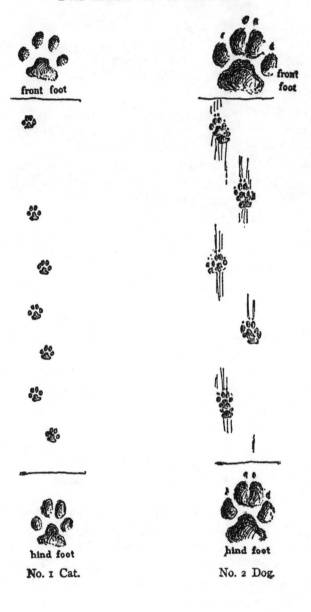

front foot

front foot

hind foot

hind foot

No. 1 Cat.

No. 2 Dog.

of setting the feet we can distinguish the predacious and
the marsh-frequenting quadrupeds.

The next track likely to be seen is that of the dog
(Illustration 2). In this the harder, less pliant foot and
the non-retractile claws are clearly seen. But the trail
shows the dog is not a correct walker. His tracks are
"out of register" as a printer would say. And he has
a glaring defect — the result no doubt of domestication,
of long generations on pavements and in houses — he drags
his toes. All these things contribute to make the dog
a noisy walker in the woods.

WOLF

It is well at this time to compare the track of the dog
with that of the wolf. I have made dozens of drawings,
casts, prints, photographs, and studies of wolf and dog
tracks; and have not found a single reliable feature that
will distinguish them. One hunter says the wolf has the
relatively small outer toes. Yes, sometimes; but not
when compared with a collie. Another says that the
wolf's foot is longer; but not when compared with that
of a greyhound, staghound, or lurcher. Another, the
wolf's foot is larger; yet it will not rank in size with that
of a St. Bernard or a great Dane. The wolf lifts his feet
neatly without dragging his toes; but so do many dogs,
especially country dogs. Thus all these diagnostics fail.
On the whole a wolf is a better walker than a dog. His
tracks do usually register, but not always, and in some
wolves rarely.

If a wolf-track in the snow be followed for a mile or two,
it will be found to go cautiously up to an unusual or
promising object. (Illustration 3.) It is obviously the
trail of a suspicious, shy creature while the dog-trail

is direct, and usually unafraid. But this does not apply to the dogs which poach or kill sheep. There is therefore no sure means of distinguishing them,

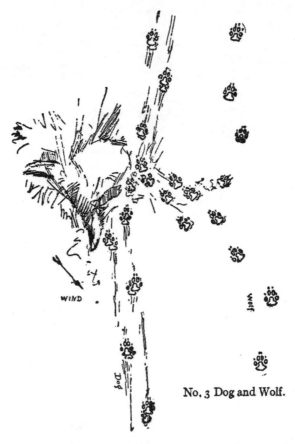

No. 3 Dog and Wolf.

even in the wilderness. One can only judge by probabilities.

I have often heard inexperienced hunters boast that they could "tell them every time"; but old hunters usually say, "No man can tell for sure."

RABBITS AND HARES

America is well provided with rabbits and hares. A score or more of species are now recognized, and two very well-known types are the cottontail of the woods and the jack-rabbit of the plains.

The cottontail is much like an English rabbit, but it is a little smaller, has shorter ears, and the whole under part of the tail is glorified into a fluffy, snowy powder-puff. It leads the life of a hare, not making burrows, but entering burrows at times under the stress of danger. The track of a New England cottontail is given in Illustration 4.

As the cottontail bounds, the hind feet track ahead of the front feet, and the faster he goes the faster ahead his hind feet get. This is true of all quadrupeds that bound, but is more obvious in the rabbits, because the fore and hind feet differ so much in size.

The jack-rabbit of Kansas is the best known of the long-eared jacks. His trail, compared with that of the cottontail, would be as in Illustrations 5 and 6.

The greater size of the marks and the double length of the bounds are the obvious but not important differences, because a young jack would come down to the cottontail standard. The two reliable differences I found are:

First, the jack's feet are rarely paired when he is bounding at full speed, while the cottontail pairs his hind feet but not his front ones. (Animals which climb usually pair their front feet in running, just as tree-birds hop when on the ground.)

Second, the stroke that is shown (x in Illustration 5) is diagnostic of the southern jack-rabbit; it is the mark made by the long hanging tail.

Each of the four types of hare common in the temperate

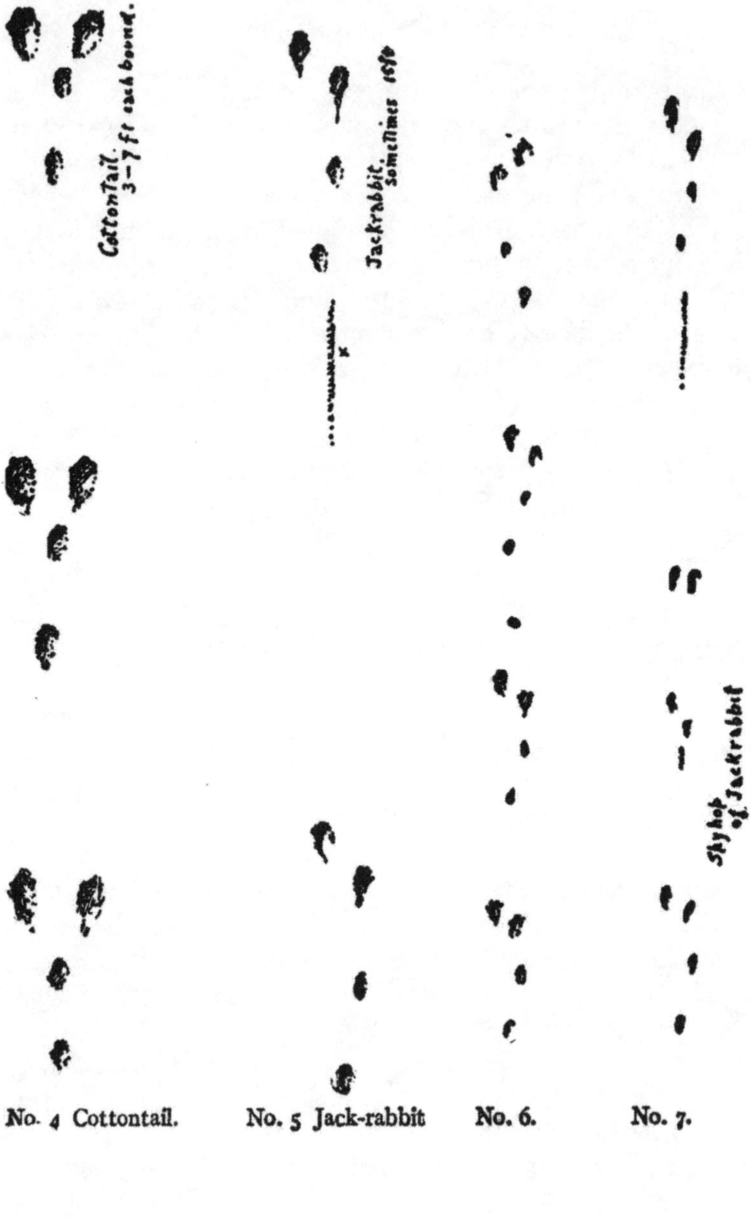

Cottontail.
3–7 ft each bound.

Jackrabbit, sometimes 16ft

Shyhop of Jackrabbit

No. 4 Cottontail.   No. 5 Jack-rabbit   No. 6.   No. 7.

parts of America has its own style of tail and fashion of wearing it:

The northern or white-tailed jack carries his snowy-white tail out straight behind, so its general pure-white is visible;

The southern or black-tailed jack has his tail jet-black on the upper part, and he carries it straight down;

The varying hare has an inconsequent, upturned tuft, like a tear in his brown pantaloons, showing the white undergarment;

The cottontail has his latter end brown above, but he keeps it curled up tight on his back, so as to show nothing but the gleaming white puff of cotton on a helpful background of rich brown. The cottontail's tail never touches the ground except when he sits down on it.

The most variable features of any animal are always its most specialized features. The jack-rabbit's tail-piece is much subject to variation, and the length and depth of the little intertrack-ial dash that it makes in the snow is a better guide to the individual that made it than would be the tracks of all four feet together.

THE NEWTON JACK-RABBIT

During February of 1902, I found myself with a day, to spare in the hotel office at Newton, Kan. I asked the usual question, "Any wild animals about here?" and got the usual answer, "No, all been shot off." I walked down the street four blocks from the hotel, and found a jack-rabbit trail in the snow. Later I found some cottontail tracks, though still in town. I walked a mile into the country, met an old farmer who said that "No rabbits were ever found around here." A quarter of a mile away was an orchard, and beside it a fence half buried in snow drifts that were yellow with tall dead grass sticking through. This was promising, so I went thither, and on the edge of the drift found a jack-rabbit form or den, with fresh tracks leading out and away at full speed. There were no tracks leading in, so he must have gone in there before the last snow came, and that was the night before.

When a jack runs without fear of any enemy at hand, he goes much like a fox or an antelope, leaving a trail, as in No. 5. But when an enemy is close at hand he runs with long, low hops, from six to seven in succession, then gives an upright leap to take an observation, leaving a trail thus. (Illustration 7.)

A silly young jack will lose time by taking one in three for observation, but a clever old fellow is content with one in ten. Here was the trail of this jack straight away, but taking about one observation in twelve hops. He had made a fence a quarter-mile off, and there had sat for some time observing, had then taken alarm and run toward a farmyard, a quarter-mile farther, taking occasional observations. A dog was lying on a doorstep by the road, and past this dog he had run, doing twenty-foot leaps. Two hundred yards down this road he had turned abruptly, as though a human still in sight had scared him. I now began to think the jack was near at hand, although so far I had not seen him. The trail led through several barbed-wire fences and some hedges, then made for another barn-yard half a mile off. I was now satisfied that he was only a little ahead of me, therefore I ceased watching the track so closely, watching rather the open plain ahead; and far on, under a barbed-wire fence, sitting up watching me, I soon saw my jack. He ran at once, and the line of his hops, was so — (Illustration 8) — the high ones being for observation.

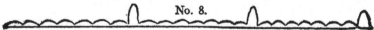

No. 8.

He never let me get within two hundred yards, and he wasted but little time in observation. He had now taken me on a two-mile circuit and brought me back to the starting point. So he had taught me this — a cunning old jack-rabbit lived in the region around which I had followed him, for they keep to their homeground. All his ways of running and observing, and of using barbed-

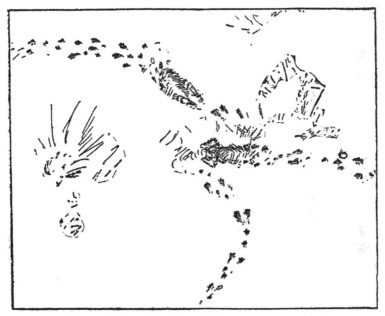

No. 9.   Where the Jack-rabbit's track was doubled

wire fences, barnyards, and hedges, showed that he was very clever; but the best proof of that was in the fact that he could live and flourish on the edge of a town that was swarming with dogs and traveled over daily by men with guns.

The next day I had another opportunity of going to the jack-rabbit's home region. I did not see himself; but

I saw his fresh tracks. Later, I saw these had joined on to the fresh tracks of another rabbit. I sketched all the salient points and noted how my big jack had followed the other. They had dodged about here and there, and then one had overtaken the other, and the meeting had been the reverse of unfriendly. I give the record that I sketched out there in the snow. I may be wrong, but I argue from this that the life of the hardy jack was not without its pleasures. (Illustration 9.)

FOX

Of more general interest perhaps is the track of the fox.

I have spent many days — yes, and nights — on the trail, following, following patiently, reading this life of the beast, using notebook at every important march and change. Many an odd new sign has turned up to be put on record and explained by later experience. Many a day has passed with nothing tangible in the way of reward; then, as in all hunting, there has come a streak of luck, a shower of facts and abundant reward for the barren weeks gone by, an insight into animal ways and mind that could not have been obtained in any other way. For here it is written down by the animal itself in the oldest of all writing — a chapter of the creature's normal life.

One day, soon after the snow had come, I set out on one of the long decipherments. The day before I had followed a fox-trail for three or four miles, to learn only that he tacked up wind and smelt at every log, bump, and tree that stuck through the snow; that he had followed a white hare at full speed, but was easily left behind when the hare got into his ancient safety — the scrubby, brushy woods.

This morning I took up another fox-trail. The frost was intense, the snow was dry and powdery and as each foot was raised it fell back; so that the track was merely shapeless dimples in the whiteness. No tell-tale details of toes and claws were there, but still I knew it for a fox-trail. It was too small for a coyote. There were but two others that might have been confounded with it; one a very large house-cat, the other a very small house-dog.

The fox has the supple paw of the cat. It spreads even more, but it shows the long, intractile claws. As a stepper the fox ranks close to the cat. His trail is noted also for its narrowness — that is, the feet are set nearly in one straight line. This in a trail usually means a swift animal; while the badly spread marks, seen at a maximum in the badger, stand for great but sluggish strength. (Illustration 10.)

The region put the cat out of the reckoning. Besides, at one or two places, the paw had grazed the snow, showing two long furrows, the marks of claws that do not sheathe: dog-marks, perhaps, but never a cat's. The marks were aligned like a cat's, but were fourteen inches apart, while it is rare for a cat to step more than ten.

They were not dog-marks: first, the probabilities were against it; second, the marks were nearly in a line, showing a chest too narrow for a dog. Then the toes did not drag, though there was four inches of snow. The register could not be distinguished, but there was one feature that settled all doubt — the big, soft, shallow marks of the fox's brush, sometimes sweeping the snow at every yard, sometimes not at all for fifty steps, and telling me with certainty, founded in part on the other things — "This is the trail of a fox."

Which way is he going? is the next question, not easy

to answer when the toe-marks do not show; but this is settled by the faint claw-marks already noted. If still in doubt, I can follow till the fox chances on some place under a thick tree or on ice where there is very little snow, and here a distinct impression may be found. I have

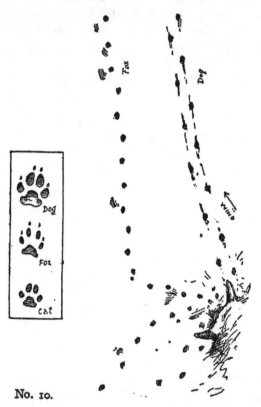

No. 10.

often seen a curiously clear track across ice made by a gentle breeze blowing away all the snow except that pressed down hard by the impact of the toes, so that the black ice under has a row of clear-cut, raised tracks, a line of fox-track cameos, cut sharp on a black-ice base.

THE FOX'S HUNT

For a mile or two I followed my fox.   Nothing happened.
I got only the thought that his life was largely made up
of nose investigation and unfavorable reports from the
committee in charge.   Then we came to a long, sloping
hollow.   The fox trotted down this, and near its lower
end he got a nose report of importance for he had swung
to the right and gone slowly — so said the short steps —
zigzagging up the wind.   Within fifteen feet, the tacks
in the course shortened from four or five feet to nothing,
and ended in a small hole in a bank.   From this the
fox had pulled out a common, harmless garter-snake,
torpid, curled up there doubtless to sleep away the winter.
The fox chopped the snake across the spine with his
powerful meat-cutters, killed it thus, dropped it on
the snow, and then, without eating a morsel of it as
far as I could see, he went on with his hunt. (Illustration 11 A.)

Why he should kill a creature that he could not eat
I could not understand.   I thought that ferocious sort of
vice was limited to man and weasels, but clearly the fox
was guilty of the human crime.

The dotted guide led me now, with many halts and
devious turns, across a great marsh that had doubtless
furnished many a fattened mouse in other days, but now
the snow and ice forbade the hunt.   On the far end the
country was open in places, with clumps of timber, and into
this, from the open marsh, had blown a great bank of
soft and drifted snow.

Manitoban winters are not noted for their smiling
geniality or profusion of outdoor flowers.   Frost and snow
are sure to come early and continue till spring.   The
thermometer may be for weeks about zero point.   It

may on occasion dip down to thirty, yes, even forty, degrees below, and whenever with that cold there also comes a gale of wind, it conjures up the awful tempest of the snow that is now of world-wide fame as—the blizzard.

No. 11. The record of the Fox's hunt.

The blizzard is a terror to wild life out on the plains. When it comes the biggest, strongest, best clad, rush for shelter. They know that to face it means death. The prairie chickens or grouse have learned the lesson long ago. What shelter can they seek? There is only one — an Eskimo shelter — a snow house. They can hide in the shelter of the snow.

As the night comes, with the fearful frost and driving clouds of white, the chickens dive into a snowdrift; not on the open plain, for there the snow is hammered hard by the wind, but on the edge of the woods, where tall grass spears or scattering twigs stick up through and keep the snow from packing. Deep in this the chickens dive, each making a place for itself. The wind wipes out all traces, levels off each hole and hides them well. There they remain till morning, warm and safe, unless — and here is the chief danger — some wild animal comes by during the night, finds them in there, and seizes them before they can escape.

This chapter of grouse history was an old story to the fox and coming near the woodland edge, his shortened steps showed that he knew it for a Land of Promise. (Illustration 11, B.)

At C he came to a sudden stop. Some wireless message on the wind had warned him of game at hand. He paused here with foot upraised. I knew it, for there was his record of the act. The little mark there was not a track, but the paw-tip's mark, showing that the fox had not set the foot down, but held it poised in a pointer-dog pose, as his nose was harkening to the tell-tale wind.

Then from C to D he went slowly, because the steps were so short, and now he paused: the promising scent was lost. He stood in doubt, so said the tell-tale snow in the only universal tongue. Then the hunter turned and slowly worked toward E, while frequent broad touches in the snow continued the guarantee that the maker of these tracks was neither docked nor spindle-tailed.

From E to F the shortened steps, with frequent

marks of pause and pose, showed how the scent was warming — how well the fox knew some good thing was near.

At F he stood still for some time with both feet set down in the snow, so it was written. Now was the critical time, and straight up the redolent wind he went, following his nose, cautiously and silently as possible, realizing that now a single heedless step might spoil the hunt.

CLOSING IN

At G were the deeply imprinted marks of both hind feet, showing where the fox sprang just at the moment when, from the spotless snowdrift just ahead, there broke out two grouse that had been slumbering below. Away they went with a whirr, whirr, fast as wing could bear them; but one was just a foot too slow; the springing fox secured him in the air. At H he landed with him on the prairie, and had a meal that is a fox's ideal in time of plenty; and now, in deep hard winter, it must have been a banquet of delight.

Now for the first time I saw the meaning of the dead garter-snake far back on the trail. Snake at no time is nice eating, and cold snake on a cold day must be a mighty cold meal. Clearly the fox thought so. He would rather take a chance of getting something better. He killed the snake; so it could not get away. It was not likely any one would steal from him that unfragrant carcass, so he would come back and get it later if he must.

But as we see, he did not have to do so. His faith and patience were amply justified. Instead of a cold, unpleasant snake, he fed on a fine hot bird.

Thus I got a long, autobiographical chapter of fox-life by simply following his tracks through the snow (see heading).

1. Tracks of old man.
2. "   " a young hunter.
3. "   " a city woman.
4. "   " dog.
5. "   " cat.

Snapping Turtle.   Brook Turtle.

I never once saw the fox himself that made it, and yet I know — and you know — it to be true as I have told it.

Deer.   Sheep.   Pig.

BOOKS AND ARTICLES RECOMMENDED

"Tracks in the Snow," By E. T. Seton, *St. Nicholas*, March, 1888, p. 338, many diagrams, etc.

"American Woodcraft," By E. T. Seton. 2 articles on tracks of animals. *Ladies' Home Journal.* May and June, 1902, many illustrations.

"The Life Histories of Northern Animals," Two large volumes by Ernest Thompson Seton, dealing with habits of animals, and give tracks of nearly all. *Scribners,* 1909.

"Tracks and Tracking," Joseph Brunner.

"The Official Handbook," Boy Scouts of America. The American News Co. 50 cents.

"Mammals of the Adirondacks," By C. Hart Merriam, M.D. Henry Holt & Co., New York City, Price $2.

XII. Mushrooms, Fungi, or Toadstools

Abundance

SUPPOSE that during the night a swarm of fairies were to enter our home woods and decorate it on ground and trunk, with the most strange and wonderful fruits, of new sorts, unheard of in shapes and colors, some like fans, with colored lacework, some like carrots, others like green and gold balloons, some like umbrellas, spring bonnets, birds' nests, barbers' poles, and Indian clubs, many like starfish and skulls, others imitating corals and others lilies, bugles, oysters, beefsteaks, and wine cups, resplendent with every color of the rainbow, delicious to eat, coming from nowhere, hanging on no plant and disappearing in a few days leaving no visible seed or remnant — we should think it very strange; we might even doubt our eyesight and call it all a pure fairy tale. Yet this very miracle is what happens every year in our land. At least 2,000 different kinds of toadstools or mushrooms spring up in their own mysterious way. Of this 2,000 at least 1,000 are good to eat. *But* — and here is the dark and dangerous fact — about a dozen of them are Amanitas, which are known to be deadly poison. And as ill-luck will have it these are the most widely diffused and the most like mushrooms. All the queer freaks, like clubs and corals, the cranks and tomfools, in droll shapes and satanic colors, the funny poisonous looking morels, ink-caps and boleti are good wholesome food but the deadly Amanitas are like ordinary mushrooms, except that they have grown a little thin, delicate and anæmic.

DANGERS

The New York papers have told of over twenty deaths this August (1911) through toadstool poisoning. The explanation possibly lies in a recorded conversation that took place between a field naturalist and a little Italian who was indiscriminatingly collecting toadstools.

"You are not going to eat those toadstools, I hope?"

"No! me no eata de toad.   My mudder she eata de toad and die; me no eata de toad; me sella de toad."

All American boys are brought up with a horror of toadstools that compares only with their horror of snakes and it is perhaps as well.   I do not want to send our boys out heedlessly to gather toadstools for the table, but I want to safeguard those who are interested by laying down one or two general rules.

This is the classification of toadstools that naturally occurs to the woodcrafter: *Which are eatable* and *Which are not*.

Those which are not fit for food, may be so, first, because *too hard* and woodlike, and, second, because *poisonous*.

The great fact that every boy should know is which are the poisonous toadstools.   Mark Twain is credited with suggesting a sure test: "*Eat them.   If you live they are good*, if you die they are *poisonous*."   This is an example of a method that can be conclusive, without being satisfactory.

What way can we suggest for general use?

First, remember that there is nothing at all in the popular idea that poisonous mushrooms turn silver black.

Next, "not one of the fungi known to be deadly gives warning by appearance or flavor of the presence of poison." (McIlvaine.)

The color of the cap proves nothing. The *color of th* *spores*, however, does tell a great deal; which is unfortunate as one cannot get a spore print in less than several hours. But it is the first step in identification; therefore the Scout should learn to make a spore print of each species he would experiment with.

To make spore prints. Cover some sheets of blue or dark gray paper with a weak solution of gum arabic — one tablespoonful of dry gum to one pint of water; let this dry. Unless you are in a hurry in which case use it at once.

Take the cap of any full-grown toadstool, place it gill side down upon the gummed paper, cover tightly with a bowl or saucer and allow to stand undisturbed for eight or ten hours. The moisture in the plant will soften the gummed surface if it is dry; the spores will be shed and will adhere to it, making a perfect, permanent print. Write the name, date, etc., on it and keep for reference. Some of the papers should be black to show up the white spored kinds.

It will be found most practical for the student to divide all mushrooms, not into two, but into three, groups.

First. A very small group of about a dozen that are *poisonous* and must be let alone.

Second. A very large group that are good *wholesome* food.

Third. Another very large group that are probably good and *worthy of trial* if it is done judiciously, but have not yet been investigated.

Scientists divide them into:

Gilled toadstools

Pore bearers

Spiny toadstools
Coral toadstools
Puffballs

All the virulently poison ones as well as the most delicious are in the first group.

The only deadly poisonous kinds are the Amanitas. Others may purge and nauseate or cause vomiting, but it is believed that every recorded death from toadstool poisoning was caused by an Amanita, and unfortunately they are not only widespread and abundant, but they are much like the ordinary table mushrooms. They have, however, one or two strong marks: Their stalk always grows out of a *"poison cup,"* which shows either as a cup or as a *bulb;* they have *white* or *yellow* gills, a ring around the stalk, and *white spores.*

First of these is the

Deathcup, Destroying Angel, Sure-Death or Deadly Amanita (*Amanita phalloides*), one and one half to five inches across the cup; three to seven inches high; pure white, green, yellowish, olive, or grayish brown; smooth, but sticky when moist; gills below; spores white; on the stem is an annulus or ring just white the cap, and the long stalk arises out of a hollow bulb or cup; usually it is solitary.

A number of forms have been described as separate, but which are considered by Professor McIlvaine as mere varieties of the *phalloides* — namely, the *Virulent Amanita* (*virosa*), shining white with a cap at first conical and acute; *Spring Amanita* (*verna*), like *virosa*, but showing a more persistent and closely sheathing remains of the wrapper at the base of the stem; *Big-veiled Amanita* (*magnivelaris*), like *verna*, but has a large persistent annulus, and the bulb

of the stem is elongated tapering downward; the *Napkin Amanitas* (*nappa*), volva circularly split; but all will be known by the four characters, poison-cup, ring, white or yellowish gills, and the form shown in the diagram — and *all are deadly poison.*

Amanita phalloides.

This wan demon of the woods is probably the deadliest of all vegetable growths. To this pale villain or its kin is traced the responsibility for all deaths on record from toadstool poisoning. There have been cases of recovery when a strong man got but a little of the poison, but any one making a meal of this fungus, when beyond reach of medical aid, has but a poor chance of escape. Its poison is a subtle alkaloid akin to rattlesnake venom, it rarely begins to show its effects, until too late for treatment, the victim is beyond human help, and slowly succumbs. For centuries its nature has been a mystery; it has defied all remedies, only lately have we begun to win a little in the fight with this insidious assassin.

There are thousands of tons of delicious food spread in our

Fly amanita.

woods and pastures every year, and allowed to go to waste because of the well-founded terror of the Deathcup. Every one should make a point of learning its looks and smashing all he can find, together with the half-formed young ones about it. We may not succeed in exterminating the pale fiend, but we can at least put that individual beyond doing mischief or giving forth seeds.

Hated Amanita (*A. spreta*). (Poisonous.) Four to six inches high, three to five inches across the cap, with a bump in the middle, whitish or pale or rich brown, gills white, a large loose yellowish poison cup; the stem tapers above the ring and at the base and is tinged reddish brown in the middle.

Fly Amanita (*A. muscaria*). (Poisonous.) About the same size; mostly yellow but ranging from orange red to almost white usually with raised white spot sor scales on the top; gills white—or tinged yellow, spores white; flesh, white.

Frost's Amanita (*A. frostiana*). (Poisonous.) This is another gorgeous demon, small but brilliant and deadly. It is two to three inches high, with the cap one to two inches broad. The cap is brilliant scarlet, orange or yellow and warty, fluted on the margin. The gills are white or tinged yellow, the spores white; the stem white or yellow and the bulb margined above with a smooth collar or ring. A woodland specimen, no doubt responsible, McIlvaine thinks, for the bad reputation of the scarlet Russula which is harmless but resembles this.

Tall Deathcup (*A. excelsa*). (Poisonous.) This tall and lonely pirate of the beech woods is about four to six inches in stature as it stands in its cup, and four to five inches across the top which is brownish gray, fleshy and sticky, often wrinkled and covered with tiny warts, edge of cap fluted; gills white; stem covered with scales on its lower parts at least.

There are about twenty more of the Amanitas, varying in size and color, but most have the general style of tall flat mushrooms, and the label marks of poison viz: *White* or *yellow gills*, a *poison cup*, and *white spores*. They are not known to be poisonous. Some of them are good eating. One of them, the

King Cap or Royal Mushroom. (*A. Caesarea*), is said to be the finest of all mushrooms. This magnificent and famous toadstool is three to eight inches across the cap which is smooth and of a gorgeous red orange or yellow color; gills yellow, though the spores are white; stem yellow; the cap is very flat when fully expanded and always is finely grooved or fluted on the upper edge. This is not only eatable but famous, yet it is so much like certain poisonous forms that it is better let alone. Indeed it is best for the beginner to accept the emphatic warning given by McIlvaine and Macadam, in their standard work "1000 American Fungi" (p. XVII):

"Any toadstool with white or lemon-yellow gills, casting white spores when laid — gills downward — upon a sheet of paper, having remnants of a fugitive skin in the shape of scabs or warts upon the upper surface of its cap, with a veil or ring, or remnants or stains of one, having at the base of its stem — in the ground — a loose, skinlike sheath surrounding it, or remnants of one," *should be considered deadly poison* till the contrary is proved by good authority. This may make you reject some wholesome kinds, but will surely keep you from danger.

If by ill chance any one has eaten a poisonous Amanita, the effects do not begin to show till sixteen or eighteen hours afterward — that is, long after the poison has passed through the stomach and begun its deadly work on the nerve centres.

Symptoms. Vomiting and purging, "the discharge from the bowels being watery with small flakes suspended, and sometimes containing blood," cramps in the extremities. The pulse is very slow and strong at first, but later weak and rapid, sometimes sweat and saliva pour out. Dizziness, faintness, and blindness, the skin clammy, cold and bluish or livid; temperature low with dreadful tetanic convulsions, and finally stupor. (McIlvaine and Macadam p. 627.)

Remedy: "Take an emetic at once, and send for a physician with instructions to bring hypodermic syringe and atropine sulphate.   The dose is $\frac{1}{180}$ of a grain, and doses should be continued heroically until $\frac{1}{20}$ of a grain is administered, or until, in the physician's opinion, a proper quantity has been injected.   Where the victim is critically ill the $\frac{1}{20}$ of a grain may be administered."   (McIlvaine and Macadam XVII.)

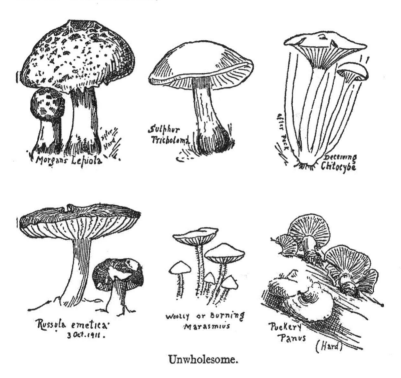

Morgans Lepiota

Sulphur Tricholoma

Deceiving Clitocybe *after Peck*

Russula emetica 3 Oct. 1911.

Woolly or Burning Marasmius

Puckery Panus (Hard)

Unwholesome.

UNWHOLESOME BUT NOT DEADLY TOADSTOOLS

There is another group that are emetic or purgative or nauseating, but not deadly.   These it is well to know.

Morgan's Lepiota (*Lepiota morgani*), six to eight inches high and five to nine or even twelve inches across the cap:

Cup, white dotted over with fragments of a brownish or yellowish skin; gills, white at first, then green; *spores, green;* flesh, white, but changing to a reddish then yellowish when cut or bruised. This immense toadstool is found in meadows all summer long, usually in rings of many individuals; it is poisonous to some and not to others, but is never deadly so far as known.

Sulphur Tricholoma (*Tricholoma suphureum*), two to four inches high: cap one to four inches apart, dingy or reddish sulphur yellow above; flesh, thick and yellow; spores, white; stem, yellow inside and out; has a bad smell and a worse taste; is considered noxious if not actively poisonous. It is the only inedible *Tricholoma* known.

Deceiving Clitocybe (*Clitocybe illudens*). This grows in clusters on rotten stumps or trees from August to October. It is everywhere of a deep yellow or orange, often it is phosphorescent. Each plant is four to six inches across the cap and five to eight inches high. It is usually nauseating and emetic.

Russula (*Russula emetica*). This is known at once by its exquisite rosy red cap, and its white gills, flesh and stalk. Sometimes the last is tinged rosy. It is a short stemmed mushroom two to four inches high; its cap pinkish when young, dark red or rosy red when older, fading to straw color in age; its gills and spores, white. Its peppery taste when raw is a fairly safe identification. In most books it is classed as "slightly poisonous," but McIlvaine maintains that it is perfectly wholesome. I know that I never yet saw one that was not more or less gnawed by the discriminating little wood folk that know a good thing when they smell it.

Woolly or Burning Marasmius (*Marasmius urens*), two to three inches high; cap two to three inches wide, pale yellowish, becoming paler; spores, white; gills, brown, paler at first; stem, woolly pungent. Poisonous to some persons but never deadly.

Puckery Panus (*Panus stipticus*). Cap one half to one inch across, cinnamon color; gills, cinnamon; spores, white; stem, under one inch long, paler than the gills; grows on stumps and in bunches: noted for its extreme acridity; said to be a purgative *poison*.

Sticky Volva (*Volvaria gloiocephelus*). Cap about three inches across; with a grayish bump in the middle, dark opaque brown and sticky and lined at the edge; stem, six or more inches high and one half an inch thick, brownish, a few fibres on outside; gills, reddish; spores, pink; volva or poison cup, downy, splitting into several unequal lobes. Said to be *poisonous*.

The Entolomas or the Fringed Entolomas. There are several of this genus that are poisonous or at least suspicious. They are of any size up to six or seven inches high and four or six inches broad, with *pink spores and gills* and *sinuate gills*.

About twenty species are described and though some are edible they are better let alone, unlike most of the unwholesome kinds their odor is agreeable.

Pie-Shaped Hebeloma. (*Hebeloma crustoliniforme*). Cap, pale tan, yellow, or brick color, a bump in middle; gills, whitish, then clay color, variable in size; spores, yellow. Smells strongly and unpleasantly of radish.

This completes the list of gilled mushrooms given as unwholesome in McIlvaine and Macadam.

White Clavaria (*Clavaria dichotoma*). Of all the coral mushrooms this is the only one known to be poisonous. It is not deadly but very unwholesome. It grows on the ground under beeches and is fortunately very rare. It is known by its white color and its branches dividing regularly by pairs.

WHOLESOME TOADSTOOLS

With all these warnings and cautions about the poisonous kinds before us, we shall now be able to approach in a
proper spirit, the subject of Toadstool eating, and consider

Oyster Mushrooms.

the second of our groups. These are the good safe Toadstools or Mushrooms — for it is the same thing.

The Common Mushroom (*Agaricus campestris*). Known.
at once by its general shape and smell, its pink or brown
gills, white flesh, brown spores and solid stem. It grows
in the open, never in the woods.

Oyster Mushroom (*Pleurotus ostreatus*). Many of us

have oyster beds in our woods without knowing it, and the oyster mushroom is a good example of valuable food going to waste. It is found growing in clusters on old dead wood, logs or standing trunks. Its cap is smooth, moist and white or tinged with ash or brown. The gills and spores are white. The flesh is white and tough. It measures two or six inches across. Sometimes it has no stem. It is a favorite for the table. It needs careful cleaning and long cooking. There is no poisonous species at all like it.

Also, belonging to the Gilled or true mushroom family, are the Ink-caps of the Genus *Coprinus*. They grow on dung piles and rich ground. They spring up over night and perish in a day. In the last stage the gills turn into a black fluid, yes, into ink. At one time this was used for ink, a quantity of the black stuff being boiled and strained for the purpose. It is still a good scout dye for roots, quills, etc. The spores of *Coprinus are black*. It is strange that such poisonous looking things should be good food. Yet all the authorities agree that the Ink-caps are safe, delicious, easily identified and easily cooked. There is no poisonous mushroom with black spores at present known in North America.

Inky Coprinus (*Coprinus atramentarius*). This is the species illustrated. The example was from the woods; often it is much more

Inky coprinus.

tall and graceful. The cap is one to three inches in diameter, grayish or grayish brown, sometimes tinged lead color.

Stew or bake from twenty to thirty minutes after thorough washing, is the recognized mode of cooking it.

Beefsteak Mushroom (*Fistulina hepatica*). This juicy red mushroom grows chiefly on the chestnut stumps. In color it varies from strawberry red to liver brown, not unlike raw meat, paler below. When wounded it bleeds.

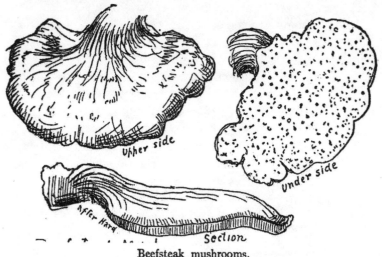

Beefsteak mushrooms.

Note that it has tubes, not gills, below. "When properly prepared it is equal to any kind of meat. It is one of our best mushrooms." (M. E. Hard.) Sometimes sliced and served raw as a salad.

All the *Clavarias* or *Coral Mushrooms* are good except *Clavaria dichotoma* which is *white*, and has its branches *divided in pairs* at each fork. It grows on the ground under beeches and is slightly poisonous and very rare.

The edible ones are of the types illustrated. They are yellow, buff or dingy brown; two to four inches high.

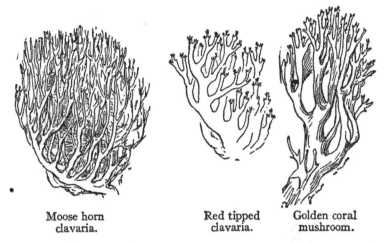

Moose horn
clavaria.

Red tipped
clavaria.

Golden coral
mushroom.

To cook Clavarias. Wash thoroughly, but do not peel. Fry or stew without salt, on a slow fire for half an hour, then add salt and other seasoning.

Morels. According to M. E. Hard the morels are easily known by their deeply pitted naked heads. All are yellowish brown when young; the stems are stout, hollow and whitish. McIlvaine & Macadam in discussing dangerous mushrooms, say: "Not one of the morels is even suspicious," except *Gyromitra esculenta*; avoid it.

To cook morels: Thoroughly wash to remove all grit from the pits and crannies, slice and stew for an hour.

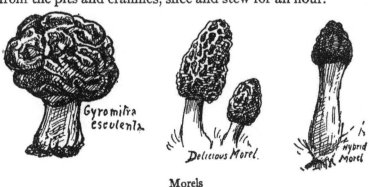

Gyromitra esculenta.

Delicious Morel.

Hybrid Morel.

Morels

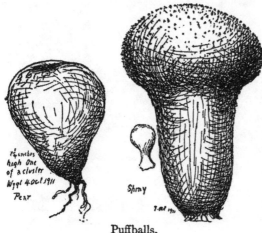

Puffballs.

Puffballs (*Ly-coperdaceae*). The next important and *safe* group are the Puffballs before they begin to puff. All our puffballs when young and *solid white inside* are good, wholesome food. Some of them, like the Brain Puffball or the *Giant Puffball*, are occasionally a foot in diameter, and yield flesh enough to feed a dozen persons. They are well known to all who live in the country, their smooth, rounded exterior without special features, except the roots, and their solid white interior are easily remembered. But one must take great care in gathering the very small ones as the poisonous toadstools in the button stage resemble small puffballs externally. However, a section shows the cap, stem, etc., of the former, whereas puffballs are solid without any obvious inner structure.

The principal kinds are these:

Pear Puffball (*Lycoperdon pyriforme*). Usually found in masses on the ground or on old timber. It is pinkish brown, and rarely over one inch in diameter.

Brain Puffball (*Calvatia craniiformis*). On the ground in woods. Pale grayish often with a reddish tinge, sometimes wrinkled on top, sometimes smooth. Commonly six to eight inches high.

Giant Puffball (*Calvatia gigantea*). Eight to twenty inches in diameter. McIlvaine found one weighing nine pounds and heard of one weighing forty. In color it is white becoming grayish, yellowish or brown. In shape nearly round with a strong root. It is found in grassy places. McIlvaine says that we can cut slices from a growing one, day after day, and, if we do not disturb the root, it keeps on neither dying nor ripening for many days.

Cuplike Puffball (*Calvatia cyathiformis*). Three to six inches in diameter, dull pinkish or ashy brown, often covered with a network of white cracks. Common on open grassy places.

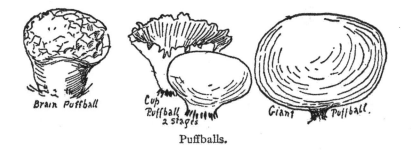

Puffballs.

To cook Puffballs: Wash clean, *peel* (other kinds are not peeled), cut out any discolored parts, slice and fry in lard or butter with seasoning.

UNCERTAIN KINDS

Now for the vast number of uncertain toadstools. Remembering always that any harmless-looking species, like a long-legged anæmic mushroom or like a pretty white parasol, is probably deadly Amanita or Sure-death, and that an odd poisonous-looking freak like a coral, a poker, a bugle, a bird's nest, a spring bonnet or an Indian club, is likely to be wholesome, we may follow the suggestions of the authors already cited (p. xxxii), as follows:

"There is but one way to determine the edibility of a species. If it looks and smells inviting, and its species cannot be determined, taste a very small piece. Do not swallow it. Note the effect on the tongue and mouth. But many species, delicious when cooked, are not inviting raw. Cook a small piece; do not season it. Taste again; if agreeable eat it (unless it is an *Amanita*). After several hours, no unpleasant effect arising, cook a larger piece, and increase the quantity until fully satisfied as to its qualities. Never vary from this system, no matter how much tempted. No possible danger can arise from adhering firmly to it."

Safety lies in the strict observance of two rules:

"Never eat a toadstool found in the woods or shady places, believing it to be the common mushroom: Never eat a white — or yellow-gilled toadstool in the same belief. The common mushroom does not grow in the woods, and its gills are at first pink, then purplish brown, or black."

Also there are many mushrooms of the Genus Boletus that are like ordinary mushrooms of various pale and bright colors, but instead of gills they have *tubes underneath*. Some are eatable, some are dangerous. Avoid all that change color as being wounded or that have red-mouthed tubes or that taste peppery or acrid.

"There is no general rule by which one may know an edible species from a poisonous species. One must learn to know each kind by its appearance, and the edibility of each kind by experiment," says Nina L. Marshall in the "Mushroom Book" (page 151), and gives the following:

CAUTIONS FOR THE INEXPERIENCED

Never use specimens which are decomposed in the slightest degree.

Never use those which are at all burrowed by insects.

Never collect for food mushrooms in the button stage, as it is difficult for a novice to distinguish the buttons of poisonous species from buttons of harmless species.

Never use fungi with swollen bases surrounded by saclike or scaly envelopes.

Never use fungi with milky juice or any juice unless it is the reddish.

Never use fungi with caps thin in proportion to the width of the gills when the gills are nearly all of equal length, especially if the caps are bright colored.

Never use for food tube-bearing fungi in which the flesh changes color when cut or broken, nor those with the tubes reddish. Be very cautious with all fleshy tube-bearing fungi.

Never use for food fungi with web-like ring around the upper part of the stem.

MUSHROOM GROWING

Mushroom growing is a good way to make some money, provided one has a cellar or roothouse at one's disposal. To learn how, send to the United States Department of Agriculture, for *Farmers' Bulletin, No. 204*, "The Cultivation of Mushrooms."

BOOKS RECOMMENDED

The following are standard and beautifully illustrated works on mushrooms and toadstools; they have been freely used for guidance and illustrations in the preparation of the above:

"Edible and Poisonous Fungi of New York," by Charles H. Peck. Published by New York State Museum, Albany, 1895.

"Edible Fungi of New York." by Charles H. Peck. Published by New York State Museum, Albany, 1900.

"The Mushroom Book." by Nina L. Marshall. Published 1902 at New York by Doubleday, Page & Co. $3.50.

"One Thousand American Fungi," by McIlvaine & Macadam. $5. Published by the Bobbs-Merrill Company of Indianapolis, 1902; add 40 cents express.

"Mushrooms," by G. F. Atkinson. Holt & Co.

"The Mushroom," by M. E. Hard. The Ohio Library Company. Columbus, Ohio.

XIII. Forestry

One Hundred of the Best Known Native Timber Trees of Northeastern America

(That is, North America east of Long. 100° west, and north of North Lat. 36°)

ALL the common forest trees of the region defined are given herein. I have, however, omitted a few rare stragglers on the South and West and certain trees that are big in the Gulf States but mere shrubs with us.

Remember when using this list as a key, that you will not often find a leaf exactly like the one in the book; look rather for an illustration of the same *general character* as the one in your hand; place your leaf with the one *most nearly* like it. Avoid the leaves of stump-sprouts and saplings; they are rarely typical; and especially get the fruit when possible; *"the tree is known by its fruit."* In some cases nothing but the fruit can settle what your species is.

In each (with five exceptions) the fruit is given of exact natural size. The exceptions are the Osage Orange or Bodarc, the Mountain Magnolia, Red-bud, Honey Locust, and Kentucky Coffee-tree, all of which are given in half size.

In giving the weight of each kind of timber it is assumed to be dry and seasoned. All of our woods are lighter than water when seasoned: but many of them sink when green. The heaviest of our list is Yellow Oak, 54 lbs. per cubic foot; the lightest is Northern Cedar, 20 lbs. A cubic foot of water weighs 63 lbs., and for further interesting comparison, a cubic foot of iron weighs 470 lbs., lead 718 lbs., gold 1228 lbs., and platinum, 1323 lbs.

I. PINACEÆ — CONIFERS OR PINE FAMILY

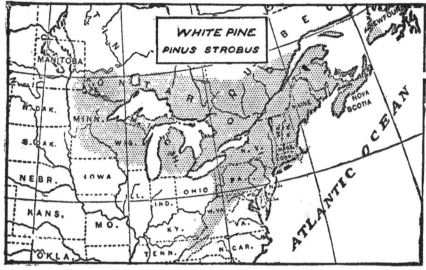

WHITE PINE, WEYMOUTH PINE. (*Pinus Strobus*)

A noble evergreen tree, up to 175 feet high. The lumberman's prize. Its leaves are in bunches of 5, and are 3 to 5 inches long; cones 4 to 8 inches long. Wood pale, soft, straight-grained, easily split. Warps and checks less than any other of our timbers. A cubic foot weighs 24 lbs.

Pine knots are hard masses of rosin, they practically never rot; long after the parent log is reduced to dust by the weather, the knots con-

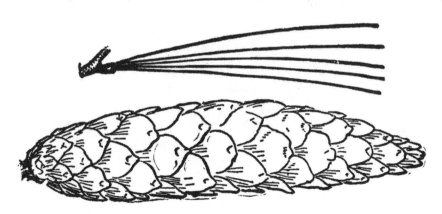

tinue hard and sound. They burn freely with hot flame and much smoke and are the certain fuel for a fire in all weathers. In a less degree the same remarks apply to the larger roots.

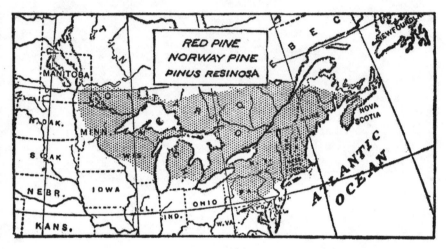

RED PINE, CANADIAN PINE, NORWAY PINE. (*Pinus resinosa*)

Evergreen; somewhat less than the White Pine, with leaves 4 to 6 inches long, in bunches of 2, cones 1½ to 2½ inches long. Wood darker, harder, and heavier. A cubic foot weighs 30 lbs.

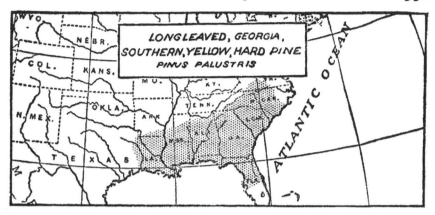

LONG-LEAVED PINE, GEORGIA PINE, SOUTHERN PINE, YELLOW PINE, HARD PINE. (*Pinus palustris*)

A fine tree, up to 100 feet high; evergreen; found in great forests in the Southern States; it supplies much of our lumber now; and most of our turpentine, tar and rosin. Wood strong and hard, a cubic foot weighs 44 lbs. Its leaves are 10 to 16 inches long, and are in bunches of 3's; cones, 6 to 10 inches long.

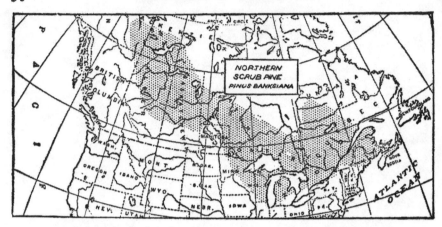

JACK-PINE, BANKSIAN PINE, GRAY PINE, LABRADOR PINE, HUDSON
BAY PINE, NORTHERN SCRUB PINE. (*Pinus Banksiana*)

Evergreen; 40 to 60 feet high; rarely 100. Leaves in bunches of
2, and 1 to 2½ inches long; cone, 1 to 2 inches long. Dr. Robt. Bell
of Ottawa says its seeds germinate better when the cone has been
scorched. Wood, soft, weak. A cubic foot weighs 27 lbs.

In 1907 on Great Slave River, N. latitude 60, we cut down a Jack-pine

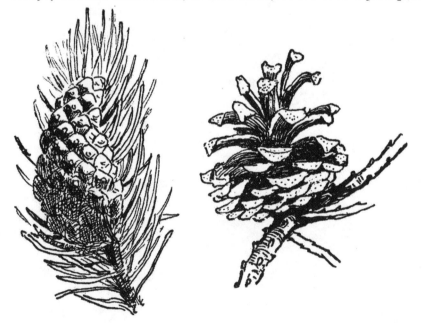

12 feet high, it was one inch thick and had 23 rings at the bottom.
Six feet up it had 12 rings and 20 whorls — in all it appeared to have
43 whorls, of these 20 were on the lower part. This tree grew up in a
dense thicket under great difficulties and was of very slow growth, the
disagreement between rings and whorls was puzzling.

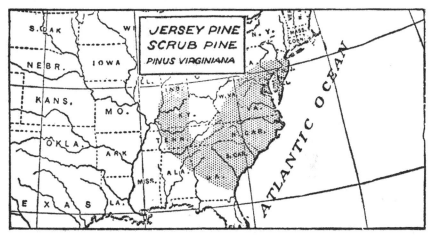

JERSEY PINE, SCRUB PINE. (*Pinus virginiana,*)

Usually a small tree. Leaves 1½ to 2 inches long and in bunches
of 2's; cones 1½ to 2½ inches long. Wood soft, weak, light orange;
a cubic foot weighs 33 lbs. In sandy soil.

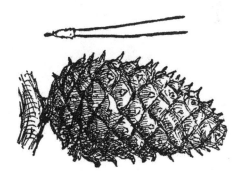

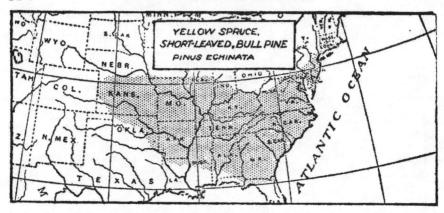

YELLOW PINE, SPRUCE PINE, SHORT-LEAVED PINE, BULL PINE. (*Pinus echinata*)

A forest tree, up to 100 feet high. Leaves 3 to 5 inches long, and in bunches of 2's or 3's; cones about 2 inches long. Wood heavy, strong, orange; a cubic foot weighs 38 lbs. Valuable timber.

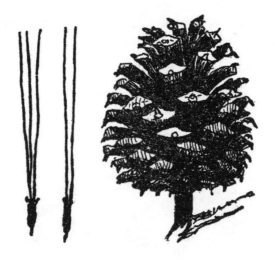

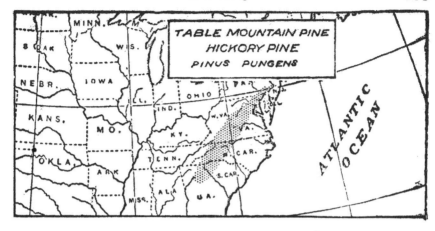

TABLE MOUNTAIN PINE, HICKORY PINE. (*Pinus pungens*)

A small tree, rarely 60 feet; leaves $2\frac{1}{2}$ inches long; mostly in bunches of 2's or sometimes 3's; cones $3\frac{1}{2}$ to 5 inches long. In the mountains New Jersey to North Carolina. Wood, weak, soft, brittle, a cubic foot weighs 31 lbs.

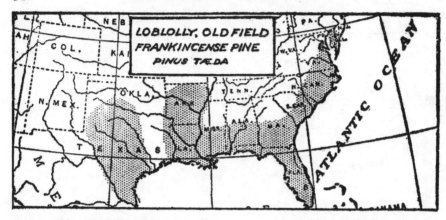

LOBLOLLY, OLD FIELD PINE, FRANKINCENSE PINE. (*Pinus Tæda*)

A fine forest tree, up to 150 feet. Leaves 6 to 10 inches long, and in bunches of 3's, rarely 2's; cones 3 to 5 inches long. Wood, weak, brittle, coarse, light brown, a cubic foot weighs 34 lbs.

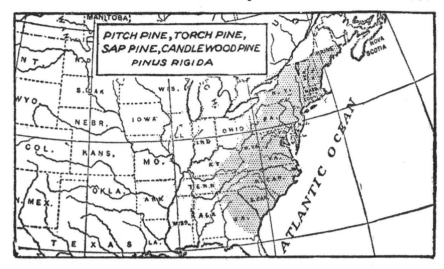

PITCH PINE, TORCH PINE, SAP PINE, CANDLEWOOD PINE.   (*Pinus rigida*)

A small tree, rarely 75 feet high; evergreen; leaves 3 to 5 inches long and in clusters of 3, rarely 4; cones 1½ to 3 inches long.   So charged with resin as to make a good torch.   Remarkable for producing shoots from stumps.   Wood, soft, brittle, coarse-grained, and light.   A cubic foot weighs 32 lbs.   "It is the only pine that can send forth shoots after injury by fire."   (*Keeler*).   The pine of the "pine-barrens" of Long Island and New Jersey.

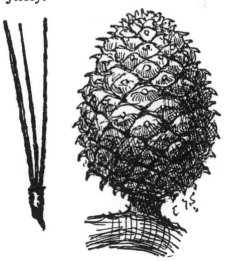

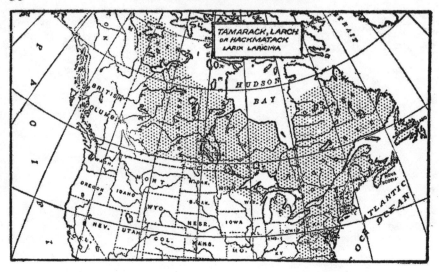

Tamarack, Larch or Hackmatack. (*Larix laricina*)

A tall, straight, tree of the northern swamps yet often found flourishing on dry hillsides.   One of the few conifers that shed all their leaves each fall.   Leaves $\frac{1}{2}$ to 1 inch long; cones $\frac{1}{2}$ to $\frac{3}{4}$ inch.   Wood very resinous heavy and hard, "a hard, soft wood" very durable as posts, in Manitoba I have seen tamarack fence posts unchanged after twenty years' wear. It is excellent for firewood, and makes good sticks for a rubbing stick fire.   A cubic foot weighs 39 lbs.   Found north nearly to the limit of trees; south to northern New Jersey and Minnesota.

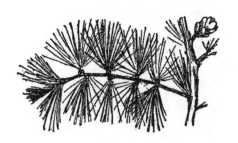

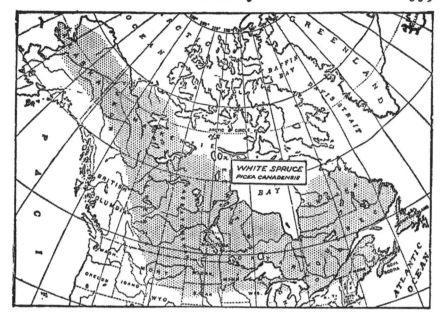

WHITE SPRUCE. (*Picea canadensis*)

Evergreen; 6c to 70 or even 150 feet high. Leaves ½ to ¾ inch long; cones 1½ to 2 inches long, are at the tips of the branches and deciduous; the twigs smooth. Wood white, light, soft, weak, straight-grained, not durable; a cubic foot weighs 25 lbs. Its roots afford the *wattap* or cordage for canoe-building and camp use generally.

Spruce roots to be used as "*wattap*" for lacing a canoe, making birch-bark vessels or woven baskets, may be dug up at any time and kept till needed.

An hour before using, soak in hot water till quite soft. They should be cleared of the bark and scrubbed smooth. *Beautiful and strong baskets* may be made of this material. It may be colored by soaking in dyes made as follows:

Red by squeezing the juice out of berries, especially *blitum* or squaw-berries.

Dull red by soaking in strong tea made from the pink middle bark of hemlock.

Black can be boiled out of smooth red sumac or out of butternut bark.

Yellow by boiling the inner bark of black oak or the root of gold seal or hydrastis.

Orange by boiling the inner bark of alder, of sassafras or of the yellow oak.

Scarlet by first dyeing yellow, then dipping in red.

Nearly every tree bark, root bark and fruit has a peculiar dye of its own which may be brought out by boiling, and intensified with vinegar, salt, alum, iron or uric salts. Experiments usually produce surprises.

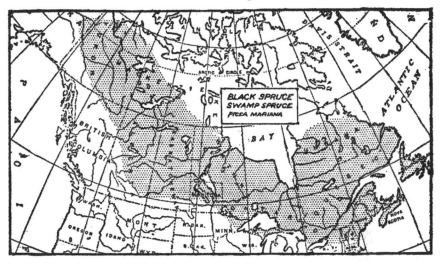

BLACK SPRUCE. (*Picea Mariana*)

Evergreen. Somewhat smaller than the preceding, rarely 90 feet high, with small rounded cones 1 to 1¼ inches long; they are found near the trunk and do not fall off; edges of scales more or less indented. In their September freshness the cones of Black Spruce are like small purple plums and those of White Spruce like small red bananas; twigs, stout and downy; wood and roots similar to those of White Spruce. Leaves about ½ inch long with rounded tops.

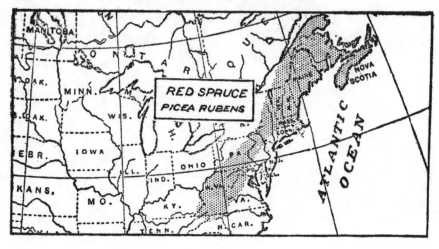

RED SPRUCE.   (*Picea rubens*)

Evergreen.   Much like the Black Spruce but with larger, longer
cones about $1\frac{1}{2}$ inch long and red when young, they are half way between
tip and trunk on the twigs; edges of scales smooth and unbroken; twigs
slender, leaves sharp pointed.   Roots as in White Spruce, but wood
redder and weigh 28 lbs.   An eastern tree.   In many ways half way
between the White and Black Spruces.

HEMLOCK. (*Tsuga canadensis*)

Evergreen; 60 to 70 feet high; occasionally 100; wood pale, soft, coarse, splintery, not durable. A cubic foot weighs 26 lbs. Bark full of tannin. Leaves ½ to ¾ inch long; cones about the same. Its knots are so hard that they quickly turn the edge of an axe or gap it as a stone might; these are probably the hardest vegetable growth in our woods. It is a tree of very slow growth — growing inches while the White Pine is putting forth feet. Its topmost twig usually points easterly. Its inner bark is a powerful astringent. A tea of the twigs and leaves is a famous woodman's sweater.

"As it bears pruning to almost any degree without suffering injury, it is well suited to form screeens for the protection of more tender trees and plants, or for concealing disagreeable objects.

"But the most important use to which this bark is applied, and for which it is imported from Maine, is as a substitute for oak bark in the preparation of leather. It contains a great quantity of tannin, combined with a coloring matter which gives a red color to the leather apt to be communicated to articles kept long in contact with it." (*Emerson.*)

There is another species in the South (*T. Caroliniana*) distinguishable by its much larger cones.

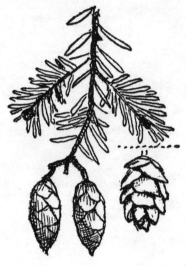

Twig and cones of Hemlock (life size)

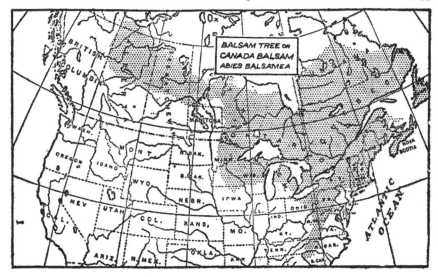

BALSAM TREE OR CANADA BALSAM. (*Abies balsamea*)

Evergreen; famous for the blisters on its trunk, yielding Canada Balsam which makes a woodman's plaster for cuts or a waterproof cement; and for the exquisite odor of its boughs, which also supply the woodmen's ideal bed. Its *flat* leafage is distinctive. Wood pale, weak, soft, perishable. A cubic foot weighs 24 lbs. The name "balsam" was given

because its gum was long considered a sovereign remedy for wounds, inside and out. It is still used as a healing salve. In the southern Alleghanies is a kindred species (*A. fraseri*) distinguished by silvery underside of leaves, and smaller rounder cones.

The Conifers illustrate better than others of our trees tne process and plan of growth. Thus a seedling pine has a tassel or two at the top of a slender shoot, next year it has a second shoot from the whorl that finished last year. So each year there is a shoot and a whorl corresponding exactly with its vigor that season, until the tree is so tall that the lower whorls die, and their knots are overlaid by fresh layers of timber. The timber grows smoothly over them, but they are there just the same, and any one carefully splitting open one of these old forest patriarchs, can count on the spinal column the years of its growth, and learn in a measure how it fared each season.

In working this out I once cut down and examined a tall Balsam in the Bitterroot Mountains of Idaho. It was 84 feet high, had 52 annual rings; and at 32 inches from the ground, that is, clear of the root bulge, it was 15 inches in diameter.

The most growth was on the N.E. side of the stump — 9 in.
" next " " " " E. " " " " — 8½ in.
" " " " " " S. " " " " — 8 in.
" " " " " " N. " " " " — 6½ in.
" " " " " " W. " " " " — 6½ in.
" least " " " " N.W. " " " " — 6 in.

There were 50 well-marked whorls and 20 not well marked; there were altogether 70 whorls, but 20 were secondary. The most vigorous growth on the tree trunk corresponded exactly with the thickest ring of wood on the stump. Thus annual ring No. 33 on the stump counting from the centre coincided with an annual shoot of more than 2 feet length, which would be that of the wet season of 1883. Some of the annual shoots were but 6 inches long and had correspondingly thin rings. There was, of course, one less ring above each whorl or joint.

Similar studies made on Jack Pine and Yellow Pine gave similar results.

On hardwood trees especially those of alternate foliage one cannot so study them except when very young.

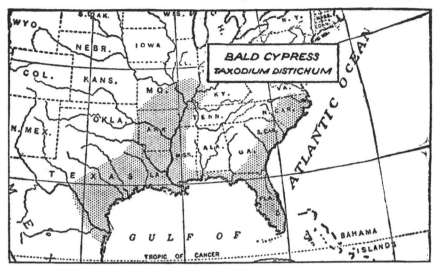

BALD CYPRESS. (*Taxodium distichum*)

A fine forest tree, up to 150 feet, with thin leaves somewhat like those
of Hemlock, half an inch to an inch long; cones rounded about an inch
through.   Sheds its leaves each fall so is "bald" in winter, noted for
the knees or upbent roots that it develops when growing in water.
Timber soft, weak, but durable and valuable; a cubic foot weighs
27 lbs.   In low wet country.

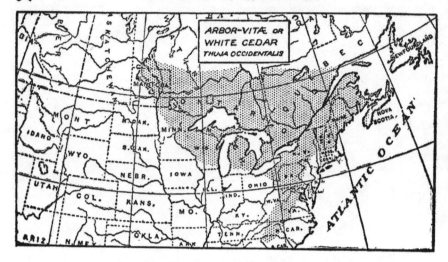

ARBOR-VITÆ OR WHITE CEDAR. (*Thuja occidentalis*)

Evergreen, 50 or 60 feet high. Wood soft, brittle, coarse grained, extremely durable as posts; fragrant and very light (the lightest on our list). Makes good sticks for rubbing stick fire. A cubic foot weighs only 20 lbs. The scale-like leaves are about 6 or 8 to the inch; the cone half an inch long or less. There is a kindred species (*Chamaecyparis thyoides*) of more southern distribution. It has much smaller cones and leaves.

The Northern or White Cedar is noted for the dense thickets it forms in the hollows and hillsides of the eastern Canadian region. These banks, like evergreen hedges, are so close that they greatly modify the winter climate within their bounds — outside there may be a raging blizzard that no creature can face, while within all is dead calm and the frost less intense. The Cedar feeds its protegés too, for its evergreen boughs and abundant nuts are nutrient food despite their rosin smell and taste. Never do the deer and hares winter better than in cedar cover, and if there is great thicket in their region, they surely gather there as sparrows at a barn, or as rats around a brewery.

Enlarged leaves
Twigs and cones of Northern Arbor-vitæ

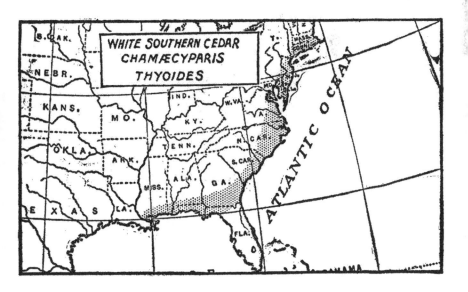

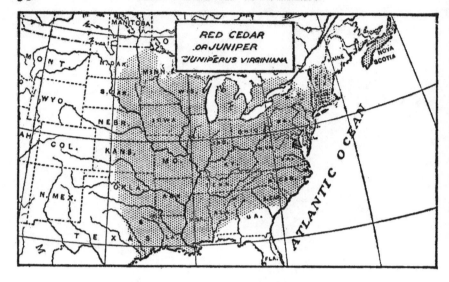

RED CEDAR OR JUNIPER.   (*Juniperus Virginiana*)

Evergreen. Any height up to 100 feet. Wood, heart a beautiful bright red; sap wood nearly white; soft, weak, but extremely durable as posts, etc. Makes good sticks for rubbing stick fire. The tiny scale-like leaves are 3 to 6 to the inch; the berry-like cones are light blue and a quarter of an inch in diameter.

The berries of the European species are used for flavoring gin, which word is an abbreviation of Juniper.

"The medicinal properties of both are the same (Savin, of Europe) a decoction of the leaves having a stimulating effect, when used internally in cases of rheumatism and serving to continue the discharge from blisters, when used in the composition of cerate for that purpose." (*Emerson.*)

A cubic foot weighs 31 lbs.

Red Cedar showing fruit and two styles of twigs (life size)
on the same tree

2. SALICACEÆ—THE WILLOW FAMILY

The Willows are a large and difficult group. Britton and Brown enumerate 34 species in the limits of northeastern America, and 160 on the globe, of which 80 are found in this continent. Of the 34, 9 only attain the dignity of trees. These are Ward's Willow, Peach-leaved Willow, Shining Willow, Weeping Willow, Purple Willow, Missouri Willow and the three herein described.

Of the shrubs, two only have a special interest in woodcraft, the Pussy-Willow, because of its spring bloom, and the Fish-Net or Withy Willow.

Since the fruits of the Willows are born of catkins and are exceedingly small and difficult of study, they are not figured.

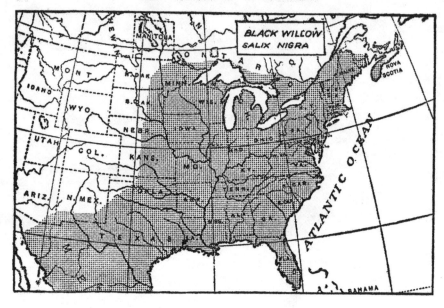

BLACK WILLOW. (*Salix nigra*)

The common Willow of stream-banks, usually 20 to 40 feet high, sometimes 100. Bark nearly black. Its long, narrow, yellow-green shining leaves are sufficiently distinctive. A decoction of Willow bark and root is said to be the best known substitute for quinine. Noted for early leafing and late shedding; leaves 3 to 6 inches long. Wood pale, weak, soft, close-grained; a cubic foot weighs 28 lbs.

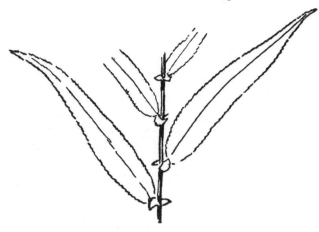

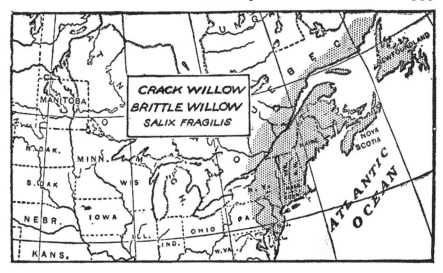

CRACK WILLOW, BRITTLE WILLOW. (*Salix fragilis*)

A tall slender tree, up to 80 feet high.   Called "Crack" etc., because its branches are so much broken by the storms; too brittle for basket work, but a favorite for charcoal used in manufacture of gunpowder, etc. Its leaves, 4 to 7 inches long, are very distinctive. This is a European species but now thoroughly naturalized in the Northeastern States.

As a rough general rule the shape of the perfect tree is closely fashioned on that of the perfect leaf, for obviously they are the same material impelled by similar laws of growth, but we have two notable exceptions in the Lombardy Poplar and the common Willow.   To conform to the rule these two leaves should change places.

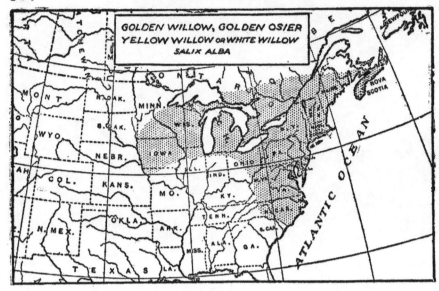

GOLDEN WILLOW, GOLDEN OSIER, YELLOW WILLOW OR WHITE WILLOW
(Salix alba)

This is a tall tree, up to 90 feet high. Leaves 2 to 4½ inches long. It is the well known willow of dams; conspicuous in spring for the mass of golden rods it presents. It comes near being evergreen as it leafs so early and sheds so late, that it is bare of leaves for less than four months. Noted for its wonderful vitality and quickness of growth. Any living branch of it stuck in the ground soon becomes a tree. On the dam at Wyndygoul are large Willows, one of them 61 inches in circumference a foot from the ground though they were mere switches when planted eight years ago. A native of Europe, now widely naturalized in the Northeastern States and southern Canada.

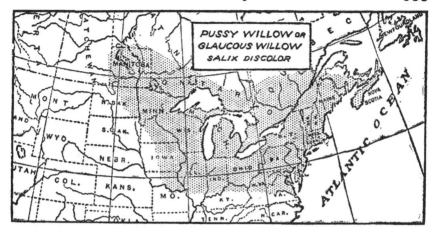

PUSSY WILLOW OR GLAUCOUS WILLOW
SALIX DISCOLOR

PUSSY WILLOW OR GLAUCOUS WILLOW. (*Salix discolor*)

Usually a shrub, occasionally a tree, up to 25 feet high. Noted for its soft round catkins an inch long and two thirds of an inch thick, that appear in early spring before the leaves. The name Pussy is given either on account of these Catkins (little cats) or from the French "Poussé" budded.

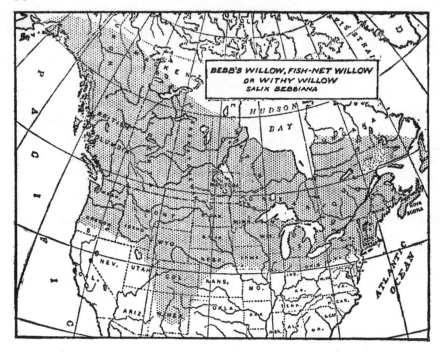

FISH-NET WILLOW OR WITHY WILLOW, BEBB'S WILLOW. (*Salix Bebbiana*)

This is a low thick bush or rarely a tree 20 feet high. It abounds near water, which seems a natural fitness, for its inner bark supplies the best native material for fish lines and fish nets in the North. It is called Withy Willow because its tough, pliant stems are used by farmers for withies or coarse cordage, especially for binding fence rails and stakes; though soft and pliant when put on they soon turn to horny hardness and last for years. Arctic to British Columbia north to Mackenzie River south to Pennsylvania and Utah.

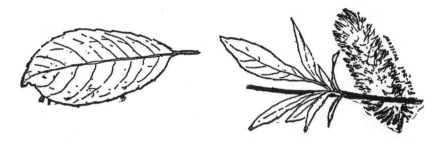

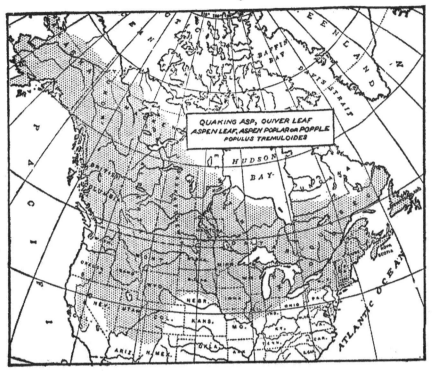

QUAKING ASP, QUIVER LEAF, ASPEN POPLAR OR POPPLE. (*Populus tremuloides*)

A small forest tree, but occasionally 100 feet high. Readily known by its smooth bark, of a light green or whitish color. The wood is pale, soft, close-grained, weak, perishable, and light. A cubic foot weighs 25 lbs. Good only for paper pulp, but burns well, when seasoned. When green it is so heavy and soggy that it lasts for days as a fire check or back-log. Leaves 1½ to 2 inches long. A tea of the bark is a good substitute for quinine, as tonic, cold cure, bowel cure and fever driver.

"Pieces of wood 2⅝ inches square, were buried to the depth of one inch in the ground, and decayed in the following order: Lime, American Birch, Alder and Aspen, in three years; Willow, Horse-Chestnut and Plane, in four years; Maple, Red Beech and Birch, in five years; Elm, Ash, Hornbeam and Lombardy Poplar in seven years; Robinia, Oak, Scotch Fir, Weymouth Pine, Silver Fir, were decayed to the depth of half an inch in seven years; while Larch, common Juniper, Virginia Juniper and Arbor-vitæ, were uninjured at the end of that time." *Balfour's Manual of Botany, 1855. P. 45.*

Quaking Asp

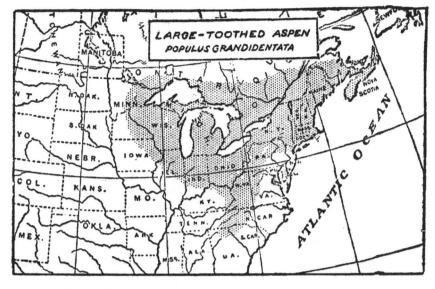

LARGE-TOOTHED ASPEN. (*Populus grandidentata*)

A forest tree, occasionally 75 feet high. Bark darker and rougher than preceding; readily distinguished by saw-toothed leaves. Wood much the same, but weighs 29 lbs. Leaves 3 to 4 inches long.

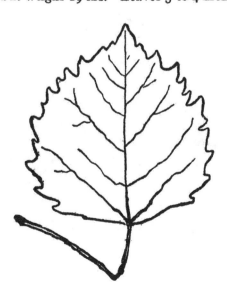

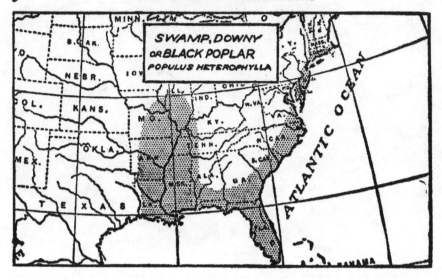

SWAMP, DOWNY OR BLACK POPLAR. (*Populus heterophylla*)

A good-sized forest tree; up to 80 feet high. A tree of cottonwood style; the young foliage excessively downy. Wood soft, weak. A cubic foot weighs 26 lbs. Leaves 5 to 6 inches long.

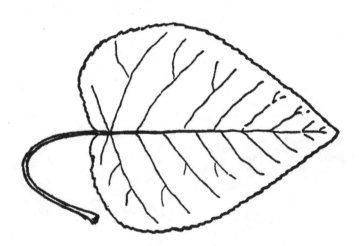

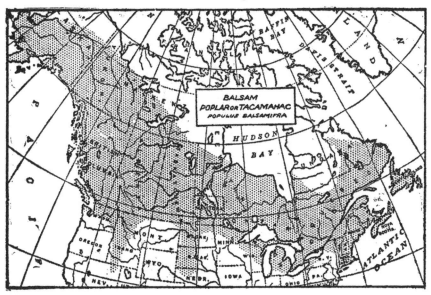

BALSAM POPLAR, BALM OF GILEAD, OR TACAMAHAC. (*Populus balsami-fera*)

Fifty or 60 feet ordinarily, but sometimes 100 feet high. Bark rough and furrowed. The great size of the buds and their thick shiny coat of fragrant gum are strong marks. Wood much as in the preceding, but weighs 23 lbs. Leaves 3 to 6 inches long. There is a narrow-leafed form called *angustifolia*.

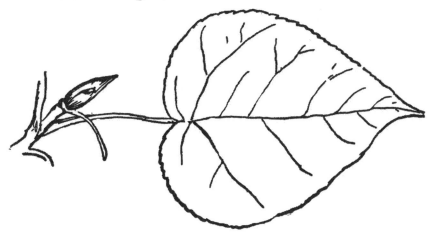

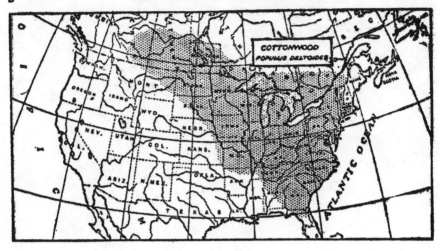

COTTONWOOD.   (*Populus deltoides*)

Small and rare in the northeast.   Abundant and large in west; even 150 feet high.   Wood as in other poplars but weighs 24 lbs.   Leaves 3 to 5 inches long.   These and most of the poplars have the leaf stalks flattened laterally so that the slightest puff of wind vibrates the leaf, this with its shiny surface clears it of dust and enables it to live in dry places where different leaves would be stifled.

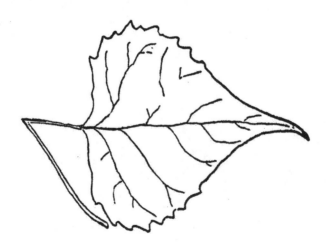

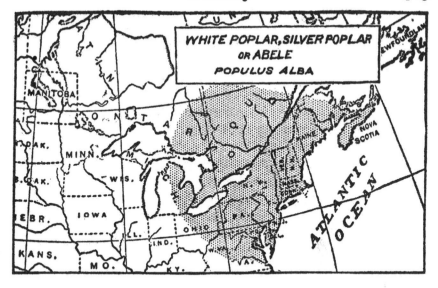

WHITE POPLAR, SILVER POPLAR OR ABELE. (*Populus alba*)

This is a species introduced from Europe. It is a tall forest tree; up to 120 feet. The dark glossy surface of the upper and the dense white velvet of the under side of leaves are strong features. Its wood is soft white and weighs 38 lbs. per cubic foot. Leaves 2½ to 4 inches long. Generally distributed in Northeastern States.

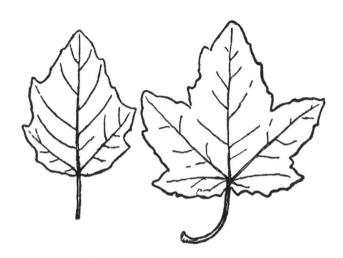

LOMBARDY POPLAR.   (*Populus dilatata*)

Introduced from Europe. Its tall form is a familiar feature of the civilized landscape in Eastern America.

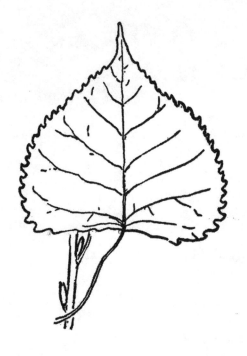

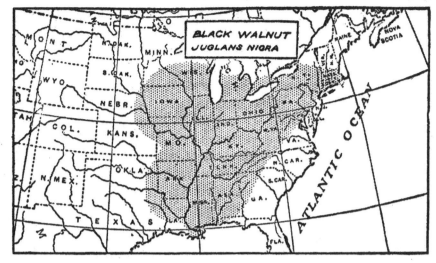

3. JUGLANDACEÆ OR WALNUT FAMILY

BLACK WALNUT. (*Juglans nigra*)

A magnificent forest tree up to 150 feet high, usually much smaller in the east. Wood, a dark purplish brown or gray; hard, close-grained; strong; very desirable in weather or ground work, and heavy. A cubic foot weighs 38 lbs. Leaflets 13 to 23; and 3 to 5 inches long. Fruit nearly round, 1½ to 3 inches in diameter.

 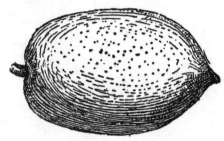

Fruit of Black Walnut   Fruit of Butternut

Both life size

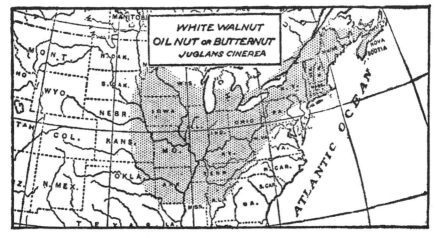

WHITE WALNUT, OIL NUT OR BUTTERNUT. (*Juglans cinerea*)

Much smaller than the last, rarely 100 feet high; with much smoother bark and larger, coarser, compound leaves, of fewer leaflets but the petioles or leaflet stalks and the new twigs are covered with sticky down.

"The bark and the nut are also used to give a brown color to wool. The Shakers at Lebanon dye a rich purple with it. Bancroft says that the husks of the shells of the Butternut and Black Walnut, may be employed in dyeing a fawn color, even without mordants. By means of them, however, greater brightness and durability are given to the color. The bark of the trunk gives a black, and that of the root a fawn color, but less powerful. From the sap an inferior sugar has been obtained. The leaves, which abound in acrid matter, have been used in the form of powder as a substitute for Spanish Flies." (*Emerson.*)

A decoction of the inner bark, preferably of the root, is a safe mild purge, a teaspoonful of it as dark as molasses is a dose.

The wood is light-brown, soft, coarse, not strong but very enduring in weather and ground work; light; leaves 15 to 30 inches long; leaflets 11 to 19 in number and 3 to 5 inches long; fruit oblong 2 to 3 inches long.

KEY TO THE HICKORIES OF NORTH AMERICA

SHAGBARKS

Bark hanging loose in broad plates; leaflets 5 to 7, broad; nut, ridged and sweet, (1) Common Shagbark.

Bark hanging loose in long narrow strips; leaflets 7 to 9; twigs, orange; foliage, downy; nut, much larger, (2) Big Shagbark.

Bark hanging loose in long narrow strips; leaflets 5 to 7; much like No. 1, but nuts not ridged, (3) Small fruited Shagbark.

RIDGED OR NET BARKS

Leaflets 11 to 15, very broad; nut smooth and without angles (4) Pecan.

Leaflets 7 to 9, very narrow, willow-like; nut smooth and without angles, (5) Bitternut.

Leaflets 9 to 13, very narrow, willow-like, top one very thin; nut with angles, (6) Water Hickory.

Leaflets 7 to 9, broad terminal bud $\frac{1}{2}$ to $\frac{3}{4}$ inches long; nut with angles, (7) Mockernut.

Leaflets 3 to 7, very broad terminal bud $\frac{1}{4}$ to $\frac{1}{2}$ inch long; nut with little or no angles, (8) Pignut.

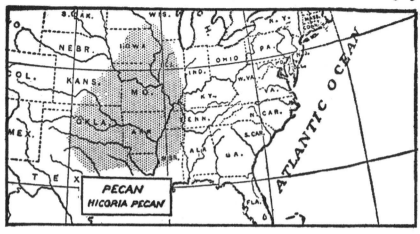

PECAN. (*Hicoria Pecan*)

A tall slender forest tree in low moist soil along streams, up to 170 feet in height: famous for its delicious nuts, they are smooth and thin shelled; fruit, oblong, cylindrical, 1½ to 2½ inches long. Its leaves are smooth when mature: leaflets 11 to 15, and 4 to 7 inches long: Wood hard and brittle, a cubic foot weighs 45 lbs.

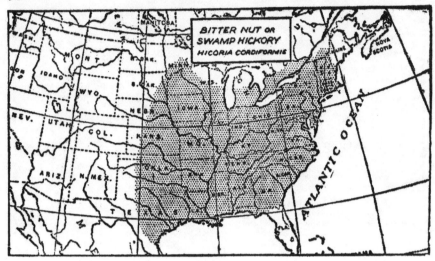

BITTERNUT OR SWAMP HICKORY. (*Hicoria cordiformis*)

A tall slender forest tree of low woods, up to 100 feet high; chiefly in Mississippi valley. Known by its small willow-like leaves; (7 to 9 leaflets); its close rough bark; its ridged fruit, and bitter kernel. Its leaves are 6 to 10 inches long, its leaflets 2 to 4 inches long. Wood, brownish, very hard, close-grained, tough, strong, and heavy; a cubic foot weighs 47 lbs. Excellent firewood.

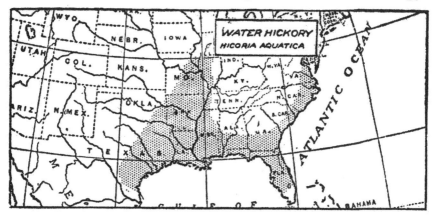

WATER HICKORY. (*Hicoria aquatica*)

A tall tree of southern swamps, up to 100 feet high; leaflets 9 to 13, 3 to 5 inches long, lance shaped, or the terminal one oblong; much like the Bitternut, but fruit longer and leaflets more numerous. Wood, soft, a cubic foot weighs 46 lbs. Virginia to Illinois, south to Texas and Florida.

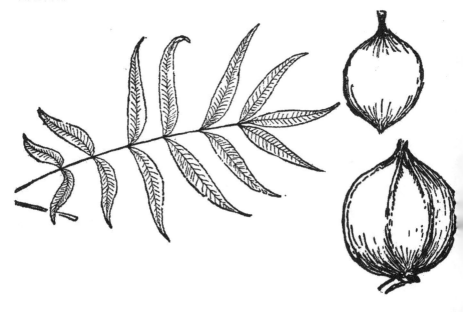

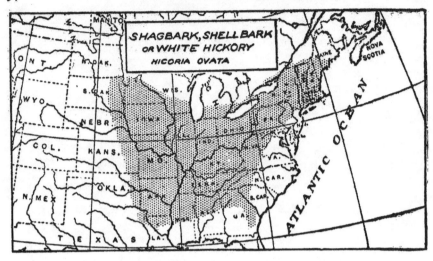

SHAGBARK, SHELLBARK OR WHITE HICKORY. (*Hicoria ovata*)

A tall forest tree up to 120 feet high. Known at once by the great angular slabs of bark hanging partly detached from its main trunk, forced off by the growth of wood, but too tough to fall. Its leaves are 8 to 14 inches long, with 5 to 7 broad leaflets. The wood is very light in color, close-grained, tough and elastic. It makes an excellent bow; is the best of fuel. A cubic foot weighs 52 lbs., so that it is the

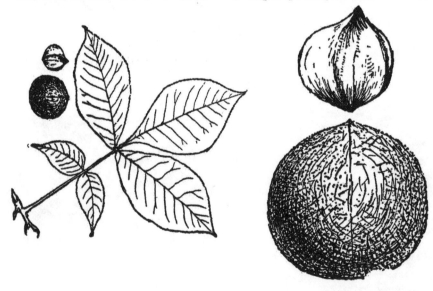

heaviest of the woods in this list except Post Oak, which is the same weight, and Yellow Oak, which is 2 lbs. heavier. It is the favorite for fork-handles and articles requiring strength and spring, but is useless for weather or ground work. Its nuts are the choicest of their kind. It is a tree of many excellencies.

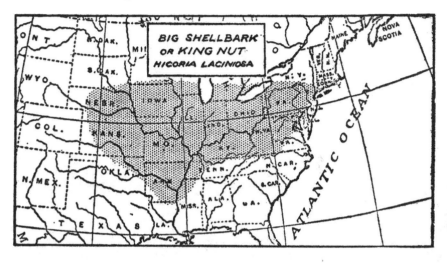

THE BIG SHELL-BARK OR KING-NUT. (*Hicoria laciniosa*)

Ranges from Central New York south and westerly. It is much like the Shagbark but known by its downy young foliage and orange twigs; its leaflets 7 to 9, rarely 5 and very large, fruit 2 to 3 inches long and oblong, while in Shagbark they are $1\frac{1}{4}$ to $2\frac{1}{4}$ inches long and rounded. Wood 50 lbs. to cubic foot. In rich soil.

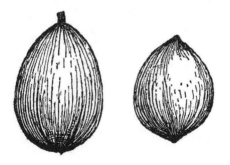

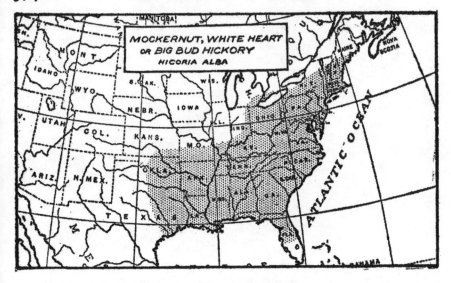

MOCKERNUT, WHITE HEART OR BIG-BUD HICKORY. (*Hicoria alba*)

A tall forest tree, up to 100 feet. Wood much like that of Shagbark, but not quite so heavy (51 lbs.). Its bark is smooth and furrowed like that of the Pignut. Its leaves like those of the Shagbark, but it has 7 to 9 leaflets, instead of 5 to 7; it has a large terminal bud $\frac{1}{2}$ to $\frac{3}{4}$ of an inch long, and the leaves have a resinous smell. Its nut in the husk is nearly 2 inches long; the nut shell is 4-ridged toward the point, has a very thick shell and small sweet kernel.

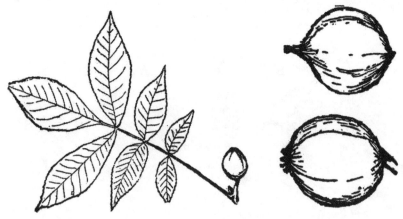

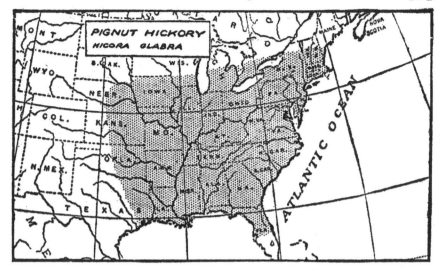

PIGNUT HICKORY. (*Hicoria glabra*)

A tall forest tree; 100 and up to 120 feet high. Wood much as in the Mockernut; bark smooth and furrowed; not loose plates. Leaves 8 to 12 inches long. Nut slightly or not at all angular, very thick shelled; the pear shape of fruit is a strong feature, 1¼ to 2 inches long.

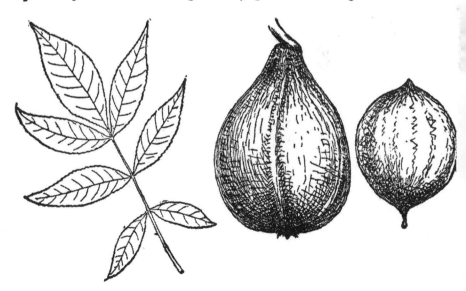

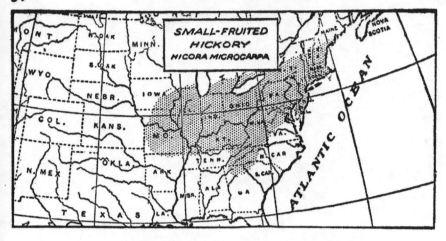

SMALL-FRUITED HICKORY. (*Hicoria microcarpa*)

A small forest tree up to 90 feet high; considered by some variety of the Pignut; leaves 4 to 7 inches long; it has a small nut *free from angles*; otherwise much like Pignut.

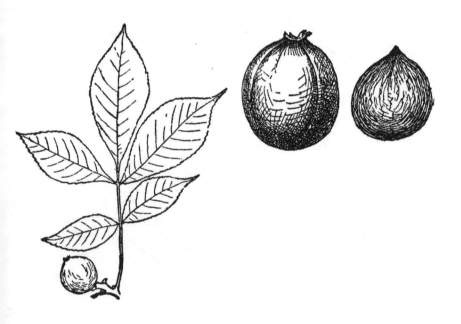

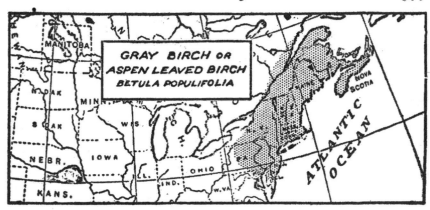

4. BETULACEÆ — BIRCH FAMILY

GRAY BIRCH OR ASPEN-LEAVED BIRCH. (*Betula populifolia*)

A small tree found on dry and poor soil; rarely 50 feet high. Wood soft, close-grained, not strong, splits in drying, useless for weather or ground work. A cubic foot weighs 36 lbs. Leaves 2 to 3 inches long. It has a black triangular scar at each armpit.

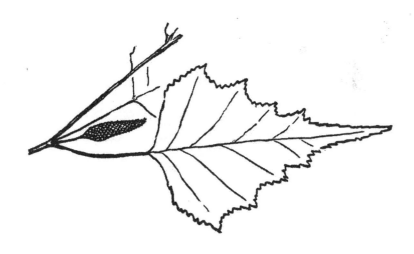

WHITE, CANOE OR PAPER BIRCH.   (*Betula papyrifera*)

A tall forest tree up to 80 feet high; the source of bark for canoes, etc. One of the most important trees in the northern forest.   Besides canoes, wigwams, vessels and paper from its bark, it furnishes syrup from its sap and the inner bark is used as an emergency food.   Every novice rediscovers for himself that the outer bark is highly inflammable as well as waterproof, and ideal for fire-lighting.   Though so much like the Gray birch, it is larger, whiter, and without the ugly black scars at each limb.   The timber is much the same, but this weighs 37 lbs.   Its leaf and catkin distinguish it; the former are 2 to 3 inches long.

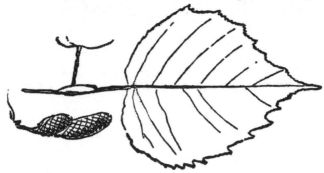

The woodman's fire in *Two Little Savages* was made thus:

> "First a curl of birch bark as dry as it can be,
> Next some sticks of soft wood dead but on the tree;
> Last of all, some pine knots to make the kittle foam,
> An' thar's a fire to make ye think yer sittin' right at home."

This is the noblest of the Birches, the white queen of the woods — the source of food, drink, transport and lodging to those who dwell in the forest; the most bountiful provider of all the trees.

Its sap yields a delicious syrup which has in it a healing balm for the lungs.

Its innermost bark is dried in famine time and powdered to a flour that has some nourishing power.

Its wood furnishes the rims for snowshoes, the frills and fuzzes of its outer bark are the best of fire kindlers, and the timber of the trunk has the rare property of burning whether green or dry.

Its catkins and buds form a favorite food of the partridge which is the choicest of game.

But the outer bark-skin, the famous birch bark, is its finest contribution to man's needs.

The broad sheets of this vegetable rawhide ripped off when the weather is warm and especially when the sap is moving — are tough, light, strong, pliant, absolutely waterproof, almost imperishable in the weather; free from insects, assailable only by fire. It roofs the settler's shack and the forest Indian wigwam, it is the "tin" of the woods and supplies pails, pots, pans, cups, spoons, boxes — under its protecting power the matches are safe and dry, and split very thin, as is easily done, it is the writing paper of the woods, flat, light, smooth, waterproof, tinted and scented; no daughter of the King has ever a more exquisite sheet to sanctify the thoughts committed to its care.

But the crowning glory of the Birch is this — it furnishes the indispensable substance for the bark canoe, whose making is the highest industrial exploit of the Indian life. It would be hard to imagine anything more beautifully made, of and for the life of the Northern woods, buildable, reparable, and usable from the Atlantic to the Pacific, in all the vast region of temperate America — the canoe whose father was the Red mind and whose mother was the birch, is one of the priceless gifts of America to the world. We may use man-made fabrics for the skin, we may substitute unlovely foreign substance for the ribs, or dangerous copper nails for the binding of spruce roots — but the original shape, the lines, the structural ribs, the lipper-turning prow, the roller-riding stern and the forward propulsion of the ever personal paddle, the buoyancy, the wonderful lightness for overland transport, the reparableness by woodland stuffs — these are the things first born of the birch canoe and for these it will be remembered and treasured until man's need of travel on the little waters has reached its final end.

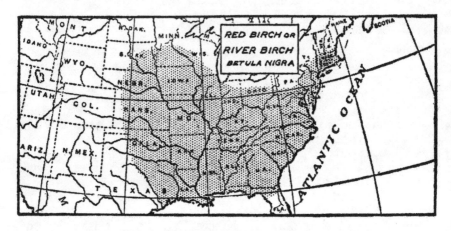

RED BIRCH OR RIVER BIRCH. (*Betula nigra*)

A tall forest tree of wet banks; up to 90 feet high. Known by its red-brown scaly bark, of birch-bark style, and its red twigs. Its wood is light-colored, strong, close-grained, light. A cubic foot weighs 36 lbs. Leaves 1½ to 3 inches long.

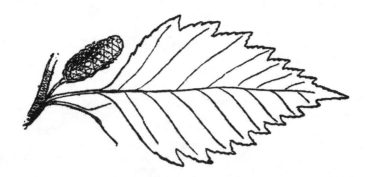

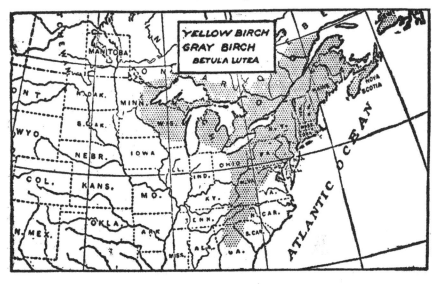

YELLOW BIRCH, GRAY BIRCH. (*Betula lutea*)

A forest tree, of 30 to 50 feet height. Bark obviously birch, but shaggy and gray or dull yellow. Wood as in the others, but reddish. A cubic foot weighs 41 lbs. Leaves 3 to 4 inches long.

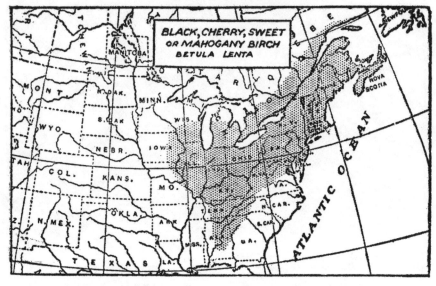

BLACK, CHERRY, SWEET OR MAHOGANY BIRCH.   (*Betula lenta*)

The largest of the birches; a great tree, in Northern forests, up to 80 feet high.   The bark is little birchy, rather like that of cherry, very dark, and aromatic.   Wood dark, hard, clear-grained, very strong; used much for imitating mahogany.   A cubic foot weighs 47 lbs.   Noted for its sweet, aromatic twigs which made into tea are a fine tonic.

"A decoction of the bark with copperas, is used for coloring woolen a beautiful and permanent drab, bordering on wine color."   (*Emerson.*)

Leaves 2½ to 6 inches long.   An oil in the bark is very good for sprains and rheumatism.

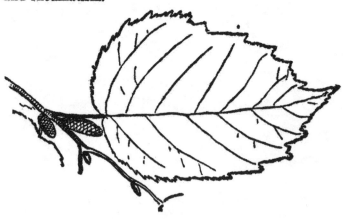

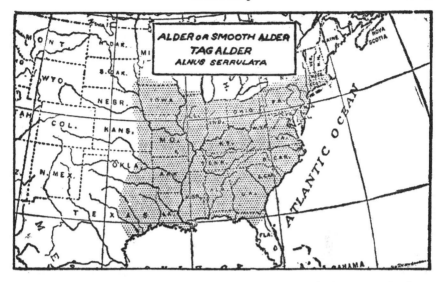

ALDER OR SMOOTH ALDER, TAG ALDER. (*Alnus serrulata*)

This is the bush so well known in thickets along the Northern streams. It is usually under 20 feet in height, but sometimes reaches 40. Its wood is soft, light brown and useless, a cubic foot weighs 29 lbs. Leaves 3 to 5 inches long. Its inner bark yields a rich orange dye. A tea made of the leaves is a valuable tonic and skin wash for pimples. In wet places or on hillsides.

Besides *serrulata* there are four alders in our limits, the Mountain Alder (*A. alnobetula*) with downy twigs, smooth leaves broad but pointed,

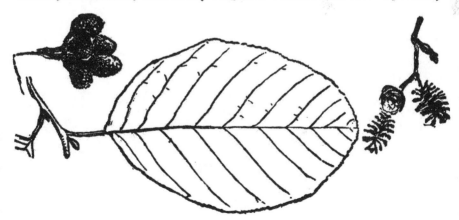

nut with wings; the Speckled Alder (*A. incana*) leaves downy beneath; the European Alder (*A. glutinosa*) with broad, rounded double-toothed leaves; (this often becomes a tall tree) and the Seaside Alder (*A. maritima*) known by its long narrow leaves.

IRONWOOD, HARD-HACK, LEVERWOOD, BEETLE-WOOD OR HOP HORN-BEAM. (*Ostrya Virginiana*)

A small tree; 20 to 30, rarely 50 feet high; named for its hardness and its hop-like fruit. Bark, furrowed. Wood, tough close-grained, unsplittable. One of the strongest, heaviest and hardest of timbers. A cubic foot weighs over 51 lbs. That is, it comes near to Shagbark Hickory in weight and perhaps goes beyond it in strength and hardness. Leaves 3 to 5 inches long. Fruit 1½ to 2½ inches long.

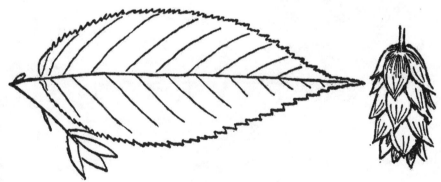

Forestry   385

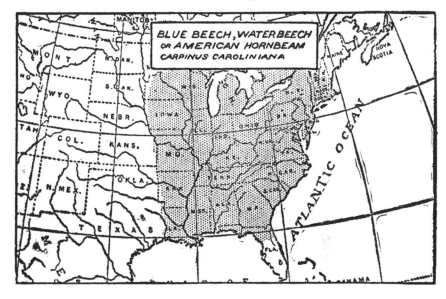

BLUE BEECH, WATER BEECH OR AMERICAN HORNBEAM. (*Carpinus caroliniana*)

A small tree, 10 to 25 feet, rarely 40 feet high; bark, smooth. Wood hard close-grained, very strong; much like Ironwood, but lighter. A cubic foot weighs 45 lbs. Leaves 3 to 4 inches long.

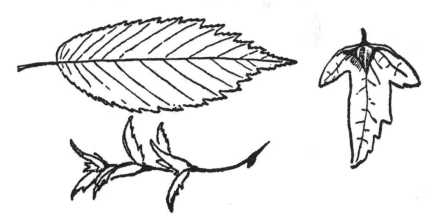

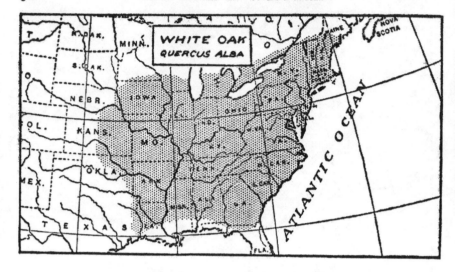

5. FAGACEÆ — BEECH FAMILY

WHITE OAK. (*Quercus alba*)

A grand forest tree; over 100 feet up to 150 feet high. The finest and most valuable of our oaks. The one perfect timber for shipbuilders, farmers and house furnishers. Its wood is pale, strong, tough, fine-grained, durable and heavy. A cubic foot weighs 46 lbs. I found that when green it weighed 68 lbs. to the cubic foot and of course sank in water like a stone. Called white from pale color of bark and wood. Leaves 5 to 9 inches long. Many of them hang all winter though dead so the White Oak contributes a little to the golden glow of the snowy woods, though not to the extent of the Black Oak. Its acorns ripen in one season. They are sweet and nutritious and eagerly sought after by every creature in the woods from bluejays, wild ducks, mice and deer to squirrels and schoolboys.

There can be little doubt that at least three out of five nut trees were planted by squirrels, chiefly the gray squirrel. All through autumn before snow falls the industrial Bannertail Gray works to bury for future use the choicest nuts he finds on the ground; ignoring the coarse and bitter, he makes sure of the sweet and delicate. Those that are not so disposed of, are usually eaten by deer, bears and other wild things. The various oaks have long competed for the squirrels' attention to their product. The Bur Oak acorn attracted by its size, Chestnut Oak by its split-ability and the White Oak by the sweetness. For a time the White

Oak fared well, for it furnished indeed the most delectable of our nuts, but now it is in an evil case. Largely through the growing scarceness of the gray squirrel the White Oak, the most valuable of its group, is no longer planted throughout its range. Its edibility is now a menace to its life, for it lies exposed and all things eagerly devour it while the other acorns lie untouched and we are now threatened with the extermination of this our noblest oak, the one that chiefly gave value to our hardwood forests, partly at least I believe through the near-extinction of the gray squirrel, its unwitting protector. The connection between these two creatures is so intimate that their ranges coincide exactly throughout the length and breadth of the land.

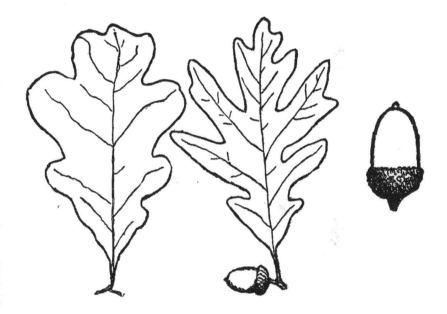

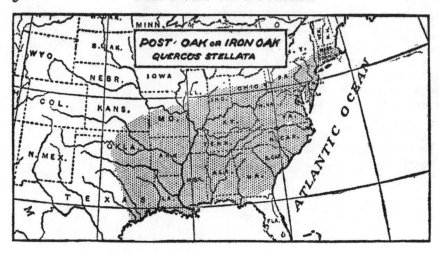

POST OAK, OR IRON OAK. *(Quercus stellata)*

A smaller tree, rarely 100 feet high; of very hard wood, durable; used for posts, etc. A cubic foot weighs 52 lbs.; that is, the same as Shagbark Hickory. Leaves 5 to 8 inches long. Acorns ripen in one season.

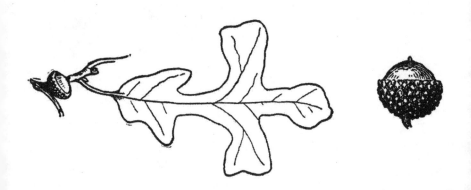

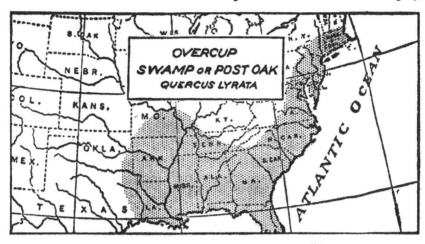

OVERCUP, SWAMP OR POST OAK. (*Quercus lyrata*)

A large tree up to 100 feet high. Wood very strong and durable; a cubic foot weighs 52 lbs. Noted for the cup covering the acorn. Leaves 6 to 8 inches long.

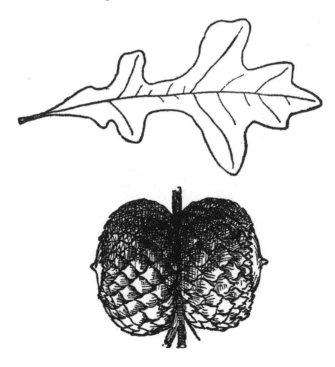

BUR OAK, CORK BARK OR MOSSY CUP. (*Quercus macrocarpa*)

A large forest tree, up to 160 feet high; known by its enormous acorns and the *corky ridges* on the twigs.   The cork of commerce is the bark of an oak found in Spain and it's not surprising to find a cork bark in our own land.   The leaves though greatly varied are alike in having two deep bays one on each side near the middle dividing the leaf nearly to the midrib so that the type is as given below; they are 4 to 8 inches long. The acorns ripen in one season.   The wood is like that of most oaks, and lasts well next the ground.   A cubic foot weighs 46 lbs.

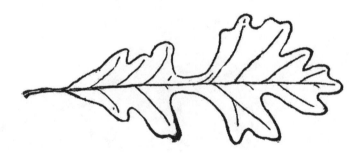

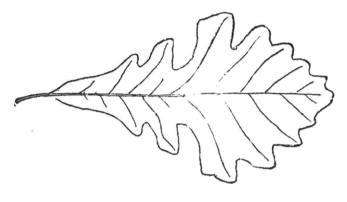

Leaf and acorn of Bur Oak
(acorn life size)

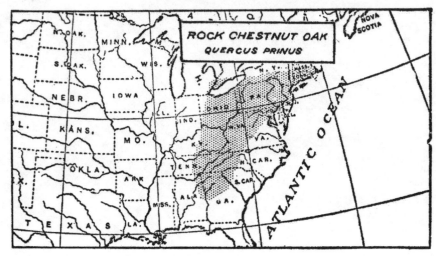

ROCK CHESTNUT OAK.   (*Quercus prinus*)

A good sized tree; up to 100 feet high.   Wood as usual.   A cubic foot weighs 47 lbs.   Its acorns are immense, 1¼ to 1½ inches long, and ripen in one season.   Leaves 5 to 10 inches long.

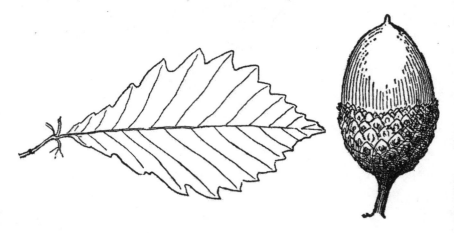

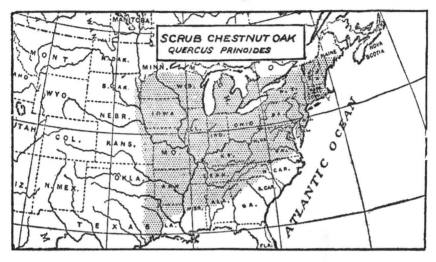

SCRUB CHESTNUT OAK.   (*Quercus prinoides*)

A mere shrub, 2 to 15 feet high.   Close akin to the preceding.
Leaves 2½ to 5 inches long.   Found in dry sandy and poor soil.

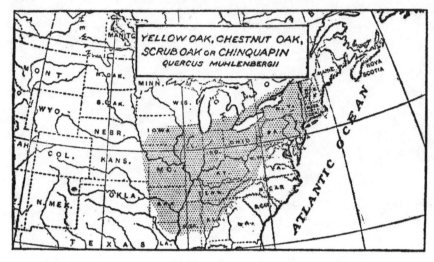

YELLOW OAK, CHESTNUT OAK OR CHINQUAPIN SCRUB OAK.
(*Quercus Muhlenbergii*)

A great forest tree; up to 160 feet high; wood as usual, but the heaviest of all, when dry; a cubic foot weighs 54 lbs; when green, it is heavier than water, and sinks at once. It is much like the true Chestnut Oak but its leaves are narrower, more sharply saw-edged and its acorns much smaller, about half the size. Its acorns ripen in one season. Leaves 4 to 6 inches long.

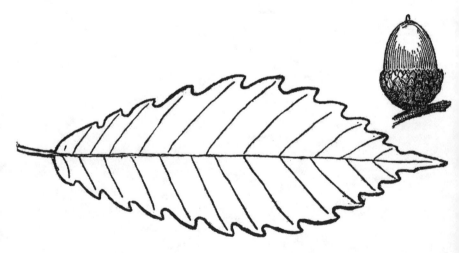

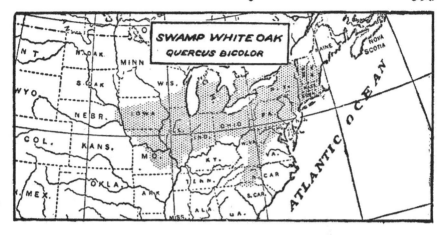

SWAMP WHITE OAK.   (*Quercus bicolor*)

A fine forest tree in swampy land; up to 110 feet high.   Wood as in preceding species, but a cubic foot weighs only 48 lbs.   It has the leaf of a White Oak, the bark of a Black.   Its smaller branches have the bark rough and loose giving a shaggy appearance to the tree.   Its acorns ripen in one season and as in all the annual fruiting oaks its wood is durable next the ground.

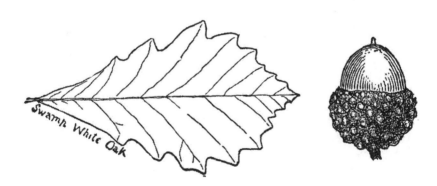

RED OAK.   (*Quercus rubra*)

A fine forest tree, 70 to 80, or even 140, feet high. Wood reddish-brown. Sapwood darker. Hard, strong, coarse-grained, heavy. A cubic foot weighs 41 lbs. It checks, warps and does not stand for weather or ground work. The acorn takes two seasons to ripen. Apparently all those oaks whose nuts take *two* seasons to ripen have wood that soon rots. The low flat shape of the cup is distinctive; in fact it has no cup, it has a saucer; leaves 4 to 8 inches long.

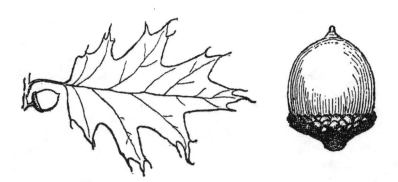

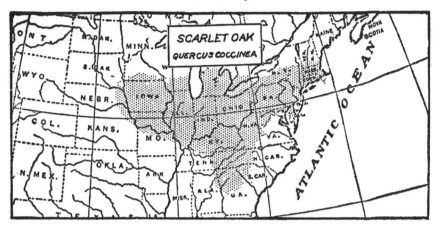

SCARLET OAK. (*Quercus coccinea*)

Seventy to 80 or even 160 feet high. Scarlet from its spring and autumn foliage color. The leaves are a little like those of the Black Oak, but are frond-like with three or four deep, nearly even, cuts on each side: The acorns of this can be easily matched among those of the Black Oak, but the kernel of the Scarlet is white, that of the Black is yellow; they take two seasons to ripen. Wood much as in Red Oak but weighs 46 lbs. per cubic foot. Leaves 4 to 8 inches long.

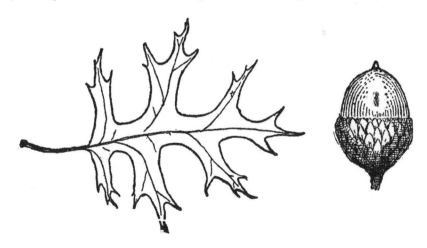

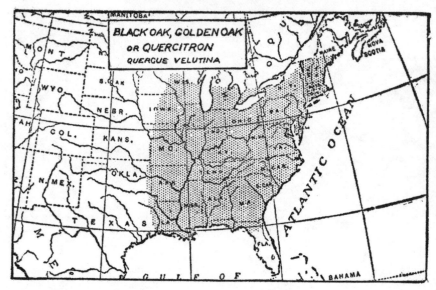

BLACK OAK, GOLDEN OAK OR QUERCITRON. (*Quercus velutina*)

Seventy to 80 or even 150 feet high. The outer bark is very rough, bumpy and blackish; inner bark yellow. This yields a yellow dye called *quercitron*. The leaf is of the Scarlet Oak style, but has uneven cuts and usually a large solid area in the outer half. The wood is hard, coarse-grained, checks, and does not stand for weather or ground work. A cubic foot weighs 44 lbs. The acorns take two seasons to ripen. Taking the White Oak acorn as a standard of white, that is a yellowish-white, the acorn of the present when cut open is a distinct golden yellow. As in all oaks the leaves vary greatly, look for the

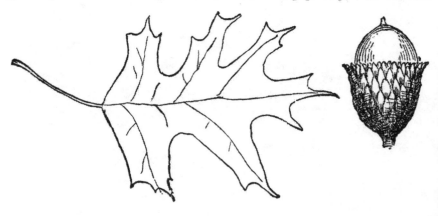

type not the exact portrait among the illustrations; they are 4 to 6 inches long.

One of the wonderful things about this oak is the persistence of its leaves. Though dead and faded they cling in numbers to the tree all winter; their exquisite old gold is one of the artist's joys and the glory of the winter landscape. This with its bright yellow inner bark, its bright yellow nut and its yellow brown winter foliage amply entitle it to be called "golden oak."

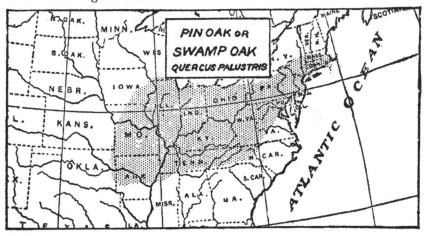

PIN OAK OR SWAMP OAK. (*Quercus palustris*)

Fifty to 70 or even 120 feet high, in swampy land. Wood hard, coarse-grained, very strong and tough; the Pin Oak is more happily named than most of its kin, first the numerous short straight branches in the lower trunk, make it seem stuck full of large pins, next, each point of its leaves has a pin on it, in each armpit of the midrib below is a tiny velvet pin cushion and finally and chiefly this exceptionally tough wood

was the best available for making the pins in frame barns. In Wyndy-goul Park I cut a Pin Oak that was 110 feet high and 32 inches across the stump and yet had but 76 rings of annual growth. Will not stand exposure next to ground. A cubic foot weighs 34 lbs. Its acorns take two seasons to ripen. Leaves 4 to 6 inches long. In moist woods and along swamp edges.

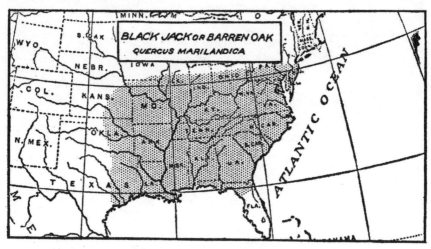

BLACK JACK OR BARREN OAK. (*Quercus marilandica*)

A small tree seldom up to 60 feet high. An unimportant tree of barren wastes. Leaves 3 to 5 lobed downy below, bristle-tipped and 3 to 7 inches long; acorns take two seasons to ripen. Wood hard and dark, not durable. A cubic foot weighs 46 lbs.

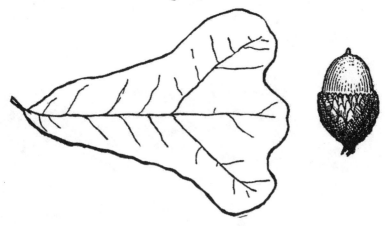

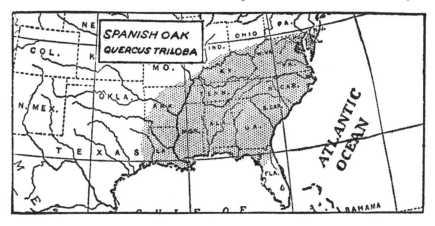

SPANISH OAK. (*Quercus triloba*)

A large tree up to 100 feet occasionally. Found on dry soil. Leaves bristle-tipped, 5 to 7 inches long, with 3 to 7 lobes. The acorns do not ripen till the second year so we may expect the wood to be undurable. A cubic foot of it weighs 43 lbs.

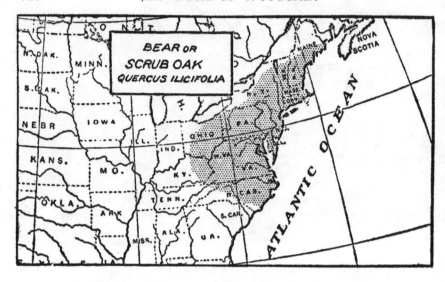

BEAR OR SCRUB OAK. (*Quercus ilicifolia*)

An insignificant tree rarely 25 feet high. Often forming dense thickets, on poor sandy or rocky soil. The leaves are bristle-tipped, 2 to 5 inches long. The acorns ripen in the second season and are so bitter that nobody cares who gets them. The bears were least squeamish so were welcome to the crop hence one of the names.

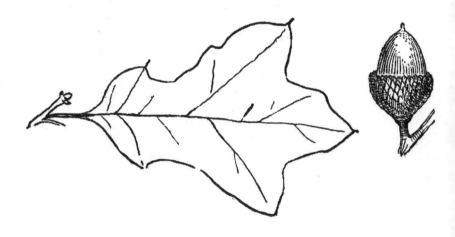

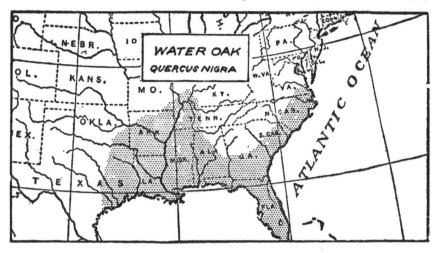

WATER OAK. (*Quercus nigra*)

A middle-sized tree, rarely 80 feet high, found chiefly along streams and swamps.   Leaves 1½ to 3 inches long; 1 to 3 lobed at the end. Wood hard and strong, a cubic foot weighs 45 lbs.   The acorns ripen in the second season so look out for its timber.   This leaf has tufts of hair in the armpits of the veins beneath.

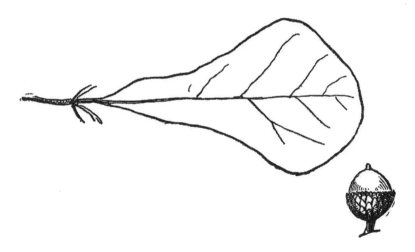

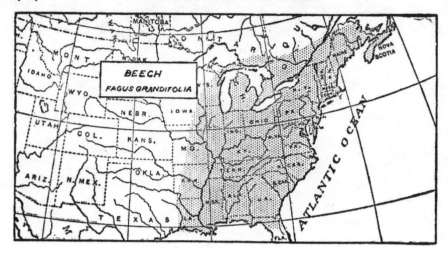

BEECH. (*Fagus grandifolia*)

In all North America there is but one species of beech. It is a noble forest tree, 70 to 80, and occasionally 120 feet high; readily distinguished by its unfurrowed ashy gray bark. Wood hard, strong, tough, close-grained, pale, heavy. Leaves 3 to 4 inches long. A cubic foot weighs 43 lbs. It shares with Hickory and Sugar Maple the honor of being a perfect firewood.

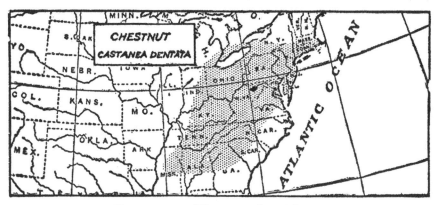

CHESTNUT. (*Castanea dentata*)

A noble tree, 60 to 80 or even 100 feet high. Whenever you see something kept under lock and key, bars and bolts, guarded and double guarded, you may be sure it is very precious, greatly coveted — the nut of this tree is hung high aloft, wrapped in a silk wrapper which is enclosed in a case of sole leather, which again is packed in a mass of shock-absorbing vermin-proof pulp, sealed up in a waterproof iron-wood safe and finally cased in a vegetable porcupine of spines, almost impregnable.

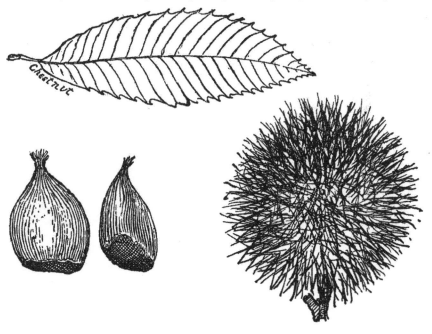

There is no other nut so protected; there is no nut in our woods to compare with it as food. Wood, brown, soft, easily worked, coarse, too easily split, very durable as posts or other exposed work, altogether a most valuable timber, the present plague that threatens to wipe it out is a fungus probably from abroad. There is no known remedy. A cubic foot of the wood weighs 28 lbs. Leaves 6 to 8 inches long.

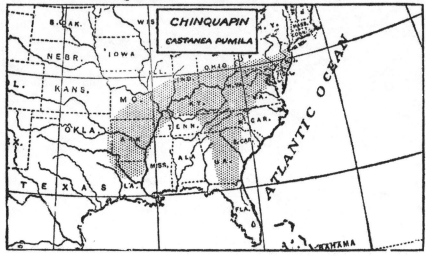

CHINQUAPIN. (*Castanea pumila*)

A small tree, rarely 45 feet high, with the general character of the common Chestnut. It is much smaller in all ways. Its leaves are 3

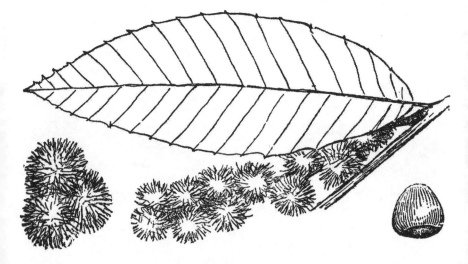

to 6 inches long; its burs less than half the size of *dentata*. Its wood is similar but darker and heavier, a cubic foot weighing 37 lbs. These two complete the list of chestnuts native to the Northeastern States.

WHITE ELM
WATER OR SWAMP ELM
ULMUS AMERICANA

6. ULMACEÆ — ELM FAMILY

WHITE ELM, WATER OR SWAMP ELM. (*Ulmus Americana*)

A tall splendid forest tree; commonly 100, occasionally 120 feet high. Wood reddish-brown; hard, strong, tough, very hard to split. This furnished the material of the hubs in O. W. Holmes's "One Hoss Shay."

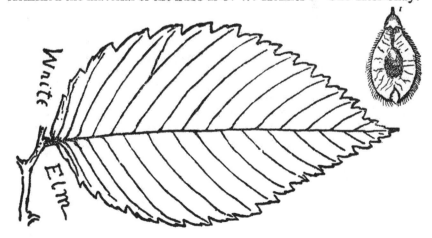

It is coarse, heavy; fairly good firewood, but sparks badly. A cubic foot weighs 41 lbs. Soon rots near the ground. Leaves 2 to 5 inches long. Flowers in early spring before leafing. Seeds ripe in May. Common in most parks.

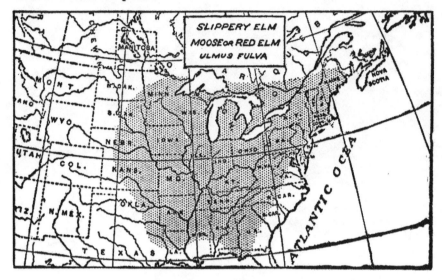

SLIPPERY ELM, MOOSE OR RED ELM. (*Ulmus fulva*)

Smaller than White Elm, maximum height about 70 feet. Wood dark, reddish; hard, close, tough, strong; durable next the ground; heavy; a cubic foot weighs 43 lbs. Its leaves are *larger and rougher* than those of the former. Four to 8 inches long, and its buds are hairy, not smooth. The seeds ripen in early spring when the leaves are half grown: they were a favorite spring food of the Passenger Pigeon. Chiefly noted for its mucilaginous buds, inner bark and seeds, which are eaten or in decoction used as a cough-remedy. This is a valuable specific in all sorts of membranous irritation: for the hard cough or bowel trouble, drink it; for sores apply it in poultice form. It can never do harm and always does some good.

The inner bark of this Elm contains a great quantity of mucilage, and is a favorite popular prescription, in many parts of the country, for dysentery and affections of the chest.

"It is much to be regretted that the Slippery Elm has become so rare. The inner bark is one of the best applications known for affections of the throat and lungs. Flour prepared from the bark by drying perfectly and grinding, and mixed with milk, like arrow-root, is a wholesome and nutritious food for infants and invalids." (*Emerson.*)

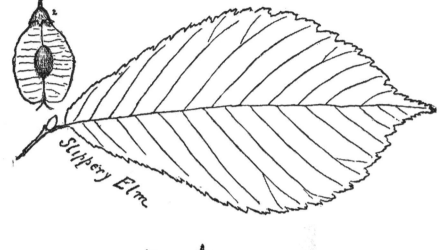

1. American Elm
2. Slippery Elm

3. Cork Elm
4. Wahoo

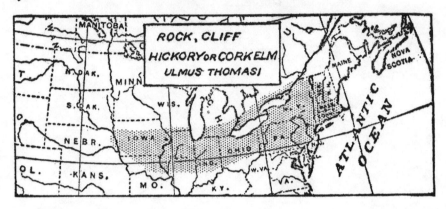

ROCK, CLIFF, HICKORY OR CORK ELM. (*Ulmus Thomasi*)

A tall forest tree on dry or rocky uplands; occasionally 100 feet high. Wood pale, reddish-brown; hard, close, strong, tough and heavy. A cubic foot weighs 45 lbs. It lasts a long time next the ground. It is regularly marked with corky ridges on the two-year-old branches, which give it a shaggy appearance. Its leaves are 2 to 5 inches long. "It possesses all the good qualities of the family, and none of the bad ones." (*Keeler*.)

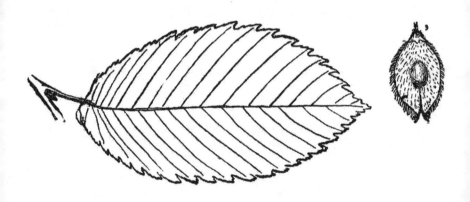

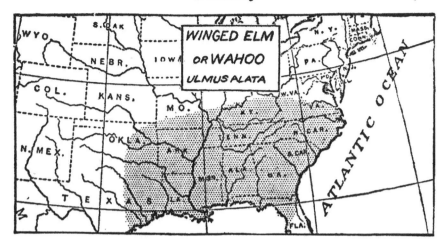

WINGED ELM OR WAHOO. (*Ulmus alata*)

A small tree, up to 50 feet high. Remarkable for the flat corky wings on most of the branches. The wood is hard, weak and brown. A cubic foot weighs 47 lbs. Its leaves are 1 to 3 inches long.

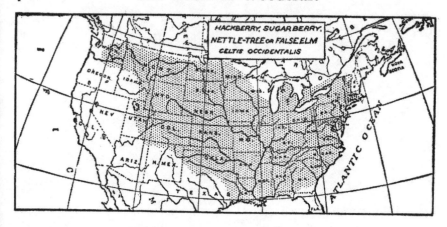

HACKBERRY, SUGARBERRY, NETTLE TREE OR FALSE ELM. (*Celtis occidentalis*)

A tall slender tree, 50 feet, rarely 100 feet high. Wood soft, pale, coarse, a cubic foot weighs 45 lbs. Leaves 2 to 6 inches long. Its style is somewhat elm-like, but it has small dark purple berries, each with a large stone like a cherry pit. The wood is "used for the shafts and axletrees of carriages, the naves of wheels, and for musical instruments. The root is used for dyeing yellow; the bark for tanning; and an oil is expressed from the stones of the fruit." (*Emerson.*) In dry soil.

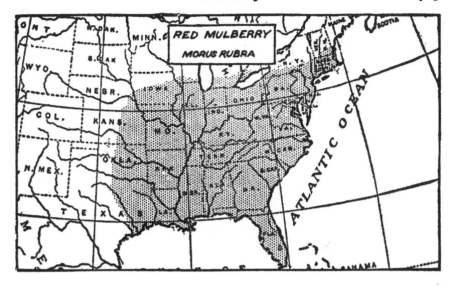

7. MORACEÆ — MULBERRY FAMILY

RED MULBERRY. (*Morus rubra*)

A fine forest tree up to 65 feet high; wood, pale yellow, soft, weak but durable; a cubic foot weighs 37 lbs.; berries 1½ inches long, dark purple red, delicious. Leaves 3 to 5 inches long. In rich soil.

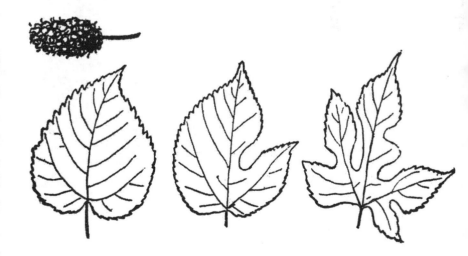

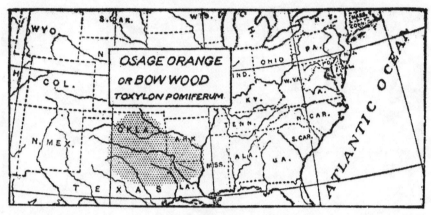

Osage Orange, Bois d'Arc, Bodarc or Bow-Wood. (*Toxylon pomiferum*)

A small tree, rarely 60 feet high.   Originally from the middle Mississippi Valley, now widely introduced as a hedge tree.   Famous for supplying the best bows in America east of the Rockies.   Wood is bright orange; very hard, elastic, enduring and heavy.   Leaves 3 to 6 inches long.   A cubic foot weighs 48 lbs.

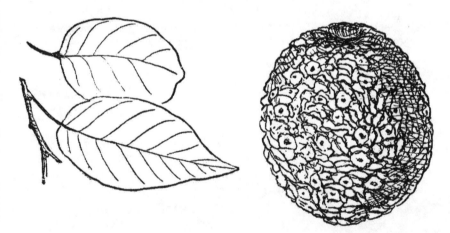

Orange, ½ of life size

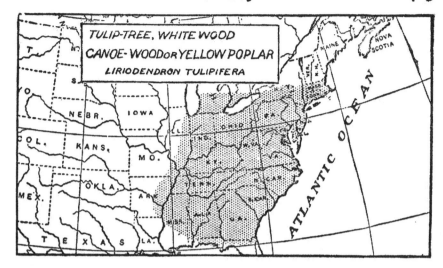

TULIP-TREE, WHITE WOOD
CANOE-WOOD or YELLOW POPLAR
LIRIODENDRON TULIPIFERA

8. MAGNOLIACEÆ — MAGNOLIA FAMILY

TULIP TREE, WHITE-WOOD, CANOE WOOD OR YELLOW POPLAR. (*Lirio-dendron Tulipifera*)

One of the noblest forest trees, ordinarily 100 feet, and sometimes 150 feet high. Noted for its splendid clean straight column; readily known by leaf, 3 to 6 inches long, and its tulip-like flower. Wood soft, straight-grained, brittle, yellow, and very light; much used where a broad sheet easily worked is needed but will not stand exposure to the weather; is poor fuel; a dry cubic foot weighs 26 lbs.

Makes a good dugout canoe, hence Indian name, "canoe wood" (*Keeler*). The inner bark and root bark either as dry powder or as "tea" are powerful tonics and especially good for worms.

Every tree like every man must decide for itself — will it live in the alluring forest and struggle to the top where alone is sunlight or give up the fight and content itself with the shade — or leave this delectable land of loam and water and be satisfied with the waste and barren plains that are not desirable.

The Tulip is one of those that believe there is plenty of room at the top and its towering trunk is one of the noblest in the woods that shed their leaves. The Laurel and Swamp Magnolia are among the shadow dwellers; and the Scrub Oaks and the Red Sumacs are among those that have lost in the big fight and are content with that which others do not covet.

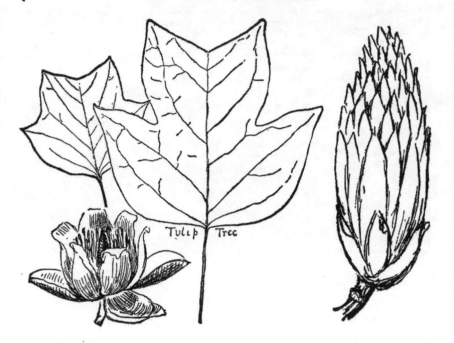

Tulip Tree

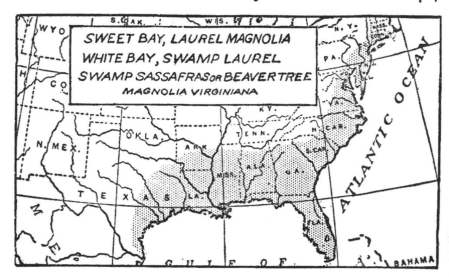

SWEET BAY, LAUREL MAGNOLIA, WHITE BAY, SWAMP LAUREL, SWAMP
SASSAFRAS OR BEAVER TREE. (*Magnolia virginiana*)

A small tree 15 to 70 feet high, nearly evergreen, noted for being a
favorite with the Beaver. "Its fleshy roots were eagerly eaten by the
Beavers, who considered them such a dainty that they could be caught
in traps baited with them. Michaux recites that the wood was used by
the beavers in constructing their dams and houses in preference to any
other." (*Keeler.*)

The wood weighs 31 lbs. to the cubic foot. The heart wood is reddish-
brown, the sap wood nearly white. The leaves are 3 to 6 inches long,
dark shiny green above, faintly downy below. Fruit cone 1½ to 2
inches high.

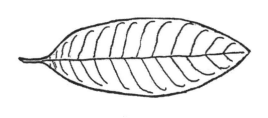

CUCUMBER TREE OR MOUNTAIN MAGNOLIA. (*Magnolia acuminata*)

A fair-sized forest tree 60 to 90 feet high. The wood weighs 29 lbs. to the cubic foot. The leaves are light green, faintly downy below, 2 to 12 inches long. Fruit cone 3 to 4 inches high.

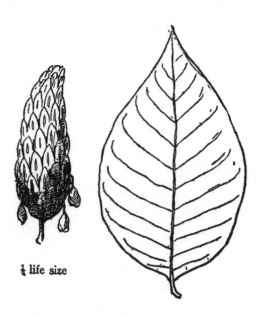

¼ life size

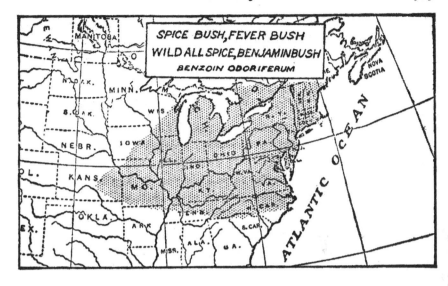

9. LAURACEÆ — LAUREL FAMILY

SPICE BUSH, FEVER BUSH, WILD ALLSPICE, BANJAMIN BUSH. (*Benzoin odoriferum*)

A small bush rarely 20 feet high. In moist woods; berries red; leaves 2 to 5 inches long. A tea made of its twigs was a good old remedy for chills and fever.

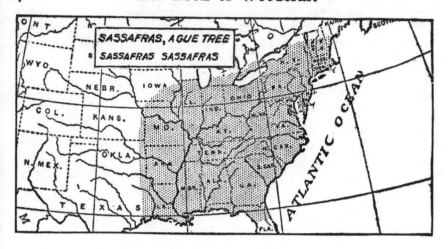

SASSAFRAS, AGUE TREE.   (*Sassafras Sassafras*)

Usually a small tree of dry sandy soil, but reaching 125 feet high in favorable regions. Its wood is dull orange, soft, weak, coarse, brittle, and light. A cubic foot weighs 31 lbs. Very durable next the ground. Leaves 4 to 7 inches long. Noted for its aromatic odor.

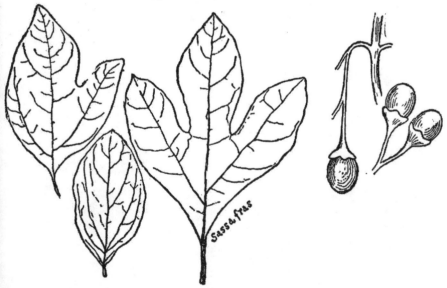

"In the Southwestern States the dried leaves are much used as an ingredient in soups, for which they are well adapted by the abundance

of mucilage they contain. For this purpose the mature green leaves are dried and powdered, the stringy portions being separated, and are sifted and preserved for use. This preparation mixed with soups, give them a ropy consistence, and a peculiar flavor, much relished by those accustomed to it. To such soups are given the names *gombo file* and *gombo zab*. (P. 321.)

"A decoction of the bark is said to communicate to wool a durable orange color." (P. 322) (*Emerson*).

Tea made of the bark is also a fine warming stimulant and sweater. Its roots are used in the manufacture of root-beer.

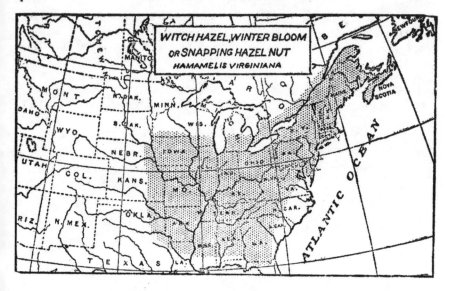

10. HAMAMELIDACEÆ — WITCH-HAZEL FAMILY

WITCH-HAZEL, WINTER BLOOM OR SNAPPING HAZEL NUT. (*Hamamelis virginiana*)

A small tree 10 to 15 feet high, usually with many leaning stems from one root. Noted for its blooming in the fall, flowers of golden threads, the nuts explode when ripe throwing the seeds a dozen feet. A snuff made of the dry leaves stops nosebleed at once, or indeed any bleeding when

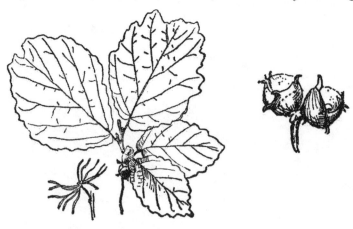

locally applied. A decoction or tea of the bark gives relief to inflammation of the eye or skin.

> Witch hazel blossoms in the fall
> To cure the chills and fever all.
> *(Two Little Savages.)*

A forked twig of this furnished the favorite divining rod whence the
name. Leaves 4 to 6 inches long.

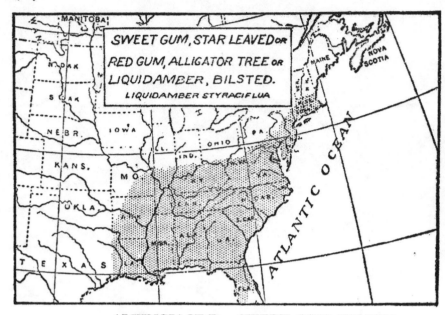

SWEET GUM, STAR LEAVED OR RED GUM, ALLIGATOR TREE OR LIQUIDAMBER, BILSTED.
LIQUIDAMBER STYRACIFLUA

11. ALTINGIACEÆ — SWEET GUM FAMILY

SWEET GUM, STAR-LEAVED OR RED GUM, BILSTED, ALLIGATOR TREE OR LIQUIDAMBAR.   (*Liquidambar Styraciflua*)

A tall tree up to 150 feet high of low, moist woods, remarkable for the corky ridges on its bark, and the unsplittable nature of its weak, warping, perishable timber.   Heart-wood reddish-brown, sap white; heavy, weighing 37 lbs. to cubic foot.   Leaves 3 to 5 inches long.

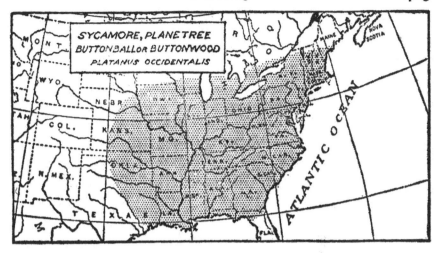

12. PLATANACEÆ — PLANE TREE FAMILY

SYCAMORE, PLANE TREE, BUTTONBALL OR BUTTONWOOD. (*Platanus occidentalis*)

One of the largest of our trees; up to 140 feet high; commonly hollow. Wood, light brownish, weak; hard to split; heavy for its strength. A cubic foot weighs 35 lbs. Little use for weather work. Famous for

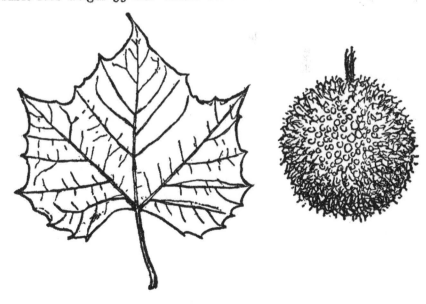

shedding its bark as well as its leaves.   Leaves 4 to 9 inches long.   Canada to the Gulf.

When a tree is a mere sapling, the bark is thin and soft; it stretches each year with the annual growth of the trunk.   But it becomes thicker and harder with age and then it cracks with the expansion of the trunk. This process continues each year till the segments of the first coat are widely separated by gaping fissures.   This is well seen in the Elm, and each of the bark ridges shows the annual layers, from the widely separated outer one to the united inmost one.

But some trees, notably the Sycamore, burst their bark, yet do not retain the fragments.   These are dropped each year, hence the smooth green surface of the trunk, hence also its success as a tree of grimy cities, for it has an annual cleaning of the skin and thus throws off mischievous accumulations that would kill a tree that retained its bark indefinitely.

The Shagbark Hickory will be remembered as a halfway shedder.

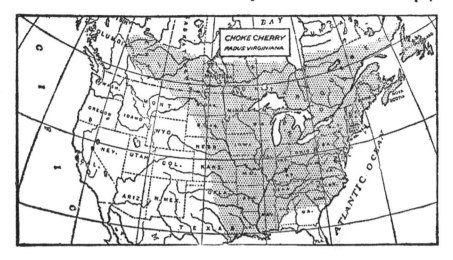

13. AMYGDALACEÆ — PLUM FAMILY

CHOKE CHERRY. (*Padus virginiana*)

A bush 2 to 19 feet high in the North. A tall tree in the Mississippi Valley. Wood, pale, hard, close-grained, and heavy. A cubic foot weighs 43 lbs. Leaves 2 to 4 inches long, the marginal teeth divaricate or outcurved. Noted for its astringent fruit. Leaf broader, fruit smaller than in Black Cherry.

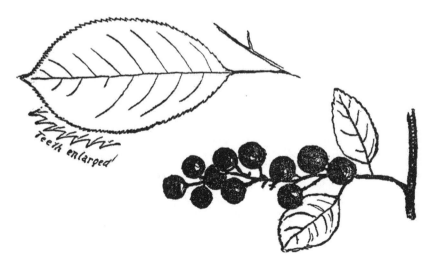

BLACK CHERRY, CABINET OR RUM CHERRY.   (*Padus serotina*)

A fine tree, even in Canada; 60 to 70 or even 90 feet high. The source of many excellent remedies, chiefly pectoral. Tea of the bark (roots preferred) is a powerful tonic for lungs and bowels; also good as

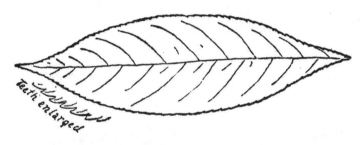

a skin wash for sores. The leaves when half wilted are poisonous to cattle. The wood is light-brown or red, strong, close-grained; much in demand for cabinet work; light. A cubic foot weighs 36 lbs. Leaves 5 inches long, the marginal teeth incurved.

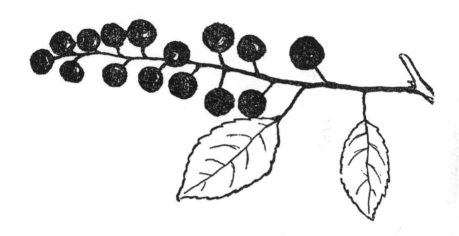

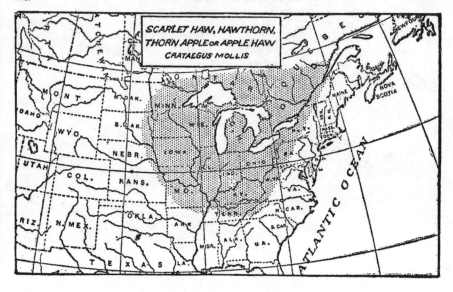

14. MALACEÆ — APPLE FAMILY

SCARLET HAW, HAWTHORN, THORN APPLE OR APPLE HAW. (*Cratægus mollis*)

A small tree, 10 to 20, rarely 30 feet high. Wood hard and heavy. A cubic foot weighs 50 lbs. Leaves 2 to 4 inches long. Noted for its beautiful deep red fruit, ¾ to 1¼ inches long, round, with pink-yellow flesh, 5 or 6 stones, quite eatable.

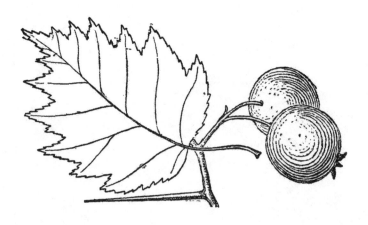

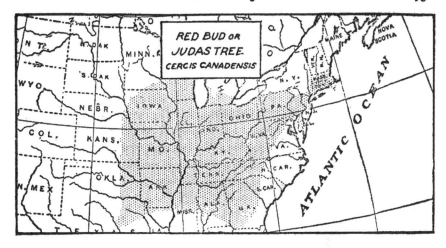

RED BUD OR JUDAS TREE. CERCIS CANADENSIS

15. CÆSALPINACEÆ — SENNA FAMILY

RED-BUD OR JUDAS TREE. (*Cercis canadensis*)

Small tree of bottom lands, rarely 50 feet high; so called from its abundant spring crop of tiny rosy blossoms, coming before the leaves, the latter 2 to 6 inches broad. "Judas tree" because it blushed when Judas hanged himself on it. (*Keeler.*) Its wood is dark, coarse and heavy.

A cubic foot weighs 40 lbs.

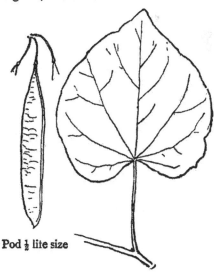

Pod ½ lite size

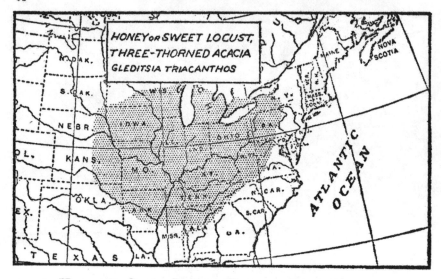

HONEY OR SWEET LOCUST, THREE-THORNED ACACIA.
(*Gleditsia triacanthos*)

A tall tree up to 140 feet high; very thorny. Wood dark, hard, strong, coarse, heavy. A cubic foot weighs 42 lbs. Leaves single or double pinnate; leaflets ¾ to 1¼ inches long. It is very durable as posts, etc. Pods 6 to 12 inches long. So called because of the sweet stuff in which its seeds are packed. Chiefly Mississippi Valley, but common in the East along roadsides.

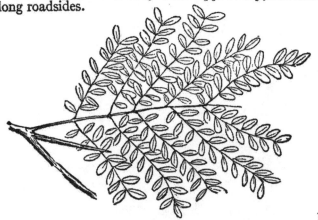

Pod is ½ life size

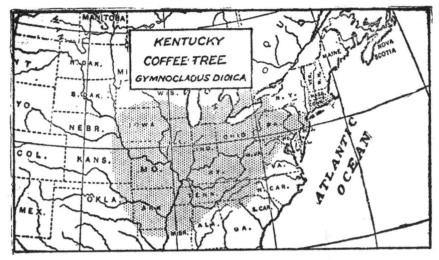

KENTUCKY COFFEE TREE. (*Gymnocladus dioica*)

A tall tree (up to 100 feet), so called because its beans were once used as coffee. Wood is light-colored, coarse-grained strong, and heavy. A cubic foot weighs 43 lbs. Leaves large and bipinnate; leaflets, 7 to 15, and 1 to 3 inches long. It is remarkably durable next the ground, as posts, etc.

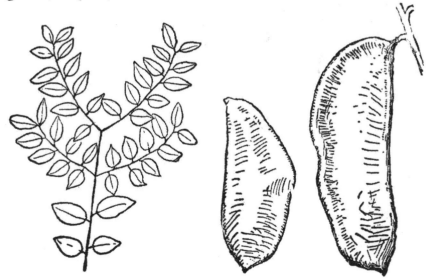

Pods ¼ life size

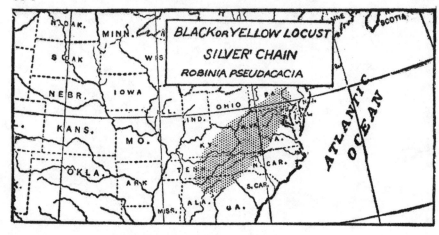

16. FABACEÆ — PEA FAMILY

BLACK OR YELLOW LOCUST, SILVER CHAIN.   (*Robinia Pseudacacia*)

A tall forest tree, up to 80 feet high: leaves 8 to 14 inches long; leaflets 9 to 19, 1 to 2 inches long; pods 2 to 4 inches long, 4 to 7 seeded. Wood greenish-brown, very strong and durable; much used for posts; weight 46 lbs. per cubic foot.

"The leaves are used in some parts of Europe, either fresh or cured, as nourishment for horses; the seeds are found very nutritious to fowls.

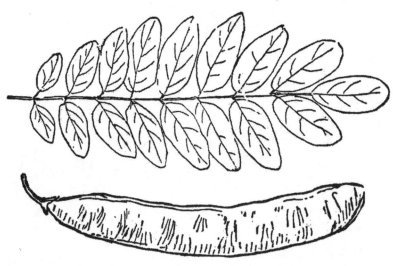

The leaves may be made a substitute for indigo in dyeing blue, and the flowers are used by the Chinese for dyeing yellow." (*Emerson.*)

Pennsylvania to Iowa and South to Georgia and common in the east along roadsides.

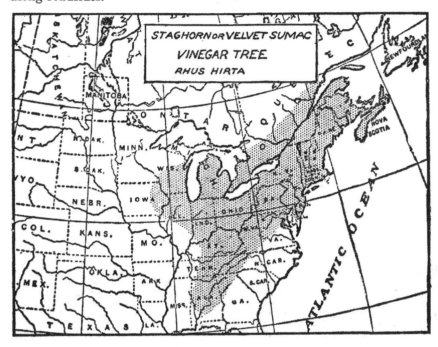

STAGHORN OR VELVET SUMAC

VINEGAR TREE

RHUS HIRTA

17. ANACARDIACEÆ — SUMAC FAMILY

STAGHORN OR VELVET SUMAC, VINEGAR TREE. (*Rhus hirta*)

A small tree 10 to 40 feet high. Noted for its red velvety berries in solid bunches and its *velvet clad stem* whence its name. Leaflets 11 to 31 and 2 to 5 inches long; the whole leaf 16 to 24 inches long.

"The berries are also used in dyeing their own color. Kalm says, that the branches boiled with the berries, afford a black, ink-like tincture." (*Emerson.*)

Nova Scotia to British Columbia, south to Florida and west to Arizona.

Somewhat like it but *quite smooth* is the Smooth or Scarlet Sumac. (*R. glabra.*)

Its berries make a safe and pleasant drink for children and tea of ͗almost any part of the tree is a powerful tonic.

Leaves and fruit of
Scarlet Sumac

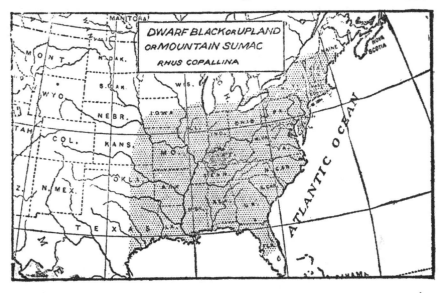

DWARF, BLACK, UPLAND OR MOUNTAIN SUMAC. (*Rhus copallina*)

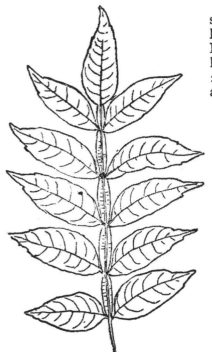

A small tree like the Staghorn; of similar range. Known by the peculiar winged stems of the leaves. Leaves 6 to 12 inches long and leaflets 2 to 4 inches long; number 9 to 21. Dry soil. Maine to Minnesota and south to Florida and Texas.

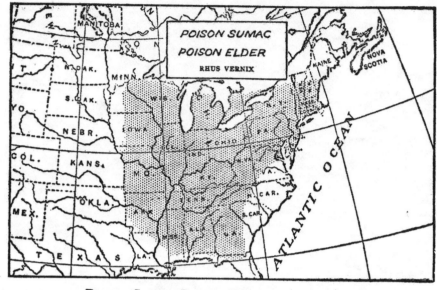

POISON SUMAC, POISON ELDER. (*Rhus Vernix*)

A small tree, 15 to 20 up to 25 feet high. Noted for being the most poisonous tree in the country. Its active principle is a fixed oil. This may be removed by washing with an alcoholic solution of sugar of lead; it is a sure cure. When this remedy is not at hand, wash the parts with water as hot as one can stand, this is also a reliable remedy. The same remarks apply to Poison Ivy or Poison Oak. Leaves 6 to 15 inches long; leaflets 7 to 13 in numbers and 2 to 4 inches long. Timber is light and worthless. A cubic foot weighs 27 lbs. Damp woods.

POISON, CLIMBING OR THREE-LEAVED IVY.   POISON OAK, CLIMATH.
(Rhus radicans)

Though a trailing vine on the ground, on fences or on trees and never itself a tree, the Poison or Three-fingered Ivy should appear here that all may know it. Its poisonous powers are much exaggerated, about three persons out of four are immune and the poison is easily cured as

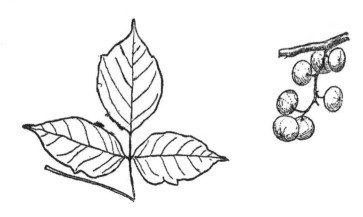

described under Poison Sumac. Its leaflets always three, are 1 to 4 inches long. Its berries are eagerly eaten by birds.

"The juice of this plant is yellowish and milky, becoming black after a short exposure to the air. It has been used as marking ink and on linen is indelible." (*Emerson.*) It grows everywhere in the open being found from Manitoba eastward and Texas northward.

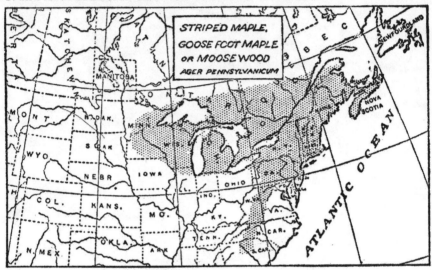

STRIPED MAPLE, GOOSE FOOT MAPLE OR MOOSEWOOD
AGER PENNSYLVANICUM

18. ACERACEÆ — MAPLE FAMILY

STRIPED MAPLE, GOOSEFOOT MAPLE OR MOOSEWOOD. (*Acer pennsylvanicum*)

A small tree up to 35 feet high, in tall woods, called "striped" because its small branches have white lines. It is much eaten by the moose. Wood, brown, soft, close-grained, light. Leaves, 5 to 6 inches long. A cubic foot weighs 33 lbs.

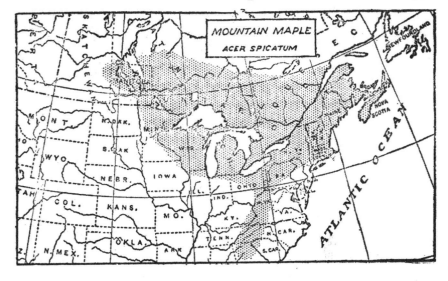

MOUNTAIN MAPLE. (*Acer spicatum*)

A shrub or small tree, rarely 30 feet high. Wood soft, pale and light, a cubic foot weighs 33 lbs. Leaves 4 to 5 inches along.

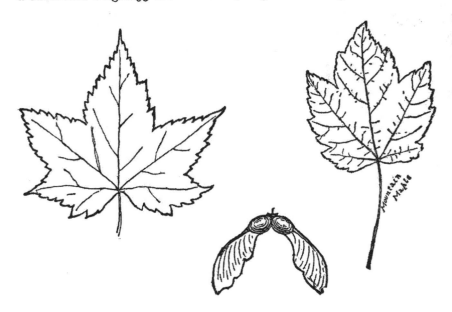

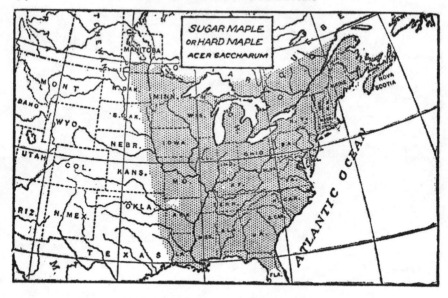

SUGAR MAPLE, ROCK MAPLE OR HARD MAPLE.   (*Acer saccharum*)

A large, splendid forest tree, 80 to 120 feet high; red in autumn. Wood hard, strong, tough and heavy but not durable. A cubic foot weighs 43 lbs. It enjoys with Beech, Hickory, etc., the sad distinction of being a perfect firewood. Thanks to this it has been exterminated in some regions.

Bird's-eye and curled Maple are freaks of the grain. Leaves 3 to 5 inches long. Its sap produces the famous maple sugar. This is the emblem of Canada.

There is a black barked variety called Black Sugar Maple (*A. nigrum*). It is of doubtful status.

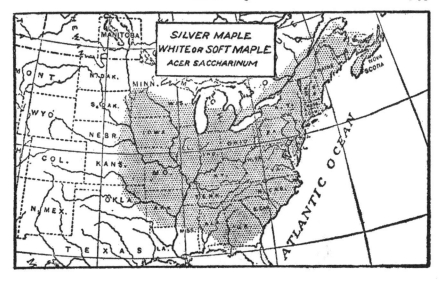

SILVER MAPLE, WHITE OR SOFT MAPLE. (*Acer saccharinum*)

Usually a little smaller than the Sugar Maple and much inferior as timber. Wood hard, close-grained. A cubic foot weighs 33 lbs. Leaves 5 to 7 inches long. This tree produces a little sugar. It is noted for its yellow foliage in autumn.

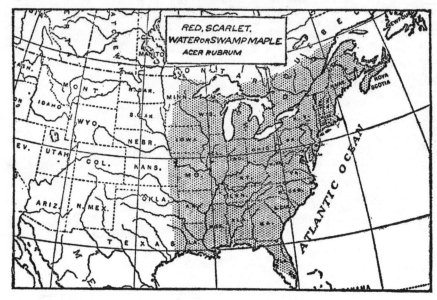

RED, SCARLET, WATER OR SWAMP MAPLE.   (*Acer rubrum*)

A fine tree the same size as the preceding. Noted for its flaming crimson foliage in fall, as well as its red leafstalks, flowers and fruit earlier. Its wood is light-colored, tinged reddish, close-grained, smooth with varieties of grain, as in Sugar Maple; heavy. A cubic foot weighs 39 lbs. Leaves 2 to 6 inches long. Produces a little sugar. In the woods there is a common bush 3 to 6 feet high, with leaves much like those of this maple, but the bush has berries on it, it is called the Maple-leaved Viburnum (see later).

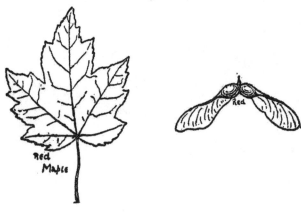

Forestry

"A small Red Maple has grown, perchance, far away at the head of some retired valley, a mile from any road, unobserved. It has faithfully discharged all the duties of a maple there, all winter and summer neglected none of its economies, but added to its stature in the virtue which belongs to a maple, by a steady growth for so many months, and is much nearer heaven than it was in the spring. It has faithfully husbanded its sap, and afforded a shelter to the wandering bird, has long since ripened its seeds and committed them to the winds. It deserves well of mapledom. Its leaves have been asking it from time to time in a whisper, 'When shall we redden?' and now in this month of September, this month of traveling, when men are hastening to the seaside, or the mountains, or the lakes, this modest maple, still without budging an inch, travels in its reputation — runs up its scarlet flag on that hillside, which shows that it finished its summer's work before all other trees, and withdrawn from the contest. At the eleventh hour of the year, the tree which no scrutiny could have detected here when it was most industrious is thus, by the tint of its maturity, by its very blushes, revealed at last to the careless and distant traveler, and leads his thoughts away from the dusty road into those brave solitudes which it inhabits; it flashes out conspicuous with all the virtue and beauty of a maple — *Acer rubrum*. We may read its title, or rubric, clear. Its virtues not its sins are as scarlet." (*Thoreau.*)

"Never was a tree more appropriately named than the Red Maple. Its first blossom flushes red in the April sunlight, its keys ripen scarlet in early May, all summer long its leaves swing on crimson or scarlet stems, its young twigs flame in the same colors and later, amid all the brilliancy of the autumnal forest, it stands preëminent and unapproachable." (*Keeler.*)

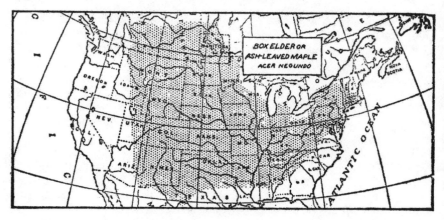

BOX ELDER OR ASH-LEAVED MAPLE. (*Acer Negundo*)

A small tree, 40 or 50 up to 70 feet high, found chiefly along streams. Wood pale, soft, close-grained, light. A cubic foot weighs 27 lbs. Poor fuel. Makes paper-pulp. Leaflets 2 to 4 inches long. Sap yields a delicate white sugar. Chiefly in Mississippi Valley and north to Manitoba, but in the eastern states as an escape from cultivation.

"It was usual to make sugar from maples, but several other trees were also tapped by the Indians. From the birch and ash was made a dark-colored sugar, with a somewhat bitter taste, which was used for medicinal purposes. The box-elder yielded a beautiful white sugar, whose only fault was that there was never enough of it." ("Indian Boyhood," p. 32, by Charles A. Eastman.)

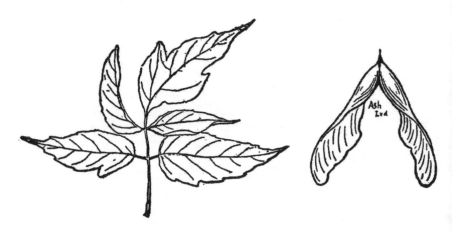

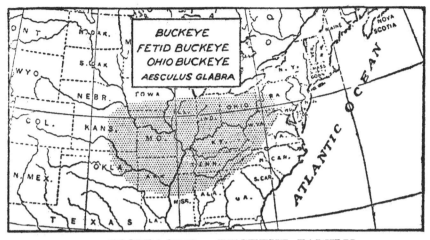

BUCKEYE
FETID BUCKEYE
OHIO BUCKEYE
AESCULUS GLABRA

19. ÆSCULACEÆ — BUCKEYE FAMILY

BUCKEYE, FETID BUCKEYE, OHIO BUCKEYE. (*Æsculus glabra*)

Not a large tree, up to 50 feet high. So called because the dark brown nut peeping from the prickly husk is like the half-opened eye of a buck. Leaflets 5, rarely 7, 3 to 6 inches long. Wood, soft, close-grained, light. A cubic foot weighs 28 lbs. Sapwood darkest, used for wooden legs and dishes.

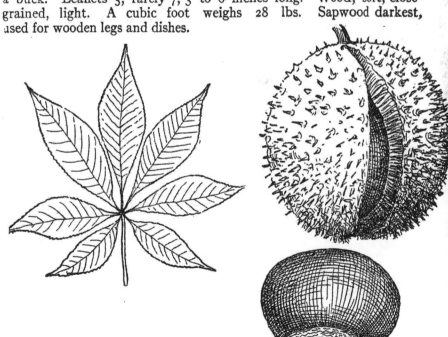

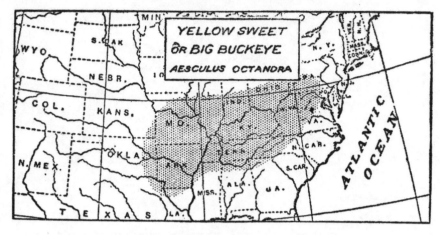

YELLOW SWEET OR BIG BUCKEYE. (*Æsculus octandra*)

A good-sized tree; up to 90 feet high. "Sweet" because its bark is less ill smelling than that of its kin. (*Keeler.*) Wood, soft and white, 27 lbs., per cubic foot, husk of nut, smooth — leaflets 5, rarely 7, 4 inches long; 2 to 3 inches wide.

HORSE CHESTNUT OR BONGAY. (*Æsculus Hippocastanum*)

A large tree sometimes 100 feet high. Wood, soft, white, close-grained; poor timber. Leaflets 5 to 7 inches long. A foreigner; now widely introduced in parks and roadsides; named either as "horse-radish," "horse-fiddle" and "horse bean" were through using the word "horse" to mean large and coarse, or possibly because the scars on the twigs look like the print of a horse's hoof.

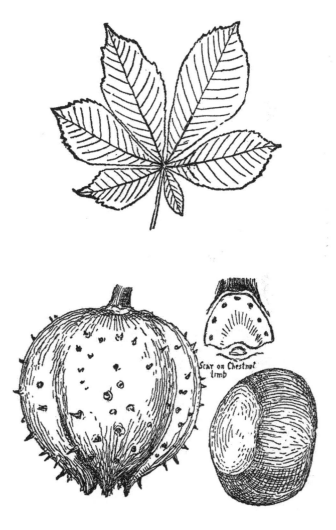

Scar on Chestnut limb

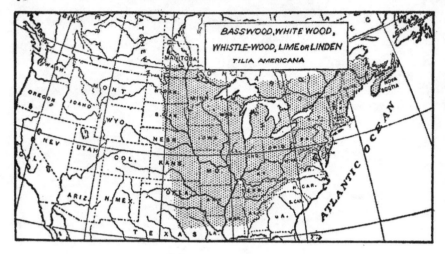

20. TILIACEÆ — LINDEN FAMILY

Basswood, White-wood, Whistle-wood, Lime or Linden. (*Tilia americana*)

A tall forest tree 60 to 125 feet high; usually hollow when old. Wood soft, straight-grained, weak, white, very light. A cubic foot weighs 28 lbs. It makes a good dugout canoe or sap trough. The hollow trunk, split in halves, was often used for roofing (see log-cabin). Poor firewood, and soon rots; makes good rubbing sticks for friction fire. Its inner bark supplies coarse cordage and matting. Its buds are often eaten as emergency food. Leaves 2 to 5 inches wide. Its nuts are delicious food, but small.

There are two other species of the family, Southern Basswood (*T. pubescens*) known by its small leaves and the Bee tree (*T. heterophylla*) known by its very large leaves.

Basswood Whistle. Take a piece of a young shoot of basswood, smooth and straight, about 6 inches long, without knots, bevel the end. Hammer this all around with a flat stick or roll it between two flat boards. Very soon the bark can be slipped off in one whole piece. Now cut the stick to the shape of a whistle plug, slip the bark on again and you have a whistle.

Make it longer and cut off the plug, add holes and you have a pipe.

The exquisite spotless purity of the wood laid bare when the bark is slipped off is so delicate and complete that a mere finger touch is a defilement. It is from this we get the phrase "clean as a whistle."

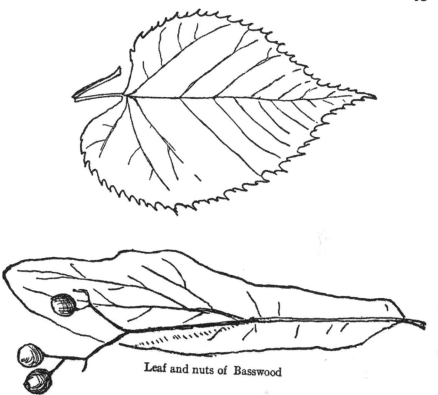

Leaf and nuts of Basswood

Nut, life size

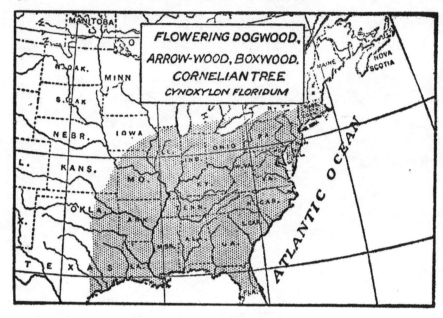

21. CORNACEÆ — DOGWOOD FAMILY

FLOWERING DOGWOOD, ARROW-WOOD, BOXWOOD, CORNELIAN TREE.
(Cynoxylon floridum)

A small tree 15 to 20 feet, rarely 40, with bark beautifully pebbled or of alligator pattern. Wood hard, close, tough, strong, and heavy, a cubic foot weighing 51 lbs. Noted for its masses of beautiful white bloom in spring. A tea of its roots is a good substitute for quinine. Leaves 3 to 5 inches long.

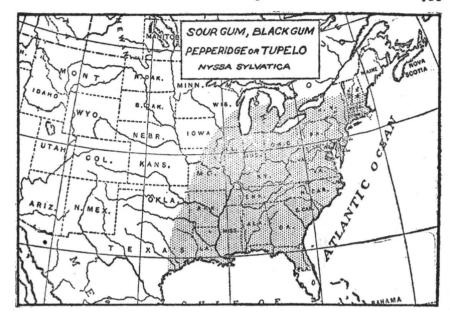

SOUR GUM, BLACK GUM, PEPPERIDGE OR TUPELO. (*Nyssa sylvatica*)

A forest tree up to 110 feet high; in wet lands. Wood pale, **very** strong, tough, unsplittable and heavy. A cubic foot weighs 40 lbs. Used for turner work, but soon rots next the ground. Leaves 2 to 5 inches long. Noted for its brilliant fiery autumn foliage.

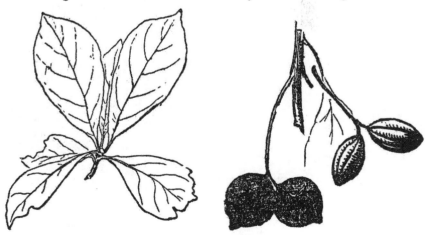

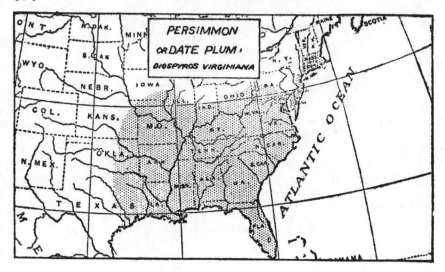

22.　EBENACEÆ — EBONY FAMILY

Persimmon or Date Plum.　(*Diospyros virginiana*)

A small tree 30 to 50 feet high, famous for the fruit so astringent and puckery when unripe, so luscious when frosted and properly mature. Leaves 4 to 6 inches long.

"In respect to the power of making heartwood, the Locust and the Persimmon stand at the extreme opposite ends of the list. The Locust changes its sapwood into heartwood almost at once, while the Persimmon rarely develops any heartwood until it is nearly one hundred years old. This heartwood is extremely close-grained and almost black.

Really, it is ebony, but our climate is not favorable to its production."
(*Keeler*.) Wood very heavy, dark and strong, a cubic foot weighs
49 lbs. Rhode Island to Florida and west to Ohio and Oklahoma where
it becomes a tall tree.

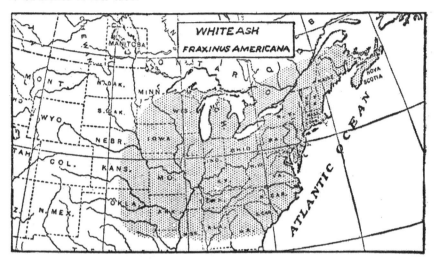

WHITE ASH
FRAXINUS AMERICANA

23. OLEACEÆ, OLIVE FAMILY (INCLUDING THE ASHES)

WHITE ASH. (*Fraxinus americana*)

A fine forest tree on moist soil: 70 to 90 or even 130 feet high.
Wood pale brown, tough, and elastic. Used for handles, springs, bows,
also arrows and spears; heavy. A cubic foot weighs 41 lbs. Soon rots
next the ground. Yellow in autumn; its leaflets have stalks, noted for
being last to leaf and first to shed in the forest. Called white for the
silvery undersides of the leaves; these are 8 to 12 inches long; each leaflet
3 to 5 inches long.

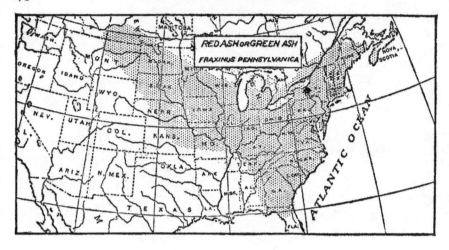

Red Ash or Green Ash. (*Fraxinus pennsylvanica*)

A small tree rarely 80 feet high. Wood light brown, coarse, hard, strong, brittle heavy. A cubic foot weighs 44 lbs. The Red Ash is downy on branchlet, leaf and leaf-stalk while the White Ash is in the main smooth, otherwise their leaves are much alike. The Green is a variety of the Red.

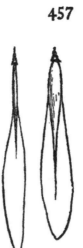

Leaf and seeds of Red Ash

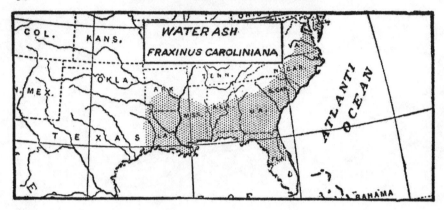

WATER ASH. (*Fraxinus caroliniana*)

A small tree rarely over 40 feet high. Wood whitish soft, weak. A cubic foot weighs 22 lbs; leaflets 5 to 7, or rarely 9; 2 to 5 inches long. In swamps and along streams.

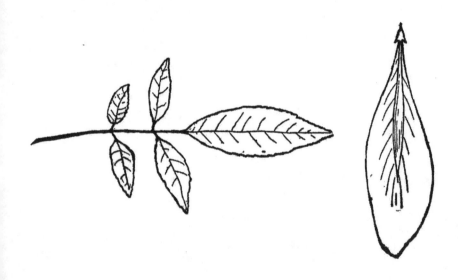

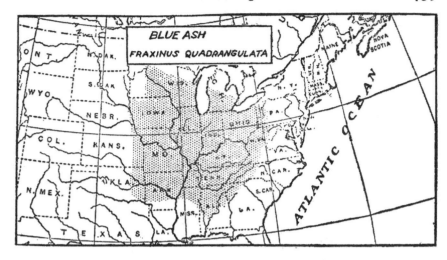

BLUE ASH.   (*Fraxinus quadrangulata*)

A tall tree of the Mississippi Valley, over 100 feet high.   Wood light yellow, hard, close, heavy.   A cubic foot weighs 45 lbs.   Leaflets 7 to 11, 3 to 5 inches long.   "The inner bark yields a blue color to water; hence its name."   "It may be distinguished among ashes by its peculiar, stout, four-angled, four-winged branches."   (*Keeler*.)

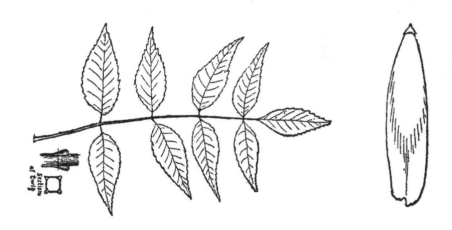

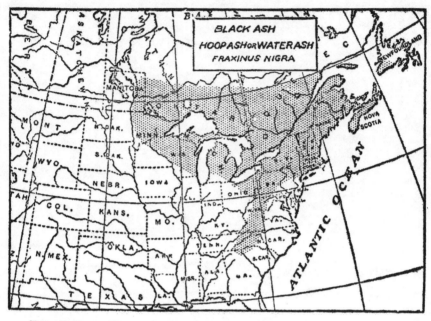

BLACK ASH, HOOP ASH OR WATER ASH. (*Fraxinus nigra*)

A tall forest tree of swampy places; 70, 80 or rarely 100 feet high. Wood dark brown, tough, soft, course, heavy. A cubic foot weighs 39 lbs. Soon rots next to the ground. Late in the spring to leaf, and early to shed in the fall. The leaves are 12 to 16 inches long; its leaflets except the last have no stalk, they number 7 to 11, are 2 to 6 inches long.

Sometimes called Elder-leaved Ash because its leaves somewhat resemble the leaves of the Elder, but they are much larger and the leaflets of the latter have slight stalks, especially those near the base and are on a succulent green stem which is deeply grooved on top. The thick bumpy twigs of the Black Ash with the black triangular winter buds are strong characters at all seasons.

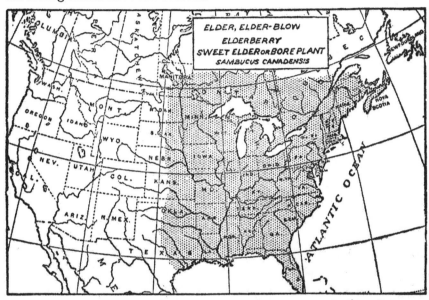

ELDER, ELDER-BLOW
ELDERBERRY
SWEET ELDER OR BORE PLANT
SAMBUCUS CANADENSIS

24. CAPRIFOLIACIÆ— HONEYSUCKLE FAMILY

ELDER, ELDER-BLOW, ELDERBERRY, SWEET ELDER OR BORE PLANT.
(*Sambucus canadensis*)

A bush 4 to 10 feet high, well known for its large pith which can be pushed out so as to make a natural pipe, commonly used for whistles,

squirts, etc.   Its black sweet berries are used for making wine.   Its leaves
are somewhat like those of Black Ash, but have a green succulent
stalk.   A tea of the inner bark is a powerful diuretic.   The young leaf-
buds are a drastic purgative; they may be ground up and taken as
decoction in very small doses.   The leaves are 8 to 12 inches long; leaflets,
5 to 11, usually 7, and 2 to 5 inches long.   There is another species with
red berries.   It is called the Mountain Elder (*S. pubens*) and is found
from New Brunswick to British Columbia, and southeast to California
and Georgia.   It has orange pith and purple leafstalks whereas *Canadensis* has yellow pith and green leafstalks.

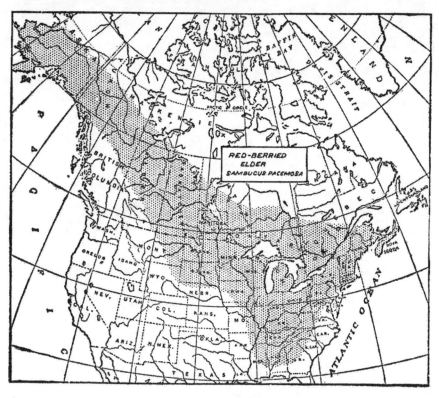

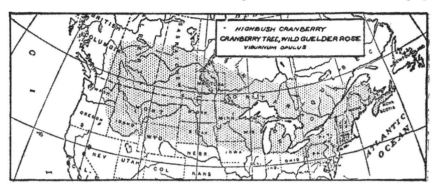

HIGH BUSH CRANBERRY, CRANBERRY TREE, WILD GUELDER ROSE.
(*Viburnum Opulus*)

A bush 10 to 12 feet high. Noted for its delicious acid fruit, bright red, translucent and in large bunches, each with a large flat seed. Leaves 2 to 3 inches long. Found in low grounds from New Brunswick to British Columbia. South to New Jersey, also in the Old World.

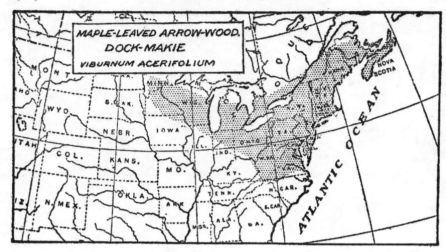

MAPLE-LEAVED ARROW-WOOD, DOCK-MAKIE.   (*Viburnum acerifolium*)

A forest bush, 3 to 6 feet high.   Chiefly noted because of its abundance in the hard woods where it is commonly taken for a young maple.   The style of its leaves however distinguish it, also its berries, these are black with a large lentil-shaped seed.   Leaves 3 to 5 inches long.

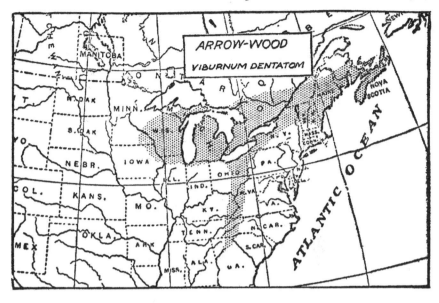

ARROW-WOOD. (*Viburnum dentatum*)

A forest bush, up to 15 feet high; its remarkably straight shoots supplied shafts for the Indian's arrows. Leaves 2 to 3 inches long. Its berries blue-black, with a large stone grooved on one side and rounded on the other. In moist soil.

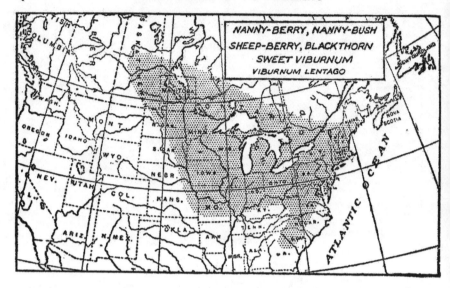

NANNY-BERRY, NANNY-BUSH
SHEEP-BERRY, BLACKTHORN
SWEET VIBURNUM
VIBURNUM LENTAGO

NANNY-BERRY, NANNY-BUSH, SHEEP-BERRY, BLACKTHORN, SWEET
VIBURNUM. (*Viburnum Lentago*)

A small tree, up to 30 feet high. Noted for its clusters of sweet rich purplish-black berries, each half an inch long, but containing a large oval, flattened seed. Leaves 2 to 4 inches long. Wood hard, a cubic foot weighs 45 lbs. It is the largest of the group.

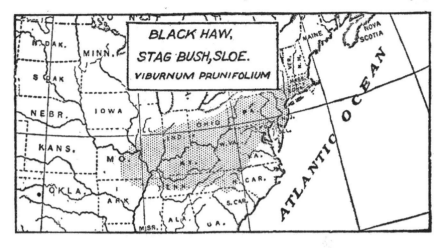

BLACK HAW, STAG BUSH, SLOE. (*Viburnum prunifolium*)

A small tree up to 20 or 30 feet high, much like the Nanny-berry;
fruit black, sweet and edible.   Leaves 1 to 3 inches long.   Wood hard,
a cubic foot weighs 52 lbs.   In dry soil.

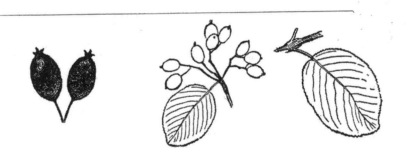

XIV. Some Indian Ways

Teepees

(From *Ladies' Home Journal*, September, 1902)

MANY famous campers have said that the Indian teepee is the best known movable home. It is roomy, self-ventilating, cannot blow down, and is the only tent that admits of a fire inside.

Then why is it not everywhere used? Because of the difficulty of the poles. If on the prairie, you must carry your poles. If in the woods, you must cut them at each camp.

General Sibley, the famous Indian fighter, invented a teepee with a single pole, and this is still used by our army. But it will not do for us. Its one pole is made in part of iron, and is very cumbersome as well as costly.

In the "Buffalo days" the teepee was made of buffalo skin; now it is made of some sort of canvas or cotton, but it is decorated much in the old style.

I tried to get an extra fine one made by the Indians, especially as a model for our boys, but I found this no easy matter. I could not go among the red folk and order it as in a department store.

At length I solved the difficulty by buying one ready made, from Thunder Bull, a chief of the Cheyennes.

It appears at the left end of the row of teepees heading this chapter.

This is a 20-footer and is large enough for 10 boys to live in. A large one is easier to keep clear of smoke, but most boys will prefer a smaller one, as it is much handier, cheaper, and easier to make. I shall therefore give the working plan of a 10-foot teepee of the simplest form — the raw material of which can be bought new for about $5.

It requires 22 square yards of 6- or 8-ounce duck, heavy unbleached muslin, or Canton flannel (the wider the better, as that saves labor in making up), which costs about $4; 100 feet of $\frac{3}{16}$-inch clothesline, 25 cents; string for sewing rope ends, etc., 5 cents.

Of course, one can often pick up second-hand materials that are quite good and cost next to nothing. An old wagon cover, or two or three old sheets, will make the teepee, and even if they are patched it is all right; the Indian teepees are often mended where bullets and arrows have gone through them. Scraps of rope, if not rotted, will work in well enough.

Suppose you have new material to deal with. Get it machine run together 20 feet long and 10 feet wide. Lay this down perfectly flat (Cut I). On a peg or nail at A in the middle of the long side put a 10-foot cord loosely, and then with a burnt stick in a loop at the other end draw the half-circle B C D. Now mark out the two little triangles at A. A E is 6 inches, A F and E F each one foot; the other triangle, A R G, is the same size. Cut the canvas along these dotted lines. From the scraps left over cut two pieces for smoke-flaps, as shown. On the long corner of each (H in No. 1, I in No. 2) a small three-cornered piece should be sewed, to make a pocket for the end of the pole.

Now sew the smoke-flaps to the cover so that M L of No. 1 is neatly fitted to P E, and N O of No. 2 to Q D.

Two inches from the edge B P make a double row of holes;

each hole is 1½ inches from its mate, and each pair is 5 inches from the next pair, except at the 2-foot space marked "door," where no holes are needed.

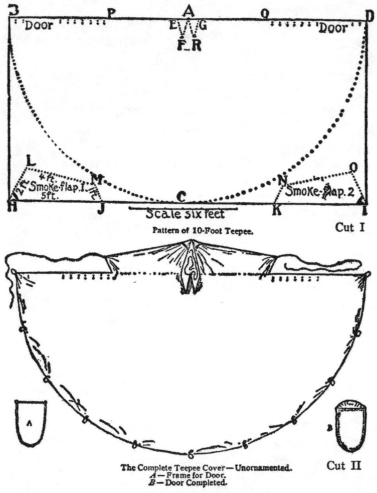

Pattern of 10-Foot Teepee.

Cut I

The Complete Teepee Cover—Unornamented.
A—Frame for Door.
B—Door Completed.

Cut II

The holes on the other side, Q D, must exactly fit on these.

At A fasten very strongly a 4-foot rope by the middle.

Fasten the end of a 10-foot cord to J and another to K; hem a rope all along in the bottom, B C D. Cut 12 pieces of rope each about 15 inches long, fasten one firmly to the canvas at B, another at the point D, and the rest at regular distances to the hem rope along the edge between, for peg loops. The teepee cover is now made.

For the door (some never use one) take a limber sapling ¾ inch thick and 5½ feet long, also one 22 inches long. Bend the long one into a horseshoe and fasten the short one across the ends (A in Cut II). On this stretch canvas, leaving a flap at the top in the middle of which two small holes are made (B, Cut II), so as to hang the door on a lacing-pin. Nine of these lacing-pins are needed. They are of smooth, round, straight, hard wood, a foot long and ¼ inch thick. Their way of skewering the two edges together is seen in the Omaha teepee at the end of the line below.

STORM CAP OR BULL-BOAT

During long continued or heavy rains, a good deal of water may come in the smoke vent or drip down the poles. To prevent this the Missouri Indians would use a circular bull-boat of rawhide on a frame of willows as a storm cap.

For a twelve-foot teepee the storm cap should be about four feet across and eighteen inches deep, made of

Storm-cap in place

canvas with a hem edge in which is a limber rod to keep it in circular shape. It is usually put on with a loose teepee pole, and sits on top of the poles as shown, held down if need be by cords to its edge.

The poles should be short and even for this.

PUTTING UP THE TEEPEE

Twelve poles also are needed. They should be as straight and smooth as possible; crooked, rough poles are signs of a bad housekeeper — a squaw is known by her teepee poles. They should be 13 or 14 feet long and about 1 inch thick at the top. Two are for the smoke-vent; they may be more slender than the others. Last of all, make a dozen stout short pegs about 15 inches long and about 1½ inches thick. Now all the necessary parts of the teepee are made.

This is how the Indian tent is put up: Tie three* poles together at a point about 1 foot higher than the canvas, spread them out in a tripod the right distance apart; then lay the other poles (except three including the two slender ones) in the angles, their lower ends forming a small circle. Bind them all with a rope, letting its end hang down inside for an anchor. Now fasten the two ropes at A Cut I to the stout pole left over at a point 10 feet up. Raise this into its place, and the teepee cover with it, opposite where the door is to be. Carry the two wings of the tent around till they overlap and fasten together with the lacing-pins. Put the end of a

---

*Some use four and find it stronger.

vent-pole in each of the vent flap pockets, outside of the
teepee.   Peg down the edges of the canvas at each loop.
Stretch the cover by spreading the poles.   Hang the door
on a convenient lacing-pin.   Drive a stout stake inside the
teepee, tie the anchor rope to this and the teepee is ready

1st Set up Tripod

3rd Set up tenth pole,
with teepee cover
fastened to it
by lash rope

2nd Set up & bind other
six poles

In hot weather raise the cover.

for weather.   In the centre dig a hole 18 inches wide and
6 inches deep for the fire.
The   fire   is   the   great   advantage   of   the   teepee,
experience will show how to manage the smoke.   Keep
the smoke-vent swung down wind, or at least quarter-
ing down.   Sometimes you must leave the door a

little open or raise the bottom of the teepee cover a
little on the windward side. If this makes too much draught
on your back, stretch a piece of canvas between two

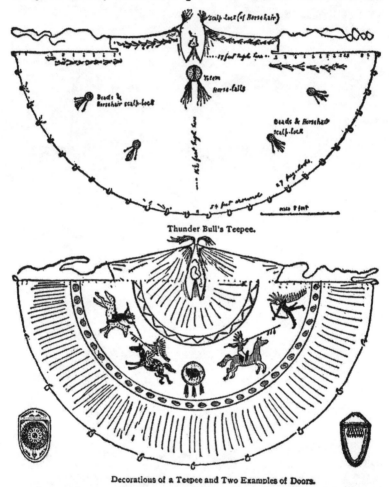

Thunder Bull's Teepee.

Decorations of a Teepee and Two Examples of Doors.

or three of the poles inside the teepee, in front of the opening
made and reaching to the ground. The draught will go up
behind this.

By these tricks you can make the vent draw the smoke.
But after all the main thing is to use only the best and
driest of wood. This makes a clear fire. There will
always be more or less smoke 7 or 8 feet up, but it worries
no one there and keeps the mosquitoes away.

RED — All parts marked so: ▥. Smoke-flaps and all tops of teepees, stem
of pipe, lower half-circle under pipe, middle part of bowl, wound on side
of Elk, blood falling and on trail; Horse, middle Buffalo, two inner bars
of pathway upback; also short, dark, cross-bars, spot on middle of two
door-hangers, and fringe of totem at top of pathway, and two black lines
on doorway.

YELLOW— All parts marked so: ▥Upper half-circle under pipe stem,
upper half of each feather on pipe; horseman with bridle, saddle and one
hindfoot of Horse; the largest Buffalo, the outside upright of the pathway;
the ground colors of the totem; the spotted cross-bars of pathway; the
four patches next the ground, the two patches over door, and the rings
of door-hanger.

GREEN — All parts marked so. ▥ Bowl of pipe, spot over it; feather
tips of same; Elk, first Buffalo, middle line on each side pathway, and
around teepee top; two dashed cross-bars on totem and dashed cross-bars
on pathway; bar on which Horse walks; lower edge and line of spots on
upper part of door.

HAIRY-WOLF'S TEEPEE

Marked with a peace pipe in Cut p. 468 is Hairy-Wolf's
teepee. I came across this on the Upper Missouri in 1897.

It was the most brilliant affair I ever saw on the Plains,
for on the bright red ground of the canvas were his totems
and medicine, in yellow, blue, green, and black. The day
I sketched it, a company of United States soldiers under

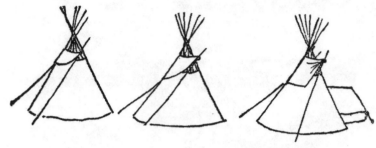

Chipewyan teepees with separate smoke flap

Blackfoot Lodge Calgary.

orders had forcibly taken away his two children "to send
them to school, according to law"; so Hairy-Wolf was going
off at once, without pitching his tent. His little daughter,
"The Fawn," looked at me with fear, thinking I was
coming to drag her off to school. I coaxed her, then gave

her a quarter.   She smiled, because she knew it would buy sweetmeats.

Then I said: "Little Fawn, run and tell your father that I am his friend, and I want to see his great red teepee."

Various tepees (smoke poles left out).

"The Fawn" came back and said, "My father hates you."

"Tell your mother that I will pay if she will put up the teepee."

"The Fawn" went to her mother, and improving my offer, told her that "that white man will give much money to see the red teepee up."

The squaw looked out. I held up a dollar and got only a sour look, but another squaw appeared. After some haggling they agreed to put up the teepee for $3. The poles were already standing. They unrolled the great cloth and deftly put it up in less than 20 minutes, but did not try to put down the anchor rope, as the ground was too hard to drive a stake into.

My sketch was half finished when the elder woman called the younger and pointed westward. They chattered together a moment and then proceeded to take down the teepee. I objected. They pointed angrily toward the west and went on. I protested that I had paid for the right to make the sketch; but in spite of me the younger squaw scrambled like a monkey up the front pole, drew the lacing-pins, and the teepee was down and rolled up in ten minutes.

I could not understand the pointing to the west, but five minutes after the teepee was down a dark spot appeared; this became a cloud and in a short time we were in the midst of a wind-storm that threw down all teepees that were without the anchor rope, and certainly the red teepee would have been one of those to suffer but for the sight and foresight of the old Indian woman.

ART

All students of the Indian art are satisfied that in this we find the beginnings of something that may develop into a great and original school of decoration. Not having learned their traditions, conventions, and inner impulse, we believe that at present we shall do best by preserving and closely copying the best of the truly native pro ductions.

Therefore, in decorating teepees, etc., we use only literal copies of the good Indian work.

Zuñi Wolf   Zuñi Deer   Zuñi Puma. 3.5M Rek   Zuñi Grizzly

INDIAN SEATS

Most boys are glad to learn of something they can make to sell for money. So I shall give you some designs for household furniture that every scout can make — they are not mission, but quite as serviceable and much more of a novelty: I mean real Indian furniture. It is very safe to say that everything you need in camp, from hair-combs to beds, blankets, and signboards, was made by the Indian in a more original way than any of us can expect to reach without help.

Very few of the Plains Indians made furniture, as we understand it, but those on the West Coast did. We may follow many of their designs exactly.

One of the simplest and most useful things is the low stool. Many of these are shown in Cuts I and II. These designs are closely copied after West Coast Indian work, though originally used to decorate boxes.

A chief's chair (e, f, g, h) is a fine thing to make for a Lodge-room or for sale, but in camp we seldom see anything so elaborate. Indeed, few fellows feel like doing cabinet work when out under the trees. They are not there for that purpose. In several cases we have made a fine throne for the chief out of rough, field stone; i in

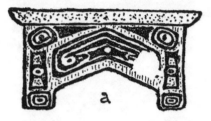

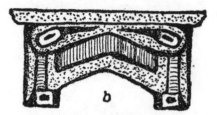

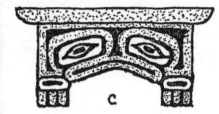

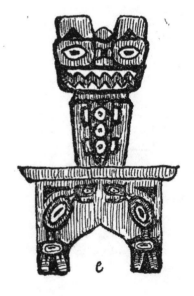

Cut I

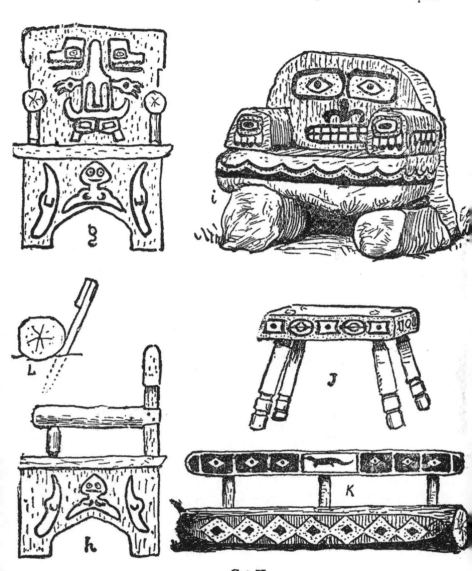

Cut II

Cut II is an example of this. The seat should be no
more than two feet from the ground, and even at that
height should have a footstool.

The stool J is of white man's construction, but Indian
decoration, in red, black and white.

The log seat, or Council seat, K, is a useful thing that each
Band should make in the Council ring. It is simply a log
flattened on top, on the front side. It has a board back,
supported on two or three stakes, as shown in L. This is
designed for the "Otters."

HEAD-BAND

Each brave needs a head-band. This holds his feathers
as they are won and his scalp if he wears one is fastened to it
behind. It consists of a strip of soft leather, long enough to
go around the head and overlap by two inches; it is fastened

at the rear, with a lace through the four holes, like the lace
of machine belting. A bead pattern ornaments the front
and it may be finished at each side in some broader design.
It is the foundation for the warbonnet and has places for
twenty-four feathers (two eagle tails). See Warbonnet
later.

The feathers are made of white quill feathers, the tip dyed dark brown or black; a leather loop is lashed to the quill end of each to fasten it on to the head-band. Each feather stands for an exploit and is awarded by the Council. An oval of paper is glued on near the high end. This bears a symbol of the feat it commemorates. If it was Grand Coup or High Honor, the feather has a tuft of red horsehair lashed on the top.

WARBONNET OR HEADDRESS — ITS MEANING

The typical Indian is always shown with a warbonnet, or warcap, of eagle feathers. Every one is familiar with the look of this headdress, but I find that few know its meaning or why the Indian glories in it so.

In the days when the Redman was unchanged by white men's ways, every feather in the brave's headdress was awarded to him by the Grand Council for some great deed, usually in warfare. Hence the expression, "a feather in his cap." These deeds are now called *coups* (pronounced *coo*), and when of exceptional valor they were *grand coups*, and the eagle's feather had a tuft of horsehair, or down, fastened on its top. Not only was each feather bestowed for some exploit, but there were also ways of marking the feathers so as to show the kind of deed.

Old plainsmen give an exciting picture in Indian life after the return of a successful war party. All assemble in the Grand Council lodge of the village. First the leader of the party stands up, holding in his hands or having near him the scalps or other trophies he has taken, and says in a loud voice:

"Great Chief and Council of my Nation, I claim a grand coup, because I went alone into the enemy's camp and learned about their plans, and when I came away I met one of them and killed him within his own camp."

Then if all the witnesses grunt and say: "*Hu!*" or "*How! How!*" ("So — it is so") the Council awards the warrior an eagle feather with a red tuft and a large red spot on the web, which tell why it was given.

The warrior goes on: "I claim grand coup because I slapped the enemy's face with my hand (thereby warning him and increasing the risk) before I killed him with my knife."

A loud chorus of "*How! How! How!*" from the others sustains him, and he is awarded another grand coup.

"I claim grand coup because I captured his horse while two of his friends were watching."

Here, perhaps, there are murmurs of dissent from the witnesses; another man claims that he also had a hand in it. There is a dispute and maybe both are awarded a coup, but neither gets grand coup. The feathers are marked with a horseshoe, but without a red tuft.

The killing of one enemy might (according to Mallery 4 Ann. Eth. p. 184) confer feathers on four different men — the first, second, and third to strike him, and the one who took his scalp.

After the chief each of the warriors comes forward in turn and claims, and is awarded, his due honors to be worn ever afterward on state occasions. All awards are made and all disputes settled by the Council, and no man would dream of being so foolish as to wear an honor that had not been conferred by them, or in any way to dispute their ruling.

In the light of this we see new interest attach to the head-dress of some famous warrior of the West when he is shown with a circle of tufted feathers around his head, and then added to that a tail of one hundred or more reaching to the ground or trailing behind him. We know that, like the rows of medals on an old soldier's breast, they are the record of wonderful past achievements, that every one of them was won perhaps at the risk of his life. What wonder is it that travelers on the plains to-day tell us that the Indian values his headdress above all things else. He would usually prefer to part with his ponies and his teepee before he will give up that array of eagle plumes, the only tangible record that he has of whatever was heroic in his past.

PLENTY-COUPS

I remember vividly a scene I once witnessed years ago in the West when my attention was strongly directed to the significance of the warbonnet. I was living among a certain tribe of Indians and one day they were subjected to a petty indignity by a well-meaning, ill-advised missionary. Two regiments of United States Cavalry were camped near, and so, being within the letter of the law, he also had power to enforce it. But this occurrence was the last of a long series of foolish small attacks on their harmless customs, and it roused the Indians, especially the younger ones, to the point of rebellion.

A Grand Council was called. A warrior got up and made a strong, logical appeal to their manhood—a tremendously stirring speech. He worked them all up and they were ready to go on the warpath, with him to lead them. I felt that my scalp was in serious danger, for an outburst seemed at hand.

But now there arose a big, square-jawed man, who had smoked in silence. He made a very short speech. It was full of plain, good sense. He told them what he knew about the United States Army — how superior it was to all the Indian tribes put together, how hopeless it was to fight it — and urged them to give up the foolish notion of the warpath. His speech would not compare with that of the other. He had neither the fire nor the words — he had not even the popular sympathy, and yet he quelled the disturbance in his few sentences, and as I looked there dawned on me the reason for his power. While the gifted orator of the big words had in his hair a single untufted eagle feather, the other, the man with the square jaw, had eagle feathers all around his head and trailing down his back and two feet

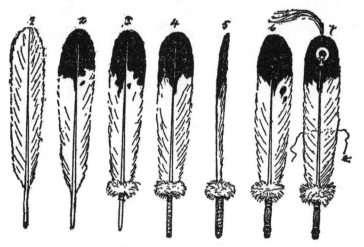

DETAILS OF THE WARBONNET

1. The plain white Goose or Turkey feather.
2. The same, with tip dyed black.
3. The same, showing ruff of white down lashed on with wax end.
4. The same, showing leather loop lashed on for the holding lace.
5. The same, viewed edge on.
6. The same, with a red flannel cover sewn and lashed on the quill. This is a "coup feather."
7. The same, with a tuft of red horsehair lashed on the top to mark a "grand coup", and (a) a thread through the middle of the rib to hold the feather in proper place. This feather is marked with the symbol of a grand coup in target shooting.

Some Indian Ways 487

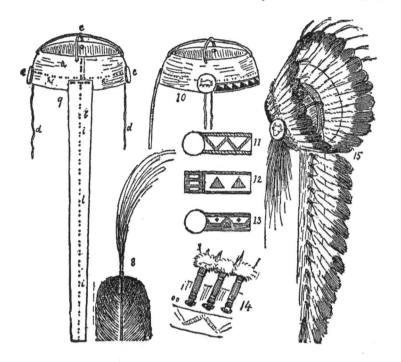

8. The tip of a feather showing how the red horsehair tuft is lashed on with fine waxed thread.

9. The groundwork of the warbonnet made of any soft leather, (*a*) a broad band, to go round the head laced at the joint or seam behind; (*b*) a broad tail behind as long as needed to hold all the wearer's feathers; (*c*) two leather thongs or straps over the top; (*d*) leather string to tie under the chin; (*e*) the buttons, conchas or side ornaments of shells, silver, horn, or wooden disks, even small mirrors and circles of beadwork were used, and some times the conchas were left out altogether; they may have the owner's totem on them, usually a bunch of ermine tails hung from each side of the bonnet just below the concha. A bunch of horsehair will answer as well; (*hh*) the holes in the leather for holding the lace of the feather; 24 feathers are needed for the full bonnet, without the tail, so they are put less than an inch apart; (*iii*) the lacing holes on the tail; this is as long as the wearer's feathers call for; some never have any tail.

10. Side view of the leather framework, showing a pattern sometimes used to decorate the front.

11, 12 and 13. Beadwork designs for front band of bonnet; all have white grounds. No. 11 (Arapaho) has green band at top and bottom with red zigzag. No. 12 (Ogallala) has blue band at top and bottom, red triangle; the concha is blue with three white bars and is cut off from the band by a red bar. No. 13 (Sioux) has narrow band above and broad band below blue, the triangle red, and the two little stars blue with yellow centre.

14. The bases of three feathers, showing how the lace comes out of the cap leather, through the eye or loop on the bottom of the quill and in again.

15. The completed bonnet, showing how the feathers of the crown should spread out, also showing the thread that passes through the middle of each feather on inner side to hold it in place; another thread passes from the point where the two straps (*c* in 9) join, then down through each feather in the tail.

on the ground behind him, and every one of them with a
bright red tuft of horsehair at its top, and I knew then that
I was listening to the voice of Plenty-Coups, the most
famous chief on the Upper Missouri, and I realized how a
few words from the man of deeds will go further than all the
stirring speeches of one who has no record of prowess to
back up his threats and fiery denunciations.

MAKING THE WARBONNET

Most modern warbonnets take the crown of a felt hat as
a basis, but the ancient way was to use a broad buckskin
band, as shown in the illustration.

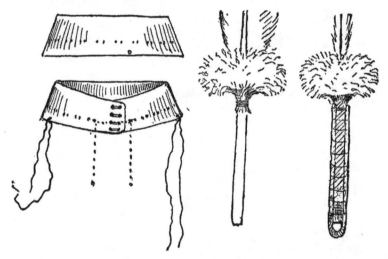

Tail feathers of the war eagle were considered essential
at one time, but many others are now used. I should be
sorry to increase a demand which would stimulate pursuit of
a noble bird already threatened with extinction.

Most of the big feather dealers have what are known as
"white quills." These are wing feathers of swans and are

sold at about 25 cents a dozen. These, when the tips are dyed brown, make a good substitute for eagle feathers. They are still more like if a little down from a white hen be lashed on.

The process of lashing a leather loop on the quill with a waxed thread, and of fastening a red tuft of horsehair on the top for the grand coup are sufficiently shown in the above illustration.

INDIAN COSTUME

War shirt. Next to the Indian warbonnet, the war shirt or coat is the most effective part of the costume. This may be made out of leather, khaki, woolen stuff, or even muslin. The finest ones used to be made of tanned deer skin, but those are very expensive. Buff-tanned calf or sheep skins, such as may be got at any leather shop, are quite as good for our purpose. It takes two or even three skins to make a war shirt. Sheep costs about 60 or 70 cents a skin, and calf at least double or even three times that, so that a good strong khaki at one third the price of sheep is likely to be more popular.

The pattern for making the war shirt is much like that of a common cotton shirt, except that it has no tucks. It fits a little more closely to the body while the sleeves are loose and without wristbands. In sewing it is usual to put into each sleeve at the back of the arm a long piece of leather three or four inches wide, and this is cut into fringe afterward. The bottom of the coat also is decorated with fringe.

The oldest style of war shirt was closed at the throat with tie strings, but some of the Indians used buttons after they saw how convenient they were.

The decorations are the most Indian part of it. Two kinds are in good usage: one, embroidery of quills or beads;

the other, painted figures. Fine effects can be secured in either way.

The first illustration shows a war shirt of the beaded style. These strips of beadwork are prepared on one of the beadlooms and sewn on afterward. The second is a quill-work device.

This is, of course, a mere suggestion. One may vary it in any way, though it will be found best always to use but

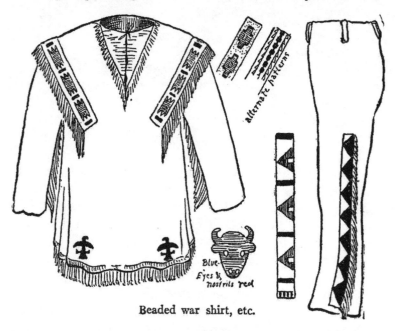

alternate patterns

Blue-
Eyes &
nostrils red

Beaded war shirt, etc.

few colors in the beads. In unskilled hands a bead pattern of two colors is better than one of four colors.

Bands of beadwork may be added on the outside of each arm in front of the fringes, as well as around the outer half of each cuff at the bottom, or they may be omitted altogether and the decorations done with paint. The Indians used native paints and dyes ground up in a mixture of rosin and grease. Black was made of soot taken from the bottom of a pot. Red, yellow, and white were made of clay

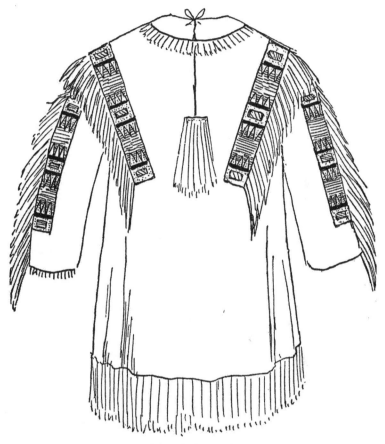

Quill worked war shirt

roasted and powdered. But common painters' oil colors will do very well if thinned out with turpentine.

Cotton costumes are used very often on the stage in Indian scenes; and when the ghost dance was danced in

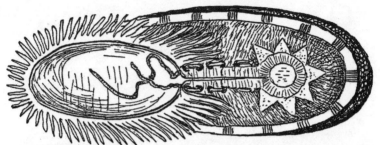

Moccasin, made of a rubber-soled shoe or sneak, embroidery of silk, red, white, blue & yellow. Around the ankle a fringe of leather.

Ojibwa Moccasin
with puckered front

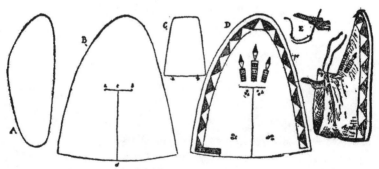

Making a Moccasin

Dakota by the Sioux, under Sitting Bull and Short Bull, nearly every one of the dancers appeared in a war shirt of painted cotton, made in some cases of old cotton flour sack.

Magnificent examples of war shirts are now to be seen in most museums. Many also are pictured in the Reports of the Bureau of Ethnology at Washington.

Leggings. The leggings are best made as ordinary trousers, embellished with fringe and beadwork on the sides.

Moccasins are a staple article of trade; but I have found nothing better or more serviceable than a pair of ordinary rubber-soled sneaks, decorated with a few beads or a fringe.

War Clubs. The only use we have for these is in the dancing or the ceremonies. They are most easily made of wood, and should be about twenty inches long. Painted with ordinary oil colors and embellished with tufts of horsehair or feathers, they are very picturesque as well as easily made.

Paddles. The best designs I ever saw for painting paddles are those of the West Coast Indians. These are shown in three colors, black, white, and red — the red being the portions cross-lined.

Drum. While an ordinary bought drum does very well for dancing, some tribes make their own, using a section of a hollow tree (or in some cases a small barrel) covered with untanned calf skin. It is soaked till soft, scraped clear of hair, and tightly stretched over each end of the hollow log. As it dries, it shrinks and becomes very tense, giving a good drum sound. Usually it is tuned up by warming at the fire before use.

The Indian Drum

Peace Pipe. The favorite peace pipe was of the red pipe stone, but I have seen many made of wood. The two shown are in my own collection.

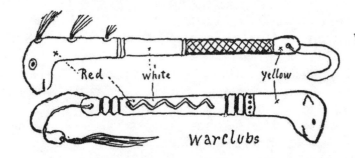

Red · white · yellow

Warclubs

Indian Paddles in black, white & red..

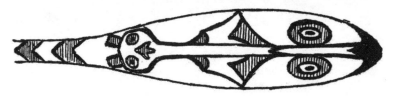

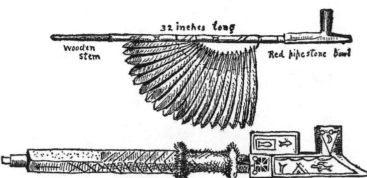

Wooden stem · 32 inches long · Red pipestone bowl

Wooden pipe spotted areas green else black with red & yellow incised lines, 33 inches long

THE INDIAN OR WILLOW BED

The only bed I know of which is light, portable, scout-like, made of wildwood stuff that can be got anywhere, and costing nothing but a little labor, is the willow or prairie bed used by all the Plains Indians.

This is how it is made: On your first short hike to the country go to some stream bank or swamp, and cut about seventy straight rods of red willow (kinnikinik), gray willow, arrow-wood, or any straight shoots, each about as thick as a pencil, when peeled, except one or two that are larger, up to half an inch thick; and all thirty inches long. Tie them up in a tight bundle with several cords until you get time to work them. Peel them, cut a slight notch in the butt of each rod, three quarters of an inch from the end, and you are ready to make the bed.

And here I may say that some fellows, who could not get to the country to cut willow rods, have used the ordinary bamboo fishing-poles. These are sawed up in 30-inch lengths and split to the necessary thinness; the butt end yields four or even five of the splints, the top, but one. This answers well, and three poles furnish material enough for the bed. This is allowable because, though the stuff is not of our own woods, it is American; it grows in the Southern States. One or two fellows in town have made the bed of dowels from a furniture factory.

Now get a ball of cord, that will stand a 25-lb. pull, a ball of fine linen thread, and a piece of shoemakers' wax, to complete your materials.

If outdoors, you can stretch your cords, between two small trees about seven feet apart, but it is much easier if you make a rough frame of strips or poles seven feet by three inside to work on.

Cut four pieces of the cord, each about twenty feet long.

Double each and tie a 3-inch hard loop in the middle. Twist these doubled cords and put them on a frame (Cut No. 1), fastened to nails as at A B, the surplus cord wrapped around the frame, and the others as at C D E F G and H.

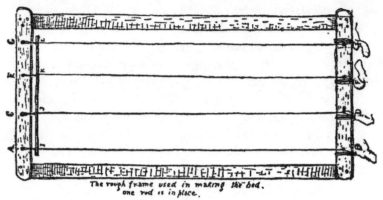

The rough frame used in making the bed. one rod is in place.

CUT NO. I.

Take one of the heaviest rods, say a half-inch one, for a starter. With a pointed stick, open the two strands of the twisted cord, and set the rod tight against the knots I J K L.

Now set a second rod in place below the first, seeing that two twists of the string are between each road and that the space separating them is one inch. Keep alternating butts and tops. At each point, that is at four places on each rod, make a lashing of waxed thread, holding rod and cords together (No. 2). I have seen beds with only two lashings, that is, one at each end, but four lashings is the sound and safe plan.

No. 2. The style of finish. All should be lashed like a & b.

When the rod-work is six feet long, it is time to taper off. Put in one big rod for a finish, and tie hard loops in the cords at this point. Then, using shorter rods, make a narrower part about eighteen inches high for a head. Finally, cover this head with a piece of brown khaki or canvas which should be decorated with the band's colors and totem, either painted or done in beadwork, or in colored cottons that are cut out and sewed on (Cuts Nos. 3 and 4).

No. 3. Various heads - canvas covering the rods.   Hook for Watch

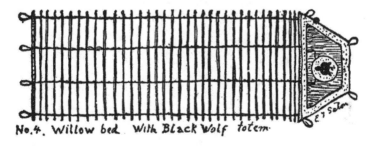

No. 4. Willow bed With Black Wolf totem

It is well to add also a wooden hook for one's watch (a and b, Cut No. 3) and a pocket for matches and money, etc., at night.

The Indians often elaborated these beds to a great extent when in permanent camps. Each rod was selected, perfectly straight, thinned at the butt end, to be uniform, and an extra piece added at the bed, head and foot, to curl up as end-boards. That at the head was elaborately deco-

rated with symbols in beadwork.   The illustration (No. 5)
shows a beautiful beaded bed-head in my possession; not
only the head, but the edges all around, are bound with red
flannel.

When in use the bed is laid with the ends of the rods

No. 5 The beaded head.

resting on two 4-inch poles, which are set firmly twenty-
six inches apart; and the bed is staked at the corners
through the loops to hold it in place (Cut No. 6).   Cut
No. 7 shows a fine specimen of an Arapaho bed all ready for
use.   When we can get no poles, we lay down a couple of
boards or rods to carry the ends of the bed, and then dig the

ground out in the middle. By means of two tall stakes the head part is held upright. When packed up the bed is rolled. It weighs about five pounds.

Of course, you always need *as much under you as over you.* Couched on such a natural spring mattress as the willow bed you sleep in perfect comfort.

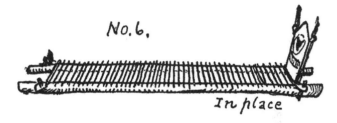

No.6.

In place

No. 7. ARAPAHO BED OF WILLOWS. 14th ANN.
Rep. Bur. Am. Ethn. P. 963

For those who wish to complete its sumptuousness a rush or grass mat may be added. (See Camp Loom.)

After long use the willows get bent, to prevent this the bed should be turned over every few days.

INDIAN PAINTS

Paints for the body are mixed with grease or tallow from some animal.

Paints for ornamenting robes are mixed with water. Clark: "Sign Language.")

Paints for lodges, totem poles, etc., were made durable by slowly melting or mixing into the grease enough rosin to make it sticky. This formed their paint oil.

Red. Before they had the white man's vermilion they used a certain stiff yellow clay (brick clay) which, when burnt, turned dull red—i. e., brick color. This they powdered and mixed with the grease oil.

In some parts of the country there are springs strongly impregnated with iron. A log of wood dug out of this — or failing that an armful of chips long soaked in it — when taken out, dried and burnt yielded ashes of a beautiful rosy color. These worked up into a very pretty red.

Yellow. Yellow clay or ochres are common in clay regions and furnish a dull yellow. Clark says that the flower of the prairie, goldenrod, yields a good yellow: also the bright yellow moss one sees on the trunks of pine trees in the Rockies. When dried and powdered this makes a sort of chrome yellow, and is also used as a dye.

"The Sioux use bull-berries" for yellow. (Clark.)

Blue. They had no good blue. Blue clays come nearest to the color. Sometimes black and white mixed were used.

Black. Soot and charcoal, ground into the paint oil, made a good black.

White. For white they used white clays, which are common in some regions, or burnt shells, finely powdered.

"Generally speaking, *Black* means joy: *White*, mourning: *Red*, beauty: and an excessive use of any of these or other colors, excitement."

"When painting for war, they use many stripes and rings of different colors, but on returning only black-colored paint is used."

"After killing an enemy, the lower part of the face might be painted black." (Clark.)

Painting was universal among Indians. They did it to beautify themselves and also to protect the skins from the weather. Though we condemn them for the practice, most of our women and a great many of our men do the same thing for the same reason.

Zuni eagles 23 Am. Rep. B. A. E.

INDIAN DYES

The dyes used to stain porcupine quills, spruce roots, and other strong material, of which they made ornaments and utensils, were very numerous, and some of them very beautiful.

Red. Soak the roots in the juice of the Squaw-berry — Blitum or Mis-caw-wa. Many other berries give red or purple.

Black. Boil the roots, etc., with the bark, branches, and berries of sumac, or the bark and chips of oak and soft maple, with some iron in the pot.

Yellow. A beautiful yellow is made by boiling the inner bark of golden or black oak. Or the root of yellowroot or hydrastis. In the Rocky Mountains the yellow moss off pine trees serves.

Orange. By boiling with the inner bark of alder or sassafras.

Scarlet. Dye yellow first then dip in red.

Most berries and barks yield a dye, and experiments with them often result in delightful discoveries.

NAMING THE CAMP — OR KEEPING THE WINTER-COUNT

When the return of the Grass-moon told the Indians that the New Year had come and that the old year had gone, the council debated the question: By what name shall we remember this last year? All names suggested by events were brought in. Smallpox Year, White-buffalo Year, Many-scalps Year, and so on. When a decision was reached the Keeper of the Winter-count made a pictograph in proper place on the Painted Robe, and so this record was kept.

In our tribes we select the name by which each Camp-out is likely to be remembered, and enter that in the Tally Book.

Thus we have: Camp-nothing-but-rain, Camp-bully-fun, Camp-robin's-nest-on-the-teepee, etc.

ARCHERY

The tribe should own a *Standard Target* — that is, 4 feet across, circular, made of straw, with a thin oilcloth cover, marked with a 9.6 inch centre of gold (called by some of our tribes "The Buffalo's Eye"); outside of that a 4.8-inch band of red, next a similar band of blue, next of black, next of white. Sometimes black rings of the right size are made to answer.

In scoring, the gold is 9, the red 7, the blue 5, the black 3, the white 1. The shortest match range for the target is 40 yards. If it is a 3-foot target the match range is reduced to 30 yards.

A target can be made of a burlap sack about five feet square. This should be stuffed full of hay or straw, then flattened by a few quilting stitches put right through with a long packing needle. On this the target is painted of exact right size.

Each brave should have a bow that pulls from 10 pounds up; about one pound for each year of his age is a safe guide for boys up to sixteen. He should have at least 6 arrows and a quiver. The arrows 25 inches long, with 3 feathers, cone-points of steel or iron; brass points are useless. A guard or bracer for the left wrist is needed, and most boys require a glove to protect the fingers of the right hand.

Bows can be bought for $1 to $5 and arrows from 15 cents to $3 each. But it is more creditable if you make them yourself.

HOW TO MAKE A BOW

Take a straight, sound piece of cedar, bodark, yew, sassafras, mulberry, apple tree, black locust, ironwood, ash, elm, hickory, or hemlock. Cut it so that it is half sap and half heartwood, flat on the sapwood side (or front) and round on the heartwood side (or back). It should be about an inch thick in the middle and tapered off to $\frac{3}{4}$ inch at each end. Cut two notches and put on a strong linen cord, either a bought bow-string or one made of many twisted linen threads. At one end it is fast to the bow by a timber hitch, at the other by a hard loop.

When strung the string should be about 5 inches from the bow.

Arrows should be 25 inches long, and $\frac{3}{8}$ of an inch thick. They are made of pine or ash. The Eastern Indians made them usually of arrow-wood or viburnum shoots.

Each should have a conical steel ferrule for head and three feathers to make it fly true. The feathers are lashed on.

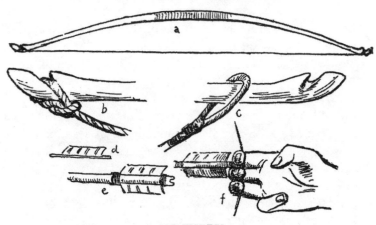

ARCHERY

a. The bow strung. b. The cord fast at the lower end. c. The cord
with loop at upper end. d. Feather ready to tie on. e. Feathers lashed
on. f. Holding.

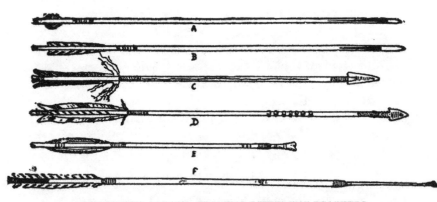

SIX SAMPLE ARROWS, SHOWING DIFFERENT FEATHERS.

A is a far-flying steel-pointed bobtail, very good in wind. *B* is another very good arrow, with a horn point. This went even better than *A* if there were no wind. *C* is an
Omaha war and deer arrow. Both heads and feathers are lashed on with sinew. The long
tufts of down left on the feathers are to help in finding it again, as they are snow-white and
wave in the breeze. The grooves on the shaft are to make the victim bleed more freely and
be more easily tracked. *D* is another Omaha arrow with a peculiar owner's mark of rings
carved in the middle. *E* is a bone-headed bird shaft made by the Indians of the Mackenzie River. *F* is a war arrow made by Geronimo, the famous Apache chief. Its shaft is
three joints of a straight cane. The tip is of hard wood, and on that is a fine quartz point;
all being lashed together with sinew.

HOLDING AND DRAWING

It is very important to begin shooting in correct form and never change from that if you wish to become a good shot.

Grasp the bow in the left hand. Put the arrow on the string with the right. Hook the first three fingers on the string one above, two below the arrow. The little finger and thumb do nothing. (f in upper cut, p. 504).

Stand perfectly upright, left side toward the target, the heels 12 inches apart and in exact line from the target. Hold the bow upright and the arrow against the left side of it, resting on the hand. Draw the cord till the head of the arrow touches the bow and the top of your thumb rests on the corner of your mouth. You must sight along the arrow for direction, but guess for elevation. Hold it one second.

Release the arrow by straightening your fingers and at the same time turn your hand back up, but keep the thumb tip at your mouth corner. Do not move the left hand a hair's-breadth till the arrow has struck.

Begin practising at very short range and slowly increase up to the standard, forty yards.

Unstring the bow when not in use.

THE WARBOW OF THE PENOBSCOTS

This warbow (Tong-bi) is as shown to me by Big Thunder, the Penobscot Chief, at Boston Sportsman's Show, December 12, 1900. He was then seventy-seven years of age, perfectly straight, and six feet four inches in height.

He said that the bow had been in his tribe for over two hundred years; fifty-five years ago it was put in his charge by his uncle, the late Chief John Nepta.

It is made of "hornbeam" in two pieces, loosely joined, with an auxiliary piece in front (AA), to which are attached two long thongs of caribou rawhide. This extra piece is bound to the arms of the main bow by a somewhat loose rawhide wrapping.

The string is three strips of rawhide, two of them loosely twisted together, the third tightly wrapped around both.

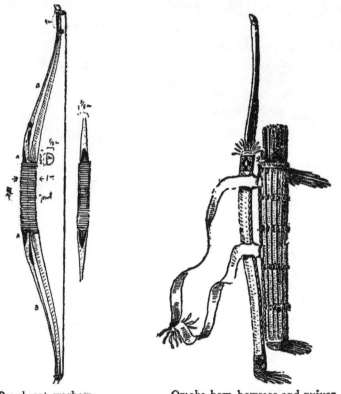

Penobscot warbow.   Omaha bow, bowcase and quiver.

The bow is 5 feet 6½ inches long, and pulls not more than 25 pounds, perhaps only 20. It seemed to me a very slow bow.

Yet the Chief told me it had killed many men and animals. He had recently shot a two-year-old moose with it.

The moose, he said, always lies down on a wound to get it next the earth, but thereby drives the arrow home.

Caribou rawhide, he claims, gets tighter when wet; and hornbeam practically never decays or loses its power with age.

The arrow he showed me was without feathers and had a stone head. The notch was very slight, showing that the pinch grip was necessary. It was 32 inches long, but the Penobscots made them up to 34 and 36 inches, usu-

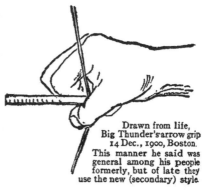

Drawn from life,
Big Thunder's arrow grip
14 Dec., 1900, Boston.
This manner he said was general among his people formerly, but of late they use the new (secondary) style.

ally with feathers. The grip by which he pulled was the Mongolian, as in the sketch.

That, he said, used to be the only one in use among his tribe, but recently they had used the grip known as the Secondary.

SCALPS

In some tribes each brave wears a long tuft of black horse-hair that answers as his scalp. The skin of this should be about one and a half inches across; it is furnished with a cord loop; the hair is as long as possible. This scalp is presented to the brave on entering the tribe. After he has promised obedience and allegiance and signed the roll the medicine man gives it to him, saying:

"This is your scalp. Treasure this as your honor. You may lose it without absolute disgrace, but not without some humiliation."

He can lose it only in an important competition, approved by the council, in which he stakes his scalp against that of some other brave. If he loses, he surrenders his tuft to the winner and goes tuftless — that is, he is dead until the council thinks proper to revive him by giving him a new scalp But he never gets back the old one, which remains the property of the winner for a teepee or other decoration.

A dead brave cannot vote or sit in council or take part in the competitions.

INDIAN WORK

For all kinds of genuine Indian work, to order if need be, send to Mohonk Lodge, Colony, Oklahoma.

XV. Campfire Stories or Glimpses of Indian Character

The Teachings of Winnemucca
Chief of the Piutes
About 1800

WINNEMUCCA was one of the famous old Chiefs who stood for valor, goodness, and courtesy; and was in himself a noble example of all his own doctrines.

Gen. O. O. Howard, who knew his people well, has recorded the teachings of Winnemucca. He ceaselessly exhorted his people:

"To love peace and make constant effort to keep it; always to be kind, one to another; always to tell the truth; and never to take for one's self what belonged to another; to treat old people with tender regard; to care for and help the helpless; to be affectionate in families, and show real respect to women, particularly to mothers." ("Famous Indian Chiefs I Have Known," p. 208–9, O. O. Howard, U. S. A., Century Co., N. Y. 1908.)

THE TEACHINGS OF WABASHA I.

In the day of his strength no man is fat. Fat is good in a beast, but in a man it is disease and comes only of an evil life.

No man will eat three times each sun if he would keep his body strong and his mind unclouded.

Bathe every sun in cold water and one sun in seven enter the sweat lodge.

If you would purify your heart and so see clearer the way of the Great Spirit, touch no food for two days or more, according to your strength. For thereby your spirit hath mastery over the body and the body is purged.

Touch not the poisonous firewater that makes wise men turn fools. Neither touch food nor taste drink that robs the body of its power or the spirit.

Guard your tongue in youth, and in age you may mature a thought that will be of service to your people.

Praise God when you rise, when you bathe, when you eat, when you meet your friends and for all good happenings. And if so be you see no cause for praise the fault is in yourself.

A proven Minisino is at all times clean, courteous and master of himself.

The wise man will not hurt his mind for the passing pleasure of the body.

If any man be given over to sex appetite he is harboring a rattlesnake, whose sting is rottenness and sure death.

By prayer and fasting and fixed purpose you can rule your own spirit, and so have power over all those about you.

When your time comes to die, sing your death song and die pleasantly, not like the white men whose hearts are ever filled with the fear of death, so when their time comes, they weep and wail and pray for a little more time so they may live their lives over again in a different manner.

THE LESSONS OF LONE-CHIEF, SKUR-AR-ALE-SHAR, GIVEN HIM BY HIS WIDOWED MOTHER

When you get to be a man remember that it is ambition that makes the man.

If you go on the warpath do not turn around when you have gone part way, but go on as far as you were going; then come back.

If I should live to see you become a man I want you to become a great man. I want you to think about the hard times we have been through.

Take pity on people who are poor, because we have been poor, and people have taken pity on us.

If I live to see you a man, and to go off on the warpath, I would not cry if I were to hear that you had been killed in battle. That is what makes a man, to fight and to be brave.

Love your friend and never desert him. If you see him surrounded by the enemy do not run away; go to him, and if you cannot save him, be killed together, and let your bones lie side by side. — ("Pawnee Hero Stories," by G. B. Grinnell, pp. 46–47.)

THE TEACHINGS OF TSHUT-CHE-NAU
CHIEF OF THE KANSAS, ABOUT 1800

On the lowest plane of all the great Indian teachers, perhaps, was Tshut-che-nau, Chief of the Kansas Indians. In 1800 he was a very old man, so probably his epoch was 1750 to 1800.

This Hammurabi of his people used to lecture the young Indians — as part of their training — and J. D. Hunter, the white boy, who was adopted into the tribe and sat at the old man's feet, has thus recorded principles there laid down:

When you become men be brave and cunning in war, and defend your hunting grounds against all encroachments.

Never suffer your squaws or little ones to want.

Protect the squaws and strangers from insult.

On no account betray your friend.

Resent insults.

Revenge yourself on your enemies.

Drink not the poisonous strong water of the white people; it is sent by the Bad Spirit to destroy the Indians.

Fear not death; none but cowards fear to die.

Obey and venerate the old people, particularly your parents.
Fear and propitiate the Bad Spirit, that he may do you no
harm.

Love and adore the Good Spirit, who made us all, who supplies our hunting grounds, and keeps us alive. — ("Captivity
Among the Indians," 1798–1816; John D. Hunter, p. 21.)

COURAGE OR THE TRAINED SCOUT

"With the Indian courage is absolute self-control. The
truly brave man, we contend, yields neither to fear nor
anger, desire nor agony. He is at all times master of
himself. His courage rises to the heights of chivalry,
patriotism, and real heroism.

" 'Let neither cold, hunger, nor pain, nor the fear of them,
neither the bristling teeth of danger nor the very jaws of death
itself, prevent you from doing a good deed,' said an old chief
to a Scout who was about to seek the buffalo in midwinter for
the relief of a starving people." ("Soul of the Indian," p. 115;
by Ohiyesa.)

AN INDIAN PRAYER

(Supplied by Miss Natalie Curtis)

O Powers that be, make me sufficient to my own occasions.

Give to me to mind my own business at all times and to
lose no good opportunity for holding my tongue.

When it is appointed for me to suffer let me take example
from the dear well-bred beasts and go away in solitude to
bear my suffering by myself.

Help me to win, if win I may, but — and this especially,
O Powers — if I may not win, make me a good loser.

GENESIS (OMAHA)

From the ritual of the Omaha Pebble Society
(Fletcher — LaFlesche, Eth. Ann. 27; p. 570)

"At the beginning all things were in the mind of Wakonda. All creatures, including man, were spirits. They moved about in space between the earth and the stars (the heavens). They were seeking a place where they could come into a bodily existence. They ascended to the sun, but the sun was not fitted for their abode They moved on to the moon and found that it also was not good for their home. Then they descended to the earth. They saw it was covered with water. They floated through the air to the north, the east, the south, and the west, and found no dry land. They were sorely grieved. Suddenly from the midst of the water uprose a great rock. It burst into flames and the waters floated into the air in clouds. Dry land appeared; the grasses and the trees grew. The hosts of spirits descended and became flesh and blood. They fed on the seeds of the grasses and the fruits of the trees, and the land vibrated with their expressions of joy and gratitude to Wakonda, the maker of all things."

THE QUICHÉ'S MYTH OF CREATION

This is the first word and the first speech: There were neither men nor brutes, neither birds, fish nor crabs, stick nor stone, valley nor mountain, stubble nor forest, nothing but the sky.

The face of the land was hidden; there was naught but the silent sea and the sky.

There was nothing joined, nor any sound, nor thing that stirred; neither any to do evil, nor to rumble in the heavens, nor a walker on foot; only the silent waters, only the pacified ocean, only it in its calm.

Nothing was, but stillness and rest and darkness and the night.

Nothing but the Maker and Moulder, the Hurler, the Bird Serpent.

In the waters, in a limpid twilight, covered with green feathers, slept the mothers and the fathers.

And over all passed Hurakan, the night-wind, the black rushing Raven, and cried with rumbling croak, "Earth!

Earth!" and straightway the solid land was there. — (From Ximenes.)

CLEAN FATHERHOOD

"This is the sum of everything that is noble and honorable — Clean Fatherhood," the words of Chief Capilano of the Squamish. (Pauline Johnson's "Legends of Vancouver," 1912, p 10.)

OMAHA PROVERBS

"Stolen food never satisfies hunger."
"A poor man is a hard rider."
"All persons dislike a borrower."
"No one mourns the thriftless."
"The path of the lazy leads to disgrace."
"A man must make his own arrows."
"A handsome face does not make a good husband."

(Fletcher — La Flesche, Eth. Ann. 27 p. 604)

THE MEDICINE MAN AND HIS WAYS

During the later Indian days the army surgeons came into close contact and rivalry with the Indian, and to the amazement of all whites, it frequently happened that the Indian doctor undertook and cured cases which the white doctors had pronounced hopeless. These were of all kinds, broken limbs, rheumatism, consumption, and obscure maladies (see "Medicine Man" in Clark's "Indian Sign Language").

This led to an investigation and a report on the ways of the medicine man. These were shown to be their chief peculiar methods:

1st: They took the patient home, giving him camp life with the daily sun-bath, and with pure air night and day.

2d: They gave him a periodic Turkish bath with purgatives.

3d: They gave him regular massage.

4th: They worked on his faith; they sang to him; they convinced him that great things were doing on his behalf. They did all in their power to set his mind at ease.

Besides which they had some knowledge of curative herbs and of dieting.

All of these have now a place among our own medical methods, yet we scoffed at them when offered to us by the Indians. They had to reach us from the East before we found them acceptable.

Of course there was a measure of quackery and fraud in many of the medicine men, but it is just possible that medical humbug was not entirely confined to the doctors of the Red Race.

THE INDIAN SILENCE

The first American mingled with his pride a singular humility. Spiritual arrogance was foreign to his nature and teaching. He never claimed that the power of articulate speech was proof of superiority over the dumb creation; on the other hand, it is to him a perilous gift. He believes profoundly in silence — the sign of a perfect equilibrium. Silence is the absolute poise or balance of body, mind, and spirit. The man who preserves his selfhood, ever calm and unshaken by the storms of existence — not a leaf, as it were, astir on the tree; not a ripple upon the surface of shining pool — his, in the mind of the unlettered sage, is the ideal attitude and conduct of life.

If you ask him, "What is silence?" he will answer, "It is the Great Mystery! The holy silence is His voice!" If you ask, "What are the fruits of silence?" he will say, "They are self-control, true courage or endurance, patience, dignity, and reverence. Silence is the cornerstone of character."

"Guard your tongue in youth," said the old Chief Wabasha, "and in age you may mature a thought that will be of service to your people!" — ("The Soul of the Indian," by Ohiyesa, pp. 89-90.)

THE INDIAN BABES IN THE WOODS

(By permission of Messers. Fleming H. Revell Company, N. Y.)

The charming story "Two Wilderness Voyagers," by F. W. Calkins, gives a true picture of the ways and powers of Indian children. Two little Sioux, a boy and a girl, Etapa and Zintkala, were stolen from their people and carried off into the land of the Ojibwa. They escaped and, though but eleven or twelve years old, wandered alone in the woods for months and eventually reached their own people on the plains.

Their ways and the thoughts of their kind toward the wonders of nature are admirably illustrated in the scene before Grandfather Rock:

In one of these short excursions the boy came upon a venerable gray boulder which stood as high as the surrounding trees and was many steps in circumference at its base. Except where the moose had eaten them off, this towering rock was thickly grown with lichens which gave it a hoary appearance of great age.

Etapa stood for some minutes, his eyes cast upward, venerating this aged and eternally enduring one which knows not time, seasons, nor change. Then the boy went softly back to Zintkala. "Come," he said, "I have found Grandfather Inyan — the very aged one. Let us smoke and pray to him!"

So they went together softly among the sand hillocks, until they confronted Grandfather Inyan. While Etapa prepared his pipe and willow bark for smoking, Zintkala stood — as a small devotee before a shrine — looking devoutly up at the everlasting one, the vast sentinel and guide, set so mysteriously among the trees.

"It is taku-wakan" (something wonderful), she said. While Etapa smoked, offering incense to the rock, sky and trees, she prayed thus:

"Behold us small ones, O Grandfather Inyan. You are doubtless very old and wise, therefore you, O Grandfather

Inyan, and ye trees, assist us greatly that we may find our way homeward.

Fire is sacred to Inyan; therefore, under the shadow of the great rock they built one of dry sticks and gathered a heap of fagots to keep the blaze going until far into the night.   Then alternately they said, "We will make a feast and dance to Grandfather Inyan, and so he shall help us."

"After they had eaten they combed their hair, greasing it with pieces of goose fat which Zintkala had saved, and then braided and tied their tresses becomingly.

After a reasonable time, by the light of the fire they had built to him, they gave a sacred dance to Grandfather Inyan and his protecting pines.   Upon a little plat of level ground, facing a broad scrap of the rock, and embowered in dark-topped evergreens, these little brown children danced.

The girl, with close drawn-blanket, with rapt face and serious air, performed her part in measured, dainty movements, dancing with her toes turned inward.

The boy, with less grace, but no less reverent face, sprang lightly from foot to foot, chanting low ejaculations of prayer.

Had the rock and the trees, sheltering their small circle of light and their brown swaying figures, possessed the ears, hearts and powers attributed to them, they must have moved even their roots to respond to the appeals for pity which these lost and revering waifs addressed to them.

When they had danced until they were weary they stretched themselves, tightly rolled in their blankets, upon the sands, and with renewed trust in the future, fell asleep." — (Pp. 112–114.)

THE STORY OF NO-HEART

(By permission of the Author)

(From "My Life as an Indian," by J. W. Schultz)

This story of No-Heart gives a realistic and kindly picture of life in an Indian village.   The heroine, a young girl nearing womanhood, had been caught with her family in a terrible thunderstorm.   When it was over all were dead but herself. In the village she had no other kins folk; thus she was left alone in the world:

Kind friends buried the dead, and the many different ones asked the girl to come and live with them; but she refused them all. "You must go and live with some one," said the chief. "No one ever heard of a young woman living by herself. You cannot live alone. Where would you procure your food? And think of what people would say, should you do so; you would soon have a bad name."

"If people speak ill of me, I cannot help it," said the girl. "They will live to take back their bad words. I have decided to do this, and I will find a way to keep from starving."

So this girl lived on alone in the lodge her parents had built, and with no company save her dogs. The women of the camp frequently visited her and gave her meat and other food, but no man, either young or old, ever went in and sat by her fire. One or two had attempted it, but only once, for she had told them plainly that she did not wish the society of any man. So the youths gazed at her from afar, and prayed the gods to soften her heart. She was a handsome young woman, a hard and cease-less toiler; no wonder that the men fell in love with her, and no wonder that they named her No-Heart.

One young man, Long Elk, son of the great chief, loved the lone girl so much that he was nearly crazy with the pain and longing for her. He had never spoken to her, well knowing that her answer would be that which she had given to others. But he could not help going about, day after day, where she could always see him. If she worked in her little bean and corn patch he sat on the edge of the river-bank nearby. If she went to the timber for wood, he strolled out in that direction, often meeting her on the trail, but she always passed him with eyes cast down, as if she had not seen him. Often, in the night, when all the camp was fast asleep, Long Elk would steal out of his father's lodge, pick up a water skin, and filling it again and again at the river, would water every row in No-Heart's garden. At the risk of his life he would go out alone on the plains where the Sioux were always prowling, and hunt. In the morning when No-Heart awoke and went out, she would find hanging in the dark entrance way, choice portions of meat, the skin of a buffalo or the deer kind.   The people talked about this, wondering who did it all.   If the girl knew she gave no sign of it, always passing the young man as if she did not know there was such a person on earth.   A few low and evil ones themselves hinted wickedly that the unknown protector was well paid for his troubles.   But they were always rebuked, for the girl had many friends who believed that she was all good.

In the third summer of the girl's lone living, the Mandans and Arickarees quarreled, and then trouble began, parties constantly starting out to steal each other's horses, and to kill and scalp all whom they could find hunting or traveling about beyond protection of the villages.   This was a very sad condition for the people.   The two tribes had long been friends; Mandan men had married Arickaree women, and many Arickaree men had Mandan wives.   It was dreadful to see the scalps of perhaps one's own relatives brought into camp.   But what could the women do?   They had no voice in the councils, and were afraid to say what they thought.   Not so No-Heart.   Every day she went about in the camp, talking loudly, so that the men must hear, scolding them and their wickedness; pointing out the truth, that by killing each other the two tribes would become so weak that they would soon be unable to withstand their common enemy, the Sioux.   Yes, No-Heart would even walk right up to a chief and scold him, and he would be obliged to turn silently away, for he could not argue with a woman, nor could he force this one to close her mouth; she was the ruler of her own person.

One night a large number of Arickarees succeeded in making an opening in the village stockade and, passing through, they began to lead out the horses.   Some one soon discovered them, however, and gave the alarm, and a big fight took place, the Mandans driving the enemy out on the plain and down into the timber below.   Some men on both sides were killed; there was both mourning and rejoicing in the village.

The Arickarees retreated to their village.   Toward evening No-Heart went down into the timber for fuel, and in a thick clump of willows she found one of the enemy, a young man badly wounded.   An arrow had pierced his groin, and the loss of blood had been great.   He was so weak that he could scarcely speak or move.   No-Heart stuck many willow twigs in the ground about him, the more securely to conceal him.

"Do not fear," she said to him, "I will bring you food and drink."

She hurried back to her lodge and got some dried meat and a skin of water, put them under her robe, and returned to the wounded one. He drank much, and ate of the food. No-Heart washed and bound the wound. Then she again left him, telling him to lie quiet, that in the night she would return and take him to her home, where she would care for him until he got well. In her lodge she fixed a place for him, screening one of the bed places with a large cow skin; she also partly covered the smoke hole and hung a skin across the entrance, so that the interior of the lodge had but little light. The women who sometimes visited her would never suspect that any one was concealed, and especially an enemy in a lodge where for three summers no man had entered.

It was a very dark night. Down in the timber there was no light at all. No-Heart was obliged to extend her arms as she walked, to keep from running against the trees, but she knew the place so well that she had little trouble in finding the thicket, and the one she had come to aid. "Arise," she said in a low voice. "Arise, and follow me."

The young man attempted to get up, but fell back heavily upon the ground. "I cannot stand." he said; "my legs have no strength."

Then No-Heart cried out: "You cannot walk! I had not thought but that you could walk. What shall I do? What shall I do?"

"You will let me carry him for you," said some one standing close behind her. "I will carry him wherever you lead."

No Heart turned with a little cry of surprise. She could not see the speaker's face in the darkness, only his dim form; but she knew the voice. She was not afraid. "Lift him then," she said, "and follow me."

She herself raised the wounded one up and placed him on the newcomer's back, and then led the way out of the timber, across the plain, through the stockade, in which she had loosened a post, and then on to her lodge. No one was about, and they were not discovered. Within a fire was burning, but there was no need of the light to show the girl who had helped her. He was Long Elk. "We will put him here," she said, lifting the skin in front of the couch she had prepared, and they laid the

sick man carefully down upon it.   Then Long Elk stood for a
little, looking at the girl, but she remained silent and would not
look at him.   "I will go now," he said, "but each night I will
come with meat for you and your lover."

Still the girl did not speak, and he went away.   But as soon
as he had gone No-Heart sat down and cried.   The sick man
raised up a little and asked, "What troubles you?   Why are you
crying?"

"Did you not hear?" she replied.   "He said that you are my
lover."

"I know you," said the man.   "They call you No-Heart,
but they lie.   You have a heart; I wish it were for me."

"Don't!" the girl cried.   "Don't say that again!   I will
take care of you, feed you.   As your mother is to you, so will
I be."

Now, when night came again, No-Heart went often out in the
passageway, staying there longer and longer each time, returning only to give the sick man water or a little food.   At last,
as she was sitting out there in the dark, Long Elk came, and,
feeling for the right place, hung up a piece of meat beyond
the reach of the dogs.   "Come in," she said to him.   "Come in
and talk with the wounded one."

After that Long Elk sat with the Arickaree every night for a
time, and they talked of the things which interest men.   While
he was in the lodge No-Heart never spoke, except to say, "Eat
it," when she placed food before them.   Day after day the
wounded one grew stronger.   One night, after Long Elk had
gone, he said, "I am able to travel; to-morrow night I will start
homeward.   I want to know why you have taken pity on me;
why you saved me from death?"

"Listen, then," said the girl.   "It was because war is bad;
because I pitied you.   Many women here, and many more in
your village, are crying because they have lost the ones they
loved in this quarrel.   Of them all, I alone have talked, begging
the chiefs to make peace with you.   All the other women were
glad of my words, but they are afraid and do not dare speak for
themselves.   I talked and feared not; because no one could bid
me stop.   I have helped you, now do you help me; help your
women; help us all.   When you get home tell what was done
for you here, and talk hard for peace."

"So I will," the Arickaree told her.   "When they learn all

that you have done for me, the chiefs will listen. I am sure they will be glad to stop this war."

The next night, when Long Elk entered the lodge, he found the man sitting up. By his side lay his weapons and a little sack of food. "I was waiting for you," he said. "I am well now and wish to start for home to-night. Will you take me out beyond the stockade? If any speak you can answer them and they will not suspect that their enemy passes by."

"I will go with you, of course," Long Elk told him. Whereupon he arose, slung on his bow and quiver, the sack of food, and lifted his shield. No-Heart sat quietly on the opposite side of the lodge, looking straight at the fire. Long Elk turned to her: "And you?" he asked. "Are you also ready?"

She did not answer, but covered her face with her robe.

"I go alone," said the Arickaree. "Let us start."

They went out, through the village, through the stockade, and across the bottom to the timber, where they stopped. "You have come far enough," the Arickaree said; "I will go on alone from here. You have been good to me. I shall not forget it. When I arrive home, I shall talk much for peace between our tribes. I hope we may soon meet again in friendship."

"Wait," said the Long Elk, as he turned to go, "I want to ask you something: Why do you not take No-Heart with you?"

"I would if she were willing," he answered, "but she is not for me. I tell you more truly this. She has been a mother to me; no more, no less. And you," he continued, "have you ever asked her to be your woman? No? Then go now, right now, and do so."

"It would be useless," said Long Elk sadly. "Many have asked her, and she has always turned them away."

"I have seen much while I lay sick in her lodge," the Arickaree continued. "I have seen her gaze at you as you sat talking to me, and her eyes were beautiful then. And I have seen her become restless and go out and in, out and in, when you were late. When a woman does that it means that she loves you. Go and ask her."

They parted; Long Elk returned to the village. "It could not be," he thought, "that the young man was right. No, it could not be." Had he not kept near her these many winters and summers? and never once had she looked at him, or smiled.

Thinking thus, he wandered on, and on, and found himself standing by the entrance to her lodge. Within he heard, faintly, some one crying. He could not be sure that was it, the sound of it was so low. He stepped noiselessly in and carefully drew aside the door skin. No-Heart was sitting where he had last seen her, sitting before the dying fire, robe over her head, and she was crying. He stole past the doorway and sat down beside her, quite close, but he dared not touch her. "Good-heart," he said, "Big-heart, don't cry."

But she only cried harder when she heard his words, and he was much troubled, not knowing what to do. After a little, he moved closer and put his arm around her; she did not draw away, so then he drew the robe away from her face. "Tell me," he said, "why you are crying?"

"Because I am so lonely."

"Ah! You do love him then. Perhaps it is not too late; I may be able to overtake him. Shall I go and call him back to you?"

"What do you mean?" cried No-Heart, staring at him. "Who are you talking about?"

"He who has just left: the Arickaree," Long Elk answered. But now he had edged up still closer, and his arm was tighter around her, and she leaned heavily against him.

"Was there ever such a blind one?" she said. "Yes, I will let you know my heart; I will not be ashamed, not afraid to say it. I was crying because I thought you would not return. All these summers and winters I have been waiting, hoping that you would love me, and you never spoke."

"How could I?" he asked. "You never looked at me; you made no sign."

"It was your place to speak," she said. "Even yet you have not done so."

"I do now, then. Will you take me for your man?"

She put her arms around his neck and kissed him, and that was answer enough.

In the morning, like any other married man, Long Elk went out and stood by the entrance to the lodge which was now his, and shouted feast invitations to his father and friends. They all came, and all were pleased that he had got such a good woman. Some made jokes about newly married ones, which made the young woman cover her face with her robe. Yet she was so happy that she would soon throw it back and laugh with the others.

In a few days came a party from the Arickarees, and the wounded young man was one of them, asking for peace. The story was told then, how No-Heart had taken in the young man and brought him to life again, and when they heard it many women prayed the gods to be good to her and give her and her man long life. Peace between the two tribes was then declared, and there was much rejoicing.— ("My Life as an Indian"; Schultz; "The Story of No-Heart," pp. 230–238.)

TECUMSEH

Of all the figures in the light of Indian history, that of Tecumseh, or Tecumtha the "Leaping Panther," the war chief of the Shawnees, stands out perhaps highest and best as the ideal, noble Redman.

His father was chief of the tribe. Tecumseh was born in 1768 at Piqua Indian Village, near the site of Springfield Ohio. Of all the Indians, the Shawnees had been most energetic and farseeing in their opposition to the encroachments of the whites. But the flood of invasion was too strong for them. The old chief fell, battling for home and people, at Point Pleasant, in 1774. His eldest son followed the father's footsteps, and the second met death in a hopeless fight with Wayne in 1794, leaving young Tecumseh war chief of his tribe. At once he became a national figure. He devoted his whole life and strength to the task of saving his people from the invaders, and to that end resolved that first he must effect a national federation of the Redmen. Too often tribe had been pitted against tribe for the white men's advantage. In union alone he saw the way of salvation and to this end he set about an active campaign among the tribes of the Mississippi Valley.

His was no mean spirit of personal revenge; his mind was too noble for that. He hated the whites as the destroyers of his race, but prisoners and the defenceless knew well that they could rely on his honor and humanity and were safe under his protection. When only a boy — for his military career began in childhood — he had witnessed the burning of a prisoner, and the spectacle was so abhorrent to his feelings that by an earnest and eloquent harangue he induced the party to give up the practice forever. In later years his name was accepted by helpless women and children as a guaranty of protection even in the midst of hostile Indians. He was of commanding figure, nearly six feet in height and compactly built; of dignified bearing and piercing eye, before whose lightning even a British general quailed. His was the fiery eloquence of a Clay and the clear-cut logic of a Webster. Abstemious in habit, charitable in thought and action, he was brave as a lion, but humane and generous withal — in a word, an aboriginal American knight-errant, whose life was given to his people.— (14 Ann. Rep. Ethn. p., 681.)

During the four years 1807 to 1811 he went from tribe to tribe urging with all his splendid powers the need for instant and united resistance.

His younger brother, Tenskwatawa the Prophet, was with him and helped in his way by preaching the regenerated doctrine of the Indian life. The movement was gaining force. But all Tecumseh's well-laid plans were frustrated by the premature battle of Tippecanoe, November 7, 1811. In this his brother, the Prophet, was defeated and every prospect of an Indian federation ended for the time.

The War of 1812 gave Tecumseh a chance to fight the hated Americans. As a British general he won many battles for his allies, but was killed leading his warriors at Moraviantown, near Chatham, Ontario, on October 5, 1813. His personal prowess, his farseeing statesmanship, his noble eloquence, and lofty character have given him a place on the very highest plane among patriots and martyrs.

If ever the great Hiawatha was reincarnated it must
have been in the form of Tecumseh.   Like Hiawatha, he
devoted his whole life to the service of his people on the
most heroic lines.   Like Hiawatha, he planned a national
federation of all Redmen that should abolish war among
themselves and present a solid front to the foreign invader.
"America for the Americans" was his cry, and all his life
and strength were devoted to the realization of his dream.
Valiant as Pontiac, wise as Metacomet, magnificent as
Powhatan, kind and gentle as the young Winona, he was a
farther-seeing statesman than they ever had had before,
and above all was the first leading Redman to put an end
to the custom for which they chiefly are blamed, the torturing of prisoners.   His people were always kind to their
own; his great soul made him kind to all the world.   He
fought his people's battles to the end, and when he knew
the cause was lost he laid aside his British uniform,
girded himself in his Indian war-chief dress for the final
scene, bade good-bye to his men and went forth, like King
Saul on Mt. Gilboa's fatal field, to fight and fighting die.
And the Star of his race had set.

Measured by any scale, judged by any facts, there can
be but one verdict: He was a great man, an Indian
without guile, a mighty soldier and statesman, loved and
revered by all who knew him.   More than a Red nobleman, he was acclaimed by all his kin who knew his life
as in very truth a Son of God.

KANAKUK, THE KICKAPOO PROPHET

"My father," he pleaded with President Monroe, "the
Great Spirit holds all the world in his hands.   I pray to
him that we may not be removed from our lands. . . .
Take pity on us and let us remain where we are."

Such was the petition of Kanakuk, peace prophet and leader in 1819, when the Kickapoos were ordered to leave the fertile corn lands of their fathers in Illinois and move out into the rugged hills of Missouri, among their traditional enemies, the Osages.

The effect of the petition was much the same as that which Naboth sent unto Ahab when that "president" of God's people coveted Naboth's heritage.

And what had they to charge against Kanakuk or his people? Their claim to the land was unquestioned. Were they objectionable or dangerous as neighbors? Surely not. No one pretended it. The doctrine Kanakuk taught his kindly people was a close parallel of the Ten Commandments, with the added clauses of non-resistance to violence, and of abstinence from drinking, gambling, and horse-racing.

Catlin, who visited the Prophet in his new home in 1831, and erronoeusly supposed the Kickapoo got these teachings from the Bible and the Christian missionaries, says (p. 697):

I was singularly struck with the noble efforts of this champion of the mere remnant of a poisoned race, so strenuously laboring to rescue the remainder of his people from the deadly bane that has been brought amongst them by enlightened Christians. How far the efforts of this zealous man have succeeded in Christianizing, I cannot tell; but it is quite certain that his exemplary and constant endeavors have completely abolished the practice of drinking whiskey in his tribe, which alone is a very praiseworthy achievement, and the first and indispensable step toward all other improvements. I was some time amongst those people, and was exceedingly pleased and surprised also to witness their sobriety and their peaceable conduct, not having seen an instance of drunkenness, or seen or heard of any use of spirituous liquors whilst I was among them.— (Catlin, Vol. II, p.98.)

In 1883 there was a great renewal of his teaching among his people, and their kin in the Indian Territory. Their ritual consisted chiefly of a ceremonial dance. The doctrine taught the same code as the Ten Commandments, but especially forbade drinking, gambling and horse-racing. — (14 Ann. Rep. B. A. E., p. 706.)

In 1885 the local Indian agent, Patrick, wrote in a curiously superior vein of this ancient faith revived.

These Indians are chaste, cleanly, and industrious, and would be a valuable acquisition to the Prairie band if it were not for their intense devotion to a religious dance started among the northern Indians some years since. This dance was introduced to the Prairie band about two years ago by the Absentee Pottawatomies and Winnebagoes, and has spread throughout the tribes in the agency. They seem to have adopted the religion as a means of expressing their belief in the justice and mercy of the Great Spirit and of their devotion to him, and are so earnest in their convictions as to its affording them eternal happiness that I have thought it impolitic, so far, to interfere with it any further than to advise as few meetings as possible and to discountenance it in my intercourse with the individuals practising the religion. It is not an unmixed evil, as, under its teaching, drunkenness and gambling have been reduced 75 per cent., and a departure from virtue on the part of its members meets with the severest condemnation. As some tenets of revealed religion are embraced in its doctrines, I do not consider it a backward step for the Indians who have not heretofore professed belief in any Christian religion, and believe its worst features are summed up in the loss of time it occasions, and the fanatical train of thought involved in the constant contemplation of the subject. — (Comr., 6.) (Mooney's "Ghost Dance Religion," 14 Ann. Rep. B. A. E., p. 706.)

CHIEF JOSEPH HINMATON OF THE SAHAPTIN OR NEZ PERCÉS

They [Nez Percés and Flat-heads] were friendly in their dispositions, and honest to the most scrupulous degree in their intercourse with the white men. . . . Simply to call these people religious would convey but a faint idea of the deep hue of piety and devotion which pervades the whole of their conduct. Their honesty is immaculate; and their purity of purpose and observance of the rites of their religion are most uniform and remarkable. They are certainly more like a nation of saints than a horde of savages.

So they were described in Captain Bonneville's narrative after his visit in 1834.

They were first officially noticed in the report of the Indian Commissioner for 1843, where they are described as "noble, industrious, sensible," and well disposed toward the whites, while "though brave as Cæsar," the whites have nothing to dread at their hands in case of their dealing out to them what they conceive to be right and equitable. — (14 Ann. Rep. Bur. Ethn., p. 712.)

About the middle of the last century their chief was Hinmaton-Kalatkit (Thunder-rolling), known more generally as Chief Joseph.

He was a splendid example of the best type of Redman, of superb physique, clinging to the ancient way, beloved by his people, feared by his enemies and, as it proved, a leader of tremendous power and resource.

In 1877, after they had sustained innumerable encroachments and flagrant violations of their treaty, a quarrel broke out between them and the whites and an Indian was killed.

Chief Joseph restrained his men and appealed for justice. For reply a band of whites raided the Indian reservation, ran off their cattle and killed the Indian in charge. So the war broke out. The first three fights were defeats for the whites, but more troops were soon rushed up. Joseph had barely one hundred warriors and three hundred and fifty helpless women and children. General Howard was behind him, General Miles in front, Colonel Sturges and the Crows

on his flank. He was obliged to retreat, and did so for
one thousand miles. "A retreat worthy to be remembered
with the story of the Ten Thousand."

After four months his starving band of warriors, now
reduced to half, surrendered to General Miles on condition
of being sent back to Idaho in the spring.

It was promised Joseph that he would be taken to Tongue
River and kept there till spring and then be returned to Idaho.
General Sheridan, ignoring the promises made on the battle-
field, ostensibly on account of the difficulty of getting supplies
there from Fort Buford, ordered the hostiles to Leavenworth
. . . but different treatment was promised them when they
held rifles in their hands. — (Sutherland, 1.)

Seven years passed before the promise was kept, and in the
meantime the band had been reduced by disease and death in
Indian Territory from about 450 to about 280.

This strong testimony to the high character of Joseph and his
people and the justice of their cause comes from the commissioner at the head of Indian affairs during and immediately after
the outbreak:

I traveled with him in Kansas and the Indian Territory for
nearly a week and found him to be one of the most gentlemanly
and well-behaved Indians that I ever met. He is bright and
intelligent, and is anxious for the welfare of his people. . . .
The Nez Percés are very much superior to the Osages and Paw-
nees in the Indian Territory; they are even brighter than the
Poncas, and care should be taken to place them where they will
thrive. . . . It will be borne in mind that Joseph has never
made a treaty with the United States, and that he has never
surrendered to the government the lands he claimed to own in
Idaho. . . . I had occasion in my last annual report to
say that "Joseph and his followers have shown themselves to
be brave men and skilled soldiers, who, with one exception, have
observed the rules of civilized warfare, and have not mutilated
their dead enemies." These Indians were encroached upon by
white settlers on soil they believed to be their own, and when
these encroachments became intolerable they were compelled,
in their own estimation, to take up arms." — (Comr. 27a.)

In all our sad Indian history there is nothing to exceed in pathetic eloquence the surrender speech of the Nez Percé chief:

"I am tired of fighting. Our chiefs are killed. Looking-Glass is dead. Toohulhulsote is dead. The old men are all dead. It is the young who say 'yes' or 'no.' He who led the young men is dead. It is cold and we have no blankets. The little children are freezing to death. My people, some of them, have run away to the hills and have no blankets, no food. No one knows where they are — perhaps freezing to death. I want to have time to look for my children and see how many of them I can find. Maybe I shall find them among the dead. Hear me, my chiefs. I am tired. My heart is sick and sad. From where the sun now stands I will fight no more forever." — (Sec. War. 3.) (Ann. Rep. Bur. Ethn. 14, p. 714-15.)

WHITE CALF, CHIEF OF THE BLACKFEET
(Died at Washington, Jan. 29, 1903)
(By George Bird Grinnell)

For sixty years, as boy, young man and fierce warrior, he had roamed the prairie, free as the other wild creatures who traversed it, and happy in his freedom.

He had been but a little fellow when the white men first came into the country to trade, but he was old enough to have been present, and was well enough thought of in the tribe, at the signing of Governor Stevens's treaty with the Prairie people in 1855, to affix his mark — as The Father — to that paper. As yet the coming of the white man meant little to him and to his people. It furnished them a market for their robes and furs, for which they received in exchange guns and ammunition, which made them more than ever terrible to their enemies. The whole broad prairie was still theirs to camp on and to hunt over. Their lodges were pitched along the streams from the Red Deer River on the north to the Elk River on the south, and their war journeys extended south to the country of the Mexicans.

More than twenty years ago happened the greatest misfortune that ever came to his tribe. The buffalo disappeared and never returned. From this time forth they were forced to depend on the food given them by the white men, and, in order to receive that food, they were obliged to stay in one place, to confine themselves to that little corner of ground, their reservation.

Long before this he had become the chief of his tribe — the father of his people. Already he was putting their welfare before his own, was thinking first of them and of himself last.

For it was the duty of a chief to look out for the well-being of his people; to care for the widows and orphans; to make peace between those who quarrel; to give his whole heart and his whole mind to the work of helping his people to be happy. Such were the duties that the old-time chief studied to perform. And since on his example and his precept so much depended, he must be a man who was brave in war, generous in disposition, liberal in temper, deliberate in making up his mind, and of good judgment. Such men gave themselves to their work with heart and soul, and strove for the welfare of those in their charge with an earnestness and a devotion that perhaps are not equaled by any other rulers of men.

And this devotion to his fellows was not without its influence on the man himself; after a time the spirit of good will which animated him began to shine forth in his countenance, so that at length, and as they grew old, such chiefs came to have the beneficent and kindly expression that we may sometimes see on the countenance of an elderly minister of God whose life has been one long, loving sacrifice of self to his Maker and to his fellowmen. And if the face was benevolent and kindly, not less sweet and gentle was the spirit that animated the man. Simple, honest, generous, tender-hearted, and yet withal on occasion merry and jolly. Such men, once known, commanded universal respect and admiration. They were like the conventional notion of Indians in nothing save in the color of the skin. They were true friends, delightful companions, wise counselors — men whose conduct toward their fellowmen we all might profitably imitate. We do not commonly attribute a spirit of altruism to Indians, but it was seen in these old-time chiefs.

Such a chief was White Calf, long chief of the Blackfeet. In his day he had been a famous warrior, and in the battle which took place in 1867, when the great chief, Many Horses, was killed, White Calf with two others had rushed into a great crowd of the enemy — the Crows and Gros-Ventres — who were trying to kill Wolf Calf, even then an old man, and, scattering them like smoke before the wind, had pulled the old man out of the crush and brought him safely off. It was not long after this that he put aside the warpath forever, and since then had confined himself to working for the good of his people by the arts of peace. No sacrifice was too great for him to make if he thought that by it the tribe might be helped; yet he possessed a sturdy independence that bullying and intimidation could not move — even that threats of soldiers and the guard house could not shake. When he was sure that he was right he could not be stirred. Yet, if reasons were advanced which appealed to his judgment, no man was quicker to acknowledge error.

Though nearly eighty years old the chief was not bowed with the weight of time nor were his natural forces greatly abated. He was still erect and walked with a briskness and an elasticity rare for one of his years. Yet in a degree he felt that his powers were failing, and he sometimes avoided the decision of important questions on the ground that he was getting old and his mind was no longer good.

A little more than two weeks ago he stood in the presence of the Chief Magistrate of the nation, who shook him warmly by the hand and talked to him and the others of his people present. A few days later, just as they were about to leave Washington for their distant prairie home, the old chief caught cold, pneumonia set in, and just before midnight on the 29th of January he peacefully passed away.

He was a man who was great in the breadth of his judgment, and in the readiness with which he recognized the changes he and his people were now obliged to face, and adapted himself to these changes; but greatest of all, in the devotion that he held for his tribe, and in the way in which he sacrificed himself for their welfare. Buffalo hunter, warrior, savage ruler and diplomat; then learner, instructor, persuader and encourager in new ways, he was always the father of the people. Just as for many years he had been constantly serving them, so now, at the end of his long chieftainship, he gave up his life in the successful effort to protect them from a great calamity.

WOVOKA, THE PROPHET OF THE GHOST DANCE

There have been many in every tribe and every time who have brought shame on their people. There have been whole tribes who forgot their race's high ideals. From time to time great prophets have arisen amongst them to stir up these backsliders, and bring them back to the faith of their fathers. The last of these was Wovoka, the Piute — the Mystic Dreamer. About 1887 he began preaching his doctrine of the coming Messiah and taught the Redmen that they must worship him by the Ghost dance. This is his own simple setting forth of the doctrine:

When the Sun died I went up into Heaven and saw God and all the people who had died a long time ago. God told me to come back and tell my people they must be good and love one another and not to fight or steal or lie. He gave me this dance to give to my people. — (Ethn. Ann. 14. p. 764.)

At Pine Ridge, S. D., in the winter of 1890, the Sioux were learning this dance with its songs and its Christ-like creed. It meant the end of war. War had been their traditional noblest pursuit. But now at the bidding of the new prophet they agreed to abjure it forever; and they prepared to take up the new religion of love.

The Indian agent, like most of his kind, was ignorant and utterly unfitted for his position. He said it was some new sort of a *war dance*. The troops were sent for and the Indian populace was gathered together at a place called Wounded Knee near Pine Ridge (Dec. 29, 1890). They had submitted and turned in their rifles. Then, maddened by the personal indignities offered them in searching for more arms, a young Indian who still had a gun fired at the soldiers. It is not stated that he hit any one, but the answer was a volley that killed half the men. A minute later a battery of four Hotchkiss machine guns was turned on the defenceless mass of virtual prisoners; 120 men, and 250 helpless women and children were massacred in broad daylight, mown down, and left on the plain, while the white soldiers pursued the remnant and the cripples, to do them to death in the hills.

Almost all the dead warriors were found lying near where the "fight" began, about Bigfoot's teepee, but the bodies of the women and children were found scattered along for two miles from the scene of the encounter, showing that they had been killed while trying to escape. — (Ethn. Ann. 14, pp. 868 – 870.)

As the men were in a separate company from the women and children, no one pretended that it was accidental.

The women, as they were fleeing with their babes, were killed together, shot right through, and the women who were very heavy with child were also killed. All the Indians fled in these three directions, and after most all of them had been killed, a cry was made that all those who were not killed or wounded should come forth and they would be safe. Little boys who were not wounded came out of their places of refuge, and as soon as they came in sight, a number of soldiers surrounded them and butchered them there. — ("Ghost Dance Religion," Mooney; Ethn. Rep. 14.   885-886.)

Nothing in the way of punishment was done by the authorities to any of the assassins. When the guards of Czar Nicholas shot down some scores of peasants who, contrary to orders, marched in a body to his palace, all America rang with horror and indignation, but nothing was said about the infinitely worse massacre at Wounded Knee.

As sure as there is a God in Heaven, this thing has to be met again, and for every drop of righteous blood spilled that day and on a thousand other days of like abomination, a fearful vengeance is being stored and will certainly break on us.

As sure as Cain struck down himself when he murdered Abel; as sure as the blood of righteous Naboth cried from the ground and wrecked the house and the kingdom and the race of Ahab; so surely has the American nation to stand before the bar of an earthly power — a power invincible, overwhelming, remorseless, and pay the uttermost price.

As sure as this land was taken by fraud and held by

cruelty and massacre, we have filled for ourselves a vial of wrath. It will certainly be outpoured on us to the last drop and the dregs. What the Persian did to rich and rotten Babylon, what the Goth did to rich and bloody Rome, another race will surely do to us.

If ever the aroused and reinspired Yellow man comes forth in his hidden strength, in his reorganized millions, overpowering, slaying, burning, possessing, we can only bow our heads and say, "These are the instruments of God's wrath. We brought this on ourselves. All this we did to the Redman. The fate of Babylon and of bloody Rome is ours. We wrote our own doom as they did."

THE APACHE INDIAN'S CASE

(From "On the Border with Crook" by Captain John G. Bourke, U. S. A. Courtesy of Messrs Charles Scribner's Sons.)

For years I have collected the data and have contemplated the project of writing the history of this people, based not only upon the accounts transmitted to us from the Spaniards and their descendants, the Mexicans, but upon the Apache's own story, as conserved in his myths, and traditions; but I have lacked both the leisure and the inclination, to put the project into execution. It would require a man with the even-handed sense of justice possessed by a Guizot, and the keen, critical, analytical powers of a Gibbon, to deal fairly with a question in which the ferocity of the savage Redman has been more than equaled by the ferocity of the Christian Caucasian; in which the occasional treachery of the aborigines has found its best excuse in the unvarying Punic faith of the Caucasian invader; in which promises on each side have been made, only to deceive and to be broken; in which the red hand of war has rested most heavily upon shrieking mother and wailing babe.

If from this history, the Caucasian can extract any cause of self-laudation I am glad of it: speaking as a censor who has read the evidence with as much impartiality as could be expected from one who started in with the sincere conviction that the only good Indian was a dead Indian, and that the only use to make of him was that of a fertilizer; and who, from studying the documents in the case, and listening little by little to the savage's own story, has arrived at the conclusion that perhaps Pope Paul III was right when he solemnly declared that the natives of the New World had souls and must be treated as human beings, and admitted to the sacraments when found ready to receive them. I feel it to be my duty to say that the Apache has found himself in the very best of company when he committed any atrocity, it matters not how vile, and that his complete history, if it could be written by himself, would not be any special cause of self-complacency to such white men as believe in a just God, who will visit the sins of parents upon their children, even to the third and fourth generation.

We have become so thoroughly Pecksniffian in our self-laudation, in our exaltation of our own virtues, that we have become grounded in the error of imagining that the American savage is more cruel in his war customs than other nations of the earth have been; this I have already intimated, in a misconception, and statistics, for such as care to dig them out, will prove that I am right. The Assyrians cut their conquered foes limb from limb; the Israelites spared neither parent nor child; the Romans crucified head downward the gladiators who revolted under Spartacus; even in the civilized England of the past century, the wretch convicted of treason was executed under circumstances of cruelty which would have been too much for the nerves of the fiercest of the Apaches or Sioux. Instances in support of what I here assert crop up all over the pages of history; the trouble is, not to discover them, but to keep them from blinding the memory to matters more pleasant to remember. Certainly, the American aborigine is not indebted to his pale-faced brother, no matter of what nation or race he may be, for lessons in tenderness and humanity.

After reviewing the methods by which the gentle, friendly natives were turned into tigers, Bourke gives this final example:

"And then there have been 'Pinole Treaties,' in which the Apaches have been invited to sit down and eat repasts seasoned with the exhilarating strychnine. So that, take it for all in all, the honors have been easy so far as treachery, brutality, cruelty and lust have been concerned. The one great difference has been that the Apache could not read or write and hand down to posterity the story of his wrongs, as he, and he alone, knew them."—("On the Border with Crook," John G. Bourke, pp. 114-15-16-17-18.)

THE WIPING OUT OF NANNI-CHADDI

(December 27th, 1872.)

(From the account by Captain J. G. Bourke, in his book "On the Border with Crook" 1892. By permission of Messrs Charles Scribner's Sons.)

For the same old reason, as always before, the Apaches of Arizona were fighting the whites, but doing it successfully. The Government at length sent against them fresh

troops under Gen. George Crook, who was said by Gen.
W. T. Sherman to be the greatest Indian fighter and
manager that the Army of the United States had had.
But, more than this, he was a man respected, admired and
beloved by every one who knew him — friend or foe.   All
the wise ones felt that the solution was in sight when Crook
took command.

Throughout the history of the matter, we find the great
General torn by two conflicting thoughts — first, "My
duty as a soldier of my country"; and, second, "These
Indians are in the right."   In his own words, "The American Indian commands respect for his rights, only so long
as he inspires terror with his rifle."

With characteristic sternness, energy and fortitude he
began the campaign, as *winter set in*, just when his pred-
ecessors had moved into comfortable quarters.

To realize that the mountains were full of Apaches that
swooped down at unexpected times, spreading fire and
slaughter and fearful destruction — was one thing and an
easy one, but to find them and strike back was a wholly
different matter.

The white soldiers under Crook would have been powerless, in spite of their far superior numbers, their superb
equipment, abundance of food and ammunition, but for
the fact that the Apaches themselves were divided, and the
white soldiers had with them a large band of these red
renegades, who did all the scouting, trailing and finer work
of following and finding the foe, as well as guarding their
white allies from surprise.

Late in December, Major Brown, with three companies
of the Fifth Cavalry, some forty Apache scouts, and about
one hundred more from the Pima nation, under their Chief,
Esquinosquizn or Bocon, set out to run down the band of
Chief Chuntz, who was terrorizing those settlers that had

encroached on the acknowledged territory of the Apaches, the Gila and Salt River valleys. They were led by Nantahay, a renegade Apache of the region, and set out fully equipped and determined to kill or capture every Apache they could find.

Led by these renegades, the soldiers crept silently up a tremendous canyon, and at last into plain view of a large, shallow cave or natural rock shed in which was a considerable band of Apache Indians, men, women, and children, only forty yards away and wholly unconscious of the enemy so near.

The men were singing and dancing in a religious ceremony; the women were preparing the midday meal. The white soldiers had ample time to post themselves and select each his victim.

"Had not the Apaches been interested in their own singing they might surely have heard the low whisper, "Ready! aim! fire!" but it would have been too late; the die was cast, and their hour had come.

The fearful noise, which we have heard reverberating from peak to peak and from crag to crag, was the volley poured in by Ross and his comrades, which had sent six souls to their last account, and sounded the death-knell of a powerful band.

*　　*　　*　　*　　*　　*　　*

Brown's first work was to see that the whole line was impregnable to assault from the beleaguered garrison of the cave, and then he directed his interpreters to summon all to an unconditional surrender. The only answer was a shriek of hatred and defiance, threats of what we had to expect, yells of exultation at the thought that not one of us should ever see the light of another day.

*　　*　　*　　*　　*　　*　　*

There was a lull of a few minutes; each side was measuring its own strength and that of its opponent. It was apparent that any attempt to escalade without ladders would result in the loss of more than half our command; the great rock wall in front of the cave was not an inch less than ten feet in height at its lowest point, and smooth as the palm of the hand; it would be madness to attempt to climb it, because the moment the assailants reached the top, the lances of the invested force could push them back to the ground, wounded to death. Three or four of our picked shots were posted in eligible positions overlooking the places where the Apaches had been seen to expose themselves; this, in the hope that any recurrence of such foolhardiness, would afford an opportunity for the sharpshooters to show their skill. Of the main body, one half was in reserve fifty yards behind the skirmish line — to call it such, where the whole business was a skirmish line — with carbines loaded and cocked, and a handful of cartridges on the clean rocks in front, and every man on the lookout to prevent the escape of a single warrior, should any be fortunate enough to sneak or break through the first line. The men on the first line had orders to fire as rapidly as they chose, directing aim against the roof of the cave, with the view to having the bullets glance down among the Apache men, who had massed immediately back of the rock rampart.

This plan worked admirably, and, so far as we could judge, our shots were telling upon the Apaches and irritating them to that degree that they no longer sought shelter, but boldly faced our fire, and returned it with energy, the weapons of the men being reloaded by the women, who shared their dangers. A wail from a squaw and the feeble cry of a little babe were proof that the missiles of death were not seeking men alone. Brown ordered our fire to cease, and for the last time summoned the Apaches to surrender, or to let their women and children come out unmolested. On their side, the Apaches also ceased all hostile demonstrations, and it seemed to some of us Americans that they must be making ready to yield, and were discussing the matter among themselves. Our Indian guides and interpreters raised the cry, "Look out! there goes the Death Song; they are going to charge!" It was a weird chant,* one not at all easy to describe, half wail and half exultation — the frenzy of despair, and the wild cry for revenge. Now, the petulant, querulous treble of the squaws kept time with the shuffling feet, and again the deeper growl of the savage bull-dogs, who represented manhood in that cave, was flung back from the cold, pitiless brown of the cliffs.

"Look out! here they come!" Over the rampart, guided by one impulse, moving as if they were all part of one body, jumped and ran twenty of the warriors — superb-looking fellows, all of them; each carried upon his back a quiver filled with the long reed arrows of the tribe; each held in his hands a bow and a rifle, the latter at full cock. Half of the party stood upon the rampart, which gave them some chance to sight our men behind the smaller rocks in front, and blazed away for all they were worth — they were trying to make a demonstration to engage our attention, while the other part suddenly slipped down and around our right flank, and out through the rocks which had so effectively sheltered the retreat of the one who had so nearly succeeded in getting away, earlier in the morning. Their motives were divined, and the move was frustrated;

---

* A Death Song, probably the one used here, is:
  "Father we are going out to die,
  Let not fear enter into our hearts.
  For ourselves, we grieve not, but for those that are left behind.
  We are going out to die."

our men rushed to the attack like furies, each seeming to be anxious to engage the enemy at close quarters. Six or seven of the army were killed in a space not twenty-five feet square, and the rest driven back within the cave, more or less wounded.

* * * * * * *

One of the charging party, seeing that so much attention was converged upon our right, had slipped down unnoticed from the rampart, and made his way to the space between our two lines, and had sprung to the top of a huge boulder, and there had begun his war-whoop, as a token of encouragement to those still behind. I imagine that he was not aware of our second line, and thought that once in our rear, ensconced in a convenient nook in the rocks, he could keep us busy by picking us off at his leisure. His chant was never fiendish; it was at once his song of glory and his death song; he had broken through our line of fire, only to meet a far more cruel death. Twenty carbines were gleaming in the sunlight just flushing the cliffs; forty eyes were sighting along the barrels. The Apache looked into the eyes of his enemies, and in not one did he see the slightest sign of mercy; he tried to say something; what it was we never could tell. "No! no! soldadoes!" in broken Spanish, was all we could make out, before the resounding volley had released another soul from its earthly casket and let the bleeding corpse fall to the ground, as limp as a wet moccasin. He was really a handsome warrior; tall, well-proportioned, finely muscled, and with a bold, manly countenance. "Shot to death," was the verdict of all who paused to look upon him, but that didn't half express the state of the case. I have never seen a man more thoroughly shot to pieces than was this one; every bullet seemed to have struck, and not less than eight or ten had inflicted mortal wounds.

The savages in the cave, with death staring them in the face, did not seem to lose their courage — or shall we say despair? They resumed their chant, and sang with vigor and boldness, until Brown determined that the battle or siege must end. Our two lines were now massed in one, and every officer and man told to get ready a package of cartridges; then, as fast as the breech-block of the carbine could be opened and lowered, we were to fire into the mouth of the cave, hoping to inflict the greatest damage by glancing bullets, and then charge in by the entrance on our right flank, back of the rock rampart which had served as the means of exit for the hostiles when they made their attack.

*   *   *   *   *   *   *

The Apaches did not relax their fire, but, from the increasing groans of the women, we knew that our shots were telling, either upon the women in the cave, or upon their relatives among the men for whom they were sorrowing.

It was exactly like fighting with wild animals in a trap; the Apaches had made up their minds to die, if relief did not reach them from some of the other "rancherias" supposed to be close by.

*   *   *   *   *   *   *

Burns and several others went to the crest and leaned over, to see what all the frightful hubub was about. They saw the conflict going on beneath them and in spite of the smoke, could make out that the Apaches were nestling up close to the rock rampart, so as to avoid as much as possible the projectiles which were raining down from the roof of their eyrie home.

It didn't take Burns five seconds to decide what should be done; he had two of his men harnessed with the sus- penders of their comrades, and made them lean well over the precipice, while the harness was used to hold them in place; these men were to fire with their revolvers at the enemy beneath, and for a volley or so they did very effec- tive work, but their Irish blood got the better of their rea- son and, in their excitement, they began to throw their revolvers at the enemy; this kind of ammunition was rather too costly, but it suggested a novel method of annihilating the enemy. Brown ordered his men to get together and roll several of the huge boulders, which covered the surface of the mountain, and drop them over on the unsuspecting foe. The noise was frightful, the destruction sickening Our volleys were still directed against the inner faces of the cave and the roof, and the Apaches seemed to realize that their only safety lay in crouching close to the great stone heap in front; but even this precarious shelter was now taken away; the air was filled with the bounding, plunging frag- ments of stone, breaking into thousands of pieces, with other thousands behind, crashing with the momentum gained in a descent of hundreds of feet. No human voice could be heard in such a cyclone of wrath; the volume of dust was so dense that no eye could pierce it, but over on our left, it seemed that for some reason we could still dis- cern several figures guarding that extremity of the enemy's line — the old Medicine Man, who, decked in all the panoply of his office, with feathers on head, decorated shirt on back, and all the sacred insignia known to his people, had defied the approach of death, and kept his place, firing coolly at everything that moved on our side, that he could see, his rifle reloaded and handed back by his assistants — either squaws or young men — it was impossible to tell which, as only the arms could be noted in the air. Major

Brown signaled up to Burns to stop pouring down his boulders, and at the same time our men were directed to cease firing and to make ready to charge; the fire of the Apaches had ceased, and their chant of defiance was hushed.   There was a feeling in the command as if we were about to rush through the gates of a cemetery, and that we should find a ghastly spectacle within, but, at the same time, it might be that the Apaches had retreated to some recesses in the innermost depths of the cavern, unknown to us, and be prepared to assail all who ventured to cross the wall in front.

Precisely at noon we advanced, Corporal Hanlon, of Company G., Fifth Cavalry, being the first man to surmount the parapet.   I hope that my readers will be satisfied with the meagrest description of the awful sight that met our eyes.   There were men and women dead or writhing in the agonies of death, and with them several babies, killed by our glancing bullets, or by the storm of rocks and stones that descended from above.   While one portion of the command worked at extricating the bodies from beneath the pile of débris, another stood guard with cocked revolvers or carbines, ready to blow out the brains of the first wounded savage who might in his desperation attempt to kill one of our people.   But this precaution was entirely useless.   All the warriors were dead or dying.

*   *   *   *   *   *   *   *

Thirty-five, if I remember aright, were still living, but in the number are included all who were still breathing; many were already dying, and nearly one half were dead before we started out of that dreadful place.   None of the warriors were conscious, except one old man, who serenely awaited the last summons; he had received five or six wounds, and was practically dead when we sprang over the

entrance wall. There was a general sentiment of sorrow
for the old Medicine Man who had stood up so fiercely
on the left of the Apache line, we found his still warm corpse
crushed out of all semblance to humanity, beneath a huge
mass of rock, which has also extinguished at one fell stroke
the light of the life of the squaw and the young man who
had remained by his side." — ("On the Border with
Crook"; Bourke; pp. 196–9).

Seventy-six, including all the men, were killed. Eighteen women and six children were taken prisoners. Thus
was wiped out a band of heroic men whose victorious foes
admitted that their victims were in the right.

THE CHEYENNES' LAST FIGHT, OR THE ENDING OF DULL KNIFE'S BAND

(Condensed by permission from E. B. Bronson's
account as given in "Reminiscences of a Ranchman."
D. P. & Co. This with "The Redblooded" by the same
author should be read by all who are interested in the
heroic days of the West.)

After the Custer fight, the American Army succeeded in
rounding up the Indians who could not or would not escape
to Canada, the one land of justice that was near, and
among these were Dull Knife's Cheyennes. They surrendered on promise of fair treatment.

But as soon as they were in the power of the American
Government (President R. B. Hayes), they were marched
six hundred miles south into Indian Territory, where they
were crowded into a region so unhealthy that it was obviously a question of but three or four years before all would

die. They were starving, too, for the promised rations were never delivered. Nearly half were sick of fevers and malaria, for medicine was refused them. The two hundred and thirty-five warriors were reduced to sixty-nine. The extermination of the tribe was being effected. They begged for succor; they asked only to go home to their own land, but, as usual, no notice was taken of their prayers.

They could not live where they were. The American Government was obviously bent on killing them off, so they decided that it would be better to die at home — taking the chance of bullets rather than the certainty of fever.

On the ninth of September, 1878, therefore, Dull Knife, their head chief, gathered in his ponies, packed up his camp, burned the last bridge, and, with warriors, women, and children, set out for home, in defiance of the soldiers of a corrupt government.

At dawn his departure was discovered, troops were ordered out, telegraph wires were busied, and then began a flight and a pursuit the story of which should thrill the world for the heroism of the fugitives, and shock humanity for the diabolical brutality of the American authorities.

Two thousand troops were sent against this handful of some sixty-nine warriors, sick and weak with starvation, and encumbered with about two hundred and fifty, more or less, sick women and children.

I do not believe there was an American soldier who was not ashamed of his job. But he had no right to an opinion. He was under orders to run down and capture or kill this band of starving Indians, whose abominable crime was that they loved their homes.

We have had fragmentary accounts of that awful flight. Night and day the warriors rode and fought. Some days they covered seventy miles and when their horses gave out, they raided the settlements for a new supply. Against them were four lines of soldiers, with railroads to keep them supplied and the United States Treasury to draw on, and yet this starving band of heroes fought them in two or three pitched battles every week; fought them when nearly even; eluded them when too strong; fooled them, and caring ever for their wives and families, left all behind; and, at last, on the fourth of October, the grand old warrior led his people across the South Platte and on to the comparative haven of the Niobrara Sandhills.

This waterless waste of sand gave them a little respite from the troops, but no chance to rest, or food to eat. They must push on, subsisting on flesh of horses, sacrificed as they had need.

Fresh cordons of troops were made in the country north of the Sandhills, and on the eighth of October army scouts reported Indian signs near Hot Creek.

On the thirteenth of October a small band of the fighters raided a store and drove off a band of horses from a place one mile east of Fort Robinson. These gave them new supplies, but it also gave their enemies the trail, and four troops of cavalry were at once sent to surround Crow Butte, the Cheyenne camp. But the Indians were not caught napping, the next morning dawned to show only that they had quietly passed all lines and were now far on the road to Canada.

Later it was learned that this was the larger part of the band, but was under Little Wolf not Dull Knife. He safely led them all, and escaped without the loss of a man to the far north and found rest.

This march is not excelled in the annals of warfare. It covered a distance of more than one thousand miles in less than fifty days, with a column encumbered with women and children, every step of the trail contested by all the troops of the United States Army that could be concentrated to oppose them; a march that struck and parted like ropes of sand the five great military barriers interposed across their path; the first across the Kansas Pacific Railway, commanded by General Pope; the second along the Union Pacific Railroad in Nebraska, commanded by General Crook; the third along the Niobrara, commanded by General Bradley; the fourth, the Bear Butte (Seventh Cavalry) column, stretched east from the Black Hills; the fifth along the Yellowstone, commanded by General Gibbon.

But Dull Knife and his band of those less able to travel— some one hundred and fifty — were still in the Sandhills. He sent an urgent prayer to Red Cloud of the Sioux for help, but the sad answer was that it was hopeless to resent the President's will.   Ten days later the troops located the Cheyennes.

(*From this to the end is quoted from Bronson.*)

In rags, nearly out of ammunition, famished and worn, with scarcely a horse left that could raise a trot, no longer able to fight or fly, suffering from cold and disheartened by Red Cloud's refusal to receive and shelter them, the splendid old war chief and his men were forced to bow to the inevitable and surrender.

Later in the day Johnson succeeded in rounding up the last of Dull Knife's scattered command and headed north for White River with his prisoners, one hundred and forty-nine Cheyennes and one hundred and thirty-one captured ponies.

The evening of the twenty-fourth, Johnson camped at Louis Jenks's ranch on Chadron Creek, near the present town of Chadron, Neb.

A heavy snowstorm had set in early in the afternoon, and the night was so bitter and the Indians so weakened by their campaign that Johnson felt safe to leave them free to take the best shelter they could find in the brush along the deep valley of Chadron Creek.

This leniency he was not long in regretting.

Dull Knife and his band had been feeding liberally for two days on troopers' rations, and had so far recovered strength of body and heart that when morning came on the twenty-fifth the sentries were greeted with a feeble volley from rifle pits in the brush, dug by Dull Knife in the frozen ground during the night!

And here in these pits indomitable old Dull Knife fought stubbornly for two days more — fought and held the troops at bay until Lieutenant Chase brought up a field gun from Fort Robinson and shelled them to a final surrender!

Thus ended the first episode of Dull Knife's magnificent fight for liberty and fatherland, and yet had he had food, ammunition, and mounts, the chances are a hundred to one that his heroic purpose would have been accomplished, and the entire band that left Reno, barring those killed along the trail, would have escaped in safety to freedom in the then wilds of the Northwest Territory.

And that, even in this apparently final surrender to hopeless odds, Dull Knife was still not without hope of further resistance, was proved by the fact that when he came out of his trenches only a few comparatively old and worthless arms were surrendered, while it later became known that twenty-two good rifles had been taken apart and were swung, concealed, beneath the clothing of the squaws!

After taking a day's rest Johnson marched his command into Fort Robinson, arriving in the evening in a heavy snowstorm, where the Cheyennes were imprisoned in one of the barracks and their meagre equipment dumped in with them, without further search for arms or ammunition. Later it was learned that that night the Indians quietly loosened some of the flooring of the barrack and hid their arms and ammunition beneath it, so that when a more careful search of their belongings and persons was made two days later, they were found to be absolutely without weapons of any description.

*   *   *   *   *   *   *

Dull Knife and his people were confined in the log barrack at the southeast angle of the parade ground [at Fort Robinson]. No doors were locked or windows barred. A small guard patroled the barrack prison night and day.

What to do with these indomitable people puzzled the Indian Bureau and the army.

*   *   *   *   *   *   *

In December a great council was held in the barrack prison. The Sioux chiefs, Red Cloud, American Horse, Red Dog, and No Flesh, came over from their agency to attend it. The Government was represented by Captains Wessells and Vroom and their juniors. The Cheyennes were gathered in a close circle, the officers and visiting chiefs near its centre, the bucks back of them, and farther back still the squaws and children.

Red Cloud was the principal Sioux speaker. He said in substance:

"Our hearts are sore for you.

"Many of our own blood are among your dead. This has made our hearts bad.

"But what can we do? The Great Father is all-powerful. His people fill the whole earth. We must do what he says. We have begged him to allow you to come to live among us. We hope he may let you come. What we have we will share with you. But, remember, what he directs, that you must do.

"We cannot help you. The snows are thick on the hills. Our ponies are thin. The game is scarce. You cannot resist, nor can we. So listen to your old friend and do without complaint what the Great Father tells you."

The old Cheyenne war chief, Dull Knife, then stepped slowly to the centre of the circle, a grim, lean figure.

Erect, despite his sixty-odd years, with a face of a classical Roman profile, with the steady, penetrating glance and noble, commanding bearing of a great leader of men, Dull Knife stood in his worn canvas moccasins and ragged threadbare blanket, the very personification of the greatness of heart and soul that cannot be subdued by poverty and defeat.

Never when riding at the head of hundreds of his wild warriors, clad in the purple of his race — leggings of golden yellow buckskin, heavily beaded, blanket of dark blue broadcloth, warbonnnet of eagles' feathers that trailed behind him on the ground, necklace of bears' claws, the spoils of many a deadly tussle — never in his life did Dull Knife look more a chieftain than there in his captivity and rags.

He first addressed the Sioux:

"We know you for our friends, whose words we may believe. We thank you for asking us to share your lands. We hope the Great Father will let us come to you. All we ask is to be allowed to live, and to live in peace. I seek no war with any one. An old man, my fighting days are done. We bowed to the will of the Great Father and went far into the south where he told us to go. There we found a Cheyenne cannot live. Sickness came among us that made mourning in every lodge. Then the treaty promises were

broken, and our rations were short.   Those not worn by
disease were wasted by hunger.   To stay there meant that
all of us would die.   Our petitions to the Great Father
were unheeded.   We thought it better to die fighting to
regain our old homes than to perish of sickness.   Then our
march we begun.   The rest you know."

Then turning to Captain Wessells and his officers:

"Tell the Great Father Dull Knife and his people ask
only to end their days here in the north where they were
born.   Tell him we want no more war.   We cannot live in
the south; there is no game.   Here, when rations are short,
we can hunt.   Tell him if he lets us stay here Dull Knife's
people will hurt no one.   Tell him if he tries to send us back
we will butcher each other with our own knives.   I have
spoken."

Captain Wessells's reply was brief — an assurance that
Dull Knife's words should go to the Great Father.

The Cheyennes sat silent throughout the council, all
save one, a powerful young buck named Buffalo Hump,
old Dull Knife's son.   With a thin strip of old canvas, that
served as his only covering, drawn tightly about his tall
figure, his bronze face aflame with sentiments of wrong, of
anger, and of hatred, Buffalo Hump strode rapidly from
one end to the other of the long barrack room, casting fierce
glances at the white men, the very incarnation of savage
wrath.   From beginning to end of the council I momen-
tarily expected to see him leap on some member of the
party, and try to rend him with his hands.

Of course nothing came of the council.   The War and
Interior Departments agreed that it would be imprudent
to permit these unsubduable people to be merged into the
already restless ranks of the Sioux.   It was therefore
decided to march them back south to Fort Reno, whence
they had come.

January opened with very bitter weather. Six or eight inches of snow covered the ground. The mercury daily made long excursions below zero. Even the troops in cantonment at Canby were suffering severely from the cold — some with frozen feet and hands. It was all but impossible weather for marching.

Nevertheless, on January 5th, Captain Wessells received orders from the War Department to immediately start Dull Knife's band, as quietly and peaceably as possible, and under proper escort, on the march to Fort Reno, six hundred miles away in the south! This was the decision of the Indian Bureau, and the Secretary of War was requested to have the decision immediately enforced. Hence the order which reached Captain Wessells.

Captain Wessells sent a guard to the barrack and had Dull Knife, Old Crow, and Wild Hog brought into his presence at headquarters. On the arrival of the Indians a council was held. Captain Wessells advised them of the order of the Department that they were to return to the Indian Territory.

Dull Knife rose to reply. His whole figure trembled with rage; his bronze cheeks assumed a deeper red; the fires of suppressed passion blazed through his eyes until they glittered with the ferocity of an enraged beast at bay. Nevertheless, he spoke slowly and almost calmly. He did not have much to say. He made no threats or gestures.

He said he had listened to what the Great Father had ordered. It was the dearest wish of him and his people to try to do what the Great Father desired, for they knew they were helpless in his hands. But now the Great Father was telling them to do what they could not do — to try to march to the Indian Territory in such weather. Many would be sure to perish on the way, and those who reached the reservation would soon fall victims to the fevers that had already brought mourning into nearly all their lodges. If, then, the Great Father wished them to die — very well, only they would die where they then were, if necessary by their own hands. They would not return to the south, and they would not leave their barrack prison.

Captain Wessells knew that Dull Knife's complaint was well founded. Still, bound by the rigid rules of the service, he had absolutely no latitude whatever. He therefore directed the interpreter to explain to Dull Knife that the orders were imperative and must be obeyed, and to assure him that the cavalry escort would do all in their power to save the Indians from any unnecessary hardship on the journey.

Dull Knife, however, remained firm, and his companions, when appealed to, only growled a brief assent to Dull Knife's views.

"Then, Interpreter," said Wessells, "tell them their food and fuel will be stopped entirely until they conclude to come peaceably out of their barrack, ready to march south as ordered."

The three chiefs silently heard their sentence, and were then quickly marched back to their barrack prison by a file of soldiers.

All this occurred shortly after "guard mount" in the morning.

Apart from its inhumanity, Wessells's order was bad policy. Hunger drives the most cowardly to violence. Then, to add to the wretched plight of the Indians, they were all but naked. No clothing had been issued to them since their capture, and they were clad only in tattered blankets and fragments of tent cloth. Requisitions for clothing had been sent to the Indian Bureau, but none had come.

Thus, half naked, without food or fires, these miserable

people starved and shivered for five days and nights, but with no thought of surrender!

Captain Wessells sent the interpreter to propose that the children be removed and fed, but this they refused; they said they preferred to die together.

For five days and nights the barrack rang with shrill, terrible death chants. It was clear that they had resolved to die, and weakening fast indeed they were under the rigors of cold and hunger, weakening in all but spirit.

The morning of the ninth of January, the fifth day of their compulsory fast, Captain Wessells again summoned Dull Knife, Old Crow, and Wild Hog to a council.

Only the two latter came.

Suspecting violence, the Indians refused to let their old chief leave the barrack.

Asked if they were ready to surrender, Wild Hog replied that they would die first.

The two chiefs were then ordered seized and ironed. In the struggle Wild Hog succeeded in seriously stabbing Private Ferguson of Troop A, and sounded his war cry as an alarm to his people.

Instantly pandemonium broke loose in the Indian barrack.

They realized the end was at hand.

The war songs of the warriors rang loudly above the shrill death chants of the squaws.

Windows and doors were quickly barricaded.

The floor of the barrack was torn up and rifle-pits were dug beneath it.

Stoves and flooring were broken into convenient shapes for use as war clubs.

The twenty-odd rifles and pistols which had been smuggled into the barrack, by slinging them about the waists of the squaws beneath their blankets, at the time of the capture, were soon brought from their hiding place and loaded.

They expected an immediate attack, but none came.

And all day long the garrison was kept under arms, ready for any sortie by the Indians.

Night at last came, and, notwithstanding the terrible warnings of the day, no extraordinary precautions were taken. A guard of only seventeen men were under arms, and of these only a few were on post about this barrack full of maddened savages.

All but Captain Wessells were so certain of a desperate outbreak that night that Lieutenant Baxter and several other officers sat fully dressed and armed in their quarters, awaiting the first alarm.

"Taps" sounded at nine o'clock, the barracks were soon darkened, and the troopers retired.

Only a few lights burned in the officers' quarters and at the trader's store.

The night was still and fearfully cold, the earth hid by the snow.

Ten o'clock came, and just as the "all's well" was passing from one sentry to another, a buck fired through a window and killed a sentry, jumped through the window and got the sentry's carbine and belt, and sprang back into the barrack. Then two or three bucks ran out of the west door, where they quickly shot down Corporal Pulver and Private Hulz, both of Troop A, and Private Tommeny, of Troop E.

At doors and windows the barrack now emptied its horde of desperate captives, maddened by injustice and wild from hunger. Nevertheless, they acted with method and generalship, and with heroism worthy of the noblest men of any race.

The bucks armed with firearms were the first to leave the

barrack. These formed in line in front of the barrack and opened fire on the guardhouse and upon the troopers as they came pouring out of neighboring barracks. Thus they held the garrison in check until the women and children and the old and infirm were in full flight.

Taken completely by surprise, the troops, nevertheless, did fearfully effective work. Captain Wessells soon had them out, and not a few entered into the fight and pursuit clad in nothing but their underclothing, hatless and shoeless.

The fugitives took the road to the sawmill crossing of White River, only a few hundred yards distant from their barracks, crossed the White River, and started southwest toward my ranch, where they evidently expected to mount themselves out of my herd of cow ponies, for they carried with them all their lariats, saddles, and bridles to this point. Here, pressed hopelessly close by the troops, their gallant rear-guard melting fast before the volleys of the pursuers, the Indians dropped their horse equipments, turned, and recrossed White River, and headed for the high, precipitous divide between Soldier Creek and White River, two miles nearer their then position than the cliffs about my ranch. They knew their only chance lay in quickly reaching hills inaccessible to cavalry.

All history affords no record of a more heroic, forlorn hope than this Cheyenne sortie.

Had the bucks gone alone, many would surely have escaped, but they resolved to die together and to protect their women and children to the last.

Thus more than half their fighting men fell in the first half mile of this flying fight. And as the warriors fell, their arms were seized by the squaws and boys, who wielded them as best they could!

In the gloom of night the soldiers could not distinguish a

squaw from a buck. Lieutenant Cummings fell into a washout near the sawmill nearly atop of two Indians. They attacked him with knives, but he succeeded in killing both with his pistol — only to find that they were squaws!

The struggle was often hand-to-hand, and many of the dead were powder-burned. For a long distance the trail was strewn thick with bodies

A sergeant and several men were pursuing two isolated fugitives who proved to be a buck and squaw. Suddenly the two fugitives turned and charged their pursuers, the buck armed with a pistol, the squaw with a piece of an iron stove! They were shot down.

This running fight afoot continued for nearly a mile, when the troops, many of them already badly frozen, were hurried back to the garrison to get needed clothing and their mounts.

[E. B. Bronson, who tells the tale, was in his ranch five miles away that night but the sound of firing at ten o'clock caused him to mount horse and hurry to the Fort with a friend.]

Presently, nearing the narrow fringe of timber that lined the stream, we could see ahead of us a broad, dark line dividing the snow: it was the trail of pursued and pursuers — the line of flight. Come to it, we halted.

There at our feet, grim and stark and terrible in the moonlight, lay the dead and wounded, so thick for a long way that one could leap from one body to another; there they lay grim and stark, soldiers and Indians, the latter lean and gaunt as wolves from starvation, awful with their wounds, infinitely pathetic on this bitter night in their ragged, half-clothed nakedness.

We started to ride across the trail, when in a fallen buck I happened to notice I recognized Buffalo Hump, Dull Knife's son.

He lay on his back, with arms extended and face up-turned. In his right hand he held a small knife, a knife worn by years and years of use from the useful proportions of a butcher knife until the blade was no more than one quarter of an inch wide at the hilt, a knife descended to domestic use by the squaws as an awl in sewing moccasins, and yet the only weapon this magnificent warrior could command in this his last fight for freedom!

As I sat on my horse looking down at Buffalo Hump, believing him dead, the picture rose in my mind of the council in which he had stalked from end to end of the barrack, burning with an anger and hatred which threatened even then and there to break out into violence, when suddenly he rose to a sitting position and aimed a fierce blow at my leg with his knife. Instinctively, as he rose, I spurred my horse out of his reach and jerked my pistol, but before I could use it he fell back and lay still — dead.

So died Buffalo Hump, a warrior capable, with half a chance, of making martial history worthy even of his doughty old father.

*　　*　　*　　*　　*　　*　　*

Immediately on hearing the fire, Vroom, at Camp Canby, had thrown two troops in skirmish order across the valley to prevent escape to the east, and hurried into Robinson himself at the head of a third troop.

Already mounted, Vroom was the first to overtake and re-engage the flying Cheyennes, whose knowledge of the geography of the country proved remarkable. They had selected a high bluff two miles west of the post as their means of escape, its summit inaccessible to horsemen for more than six miles from the point of their ascent.

Almost daily for months had I ridden beneath this bluff and would readily have sworn not even a mountain goat could ascend to its summit; but, hidden away in an angle of the cliff lay a slope accessible to footmen, and this the Indians knew and sought.

Just below this slope Vroom brought the rear guard to bay, and a brief, desperate engagement was fought.   The Indians succeeded in holding the troops in check until all but those fallen under the fire of Vroom's command were able to reach the summit.

Here on this slope, fighting in the front ranks of the rear guard, the "Princess," Dull Knife's youngest daughter, was killed!

Further pursuit until daylight being impossible, the troopers were marched back into the garrison.

By daylight the hospital was filled with wounded Indians, and thirty-odd dead — bucks, squaws, and children — lay in a row by the roadside near the sawmill, and there later they were buried in a common trench.

At dawn of the tenth, Captain Wessells led out four troops of cavalry, and, after a couple of hours' scouting, found that the Indians had followed for ten miles the summit of the high divide between White River and Soldier Creek, traveling straight away westward, and then had descended to the narrow valley of Soldier Creek, up which the trail lay plain to follow through the snow as a beaten road.

Along this trail Captain Vroom led the column at the head of his troop.   Next behind him rode Lieut. George A. Dodd, then a youngster not long out of West Point, and later for many years recognized as the crack cavalry captain of the army.   Next behind Dodd I rode.

Ahead of the column a hundred yards rode Woman's Dress, a Sioux scout.

For seventeen miles from the post the trail showed that

the fugitives had made no halt! A marvelous march on such a bitter night for a lot of men, women, and children many of them wounded, all half clad and practically starved for five days!

Presently the trail wound round the foot of a high, steep hill, the crest of which was covered with fallen timber, a hill so steep the column was broken into single file to pass it. Here the trail could be seen winding on through the snow over another hill a half mile ahead.

Thus an ambush was the last thing expected, but, after passing the crest of the second hill, the Indians had made a wide detour to the north, gained the fallen timber on the crest of this first hill, and had there entrenched themselves.

So it happened that at the moment the head of Vroom's column came immediately beneath their entrenchment, the Cheyennes opened fire at short range, emptied two or three saddles, and naturally and rightly enough stampeded the leading troop into the brush ahead of and back of the hill, for it was no place to stand and make a fight.

* * * * * * *

Nothing remained but to make a run for the brush, and a good run he made of it, but, encumbered with a buffalo overcoat and labouring through the heavy snow, he soon got winded and dropped a moment for rest behind the futile shelter of a sage bush.

Meantime, the troopers had reached the timber, dismounted, taken positions behind trees, and were pouring into the Indian stronghold a fire so heavy that Dodd was soon able to make another run and escape to the timber unscathed.

* * * * * * *

The Indian stronghold on the hilltop was soon surrounded and held under a desultory long-range fire all day, as the position was one impregnable to a charge.

No packs or rations having been brought, at nightfall Captain Wessells built decoy campfires about the Indians' position and marched the command back into the garrison.

*   *   *   *   *   *   *

He told me Lieutenant Baxter, with a detachment of ten men, had located, on the slope of a bluff a mile east of the Deadman Ranch, a camp of Indians which he believed represented a large band of hostiles still loose.

Pointing to a spur of the bluffs, three or four hundred feet high, standing well out into the valley a scant mile east of my ranch, the trooper hurried on in to the garrison for reinforcements, and I spurred away for the bluff, and soon could see a line of dismounted troopers strung along the crest of the ridge.

As I rode up to the foot of the bluff, skirmish firing began on top of the ridge.

After running my horse as far up the hill as its precipitous nature would permit, I started afoot climbing for the crest, but, finding it inaccessible at that point, started around the face of the bluff to the east to find a practicable line of ascent, when suddenly I was startled to hear the ominous, shrill buzz of rifle balls just above my head, from the skirmish line on the crest of the ridge — startled, indeed, for I had supposed the Indians to be on the crest of the bluff, farther to the south.

Dropping behind a tree and looking downhill, I saw a faint curl of smoke rising from a little washout one hundred yards below me, and, crouched beside the smouldering fire in the washout, a lone Indian.

This warrior's fight and death was characteristic of the magnificent spirit which had inspired the band, from the beginning of the campaign at Fort Reno.

In mid-afternoon, scouting to the south of the garrison

for trails, Lieutenant Baxter had discovered this campfire, and, quite naturally assuming that none but a considerable band of the Indians would venture upon building a campfire so near to the garrison, had immediately sent a trooper courier into the garrison with advice of his discovery.

Then he dismounted his command and approached the campfire in open skirmish order, until it was plain to be seen that the fire was deserted. The trail of a single Indian led into the washout, and imprints in the snow showed where he had sat, evidently for some hours, beside the fire. But of the washout's fugitive tenant no trace could be found, no trail showing his route of departure. In one direction along a sharp ridge leading toward the hogback's crest, the snow was blown away, the ground bare, and this seemed to be his natural line of flight from Baxter's detachment.

After what all believed a thorough search of the vicinity of the fire, Lieutenant Baxter left Corporal Everett and a trooper near the fire, and, remounting, led the balance of his men up the slope with the view to cut the Cheyenne's trail wheresoever it might again enter the snow.

Baxter was gone barely ten minutes when he was startled by two rifle shots in his rear, from the vicinity of the fire! Looking back, he saw his two troopers prostrate in the snow, and later learned that Everett and his mate, while stamping about to keep warm, had approached a little shallow washout within thirty yards of the fire that all vowed they had looked into, and suddenly had discovered the Indian lying at its bottom, wrapped in a length of dirty old canvas the precise color of the gray clay soil which doubtless had served to conceal him through the earlier search. The moment the Indian made sure he was discovered. he cast open his canvas wrap and fired twice with a carbine, shooting Corporal Everett through the stomach and killing him almost instantly, and seriously wounding his mate.

Thus rudely taught that humanity was useless, and that it must be a fight to the death, observing "Papa" Lawson approaching from the fort at the head of his troop, Baxter swung his own men up and along the top of the ridge, where they could better command the old Cheyenne's position, and opened on him a heavy fire — and it was just at this juncture I arrived.

Immediately after I first sighted the Indian, "Papa" Lawson swung around the foot of the hill with his troop, dismounted, and charged up on foot — thus making sixty men concentrated upon one!

The old Cheyenne kept up his rapid fire as long as he could. Toward the last I plainly saw him fire his carbine three times with his left hand, resting the barrel along the edge of the washout, while his right hand hung helpless beside him.

Suddenly I saw him drop down in the bottom of the washout, limp as an empty sack.

When we came up to him it appeared that while the shot that killed him had entered the top of his head, he nevertheless earlier in the engagement had been hit four times — once through the right shoulder, once through the left cheek, once in the right side, and a fourth ball toward the last had completely shattered his right wrist.

It was apparent that he had been making a desperate break to reach my horses, which usually ran in the very next canyon to the west, for he still carried with him a lariat and bridle; but his unprotected feet had been so badly frozen during the night that he had become entirely unable to travel farther, and, realizing himself to be utterly helpless, in sheer desperation had built a fire to get what poor, miserable comfort he could for the few minutes or hours remaining to him!

A curious incident here followed.

An ambulance had come with Lawson's troop to the field, in which the body of Everett and his wounded mate were placed, while the body of the dead Cheyenne was thrown into the boot at the back of the conveyance. Upon arrival in the garrison, Lieutenant Baxter discovered that the body of the Indian had been lost out of the boot on the short four-mile journey into Robinson, and sent back a sergeant and detail of men to recover it. But the most careful search along the trail failed to reveal any trace of the body, and whatever became of it to this day remains a mystery.

On the night of the tenth, fifty-two Indians had been captured, approximately half of them more or less badly wounded, and thirty-seven were known to have been killed, leaving a total of sixty unaccounted for.

Still without food, on the morning of the eleventh, the seventh day of their fast, and unable to march farther, Captain Wessells's column found the fugitives occupying a strong position in the thick timber along Soldier Creek at the foot of the hill upon which they had been entrenched the day before, better sheltered from the severity of the weather.

Again long-range firing was the order of the day, for a charge would have incurred needless hazard.

During this day the Indians succeeded in killing a troop horse on an exposed hillside within three or four hundred yards of their position. The rider narrowly escaped with his life.

The ground where the horse fell was so openly exposed, the carcass had to be left where it had fallen, and that night, after Captain Wessells had again marched his command back to the garrison, the carcass furnished the first food these poor wretches had eaten for seven days!

That their hearts were firm as ever and that all they needed was a little physical strength the next few days effectually proved.

The twelfth they lay eating and resting, and when on the thirteenth, Wessells's column returned to the attack, the Indians were found six miles farther to the west, well entrenched on the Hat Creek Bluffs, and there again an ambush was encountered in which two troopers were wounded.

On this day a twelve-pound Napoleon gun was brought into action, and forty rounds of shell were thrown into the Indians' position, without dislodging them.

The same day Captain Wessells and Lieutenants Crawford and Hardie crept near the rifle-pits with an interpreter and called to the Cheyennes to bring out their women and children, promising them shelter and protection. A feeble volley was the only reply!

Realizing the Indians had now reached a cattle country in which they could kill meat and subsist themselves, Captain Wessells had brought out a pack-train, with blankets and rations, to enable him to surround the Indians' position at night, and, should they slip away, to camp on their trail.

This night they were surrounded, but at dawn on the fourteenth, Lieutenant Crawford discovered the wily enemy had again slipped through the picket lines, headed southwestward along the high bluffs which lined the southern edge of Hat Creek Basin.

For six days more the same tactics on both sides prevailed; the Indians were daily followed in running fight, or brought to bay in strong positions practically impregnable of direct attack, surrounded at nightfall, only to glide away like veritable shadows during the night, and of course more or less were killed in these daily engagements.

On the twentieth, Captain Wessells's command was joined by Lieutenant Dodd and a large band of Sioux scouts.

Tuesday, the twenty-first (January, 1879), saw the finish.

At a point on the Hat Creek Bluffs, near the head of War Bonnet Creek, forty-four miles a little to the south of west of Fort Robinson, the Cheyennes lay at bay in their last entrenchment, worn out with travel and fighting, and with scarcely any ammunition left.

They were in a washout about fifty feet long, twelve feet wide, and five feet deep; near the edge of the bluffs.

Skirmishers were thrown out beneath them on the slope of the bluff to prevent their escape in that direction, and then Captain Wessells advanced on the washout, with his men formed in open skirmish order.

A summons through the interpreter to surrender was answered by a few scattering shots from the washout.

Converging on the washout in this charge, the troopers soon were advancing in such a dense body that nothing saved them from terrible slaughter but the exhaustion of the Cheyennes' ammunition.

Charging to the edge of the pit, the troopers emptied their carbines into it, sprang back to reload, and then came on again, while above the crash of the rifles arose the hoarse death chants of the expiring band.

The last three warriors alive — and God knows they deserve the name of warriors if ever men deserved it — sprang out of their defences, one armed with an empty pistol and two with knives, and madly charged the troops!

Three men charged three hundred!

They fell, shot to pieces like men fallen under platoon fire.

And then the fight was over.

The little washout was a shambles, whence the troops removed twenty-two dead and nine living, and of the living all but two (women) were badly wounded!

These were all that remained out of the sixty unaccounted for after the fighting near Fort Robinson, excepting five or six bucks, among them Chief Dull Knife, who had been cut off from the main band in the first night's fight and had escaped to the Sioux.

And among the Ogallala Sioux thereafter, till he died, dwelt Dull Knife, grim and silent as Sphinx or dumb man; brooding his wrongs; cursing the fate that had denied him the privilege to die fighting with his people; sitting alone daily for hours on the crest of a Wounded Knee bluff rising near his teepee, and gazing longingly across the wide reaches of the Bad Lands to a faint blue line, on the northwestern horizon, that marked his old highland home in the Black Hills.

The Message of the Indian

The message of the Indian for us is sixfold:

1st. *He was the great prophet of outdoor life.* He was strong when he lived in the sun; and when, under pressure, he took to a house, he was like Samson shorn of his hair. By the physical perfection of his body, he showed the truth of his way. He was a living protest against house-life. He, above all others, can show us how to get the joys, and escape the dangers, of life in the open air.

2nd. *He was a master of woodcraft* — woodcraft, the oldest of all the sciences; the one, that, above all, makes for manhood. Strength, speed, skill, courage, knowledge of the woods and its creatures, star-wisdom, water-wisdom, plant lore, and everything that makes for the well-built man in masterful touch with a large environment of blue air, is part of woodcraft. And in this above all other men, the Indian can be our guide.

3rd. *He taught the sacred duty of reverencing, beautifying and perfecting the body.*

4th. *He sought for the beautiful in everything.* He teaches us that, if we have the spirit of beauty within, we may beautify everything in every office and walk of our lives. Every weapon, tool, utensil, garment and house; yes, every gesture — he has taught us how to make beautiful. His songs, stories, dances, ceremonies, his system of etiquette and courtesy, were expressions in his daily life that proved his mind; and in the making of beautiful tents, blankets, baskets and canoes, he has easily led the world. These things were mere expressions of his broad creed that the Great Spirit is in everything, everywhere, all the time.

5th. *He solved one great economic problem that vexes us to-day.* By his life and tribal constitution, he has shown us that the nationalization of all natural resources and national interests puts a stop at once equally to abject poverty and to monstrous wealth.

6th. *He was the world's great historic protest against avarice.* Under various euphonious names we encourage greed as a safeguard against destitution. He showed that it has no bearing on the case and that it unavoidably ends in measureless crime:

That seems to be the sixfold message of the Indian; but there is also a thought that will not down, as one reads these chronicles of a trampled race.

The law of this land gives every one the right to think and decide for himself, so long as he does not infringe on the rights of others. No man may compel the conscience of another, *except that other be a soldier or a marine.* When a man joins army or navy, he must leave his conscience behind. That is the law. Why? Because those in the high place of authority know so well that the soldier or sailor, going to the front and seeing with his own eyes the abominations and human tortures that warfare really means, would be so horror-stricken that he would recoil as from a very hell. He would refuse to be a party to such unspeakable atrocities, and so army and navy, yes, the whole system back of it, would crumble.

No, sir, discipline must be maintained. The soldier and sailor must leave his conscience at home and do as he is told, stifling the voice within that tells him he is espousing the cause of Jezebel, Herod and Moloch, and pledging his manhood to the service of hell.

When General Crook set off in deep winter to hound the Dakota patriots to their death, and to slaughter their women and babies, he admitted, as we have seen, that it was a hard campaign to go on. "But," he added, "the hardest thing is to go and fight those whom we know are right."

Then why did he go?

If Crook had been ordered by the War Department to nail the Saviour to the Cross, I suppose he would have done it, and wept as he obeyed; or, under orders of Herod, he would have slaughtered the babes of Bethlehem as expeditiously as his broken heart would have allowed. The British general who led his troops against China, probably all against his better judgment, and there, by force and bloodshed, established the diabolical opium traffic, obeyed his government, indeed, and gained some money for his country's merchants. But he made an awful day of reckoning for himself and for his race.

When the French army decided that it was wise to sacrifice innocent Dreyfus for the cause of patriotism, they set the army above justice and their country in a higher place than God. And thus struck France a blow from which she never yet has recovered — we cannot tell — maybe a death-blow.

Most men agree with the Indian that courage is one of the greatest, if not the greatest, of virtues. How many of them dare live up to this belief? To most men, in some measure, there comes a time when they must decide between their duty to country and their duty to God. How many dare take the one course that they know to be right? Are there no times when man's allegiance to high principle must override his allegiance to constituted authority? No? Then, how do you justify 1776? And the martyrs, from Socrates, seditious preacher of the truth, right down to men of our own times; were they all wrong? All set their God above their country's laws, and suffered cruel, shameful deaths.

If they did not teach us by their lives and deaths that justice and truth are above every consideration of one's country and its laws, then Socrates, St. Peter, St. Stephen, St. Paul, St. John, Becket, Huss, Coligny, Latimer, Ridley, Cranmer — yes, the Lord Himself — all lived and died in vain.

THE END

INDEX

INDEX

Index

583